T0271274

"Calla Wiemer has written a highly readable, accessible, and analytically rigorous volume that will be of great value to scholars and policymakers both in East Asia and for anybody with an interest in this fascinating, diverse, and dynamic region. *Macroeconomics for Emerging East Asia* is grounded in mainstream macroeconomic theory and practice. But the author is rightly at pains to emphasize that the standard US macro textbooks are generally written with the implicit assumption that economies enjoy the 'exorbitant privilege' of possessing an internationally accepted reserve currency, and that this framework needs to be modified for the East Asian economies. An attractive feature of the volume is its application to real-world policy issues and challenges. These range from the misleading allegation, frequently directed at China and some other East Asian economies, of 'currency manipulation', to the origins and management of recent economic crises such as those of 1997–98, 2008–9, and the current pandemic. Highly recommended."

– Hal Hill, H. W. Arndt Professor Emeritus of Southeast Asian Economies, Crawford School of Public Policy, Australian National University

"This excellent work clearly explains the interplay of macroeconomics, international finance, and development in an important – yet not completely familiar – part of the world. The author, an expert long familiar with the region, compellingly lays out the models necessary for analysis, while deploying data that highlights how emerging East Asia differs from other regions in macro behavior and response to policies. This is sure to become the reference for this subject."

– Menzie Chinn, Professor of Public Affairs and Economics, University of Wisconsin–Madison

"In *Macroeconomics for Emerging East Asia*, Calla Wiemer skillfully presents theoretical concepts and policy topics in a highly lucid manner. The liberal use of examples from East Asia makes it attractive both to intermediate economics majors and to advanced students in public policy, business, and area studies."

– Shinji Takagi, Distinguished Research Professor, Asian Growth Research Institute, and Professor Emeritus of Economics, Osaka University

Macroeconomics for Emerging East Asia

Macroeconomics for Emerging East Asia presents a distinctive approach to the study of macroeconomic theory and policy. The author develops a unique analytical framework that incorporates: (1) both internal and external balance as aspects of macroeconomic stability; (2) both the exchange rate and the interest rate as monetary policy instruments, (3) government debt sustainability as a concern of fiscal policy, and (4) global capital flows as a force to be reckoned with. The framework provides students with the foundational knowledge to analyze macroeconomic issues common to emerging economies. Concepts are illustrated using the latest empirical data and extensive case study analysis for 13 economies of Northeast and Southeast Asia (Cambodia, China, Hong Kong, Indonesia, Korea, Laos, Myanmar, Malaysia, the Philippines, Singapore, Taiwan, Thailand, and Vietnam). The book's lucid exposition accommodates students of differing levels of preparation.

Calla Wiemer has taught at the University of Hawaii at Manoa, the University of the Philippines, the National University of Singapore, the KDI School of Public Policy and Management, and Claremont McKenna College. She was Editor-in-Chief of the *Journal of Asian Economics* from 2015 to 2020. As President of the American Committee on Asian Economic Studies, she moderates the Asia Economics Blog. She is bi-continental with homes in Los Angeles and Manila.

Macroeconomics
for Emerging East Asia

Calla Wiemer

CAMBRIDGE
UNIVERSITY PRESS

CAMBRIDGE
UNIVERSITY PRESS

Shaftesbury Road, Cambridge CB2 8EA, United Kingdom

One Liberty Plaza, 20th Floor, New York, NY 10006, USA

477 Williamstown Road, Port Melbourne, VIC 3207, Australia

314–321, 3rd Floor, Plot 3, Splendor Forum, Jasola District Centre, New Delhi – 110025, India

103 Penang Road, #05–06/07, Visioncrest Commercial, Singapore 238467

Cambridge University Press is part of Cambridge University Press & Assessment, a department of the University of Cambridge.

We share the University's mission to contribute to society through the pursuit of education, learning and research at the highest international levels of excellence.

www.cambridge.org
Information on this title: www.cambridge.org/highereducation/isbn/9781009152518

DOI: 10.1017/9781009152525

First published 2023

A catalogue record for this publication is available from the British Library

ISBN 978-1-009-15251-8 Hardback
ISBN 978-1-009-15253-2 Paperback

Cambridge University Press & Assessment has no responsibility for the persistence or accuracy of URLs for external or third-party internet websites referred to in this publication and does not guarantee that any content on such websites is, or will remain, accurate or appropriate.

In memory of Charles Adams,
whose knowledge lives on in these pages.

Contents

Figures

Tables

Charts

Boxes

Acknowledgments

The essence of this book is due to Charles Adams, my colleague at the Lee Kuan Yew (LKY) School of Public Policy from 2006 to 2008. Charles arrived at the LKY School after a career at the International Monetary Fund, a colleague of his there describing him as "the smartest economist I know." Not only was he that smart, he was generous with his knowledge. Charles and I were tasked by the LKY School to develop an executive program in macroeconomics and take turns teaching it in Vietnam. Charles masterminded the program, and I put together the charts and tables and prepared the slides. I thought the result was worthy of turning into a textbook, and Charles was game. He fed me ideas, and I did the writing, then got his feedback and revised. We talked for long stretches on the grounds of the LKY School where Charles would chain smoke. I was worried about how that would end, and rightly so, it turned out. I was left to carry on by myself, but Charles's knowledge and insight permeate the book.

Two reviewers have read the manuscript in full and offered transformative commentary. From the economist perspective, Shinji Takagi has offered penetrating critique, pushing me to work to get it right. Like Charles Adams, he is generous with his knowledge, and I am grateful to have absorbed as much as I could from him. I got to know Professor Takagi as my favorite reviewer when I served as editor of the *Journal of Asian Economics*. He was tough, and that was just what I wanted for my own writing. From the non-economist perspective, political scientist and Asia expert Greg Anderson has provided guidance on keeping the presentation accessible and interesting. His ideas on what else to include could make for another book. Five others – Jerry Schiff, Corina Gochoco-Bautista, Laurence Kirsch, Menzie Chinn, and William Rohlf – have contributed valuable input on select chapters. My great gratitude goes to all.

During an interlude in Los Angeles, I was granted institutional haven at the Center for Chinese Studies at the University of California, Los Angeles (2008–2010), and the U.S.-China Institute at the University of Southern California (2010–2014). I'm grateful for the collegiality offered by these institutions and the access to outstanding library collections, augmented by that of the fabulous Los Angeles Public Library. While at the University of the Philippines (2015–2018), I received support for Chapter 8 from the UPecon Foundation and for Chapter 10 from the Philippine Center for Economic Development, which I appreciate.

Students at the University of the Philippines School of Economics (2015–2017) and the KDI School of Public Policy and Management in Korea (2019) have test run draft and pre-draft material in a process that has proved immensely helpful in structuring the narrative, tightening the arguments, and ferreting out errors.

Finally, my thanks go to Joe Ng of Cambridge University Press for finding me and waving open the door to publication.

Preface

The idea for this book originated with my teaching a macroeconomics course to mostly Asian students at the Lee Kuan Yew (LKY) School of Public Policy at the National University of Singapore. For my first year teaching the course, a standard US principles text had already been adopted for our use. Teaching macroeconomics from the standpoint of a country that prints the world's reserve currency and gives no thought to external balance or debt sustainability to students from Singapore, China, and Laos seemed altogether inappropriate. To even begin thinking about macroeconomics for these countries requires an understanding of the balance of payments and exchange rates, and yet these topics were relegated to the final chapter of the text like an afterthought.

In my second year at the LKY School I had the opportunity to work with a colleague, Charles Adams, in designing a macroeconomics executive program for Vietnamese government officials. Charles had spent most of his career in Asia with the International Monetary Fund advising on macroeconomic policy in the region. He knew exactly how to structure a course in macroeconomics for Asia, and I caught on quickly enough that we were able to take turns delivering the program in Hanoi. It struck me that someone ought to write the textbook for such a course.

Around the same time, China was coming under fire for "manipulating" its exchange rate. I wrote a series of op-eds for the *Wall Street Journal* defending China's currency policy as rooted in sound macroeconomics. The anomalousness of this position prompted the paper's opinion page editor to ask me whether there was anyone else who agreed with my view. And again, it seemed to me that someone ought to write a textbook that would establish a way of thinking about macroeconomics for the Asian context.

I decided to step up. The book is designed from the outset for Emerging East Asia. It encompasses 13 economies: Cambodia; China; Hong Kong; Indonesia; Korea; Laos; Malaysia; Myanmar; the Philippines; Singapore; Taiwan; Thailand; and Vietnam. As different as they are in many ways, these economies can all be subsumed within a common framework for purposes of macroeconomic analysis. And a substantially different framework it is from the one conceived for the USA.

The economies of Emerging East Asia share the following salient features: (i) both internal balance, involving output growth at potential with inflation low and stable, and external balance, involving sustainable foreign trade and capital flows, matter for macroeconomic stability; (ii) the exchange rate figures importantly in macroeconomic policy; (iii) the role of the interest rate in monetary policy is circumscribed by the pressures of global capital flows (Singapore and Hong Kong being extreme cases) or by insensitivity of credit to interest rate movements (China being a case in point); and (iv) sustainability of public debt is a concern.

By contrast, because the USA is in the unique position of printing the world's reserve currency, external balance and debt sustainability are not at issue there. Further, because the US financial system is well developed and globally dominant, the interest rate serves as an effective, finely tuned instrument of monetary policy, while the exchange rate does not figure in.

A technical summary aimed at the initiated follows in this and the next paragraph, with the novice invited to hang on for inspiration. The book treats the balance of payments and exchange rates as foundational. Once the system of national accounts for measuring the domestic economy has been laid out, the balance of payments accounts are introduced. This sets the stage for presenting the basic identity equating an excess of national saving over domestic investment with a capital outflow that must be matched by a trade surplus. The basics of money creation are then explained with reference to the central bank balance sheet so as to illuminate the parallel between domestic bonds and foreign currencies for purposes of central bank trading operations. A full elaboration of foreign exchange markets follows with the implications of central bank intervention highlighted. Foundations thus in place, attention turns to theories of how an economy responds to shocks and why performance is prone to fluctuate over time. The policy chapters follow. Monetary policy is discussed with reference to both the interest rate and the exchange rate as instruments. Fiscal policy is examined with emphasis on debt sustainability. The coordinated exercise of monetary and fiscal policy for pursuit of combined internal and external balance is then analyzed with use of the Swan diagram. Two further chapters deal with macroprudential policy and the origins and management of crises.

To cap it off, the Epilogue circles back to a motivating issue for the book: "currency manipulation", as charged most vociferously against China, but also against Vietnam, Taiwan, and in broader brush potentially any economy that relies on central bank intervention in the foreign exchange market to pursue macroeconomic stability. That means all 13 economies covered in this text. Central bank buying of foreign currency in exchange for newly issued domestic currency stimulates the economy by expanding the money supply and by making exports cheaper and imports more expensive to favor domestic production. Central bank selling of foreign currency and withdrawal of domestic currency does the opposite. Importantly, a central bank can only sell foreign currency to the extent that it has previously bought it. And it may need to sell a lot to stabilize an exchange rate in the face of heavy capital outflows, a leading cause of which is the pull of higher interest rates in the USA when authorities there tighten monetary policy. When the USA acts, the rest of the world must react. Foreign exchange market intervention is a prime tool for such reacting and for pursuing macroeconomic stabilization more generally. This book lays the foundations for understanding and justifying the exchange rate management behavior we observe.

No prior knowledge of economics is assumed on the part of students, although novices should be prepared to get up and running quickly. Those who have taken macroeconomics courses using standard US textbooks will find the training helpful in grasping the material even as they discover much that is new here. Those who are well versed in the discipline will appreciate the substantially different approach taken in this book to fit macroeconomics to the Asian milieu.

Finally, as this book goes to press, the Covid pandemic continues to cause economic disruption and pose policy challenges. For updates on the situation applying the framework developed in the book, interested readers are referred to the *Asia Economics Blog* of the American Committee on Asian Economic Studies. The website for this textbook keeps a running tally of posts keyed by chapter. Further to those with a broad interest in Asian economies, the Blog provides an open forum for presentation of research and analysis.

1   Fitting Macroeconomics to Emerging East Asia

East Asia has given rise to some of the most spectacular economic performances of the post-World War II era. It has also borne some of the most serious setbacks. As everywhere, boom and bust follow one upon the other in recurring cycles. Notably for Emerging East Asia, as the region has become more integrated internally and with the rest of the world, the cycles have become more synchronized.

Many East Asian economies have managed to sustain double-digit growth rates for a few years at a stretch – Japan, Hong Kong, Singapore, Korea, Taiwan, China, Thailand, and as of the 2000s even Myanmar and Cambodia, are all members of this club. Singapore stands out for having achieved growth in excess of 10 percent for nine consecutive years from its independence in 1965 to 1973. More recently, Myanmar appears to have beaten this record with an 11-year run of double-digit growth beginning in 1999, if official statistics are to be believed (see end of chapter Data Note).

Typically though, boom times are short lived, and what's more, they are often followed by busts. Spurts of growth intermix with periods of sluggishness or even contraction. Singapore's storied success was punctuated by repeated setbacks, with growth going negative in 1985, 1998, 2001, and 2009. The Asian Financial Crisis of 1997–1998 plunged much of Emerging East Asia into negative growth territory. At the epicenter of the crisis, Thailand experienced a particularly virulent turn, coming through a decade of expansion at near double-digit levels only to see output growth drop to −1.4 percent in 1997 and then to −10.5 percent the following year.

Fluctuations in economic growth, and the policy measures aimed at containing them, are the central concern of this book. This chapter introduces the subject matter and explains why the treatment presented in standard US texts is a poor fit for Emerging East Asia. The 13 economies within our purview are Cambodia, China, Hong Kong, Indonesia, Korea, Laos, Malaysia, Myanmar, the Philippines, Singapore, Taiwan, Thailand, and Vietnam.

The focus of this text is on short-run deviations from long-run potential growth. For our purposes, the conceptual basis for long-run potential growth can be characterized succinctly, and we accomplish that in this first chapter. Long-run potential provides a reference against which to mark output gaps wherein an economy temporarily overshoots or undershoots a sustainable path. A high degree of volatility around the norm rate of growth is undesirable. Shortfalls involve loss of employment and income, as well as missed investment opportunities. But overshooting, too, carries costs as resources are misallocated into projects that are not ultimately viable, sowing the seeds of dislocations to come. More generally, volatility complicates planning for the future and inhibits entrepreneurial risk taking. Government policy thus seeks to stabilize growth and keep output gaps – positive or negative – to a minimum.

The first section of this chapter defines macroeconomics, drawing the contrast with microeconomics. It then presents graphically the main phenomenon to be understood: growth fluctuations for our 13 economies as viewed over the last six decades. The second section explains the concept of long-run potential growth, against which output gaps are registered, and examines the controversy surrounding how the early break-out economies of Emerging East Asia sustained their extraordinary growth rates. Theories of output gaps are introduced in the third section, with attention to why the economies of Emerging East Asia are particularly prone to volatility. The fourth section discusses stabilization policy, again with attention to the particulars of Emerging East Asia. The final section summarizes the book and provides a chapter by chapter outline, then offers guidance on finding a path through it along alternative tracks.

A   Macroeconomics Defined

An economy is made up of multitudes of diverse individuals making choices in pursuit of their own interests. Households make choices about how much of their incomes to spend or save, what products to buy or assets to hold, how to make the most of their time and talents in the marketplace. Business managers make choices about designing and producing products, employing workers, investing in plant and equipment, adopting and developing technologies, borrowing money or taking on equity investors, and distributing profits. No omniscient planner coordinates this vast array of activity, yet somehow it takes on an overall coherence. And in the aggregate, the activity coalesces to move as an integrated whole, cycling through boom-and-bust.

In this section, we flesh out the concept of macroeconomics by contrasting it with microeconomics. We then offer a first glimpse of the phenomenon at the heart of this text by charting growth fluctuations over the last six decades for the economies of Emerging East Asia.

Macro vs Micro

Macroeconomics looks at the big picture of aggregate output and the general price level, and seeks to understand movement in these indicators over time. Microeconomics focuses on the behavior of individual households and firms and how this behavior is expressed in markets to determine relative prices and patterns of resource allocation among alternative uses. Systematic parallels between macro and micro are drawn in Box 1.1.

Box 1.1 Macro vs micro

Macroeconomics deals with an economy as a whole. Attention is on aggregate production of output and overall utilization of resources. The key performance indicator is the total value of final goods and services produced during a period of time. In contrast, **microeconomics** focuses on the allocation of resources among alternative uses in the production of goods and services. Attention is on how the forces of supply and demand determine activity in particular markets.

Prices are of interest in **macroeconomics** for how they move overall. A key indicator of macroeconomic stability is the inflation rate. In **microeconomics** relative prices are what matters. Some products are relatively cheap, others relatively expensive, and microeconomics explains why.

The degree of resource utilization relative to potential is of concern in **macroeconomics**, the unemployment rate being a standard measure of this and, along with inflation, a key indicator of stability. **Microeconomics** looks at the allocation of resources among competing uses.

Finally, the external sector comes into play in **macroeconomics** with respect to an economy's overall payments position with the rest of the world. Whether an economy is running a surplus or deficit in its international trade and financial accounts has implications for macroeconomic performance and policy. In **microeconomics**, the composition of imports and exports and the role of foreign investment by sector are of interest.

	MACRO	MICRO
General Purview	size of an economy in the aggregate; long-term growth and short-term fluctuations	relative activity in particular markets as determined by forces of supply and demand
Prices	movement in the general level of prices, the inflation rate being the key indicator	relative prices, or why some things are cheap and others expensive
Resources	utilization of resources relative to capacity, the unemployment rate being a prime indicator	allocation of resources among alternative uses
External Sector	overall balance in international trade and financial flows	composition of exports and imports, and impact of trade and foreign investment by sector

Microeconomics takes households and firms, of a stylized sort, as its basic building blocks. Households are assumed to maximize utility (i.e., well-being) by selling the factor inputs to production – labor, capital, land, and entrepreneurship – and buying goods and services. Firms are assumed to maximize profits by operating on the opposite side of these exchanges, buying factor inputs and selling goods and services. Market participants bid against one another to arrive at prices that equate demands and supplies. Under competitive market conditions, microeconomic theory contends that scarce resources will be allocated to the uses in which they are most highly valued. The "Invisible Hand" of the market, in the metaphor of Adam Smith (1776), thus achieves an efficient outcome in a way that no planning authority could hope to match.

Yet, while micro theory adheres to a story of markets reaching equilibrium, macro theory is concerned with instability in an aggregate that is ostensibly the sum of its micro parts. There is a seeming disconnect in this. For macro must deal with resources at times being less than fully utilized and the price level being broadly unstable even as micro presents a vision of markets clearing through price equilibration. At the macro level, the unemployment rate and the inflation rate are standard indicators of how an economy is performing relative to its potential. An economy in a downturn experiences rising unemployment and weakening inflation or even a falling price level. Conversely, in an expansion, labor markets tighten to reduce unemployment and inflation heats up. Equilibrium seems elusive in the macro realm.

How can the disconnect between micro and macro be reconciled? The failure of the labor market to clear – that is, the existence of unemployment – may be explained by lags in adjustment to shocks or by rigidities in wage bargains that limit downward adjustment and thus compel firms to layoff workers when they must cut costs. And movements in the macro price level can occur irrespective of the structure of relative prices that pertain to micro. In any case, some disconnect between micro and macro should not be too disconcerting. Each body of thought is concerned with explaining different phenomena: micro with the way markets coordinate the allocation of resources and the distribution of products to achieve an outcome in the moment; macro with the way the aggregate of this activity moves over time. Each body of theory should be taken on its own terms with a view to its particular purpose.

For a large economy with a relatively small foreign sector, the study of macroeconomics can proceed with respect to the domestic realm, leaving an international dimension to be grafted on afterward. This is the typical approach of textbooks focused on the US economy. However, for the outward oriented economies of Emerging East Asia, external influences must be treated as integral. External shocks – for example, swings in global commodity prices, movements in exchange rates, or changing perceptions of risk that drive international capital flows – are major sources of volatility for these economies. External imbalances in trade or financial flows can be sustained to a point, and that point can be stretched with concerted macro policy action. But ultimately, vulnerabilities may develop or tipping points may be reached with disruptive consequences when corrections finally occur. External balance is thus central to the study of macroeconomics for Emerging East Asia.

Fluctuations around Potential Growth

The principal measure of macroeconomic performance is gross domestic product (GDP) which captures the value of all final goods and services produced in a given period of time. This includes both consumption and investment products. Nominal GDP growth rates are calculated based on current prices. Subtracting the rate of inflation yields real GDP growth at constant prices.

Real GDP growth rates for our 13 economies for the period 1960–2020 are presented in Chart 1.1. The scaling of the axes allows for growth as high as 15 percent and as low as –15 percent, with the numbers sometimes going off the chart in early years although not since the 1970s. The most extreme negative value was for China in 1961 at –27 percent, and indeed this is the only instance of a growth rate dropping below the negative bound of the scale. Known in China as the "difficult period," the early 1960s saw tens of millions of people lose their lives to famine as food production collapsed under Chairman Mao's ill-conceived Great Leap Forward. Later in the 1960s and the 1970s, both China and Hong Kong saw growth rates spike above 15 percent within a context of extreme volatility.

Growth has at some point reached more than 10 percent for all economies in the region except the Philippines and Vietnam (the latter on the basis of data only since 1985). And it has plunged into negative territory without exception for all those economies for which time series are available in full. Volatility is a reality no economy has escaped. Even from one year to the next, wide fluctuations in growth rates are common. Of a total 686 year-to-year points of comparison yielded by the sample, 114, or 17 percent, involve a change of more than five percentage points in one direction or the other.

For each economy, Chart 1.1 shows a trend line representing a linear approximation of the growth rate over time. The linear form of the approximation allows values to go to untenable extremes toward the ends of the time period. Subject to this caveat, the slope of the line provides a clue as to general movement in the growth rate up or down over time. Economies that reached middle income status earlier (Hong Kong, Korea, Singapore, and Taiwan) have generally experienced slowing growth rates during the period under examination whereas those emerging later (such as China, Laos, and Myanmar) have shown rising growth rates.

Patterns over time in the region-wide coincidence of fluctuations can be discerned by superimposing the growth rates of the 13 economies, as shown in Chart 1.2. The Asian Financial Crisis stands out for its severe impact across the board in 1998. And the devastating impact of the pandemic is evident in 2020. Prior to the Asian Financial Crisis, deep recessions were usually confined to a single economy, although milder growth slowdowns of a more shared nature are visible in some years (1964, 1967, 1982, and 1985). From the Asian Financial Crisis onward, synchronization is more clearcut. Subsequent sharp dips in growth rates registered broadly in 2001 and 2009. In recent decades, the economies of Emerging East Asia have become more integrated both with one another and with the rest of the world. Individual economies have thus tended to get more caught up in forces emanating from beyond their borders.

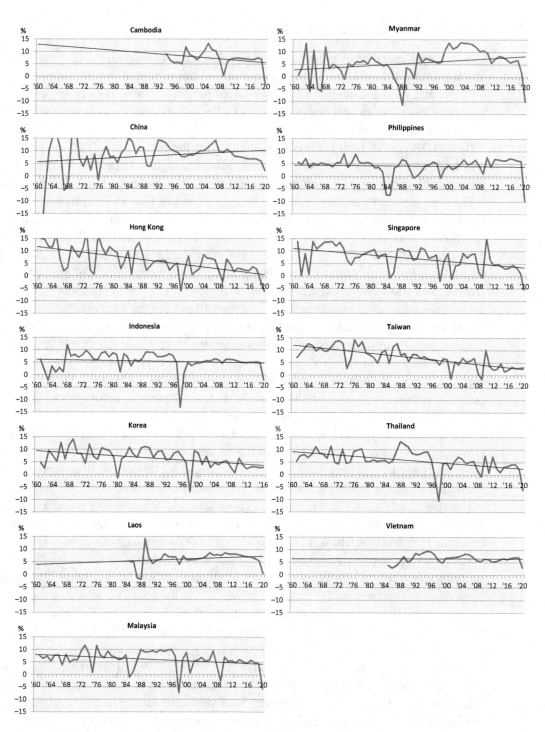

Chart 1.1 GDP growth rates, select economies, 1961–2020

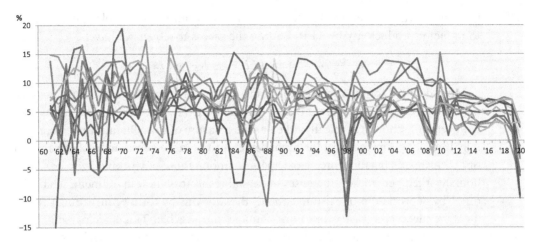

Chart 1.2 GDP growth rates superimposed, select economies, 1961–2020

B   Potential Growth

With all the variation in growth rates on display – not only from year to year for given economies but in general trends across economies – how are we to discern long-term potential? In this section we examine the underpinnings of potential growth using a formal growth accounting framework. We then review empirical applications of the framework to Emerging East Asia.

Even a formal accounting framework leaves much ambiguity about what *can* be achieved as opposed to what *has* been achieved. For purposes of macroeconomic stabilization policy, the reality is in any case more pragmatic discovery process than modeling exercise. An economy's potential growth is marked most tellingly by that threshold beyond which inflation accelerates. The goal of policy is to bring the economy as close to potential as possible without crossing the line. As a practical matter, potential is discerned by pushing the limits. Growth accounting acts as an aid in envisioning those limits.

Growth Accounting

The conceptual foundation for growth accounting, as laid out by Robert Solow (1957), rests on a distinction between increases in the factor inputs to production and increases in the productivity of those factor inputs. For growth accounting purposes, the key factor inputs are capital and labor (land not varying appreciably over time and entrepreneurship, varying or not, not readily measurable). Formally, the contribution of capital to output growth is given by the rate of increase in the capital stock, represented by $\dot{K}$, times the rate of return to capital, i.e, the profit rate, represented by π. Similarly, the contribution of labor is given by the rate of increase in labor, $\dot{L}$, times the rate of return to labor, i.e., the wage rate, w.

Output growth is given by $\dot{Y}$, and that part of output growth explained by an increase in total factor productivity by TFP. Putting the pieces together, we have:

$$\dot{Y} = TFP + \pi \cdot \dot{K} + w \cdot \dot{L} \qquad (1.1)$$

More detailed formulations of the contributions of labor and capital are possible. Labor may increase not only quantitatively, but qualitatively through human capital formation, with years of schooling typically taken as the measure of this. Quantitative increases in labor may trace to: (1) increases in the labor force due to (1a) increases in working age population or (1b) increases in labor force participation among those of working ages; or (2) changes in hours worked per worker. Increases in capital result from new investment, which is partially offset by depreciation of existing capital. Breakdowns by form of investment (plant, equipment, residences, infrastructure) and vintage are possible. This finer parsing of labor and capital inputs allows for more closely calibrated measurement of their impact on growth affording a clearer delineation of the residual element, TFP.

The TFP residual captures a wide variety of influences. Foremost among these is technological innovation. The advance of knowledge allows more to be achieved with given resources. Another influence, important in developing economies, is the transfer of labor out of subsistence agriculture into formal industrial and service sector employment. Migration from farm to factory involves a leap across a productivity chasm when poor peasants take up work in the city. Finally, institutional development can contribute dramatically to productivity growth. The strengthening of market functioning and the fostering of private enterprise are great boosters of effort, entrepreneurial energy, and efficiency in resource use.

Empirical Application to Emerging East Asia

Growth accounting exercises for Emerging East Asia have ignited a firestorm of controversy. A study by Young (1995) of Hong Kong, Korea, Singapore, and Taiwan for the period 1966–1990 traced most of the extraordinary growth recorded to increases in factor inputs leaving little, or in the case of Singapore less than nothing, to be explained by improvements in TFP. The four tigers, as they are known, invested heavily in both physical and human capital, and put more of the population to work as females increasingly entered paid labor and falling birth rates concentrated more of the population in working ages. Hard work and sacrifice, then, rather than technological advance and economic progress, were alleged to have been the basis for growth.

The finding that East Asia's success derived mainly from "perspiration" rather than "inspiration" in the words of Paul Krugman (1994) did not sit well within the societies being studied. The findings suggested that growth had come at a very high cost in terms of foregone consumption and leisure, and that in the extreme case of Singapore investment had been pushed to a point of negative returns. With saving rates and labor force participation reaching the limits of feasibility, the implication was that the East Asian development model was close to exhaustion, and that absent improvements in productivity, growth was about to hit a wall.

Results of growth accounting studies are sensitive to tweaks in methodology, and other researchers have come to less extreme conclusions. A report by the International Monetary Fund (2006) offered mixed findings on TFP for a broad selection of Emerging East Asian economies. The period under review started from an economy-specific year of growth take-off and extended to 2005. The report showed TFP growth having contributed more importantly among the four tigers than Young estimated, and very importantly with respect to China's much higher growth, although negligibly to the more modest growth of the ASEAN-4 comprising Indonesia, Malaysia, the Philippines, and Thailand. Heavy reliance on investment in physical and human capital to achieve growth remains characteristic of the region. Once that is recognized, the wedge left for attribution to TFP increases takes on significance only with very high GDP growth.

The formal growth accounting framework is useful for benchmarking potential. Projections of labor and capital increases combined with expectations about productivity growth can suggest a feasible trajectory for an economy. A modeling exercise such as this presents a loose reference point for macro stabilization policy. But more immediate, tangible indicators of output gaps take on greater influence in the practical affairs of policymaking. We now turn attention to these indicators.

C   Output Gaps

Growth above potential is indicated by accelerating inflation, growth below potential by resource under-utilization. We elaborate on the manifestations of output gaps in this section with attention to the particulars of emerging market economies. We then approach the controversial subject of how to interpret fluctuations in growth. Much disagreement revolves around what causes fluctuations and whether or not an economy will tend to self-correct and return to its potential path automatically. Differences in views on these theoretical issues lead to differences in positions on how to conduct stabilization policy.

Measuring Output Gaps

Overperformance relative to long-run potential results in a positive output gap, underperformance a negative output gap. A positive output gap is also known as an inflationary gap. As growth outstrips potential, bottlenecks develop in markets for labor and other resources. This puts upward pressure on wages and prices. Low levels of inflation, on the order of 2–4 percent, are generally conducive to healthy economic development. A little inflation allows for easy adjustment in relative prices to reflect changes in costs or other market conditions. Higher and accelerating inflation becomes problematic, however, especially as uncertainty mounts and this clouds decision-making. Lenders worry about lost purchasing power of funds being repaid them and call for higher interest rates, which borrowers may be reluctant to take on. Investment consequently tends to shift to riskier endeavors in an inflationary environment. Keeping inflation low and stable is therefore an important macro policy objective.

A negative output gap is known also as a deflationary or recessionary gap. In mature market economies, the unemployment rate is the most closely watched indicator of a negative output gap. In emerging market economies, however, reported unemployment rates are generally not very meaningful. Much of the labor force is absorbed in agriculture or informal urban activities such as street vending or day labor. For the stratum of society eking out an existence in such pursuits, work is often erratic and insecure. People nevertheless have to survive somehow, and unemployment strictly speaking is not much of an option. Official unemployment rates typically pertain to the formal segment of the labor force, members of which are entitled to benefits and officially register their unemployment status. In the emerging market context, the more telling way to gauge lagging economic performance relative to potential is by comparing the number of jobs created in the urban formal sector with some measure of potential based on demography and urbanization. If the economy is not creating enough jobs to absorb school leavers and a steady stream of those transitioning from agricultural and informal urban activities, this signals a negative output gap. The employment focus is thus on the rate of formal job creation rather than a not readily measured, or even conceptualized, unemployment rate. Job creation is in turn closely tied to GDP growth with a shortfall relative to trend the practical indicator of a negative output gap.

Explaining Output Gaps

Classical economics, rooted in the works of Adam Smith (1776), Jean-Baptiste Say (1821), and David Ricardo (1817), provides an explanation for how the decentralized decision-making of a market economy succeeds as well as it does to put people to work and provide for their needs. The upshot is that wages and prices adjust to match supplies with demands. Within this framework, such unemployment as may emerge is attributed to shocks that cause temporary dislocations. These shocks can trace to a host of forces from technological advances that bring about substitution of capital for labor to development of new products that crowd out old ones to geopolitical events or natural disasters. A shock is transmitted through the price mechanism to guide a process of resource reallocation that culminates in a return to full-employment equilibrium.

The classical paradigm largely held sway until the Great Depression of the 1930s. But when unemployment in the USA reached 25 percent in 1933 and remained at 19 percent five years later, the credibility of an autonomous mechanism to achieve full employment was seriously undermined.

John Maynard Keynes (1936) stepped into the ideological breach to offer a whole new way of thinking about economic malaise. "Animal spirits," in Keynes's view, were the driving force behind booms and busts. For risky investments to be undertaken and consumer spending to thrive, people must be optimistic about the future. When investors lack confidence that new projects will generate returns or workers are worried about losing their jobs, spending contracts all around. Negative expectations held on a broad scale are self-fulfilling. When inventories accumulate on shelves, business managers cut production. Interest rates can fall to a lower bound of near zero, and still entrepreneurs do not deign to borrow out of fear of taking on the risk of new investment. Resistance to wage cuts on the part of workers pushes employers to lay off staff to pare expenses. The future seems bleak, so spending is inhibited; but with spending inhibited, the economy indeed fails to regain momentum. The system does not self-correct as classical theory would have us believe. This opens the way for government to play a role, increasing its own spending or cutting taxes to increase the spending of households and businesses so as to stir the economy out of its doldrums.

The contemporary approach to modeling macroeconomic processes rests on an amalgam of classical and Keynesian elements. Market equilibration from classical theory provides the foundation while Keynesian theory injects lags into the adjustment process. In the classical spirit, output gaps are attributed to exogenous shocks to productivity that disturb the equilibrium course of the economy. But in the Keynesian mode, markets do not respond expeditiously to these shocks to return the economy to a stable, full-employment path. Rather, imperfect competition inhibits output adjustment; wage bargaining and contracting impede labor reallocation; and intransigence in expectations weighs on investment and consumption behavior. From this hybrid model, the Keynesian policy conclusion comes through that government action is needed to get the economy moving forward in a timely fashion.

There is an alternative way of thinking about macroeconomic fluctuations, with a long history going back to Mills (1867) and Bagehot (1874), if not much contemporary following. Rather than attributing macroeconomic ups and downs to exogenous shocks disrupting movement along an equilibrium path, the approach posits an endogenous cyclical process. The process rests on the essential role of credit in a capitalist economy. In a financial upswing, credit expansion fuels asset price increases and risky bets then pay off to encourage more lending, driving further asset price increases in a positive feedback loop. The process tends to overshoot, however, with asset prices becoming unsustainable such that ultimately a reversal takes place with loans going into default. A downturn then sets in, only to be propelled by the feedback loop going negative as tightening credit interacts with declining asset prices. The bust deepens and endures until, at last, the skies clear and a sense of opportunity germinates once again. Soon enough, another boom gets underway. The US financial crisis of 2008 brought renewed attention to the role of finance in macroeconomic fluctuations and with that a revival of endogenous cycle theory. In particular, Hyman Minsky (1986) gained prominence for his more recent articulation of the argument, with the crisis dubbed a "Minsky moment."

Perhaps an amalgam of schools of thought is again in order, this one between a shock-based exogenous process and a credit-based endogenous process. Indeed, that is what

Bagehot proposed nearly 150 years ago. As an economy ascends the peak of an expansionary credit cycle, it becomes more vulnerable to shocks landing with disastrous consequences. An economy on a sounder financial footing would weather the same shock more smoothly. Incorporation of the workings of the financial system into a theory of output gaps suggests a role for government policy aimed at regulating and supervising financial institutions to keep risks in check.

Emerging East Asia Particulars

The economies of Emerging East Asia differ in important respects from the economy that is the focus of most macroeconomic textbooks used in the region. The USA, in all its uniqueness, is possessed of: a low trade ratio to GDP; the world's dominant reserve currency; and deep and diversified financial markets that move global interest rates but are little affected by interest rates elsewhere. In contrast, the economies of Emerging East Asia are: externally oriented to a high degree; home to currencies for which maintaining confidence is a concern; and dependent on financial systems that operate under constraints unknown to the USA. These differences have critical implications for vulnerability to macroeconomic instability and the policy mechanisms suited to countering it.

Deep involvement in international trade and finance exposes the economies of Emerging East Asia to external shocks from shifts in global market conditions. Such shocks can drive volatility in domestic production and employment to powerful degree. International capital flows are especially prone to variability given their sensitivity to the fickle nature of confidence and risk tolerance. Once an emerging economy loses the faith of investors, its access to foreign credit can become strained and its currency quickly lose value. Currency depreciation in turn undermines the capacity to service foreign debt to the further alarm of creditors. This is how crises take hold.

To guard against such threats, central banks in Emerging East Asia have accumulated large troves of foreign reserves as bulwarks against loss of confidence. Central banks build reserves by intervening in currency markets, buying foreign exchange with domestic currency newly printed for the purpose. Should the local currency come under threat, reserves can then be sold off in a reversal of the transaction to stabilize the exchange rate. More generally, maintaining a reasonably stable exchange rate against the vagaries of the market – provided the rate does not diverge persistently from a credible long-run level – can facilitate business planning and investment by reducing uncertainty.

Financial systems within the Emerging East Asia region differ greatly in depth and global integration. At one extreme Hong Kong and Singapore have become major international financial centers. At the opposite extreme China imposes controls on the flow of capital in and out under a state-dominated financial system that limits the role of market forces in determining interest rates and the allocation of credit. Regionwide, the process of financial liberalization and development has been prone to fits and starts over a span of decades, with credit growth sometimes erratic. Weak regulatory frameworks and implicit government bailout guarantees complicate the opening of immature markets to the riptide forces of global capital.

In summary, Emerging East Asian economies are vulnerable to sources of instability that textbooks on the US economy need never consider. Exchange rate management can help to moderate volatility, but with critical implications for the conduct of macroeconomic stabilization policy. The state of development of the financial system factors into volatility and policymaking as well. The following section on policy elaborates.

D   Stabilization Policy

Two principle arms of policy exist for stabilizing economic growth: monetary policy and fiscal policy. Stabilization policy acts through its effect on aggregate demand, as given by total spending on final goods and services. For monetary policy, the channel involves central bank influence over credit creation by commercial banks. For fiscal policy, it involves government spending and taxation. We discuss each policy arm in turn in this section, highlighting features that distinguish the Emerging East Asia policy milieu.

Monetary Policy

Classical economics regards the supply of money as affecting the price level only and not real economic activity. The evidence, however, is compelling that certainly in the short run, changes in money supply affect real output even if the effect is ultimately channeled into prices. Against this conceptual backdrop, some central banks are mandated to focus narrowly on achieving an inflation target with an eye to the medium term while others have leeway to balance competing goals on inflation and output growth under a nearer term perspective.

Monetary policy works through central banks manipulating reserves of commercial banks so as to influence their capacity to lend. In the USA, the overnight interest rate on inter-bank lending serves as the principle instrument to guide reserve creation. Expansion of bank reserves lowers the interest rate and stimulates bank lending to speed up economic growth. Conversely, tightening of bank reserves raises the interest rate to restrain bank lending and slow down economic growth. This process works well for the USA with its sophisticated financial system, advanced market economy, and indomitability to external trade and capital shocks.

Nowhere in Emerging East Asia does this combination of circumstances obtain. Circumstances in fact vary a great deal across the region, and accordingly, so do institutional arrangements for the conduct of monetary policy. Hong Kong and Singapore are distinguished by their globally integrated financial systems which preclude any influence by domestic authorities over interest rates. Instead, the exchange rate serves to anchor monetary policy, although under arrangements that differ between the two jurisdictions. In Hong Kong the exchange rate is fixed to the US dollar whereas in Singapore it is managed by the monetary authority relative to a basket of currencies. In the Hong Kong case, the authority has no discretion over the supply of money; Hong Kong dollars are automatically issued or withdrawn in response to market demand for them relative to supply at the exchange rate peg. By contrast, in Singapore the authority exercises discretion in setting a target path for the exchange rate. A path of appreciation of the Singapore dollar reduces demand for it and lowers issuance thereby slowing growth in the economy and damping down inflation. Conversely, a path of depreciation increases demand and raises currency issuance to stimulate the economy. This general principle has broad applicability for the exchange rate as an instrument of monetary policy.

Elsewhere in the region, use of the interest rate as an instrument of monetary policy is limited not because of full global integration of financial markets but the opposite. Where financial systems are immature and not so market driven, controls on international capital flows can create an effective buffer between domestic activity and international forces. China is the foremost case in point. Under the country's system of state capitalism, a degree of government control extends to interest rates and the allocation of credit, which diminishes the functionality of the interest rate as an instrument of monetary policy. In these circumstances too, then, the exchange rate takes on greater import as an instrument of macro stabilization.

Broadly speaking, the exchange rate is an important instrument of monetary policy throughout Emerging East Asia under widely varying conditions of financial market openness and functionality. The International Monetary Fund classifies economies by the degree of official intervention in foreign exchange markets using three broad categories and a number of sub-categories. As of 2020, Hong Kong was classified as having a hard peg to the US dollar; Cambodia, China, Laos, Myanmar, Singapore, and Vietnam as having soft pegs, tied either to the US dollar or to a basket of currencies; and Indonesia, Korea, Malaysia, the Philippines, and Thailand as having "floating" exchange rates, but not "free floating," meaning their exchange rates are mostly market determined but with intervention at the discretion of authorities.

Throughout the region as well, the space in which authorities conduct monetary policy is circumscribed. A number of factors enter in, most importantly: the exchange rate regime; the degree of openness to international capital flows; and the development of the domestic financial system. Macroeconomic textbooks focused on the USA take for granted: a freely floating exchange rate; financial markets that are globally integrated, and yet not subordinated to external forces; and a mature financial system. In this environment, the USA conducts monetary policy with a focus on domestic interest rates and without regard for exchange rates. This model is not relevant for Emerging East Asia. In this text, our approach to macroeconomic policy takes exchange rate management as a pillar and accords due attention to the degree of openness to international capital flows and the limitations of domestic financial systems.

Fiscal Policy

The Keynesian view that recovery from a downturn is by no means automatic or assured looks to the fiscal arm of macroeconomic stabilization policy for deliverance. For Keynesians, increases in government spending or decreases in taxation have the power to boost aggregate demand and get an economy out of a slump. The initial fiscal impetus works with a multiplier effect as new government spending generates additional income which in turn leads to more spending and more income in successive rounds. Though over the years, activist fiscal policy has had its detractors, the Great Financial Crisis of 2008 saw a rallying to Keynesian remedies worldwide. The pandemic induced crisis of 2020 is invoking a similar response as of this writing.

The big concern with fiscal policy is that it inclines toward budget deficits, due to stimulatory spending increases and tax cuts, that must be financed. Government borrowing saddles future generations with the burden of debt repayment with interest. If debt-fueled spending leads to growth that expands the tax base sufficiently to cover the cost of debt service, the debt load will remain manageable. Putting unemployed resources to work productively during a recession may well achieve this. However, skepticism arises for a number of reasons: government spending works with lags in execution and impact; political factors influence spending choices, to the possible detriment of efficiency; and to the extent that resources are diverted from private sector activities, net gains are diminished.

Emerging market economies present a special sensitivity to rising public debt loads. Concerns about fiscal sustainability can lead creditors to demand higher interest rates. To pay back creditors, government must rely on tax revenues. To pay back foreign creditors in particular, government must further acquire foreign exchange generated through exports or new capital inflows and must do so in competition with potential private users of foreign exchange wishing to purchase imports, invest in foreign assets, or service their own foreign debts. Budget deficits are easy enough to incur, but not so easy politically to rein in again. Governments, especially in emerging markets, must therefore be cautious in exercising deficit spending as a means of stimulating growth.

A key indicator of fiscal policy space is the ratio of the stock of public debt to GDP. The safe zone for this ratio depends on such factors as the GDP growth rate and the interest cost of public sector borrowing. Governments with high debt-to-GDP ratios accumulated through past borrowing will hit up against limits for fiscal activism. The issue of fiscal sustainability is pertinent for many of the economies under our purview, and not touched on in US textbooks.

E Overview of Macroeconomics for Emerging East Asia

We conclude this chapter with a few general words of overview followed with a chapter by chapter outline and then some guidance on navigating a path.

General Overview

This text focuses on short-run growth fluctuations and stabilization policy in Emerging East Asia. Key features of the setting are: a high degree of openness to international trade and capital, and with that vulnerability to external shock; macroeconomic stabilization policies involving exchange rate management; and financial sectors that, whether sophisticated and globally integrated or ringed by capital controls and subject to administrative intervention, pose limits on the scope for an interest rate focused monetary policy.

The book is rich in empirical documentation of the Emerging East Asian experience. Only two out of 16 chapters, Chapters 3 and 9, are confined to pure theory. The remaining chapters illustrate concepts with comparative data for the 13 economies of the region, with most also featuring one economy in particular for in-depth analysis.

Most chapters are followed by a data note and a bibliographic note. The data note identifies the sources for the empirical content of the chapter and offers any comments or caveats. The bibliographic note discusses the origins of the ideas contained in the chapter.

Chapter Outline

Chapter 2 takes the broad economic measure of Emerging East Asia. The economies of the region differ greatly with respect to size, level of development, engagement in international trade and finance, and roles of state versus market. These factors are examined for their bearing on macroeconomic volatility and the policy environment.

Chapter 3 lays out the fundamentals of microeconomics. The focus is on the mechanics of demand and supply and development of the argument that competitive markets achieve efficiency in the allocation of resources. The tools of microeconomics find application in macroeconomics for analyzing markets that pertain to the economy as a whole. These include: the market for labor in which the wage rate is determined; the market for loanable funds in which the interest rate is determined; and the market for foreign exchange in which the exchange rate is determined. This is the first of two chapters that are purely theoretical.

The next two chapters deal with measuring and categorizing economic activity. Chapter 4 covers the national income and product accounts which yield the key aggregate indicator, GDP (gross domestic product). This aggregate is arrived at through three different approaches that involve summing activity along three different dimensions: the product approach based on sector of production, the broad divisions being agriculture, industry, and services; the expenditure approach defined over consumption, investment, government, and exports net of imports; and the income approach encompassing wages, interest, rents, and profits. The diversity of Emerging East Asia comes across vividly in comparisons of the region's economies along these lines. Historic data for Taiwan capture systematic changes associated with the economic development process.

Chapter 5 lays out the balance of payments accounts. These accounts capture cross-border trade and financial flows including the accumulation of official reserves by the monetary authority. Comparison across economies shows most Emerging East Asian economies having run substantial balance of payments surpluses through recent decades resulting in the amassing of vast official reserves. Because China's reserve accumulation has been so extraordinarily large and politically charged, with later reversals in this accumulation so sharp, we examine its balance of payments history in detail.

Chapter 6 deals with money. We begin by defining money as debt and explaining that it derives from the banking system issuing liabilities against itself. We then consider the age old debate in economics as to the effect of money supply increases on the price level versus real output. Data across our set of economies show a clear correlation between money and prices, that is nevertheless not without aberrations. Myanmar makes for an interesting case study because money supply growth there has been so erratic over time.

The importance of finance in macroeconomics came to the fore with the Great Financial Crisis of 2008, textbooks not having given it much attention before then. Chapter 7 considers the role of the financial system in creating debt beyond that narrowly defined as money with the potential to generate destabilizing impulses. The chapter also provides foundations in the functioning of financial markets to determine interest rates and asset values. Hong Kong, as one of the world's leading financial centers, gets a close look.

Exchange rates are the subject of Chapter 8. We begin by studying how market forces act to determine exchange rates and achieve balance in international payments. We then proceed to consider the implications of government intervention in foreign exchange markets and come to understand how external balance can be achieved even under a pegged exchange rate. Our focus economy, Indonesia, has transitioned from a fixed exchange rate to a floating rate, and we examine how the country has contended with external shocks under these alternative regimes.

Chapter 9 is the second of two purely theoretical chapters. In it we review macroeconomic models of equilibrium and disequilibrium. The model of aggregate demand and supply is a model of equilibrium in the classical spirit in which prices adjust to clear markets and the economy rebounds spontaneously from shocks to recover its potential growth path. In contrast, the income-expenditure model, based on the work of Keynes, depicts an economy that is prone to sustained sub-optimal performance. In this model, wages and prices fail to adjust to achieve full employment in any timely fashion, and aggregate demand thus falls short of inducing production at potential. Finally, the IS-LM (investment/saving-liquidity/money) model elaborates on the Keynesian framework to highlight the role of the interest rate in policy, and the Mundell–Fleming extension of the model brings in a foreign sector with a role for the exchange rate. This model is later put through its paces in Chapter 12 on fiscal policy.

The models of Chapter 9 are comparative static in nature. They capture an initial situation, introduce an exogenous shock, and compare the outcome with the baseline suppressing the passage of time. By contrast, the models of business cycles presented in Chapter 10 are dynamic. They describe a process of movement with an explicit time dimension. The dominant paradigm for business cycle modeling extends comparative static analysis in a straightforward manner, taking an equilibrium path as the norm and ascribing deviations from it to exogenous shocks. Classical versus Keynesian variations on this theme are distinguished by the speed with which equilibrium is restored post-shock. An alternative approach posits endogenous laws of motion that push an economy to overshoot its potential to the point that finally a correction must occur, and when it does a downward spiral of job loss and business failure leads again to overshooting such that the economy becomes mired below its potential until, eventually, a recovery takes hold and the cycle begins anew. We develop both the standard exogenous shock-based paradigm and the alternative endogenous cycle paradigm, then bring the two together in a synthesis. The synthesis involves a cyclical process that affects an economy's vulnerability to shocks such that the shocks play out differently depending on the state of this vulnerability. We apply these theories to interpreting the Philippine experience.

The next three chapters cover macroeconomic stabilization policy. Stabilization policy involves monetary and fiscal action to exert expansionary or contractionary pressure on aggregate demand. Chapter 11 deals with monetary policy, treating the exchange rate and the interest rate as intertwined policy instruments. The options for monetary policy framework are governed by the Trilemma which asserts the impossibility of adopting all three of: a fixed exchange rate; free mobility of international capital; and an independent monetary policy. The trade-offs are managed differently by the economies of Emerging East Asia. At one extreme, Hong Kong, as a global financial hub, fixes its currency to the US dollar and forfeits any discretion over monetary policy. China takes a different tack by imposing controls on capital flows which increases the space for discretionary monetary policy despite a stabilized exchange rate. Most economies in the region have fairly open financial markets and finesse the trade-off between exchange rate stabilization and monetary policy discretion. Singapore's finely honed relationship between exchange rate management and monetary policy under an open financial market provides the case study for this chapter.

Chapter 12 takes up fiscal policy, which involves the use of government spending and taxation to steer aggregate demand. To some extent, automatic stabilizers are built into the tax system and government welfare programs in that booms are restrained by rising tax revenues and falling welfare spending and conversely busts are ameliorated by falling tax revenues and rising welfare spending. More activist policy, when aimed at promoting stimulus, must be attentive to the sustainability of public debt. We examine debt-to-GDP ratios for the economies of Emerging East Asia and assess the space for fiscal policy reach. Vietnam in the 2010s was on a path of sharply rising debt which it managed to temper, and we examine how that was achieved and the prospects for sustainability.

Monetary and fiscal policy work in complementary fashion to address internal and external imbalances. We analyze the process in Chapter 13 using the Swan diagram. The Swan diagram defines four "zones of economic discomfort" based on the four possible combinations of internal overheating versus underperformance relative to GDP growth potential and external overshooting versus undershooting of a target within the balance of payments. Based on an economy's position within the Swan diagram, prescriptions for expansionary versus contractionary monetary and fiscal policy can be derived. In the Malaysian case for the late 2010s, the recommendation was for a contractionary monetary policy and an expansionary fiscal policy. We note, however, that Malaysia's space for such action was constrained, and so we pull back to consider other strategies from a broader perspective.

The essentials of a macroeconomics for Emerging East Asia are covered in Chapters 4–13. Two further chapters explore special topics. Chapter 14 takes up macroprudential policy which involves regulation and supervision of financial institutions to safeguard stability in the financial system as a whole. Systemic risk tends to build in boom times and subside in busts. Such fluctuations are amplified in the Emerging East Asia setting by global capital flows. Macroprudential policy aims at moderating the fluctuations. We analyze the Korean experience for lessons.

Chapter 15 is devoted to crises. Generally, crises originate in financial overshoot when mounting debt becomes unsustainable. Despite centuries of catastrophic experience with this phenomenon, policymakers have not figured out how to avoid it with consistency. This chapter inquires into why that is. It then looks at monetary and fiscal policy responses put to their ultimate test. Emerging East Asia suffered a regional financial crisis in 1997. As the epicenter of this crisis, Thailand offers a window into the incubation and eruption of a financial crisis and the lessons learned about policy response. From 2020, a crisis of a different sort has been unfolding in the form of a shock to the the real economy from a pandemic. We consider the policy response, with attention to the limits on policy space, as an application of the analytical tools developed in this text.

Chapter 16 is the epilogue. This chapter sums up the basics of macroeconomics for Emerging East Asia, then takes on the politically charged topic of currency manipulation. Technically, this term is applied when an economy depresses the value of its currency with the intent of gaining an unfair advantage in exporting. The principles laid out in this text provide a foundation for arguing that the intent of foreign exchange market intervention in Emerging East Asia is instead to achieve macroeconomic stabilization, which is perfectly allowable under the prevailing rules of the International Monetary Fund.

Navigating This Text

This text is meant to accommodate students of widely differing backgrounds in US-centric macroeconomic instruction. Those entering the discipline of economics for the first time through this doorway will do well to keep their focus on a narrow Emerging East Asia track and treat as peripheral the doctrinal material. Those already versed in standard doctrine will appreciate the originality of the approach to Emerging East Asia.

The two tracks differ most sharply at Chapter 9, which presents a compact summary of the core models of conventional macroeconomics. These models help us understand why an economy diverges from its potential. The uninitiated may skate lightly over this material to gain a superficial sense of the models for reference. The workhorse of US-centric macro modeling is the IS-LM model which focuses on the interest rate as the key policy variable. The Mundell–Fleming extension of the model brings in the exchange rate. While these models have their place, it is the premise of this text that they do not do the best job of affording insight into Emerging East Asia. Rather, the main track of the text builds foundations in external balance and exchange rates to arrive at the Swan diagram of Chapter 13. For those who must prioritize carefully in their study of Emerging East Asia, this model should take pre-eminence over the models of Chapter 9.

Chapter 10 on business cycles extends the static analysis of Chapter 9 on why an economy diverges from its potential into a dynamic framework to describe movement relative to potential over time. The conventional approach to the subject treats exogenous productivity shocks to the static models of Chapter 9 as the driving force. An alternative approach drawn from the historical literature avoids the models of Chapter 9 altogether to tell a story of endogenous movement wherein the interaction between credit and asset prices acts as the driving force. This alternative gained interest in the West with the Great Financial Crisis of 2008. For Emerging East Asia, the emphasis on finance takes on greater relevance given the importance of cross-border capital flows in economic fluctuations. This is further justification for skipping lightly over Chapter 9.

For the novice in economics with a predominant interest in Emerging East Asia, the foregoing discussion points to a streamlined path through the text that culminates in the monetary and fiscal policy chapters. All readers will need the solid foundations in the mechanics of supply and demand expounded in Chapter 3. Chapter 4 on national income accounting is also foundational and should be readily accessible even to the novice. Then, Chapter 5 on the balance of payments along with Chapter 8 on exchange rates provide the tools for thinking about the issue of external balance that is key to the distinctive approach of this text. Chapter 6 on money is a precursor to Chapter 8 with the material tailored to the Emerging East Asia context. From there, Chapters 9 and 10 can be approached with discretion subject to reader preparation and time availability. Chapter 11 on monetary policy draws on the required grounding in balance of payments and exchange rates. Chapter 12 on fiscal policy contains an optional application of the IS-LM/Mundell–Fleming model. Students who have skated over this model superficially in Chapter 9 can similarly skate over this application of it with attention confined to the verbal reasoning. The remainder of Chapter 12 should be broadly accessible, including the treatment of public debt sustainability. Chapter 13 wraps up with the Swan diagram which brings together monetary and fiscal policy to address internal and external imbalance simultaneously.

A secondary narrative thread incorporates finance into the analysis. Foundations are laid in Chapter 7. Chapter 10 on business cycles contains a finance-based treatment as an alternative to the standard productivity shock approach. Chapter 14 on macroprudential policy examines regulation and supervision of financial institutions as a means of keeping the economy on an even keel. And Chapter 15 presents a finance-based treatment of crises along with discussion of the pandemic as a crisis resulting from shock to the real economy. The financial sector plays an especially important role in macroeconomic processes in Emerging East Asia due to the influence of international capital flows. Time permitting, study of this material can add appreciably to an understanding of the region's macroeconomic dynamics. No prior knowledge of finance is assumed, although previous study is helpful.

Chapter 16 provides a wrap-up for every path taken.

Data Note

The matter of data reliability must be addressed at the outset. We rely on official government statistics throughout this text. Compiling accurate macroeconomic statistics is a difficult undertaking even in advanced economies, and more difficult by far in cash-based economies with large informal sectors. That said, local statistical authorities have access to a great deal more information than their detractors on the outside. These authorities are in a position to provide the best possible numbers, so we use them, albeit questioningly at times.

GDP growth rates in Charts 1.1 and 1.2 are from the World Bank World Development Indicators database for all but Taiwan for which data are from the Macro Database of the R.O.C. (Taiwan) Directorate-General of Budget, Accounting and Statistics.

US unemployment rates during the Great Depression are from the US Bureau of the Census (1975).

Classification of economies by their exchange rate arrangements and monetary policy frameworks is done by the International Monetary Fund and published in its *Annual Report on Exchange Arrangements and Exchange Restrictions*.

BIBLIOGRAPHIC CITATIONS

Bagehot, Walter, 1910[1874]. *Lombard Street: A Description of the Money Market* (New York: E.P. Dutton). https://archive.org/details/lombardstreetd00bage

Fleming, J. Marcus, [1962] 1969. "Domestic Financial Policies under Fixed and Floating Exchange Rates," reprinted in Richard N. Cooper, ed., *International Finance* (New York: Penguin Books).

International Monetary Fund, 2006. World Economic Outlook: Financial Systems and Economic Cycles, Chapter 3.

International Monetary Fund, 2019. Annual Report on Exchange Arrangements and Exchange Restrictions, 2019, pp. 6–8. www.imf.org/en/Publications/Annual-Report-on-Exchange-Arrangements-and-Exchange-Restrictions/Issues/2020/08/10/Annual-Report-on-Exchange-Arrangements-and-Exchange-Restrictions-2019-47102 (accessed July 24, 2021).

Keynes, John Maynard, [1936] 1964. *The General Theory of Employment, Interest, and Money* (New York: Harcourt, Brace & World).

Krugman, Paul, 1994. "The Myth of Asia's Miracle," *Foreign Affairs*, Vol. 73, No. 6 (November/December), pp. 62–78.

Mills, John, 1867. "On Credit Cycles and the Origin of Commercial Panics," *Transactions of the Manchester Statistical Society*, Session 1867–1868, pp. 5–40.

Minsky, Hyman, 2008[1986]. *Stabilizing an Unstable Economy* (New York: McGraw Hill).

Mundell, Robert, 1963. "Capital Mobility and Stabilization Policy under Fixed and Flexible Exchange Rates," *Canadian Journal of Economic and Political Science*, Vol. 29, No. 4, pp. 475–485.

R.O.C. (Taiwan) Directorate-General of Budget, Accounting and Statistics, 2021. Macro Database. https://nstatdb.dgbas.gov.tw/dgbasall/webMain.aspx?k=engmain (accessed July 20, 2021).

Smith, Adam, 1776. *An Inquiry into the Nature and Causes of the Wealth of Nations* (London: W. Strahan and T. Cadell).

Ricardo, David, 1821[1817]. *On the Principles of Political Economy and Taxation*, 3rd edition (John Murray: Albemarle-Street). https://archive.org/details/onprinciplespol00ricagoog.

Say, Jean-Baptiste, 1821. *A Treatise on Political Economy; or the Production, Distribution, and Consumption of Wealth*, Translated from the Fourth Edition of the French by C.R. Prinsep (London: Longman, Hurst, Rees, Orme, and Brown). https://archive.org/details/atreatiseonpoli01unkngoog.

Solow, Robert, 1957. "Technical Change and the Aggregate Production Function," *Review of Economics and Statistics*, Vol. 39, No. 3 (August), pp. 312–320.

Swan, T. W., 1963. "Longer-Run Problems of the Balance of Payments," in H. W. Arndt and W. M. Corden, eds., *The Australian Economy: A Volume of Readings* (Melbourne: Cheshire Press), pp. 384–395.

US Bureau of the Census, 1975. Historical Statistics of the United States: Colonial Times to 1970 (Washington, DC: US Department of Commerce), p. 135.

World Bank, 2013. World Development Indicators database. http://databank.worldbank.org/data/views/variableSelection/selectvariables.aspx?source=world-development-indicators.

Young, Alwyn, 1995. "The Tyranny of Numbers: Confronting the Statistical Realities of the East Asian Growth Experience," *Quarterly Journal of Economics*, Vol. 110, No. 3 (August), pp. 641–680.

2   Taking the Measure of Emerging East Asia

The economies of Emerging East Asia differ greatly with respect to size, stage of development, and degree of international integration. These differences bear on vulnerability to external shock and the tendency toward volatility. Nevertheless, the same principles of macroeconomics apply, and we can subsume the whole lot within a common analytical framework.

The world's second biggest economy, China, accounts for more than 70 percent of Emerging East Asian GDP, while Cambodia and Laos weigh in at just a fraction of a percent. Adjusted for purchasing power, Singapore's per capita GDP outranks that of the USA, while elsewhere in the region per capita incomes of a few dollars a day mean that life is a constant struggle to survive. A child born in Hong Kong can expect to live nearly two decades longer than one born in Myanmar or Laos. The entrepots of Hong Kong and Singapore sustain trade-to-GDP ratios of more than 300 percent, whereas the ratio is less than 40 percent for China. Similarly for foreign assets and liabilities, the ratios to GDP are larger by an order of magnitude for Hong Kong and Singapore than for most other economies in the region.

In this chapter we compare economies along three dimensions: size and growth; stage of development; and degree of global integration. In every aspect, the Emerging East Asia region extends to extremes.

A   Size and Growth

China is the behemoth of Emerging East Asia, and its dominance has only increased over recent decades. Against China's strong growth performance, most other economies in the region have lost output share, although two have managed to gain. We look first at size, then at growth, in terms relative to the region for both indicators.

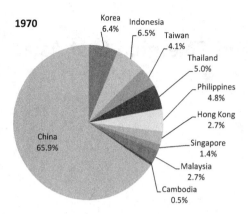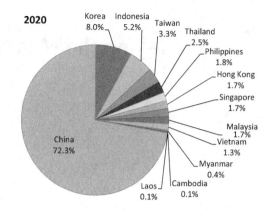

Chart 2.1 Shares in regional GDP, select economies, 1970 and 2020

Size

Chart 2.1 shows regional shares in GDP for the economies of Emerging East Asia for the years 1970 and 2020. In 2020, China accounted for 72.3 percent of the total. Korea took the second spot with 8.0 percent, followed by Indonesia at 5.2 percent, and Taiwan at 3.3 percent. Clustered in the 1.0–2.5 percent range were Thailand, the Philippines, Hong Kong, Singapore, Malaysia, and Vietnam. That leaves Myanmar, Cambodia, and Laos with less than half a percent each.

Within a region that has become increasingly integrated through the supply chain and more generally tied into global networks of trade and finance, disruptions in one economy can reverberate throughout the region. China's mass creates obvious potential to stimulate regional growth or to send shock waves. Yet far smaller economies have managed to trigger upheaval across boarders as well. Of particular note, Thailand was the epicenter of the 1997 Asian Financial Crisis.

Growth

The Emerging East Asia region as a whole has achieved impressive growth over the last five decades. Against this oversized benchmark some economies have outperformed to gain share, while others have lagged to lose it between 1970 and 2020. The addition by 2020 of Vietnam, Myanmar, and Laos, for which 1970 data are not available, impinges very slightly on the shares of all others. Growth over the period was most outstanding for Korea and Singapore, which saw share gains despite China's major encroachment. The most serious laggards were Thailand and the Philippines with share declines of half or more.

To be sure, were a later base year chosen, relative growth performances would stack up differently as some economies began their take-offs earlier and others later, while some that enjoyed early success hit setbacks later on from which they were slow to regain momentum.

High long-term growth is often accompanied by significant volatility. In part, this is because the inevitable slowdown when it comes registers as a sharper break from a history of strong growth than from a history of weak growth. But in part also the forces that help to generate a boom can sow the seeds of a bust. Credit growth is an important driver of expansions, with a rapidly growing economy in turn facilitating repayment of debt in a self-reinforcing cycle. Creditors respond by taking on more risk, and overall debt loads rise. However, as asset prices soar, lending becomes ever more speculative. Eventually, the process runs out of steam. Loans begin to go bad and asset prices go into reversal. Credit tightens and the economy can go into a downward spiral. As unsettling as such boom-and-bust cycles may seem, they are commonly embedded within very successful long-term performance records.

B Stage of Development

Some of the world's richest societies exist alongside some of the poorest within the Emerging East Asia region. In this section we compare levels of economic development, first with respect to GDP per capita, then on the basis of broader indicators of the human condition.

GDP per Capita

Comparing GDP across economies is complicated by the need to convert economic activity recorded in different currencies to a common unit of measurement. The simplest way to accomplish this is to apply market exchange rates, typically standardizing on US dollars. The appeal of this approach lies in its reliance on readily available data and a transparent methodology. There are a number of drawbacks, however. One is that exchange rates can fluctuate a great deal, creating the appearance that relative incomes are highly unstable across economies. The fluctuations tend to be driven largely by currency trading to support financial transactions, however, as opposed to shifts in the real goods and services an economy produces. Another problem is that government intervention in foreign exchange markets can distort exchange rates relative to market valuations. Finally, even apart from the influence of financial transactions and government intervention, market exchange rates derive only from traded goods and services, whereas much of what is produced in an economy is non-tradable. Traded goods and services tend to be expensive in less developed economies relative to domestically produced and consumed products, such as haircuts or restaurant meals, prices for which reflect relatively low local wages. In other words, a US dollar will buy more in the way of non-traded items in an emerging market setting than in an advanced economy even as the purchasing power of a dollar for traded products is close to parity when converted at exchange rates.

An alternative to the exchange rate approach involves imputing currency conversion rates based on broad purchasing power parity. Under this approach a basket of goods and services that spans the gamut of traded and non-traded goods and services – from food and utilities to housing and education – is priced in local currency for each of the economies to be compared. The ratio of this basket price in an economy to that of the same basket in the USA is then used to convert GDP expressed in local currencies to a common US dollar measure. This is known as the purchasing power parity (PPP) approach.

Chart 2.2 GDP per capita at exchange rate and purchasing power parity valuations, select economies, 2020

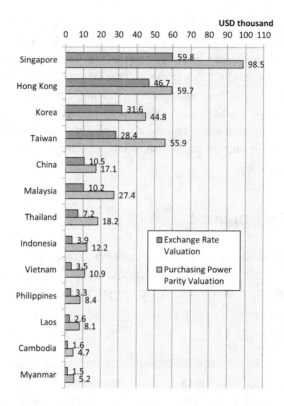

Chart 2.2 presents GDP per capita at both exchange rate and PPP valuations for the economies of Emerging East Asia. For the USA, with its benchmark currency, exchange rate and PPP valuations are equivalent at about $63,000 a year. For all Emerging East Asia economies, GDP expressed in PPP terms exceeds that expressed in exchange rate terms. This indicates that a dollar converted at the market exchange rate can buy more in the Asian economy using local currency than it can buy in the USA. Output for the Asian economies is thus higher in purchasing power terms than an exchange rate–based conversion suggests.

The disparity across the region is striking. In exchange rate terms, GDP per capita ranges from $1500 a year to nearly the US level. In PPP terms, Singapore's GDP substantially exceeds that of the USA, while Hong Kong's is close to the US mark. Korea and Taiwan are roughly on par at the next tier. From there, the downward gradient is sharp to China and Malaysia, then to Thailand, then Indonesia, Vietnam, and the Philippines, and finally Laos, Cambodia, and Myanmar. The region still holds much potential for growth if lagging economies can make strides in catching up to frontrunners.

Human Development Indicators

GDP per capita, even in PPP terms, is a very limited measure of economic development. The Human Development Index devised by Nobel laureate Amartya Sen offers a broader

Table 2.1 Human development indicators, select economies, 2019

	Human Development Index	Life expectancy at birth	Expected years of schooling	Mean years of schooling of adults
Hong Kong	0.95	84.9	16.9	12.3
Singapore	0.94	83.6	16.4	11.6
Korea	0.92	83.0	16.5	12.2
Malaysia	0.81	76.2	13.7	10.4
Thailand	0.78	77.2	15.0	7.9
China	0.76	76.9	14.0	8.1
Indonesia	0.72	71.7	13.6	8.2
Philippines	0.72	71.2	13.1	9.4
Vietnam	0.70	75.4	12.7	8.3
Laos	0.61	67.9	11.0	5.3
Cambodia	0.59	69.8	11.5	5.0
Myanmar	0.58	67.1	10.7	5.0

indicator of progress. Sen premised his index on a notion of development that involves the advance of human capabilities. This notion of capabilities is conceived as enabling people to live lives they have reason to value. In this spirit, Sen incorporated measures of health and education into his index in combination with the more standard per capita income in PPP terms.

Table 2.1 presents values for the Human Development Index and three of its components: life expectancy at birth; expected years of schooling for children entering school age; and mean years of schooling of adults. Hong Kong and Singapore top the chart, with global rankings of fourth and eleventh, respectively. Korea follows close behind, making up for a lower per capita income with outstanding educational attainment, its adult population benefiting from an average 12.2 years of schooling with today's children projected to receive 16.5 years of schooling. Another economy that performs well on education relative to income is the Philippines with an average 9.4 years of schooling for adults. At the lower end of the spectrum, aligning roughly with lower incomes, a number of economies in the region show schooling for adults of less than six years. Life expectancy similarly follows a pattern broadly in accord with income rankings, although not without aberrations. Vietnam exhibits an exceptionally high life expectancy for a lower income economy, which helps to offset a poorer performance on education. Disparity in life expectancy within the region is such that a child born in Hong Kong can look forward to nearly 18 years more on this earth than one born in Myanmar.

Economies that operate deep inside the global frontier for technology and social organization have the potential to grow rapidly. However, with rapid growth comes the prospect of greater volatility. Economies at or near the frontier inevitably grow more slowly but with less tendency toward instability. For lagging economies, development involves adopting and adapting existing technologies, relying on global frontrunners to do most of the innovating. It also involves building effective economic and political institutions. Forging a path relies on idiosyncratic trial and error, with the process prone to lurches and setbacks.

C   International Economic Integration

Opening up to international trade and investment can act as a springboard to economic development. But engaging internationally also brings exposure to external shock. Chart 1.2 captures vividly the synchronization of business cycles in Emerging East Asia that has followed from increased external engagement. In this section we examine trade and investment flows relative to GDP to get a sense of the variation in international integration within the region.

Foreign Trade

For the world as a whole, the combined value of exports and imports of goods and services is about 53 percent of GDP. The economies of Emerging East Asia exhibit ratios generally above this level, and in some cases far above it, although several countries fall short, as shown in Chart 2.3. The region is home to the world's two great entrepot economies – Singapore and Hong Kong. Much of what is imported by these entrepots is in turn exported with little value added locally. The resulting two-way trade ratios for these economies exceeded 300 percent of GDP in 2020. Trade ratios near or above 100 percent were

Chart 2.3 Trade ratios to GDP, select economies, 2020

registered by Vietnam, Cambodia, Malaysia, Taiwan, and Thailand. Generally speaking, larger economies tend to be less trade oriented than smaller ones because they can achieve economies of scale in production for a broader range of industries domestically. This explains the relatively low trade ratio for China, which at 34.5 percent was nevertheless significantly above the 23.4 percent registered by the USA in 2020.

Most of the economies in the region ran trade surpluses in 2020, although deficits were recorded for Cambodia and the Philippines. A broader measure of current transactions includes income payments for overseas labor and investment with the Philippines generating large inflows from its nationals working abroad which reduce the size of its deficit.

A trade deficit must be financed with inflows of financial investment. Such inflows are attracted to capital-scarce developing economies by opportunities for high returns, although risks tend to be high as well given weak institutional infrastructure. From a position of trade deficit at low income, rapid economic development is accompanied by a rising saving rate that reduces reliance on foreign investment inflows and turns the trade balance toward surplus. A trade surplus implies a net outflow of investment funds and the accumulation of foreign assets or the pay down of foreign debt. The large trade surpluses common among the economies of Emerging East Asia reflect a concerted effort to build up foreign reserves.

While offering gains from specialization and the pursuit of comparative advantage, trade carries with it increased exposure to the vicissitudes of the international marketplace. The ramifications were brought home forcefully by the Great Financial Crisis of 2008. The economies of Emerging East Asia were little exposed to the financial debacle directly. Rather, the sharp slowdown that hit the region (visible in Chart 1.2) was due mainly to the trade shock that followed in the aftermath. Worldwide, trade volume fell by 19 percent in 2009 relative to the previous year. Emerging East Asia suffered the consequences.

Foreign Investment

Trade flows involve real goods and services moving across borders in support of current consumption or capital formation. The activity is completed in a one-way transaction. Financial investment flows, by contrast, involve transfer across borders of title to assets. Positions are taken, and holdings may be accumulated over time, but flows are then open to reversal. Psychological factors weigh heavily on investment flows as opposed to the more practical concerns that motivate trade flows. This makes for far greater volatility and unpredictability in investment flows than in trade flows with sudden large movements of funds either in or out wreaking havoc on an economy.

An outflow of foreign investment results in an asset position on an economy's balance sheet, an inflow a liability position. The net international investment position for an economy may be positive (meaning the economy is a net creditor to the world), negative (meaning it is a net debtor), or zero.

Different forms of investment are characterized by differences in liquidity and the prospective reversal of flows. Direct investment involves a substantial equity stake in a business that is not easily liquidated. Portfolio investment pertains to the purchase of securities traded on markets, with funds thus more readily repatriated. Loans generate a commitment of interest and principle repayment according to a specified timetable. Derivatives represent contracts for payment to be made in the future under specific terms and conditions, for example, for the purchase of an asset at a predefined price at the option of either the buyer or the seller. A final form of investment tracked only on the asset side is official reserves involving foreign assets held by a monetary authority.

International investment positions relative to GDP for the economies of Emerging East Asia are presented in Chart 2.4. Hong Kong and Singapore are again outliers, so much so that we measure them against a different axis calibrated higher by a factor of almost five, and we bring in Taiwan here too as it's caught in the middle. Hong Kong and Singapore serve as international financial hubs. For Hong Kong, foreign assets surpassed 1,800 percent

Chart 2.4 International investment position, select economies, 2020

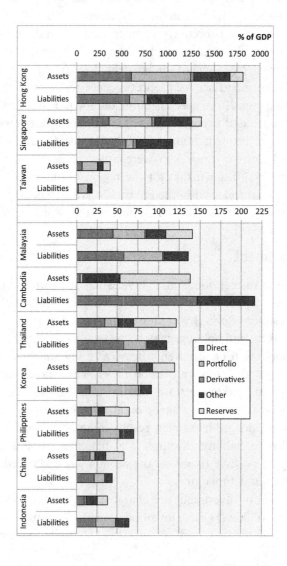

of GDP in 2020 while for Singapore they exceeded 1,300 percent. Strong net creditor positions are evident for both. Taiwan is a net creditor to an even greater degree proportionally with assets more than double liabilities.

Net debtor positions show up substantially for Cambodia and Indonesia and to a minor degree for the Philippines. For Cambodia, the liabilities are mostly in the form of direct investment which is not vulnerable to ready reversal. China is a major contributorin this. For Indonesia, although liabilities are large relative to assets, they are not large relative to GDP.

Erratic movement of funds across borders can be seriously destabilizing for emerging market economies. The need to convert currencies when money crosses borders exerts pressure on exchange rates. An inflow of foreign funds pushes the value of the local currency up putting a squeeze on exporters and on producers for the domestic market that must compete with cheapened imports. On the other hand, an outflow of funds undermines the value of the local currency straining borrowers and others with payment obligations set in foreign currency terms. To limit vulnerability, many governments in the Emerging East Asia region impose controls on cross-border capital movements. They also prepare to meet any urgent demand for foreign currency in the event of a significant capital outflow by stockpiling official reserves.

As of 2020, Hong Kong held official reserves at the extraordinarily high level of 140 percent of GDP. Hong Kong conditions the issuance of local currency on receipt of US dollars by the monetary authority, and thus its monetary base is fully backed by US dollars. China's reserves in absolute terms were by far the world's largest at more than US$3.4 trillion as of 2020, although relative to GDP the country is not an outlier for reserve assets. At the low end, Indonesia held reserves of 12.8 percent of GDP with all others registering above 20 percent.

The Asian Financial Crisis was a major factor in motivating the accumulation of reserve assets. During the crisis, some economies found their currencies collapsing and their growth rates plummeting as foreign investment fled and credit to finance trade and other short-term working capital needs dried up. Governments in the region became intent on avoiding such vulnerability in the future. Amassing substantial reserve assets not only allows authorities to supply foreign currency into the foreign exchange markets if and when investors seek to withdraw en masse, it can actually forestall the need for intervention by promoting confidence that foreign currency shortages are not a risk.

Government controls on cross-border movement of capital are another mechanism for guarding against the disruptive movement of funds. On the inbound side, direct investment is typically cultivated as being more stable and supportive of development goals whereas, by contrast, portfolio investment is subjected to limitations via transaction caps, holding periods, and stringent approval procedures. Long-term borrowing is treated more favorably than short-term borrowing which may be in need of rollover at potentially higher interest rates. Chart 2.4 shows differing profiles across economies with respect to liabilities. China has historically relied more narrowly on direct investment, whereas the mature financial markets of Taiwan, Malaysia, and Korea offer greater accommodation to portfolio inflows. The category "Other" captures loans and deposits. The substantial role of this category in

Hong Kong and Singapore on both asset and liability sides indicates the importance of these economies in regional financial intermediation, as does the growing presence of derivatives on their balance sheets.

D   Macroeconomic Ramifications

The boom-and-bust episodes common to all economies are driven by a complex web of factors, both domestic and external. For Emerging East Asia, the increasing importance of the external is clear from the synchronization of business cycles dating to the Asian Financial Crisis (see Chart 1.2). The Crisis first struck Thailand, then rippled across the region, pushing GDP growth into negative territory in 1998 for seven of our 13 economies and bringing it down sharply for most others. The economies hit hardest were those most dependent on short-term foreign financing which suddenly became difficult to roll over by taking out new loans. The next shock landed in 2001 with the bursting of the technology stock bubble in the USA. The hardest hit economies in this case were those most integrated into the global supply chain for information and communication products, notably Taiwan, Singapore, Hong Kong, and Malaysia. Then came the Great Financial Crisis of 2008. The financial fallout as such was not serious; rather it was the subsequent downturn in international trade in 2009 that took a heavy toll. Five economies in the region fell into contraction and others escaped with barely positive growth.

The openness of Emerging East Asia to International trade and investment exposes the region to external shock even as it fuels long-term growth. Smaller economies are particularly dependent on trade to achieve scale economies and make the most of their comparative advantage. Developing economies gain vital access to technology and managerial resources through foreign investment. And regardless of size or stage of development, all economies are prodded by global competition to become more efficient and innovative.

The challenge then is to find ways of coping with external shock while still reaping the benefits of openness. Given the vast differences in size and stage of development represented in Emerging East Asia, the mechanisms for buffering and managing shock naturally vary as well. Some economies (Hong Kong and Singapore) have found success in opening up to investment flows and cultivating a role in financial services while others continue to enforce extensive controls on capital flows (China). All economies in the region rely on exchange rate management to a degree, but forms range from the hard dollar peg of Hong Kong to the more strategic intervention of those classified by the International Monetary Fund as having floating – but not free floating – exchange rates (Indonesia, Korea, Malaysia, the Philippines, and Thailand, and similarly Taiwan though it lacks formal classification). Much variation exists, too, in institutions for managing domestic money and credit issuance. Nevertheless, a common body of macroeconomic principles applies. The chapters to come expound these commonalities, while at the same time documenting the particulars through case studies and empirical comparison across economies.

Data Note

The table and charts presented in this chapter draw on databases maintained by various multilateral organizations, supplemented by data from Taiwan government sources. Details are given below.

Chart 2.1   GDP data are from the World Bank's World Development Indicators database, which extends back to 1960. Data for Taiwan are from the Republic of China (Taiwan) Statistical Bureau.

Chart 2.2 GDP per capita data are from the International Monetary Fund's World Economic Outlook database, which includes Taiwan.

Table 2.1 Data on human development are from the United Nations Development Programme's Human Development Reports website.

Chart 2.3   Trade data are from the World Bank's World Development Indicators database. Data for Taiwan are from the Central Bank of the Republic of China (Taiwan) balance of payments data.

Chart 2.4   International investment data are from the IMF's Balance of Payments and International Investment Position Statistics database. Data for Taiwan are from the Central Bank of the Republic of China (Taiwan).

The purchasing power parity measures of GDP per capita presented in Chart 2.2 merit elaboration. The estimation exercise rests on collection of prices expressed in local currency for roughly 1,000 meticulously specified products for each participating economy. The effort to price identical baskets of goods and services across economies dates back to a 1968 collaboration between the University of Pennsylvania and the United Nations Statistical Division. The International Comparison Program, as it is known, was later taken over by the World Bank for most of the world and by Eurostat and the Organization of Economic Cooperation and Development (OECD) for their member countries. The most recent round of data compilation by the World Bank took place in 2017 with rounds before that in 2011 and 2005.

Bibliographic Note

Regular status reports by economy, with supporting datasets, are prepared by a number of multilateral organizations. The World Bank's *World Development Report*, published annually since 1978, takes up a different theme each year and contains a wealth of data on all aspects of development. The International Monetary Fund's semi-annual *World Economic Outlook* offers macroeconomic analysis and medium-term forecasts. Finally, the Asian Development Bank's annual *Asian Development Outlook* focuses on macroeconomic and development issues for ADB developing member countries.

Human Development Index creator Amartya Sen laid out his views on human development in the book *Development as Freedom*. Sen maintains that the goal of development should be to increase the opportunities available to people by enhancing their capabilities.

The notion of "capabilities" encompasses: (1) the capability to live a long and healthy life; (2) the capability to acquire education and skills and share in the benefits of social progress; (3) the capability to escape poverty and enjoy a rising standard of living. Indicators of national achievement that reflect these capabilities are the basis for the Human Development Index. More broadly, Sen champions political liberty and civil rights as fundamental to the exercise of human capabilities.

BIBLIOGRAPHIC CITATIONS

Asian Development Bank, multi-year. Asian Development Outlook (Manila). www.adb.org/publications/series/asian-development-outlook (accessed November 5, 2021).

Central Bank of the Republic of China (Taiwan), 2021. Balance of Payments, Analytic Presentation by Year. www.cbc.gov.tw/content.asp?CuItem=2071 (accessed November 4, 2021).

International Monetary Fund, 2021. Balance of Payments and International Investment Position Statistics. https://data.imf.org/?sk=7A51304B-6426-40C0-83DD-CA473CA1FD52&sId=1390030341854 (accessed November 4, 2021).

International Monetary Fund, 2021. World Economic Outlook database. www.imf.org/external/pubs/ft/weo/2018/02/weodata/index.aspx (accessed November 4, 2021).

International Monetary Fund, multi-year. *World Economic Outlook*. (Washington, DC). www.imf.org/en/Publications/WEO (accessed November 5, 2021).

Republic of China (Taiwan) Statistical Bureau, 2021. https://eng.stat.gov.tw/ct.asp?xItem=37408&CtNode=5347&mp=5 (accessed November 4, 2021).

Sen, Amartya, 1999. *Development As Freedom* (New York: Knopf).

United Nations Development Programme, 2021. Human Development Data Center. http://hdr.undp.org/en/data (accessed November 4, 2021).

World Bank, 2021. International Comparison Program. www.worldbank.org/en/programs/icp#1 (accessed November 5, 2021).

World Bank, 2021. World Development Indicators database (Washington, DC: World Bank). https://databank.worldbank.org/source/world-development-indicators (accessed November 4, 2021).

World Bank, multi-year. *World Development Report* (Washington, DC). www.worldbank.org/en/publication/wdr/wdr-archive (accessed November 4, 2021).

3   Microeconomic Fundamentals

Microeconomics deals with how resources are allocated and incomes are distributed. Demand and supply are the crux of the matter.

Resources are scarce and human wants unlimited – this is the fundamental economic problem. It follows that choices must be made. A couple's choice to save money for a future down payment on a home means giving up vacation travel today. An aspiring young author's choice to write a novel means foregoing the steady wages of an office job. A farmer's choice to plant vegetable crops means diverting land from the production of grain. A society's choice to fight a war means sacrificing consumption. The notion of cost in economics is based on this principle that every choice involves giving up other opportunities. *Opportunity cost* is defined as the best alternative foregone in the exercise of a choice.

In a market economy, choices on how to allocate resources are conveyed through demand and supply. In this chapter, we outline the mechanics of demand and supply focusing initially on product markets under conditions of perfect competition. Free markets operating under perfect competition yield an allocation of resources that is efficient in the sense that just the right amount of a good or service is produced so that the value of the marginal unit to users is equal to the cost of producing it. Against this stylized vision of a market economy we consider how in reality impediments to perfect competition arise and what that means for efficiency. We then shift attention from product markets to the markets for factor inputs to production. Finally, we conclude by explaining why an understanding of microeconomics is important to the study of macroeconomics.

A   Demand and Supply in Competitive Product Markets

Demand and supply interact in markets to determine the prices and quantities of goods and services traded. A strengthening of demand pushes the price of an item up attracting more resources into production of it. An expansion of supply brings the price down enticing customers to make additional purchases. Microeconomics provides a systematic framework for understanding these processes.

We focus initially on perfectly competitive product markets. Under perfect competition, individual buyers and sellers are *price takers* in the market. Being small relative to the overall size of the market, individual players are unable to influence price. In many situations the assumption of perfect competition is reasonable. One shopper cannot bargain for lower prices at the supermarket by threatening to take his business elsewhere; nor can one wheat farmer force crop prices up by withholding her output. In these situations, market participants must accept prevailing prices and can transact any volume of trade within their capacity without causing prices to budge.

Our focus is on product markets initially as distinct from factor markets. In product markets households are the buyers and business firms the sellers. The demand side of product markets thus embodies household preferences while the supply side reflects business costs. Conversely, in factor markets households are the sellers and firms the buyers. Households exercise property rights over the sale of labor, capital, land, and entrepreneurial talent which firms buy as the factor inputs to production. In factor markets then, the supply side conveys household preferences while the demand side reflects businesses responding to the final demand in product markets for the goods and services they produce. (In this simple scheme, we ignore government as a buyer or seller.)

Demand

Demand in product markets is an expression of consumer preferences. People buy things to gain satisfaction, or in the language of economics, *utility*. Utility cannot be directly observed or measured. It cannot be compared across individuals or aggregated within societies. Rather, utility is a theoretical construct designed to aid in the interpretation of consumer behavior. Only indirectly through the way consumers reveal their preferences in the marketplace do we infer how utility plays a part.

Manifest in this utility shadow play is a gradual process of satiation. The more a person consumes of any given product, the lower the value they place on an additional unit of it at the margin. The paradox of diamonds and water famously illustrates this point. That a frivolous (or often frivolous) commodity like diamonds commands such a high price while the water essential to life is cheap by comparison may seem counterintuitive at first. But it is the relative scarcity of diamonds that makes them expensive at the margin, not their essentialness or lack thereof. Only because water is, in general, abundant does it hold such low value at the margin despite its inestimable utility in total. For a thirsty man stranded in the desert, of course, water would be worth more than its weight in diamonds.

The principle of *diminishing marginal utility* is reflected in the downward slope of the demand curve. Figure 3.1 depicts the demand for lychees. Quantity (Q) is plotted on the horizontal axis and the price (P) buyers are willing to pay for an incremental unit of lychees on the vertical axis. The first lychee consumed as the fruit comes into season is an exquisite treat and valued preciously. With each additional lychee consumed, however, the pleasure

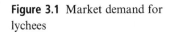

Figure 3.1 Market demand for lychees

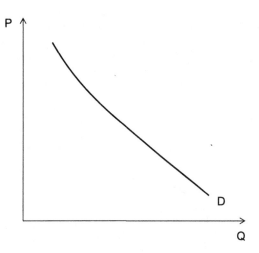

The downward slope of the demand curve reflects diminishing marginal utility to consumers.

subsides a bit more. At some point as our consumer continues to partake, a point of satiation is reached and an additional lychee brings little, if any, enjoyment. The downward slope of the demand curve indicates that as quantity increases, the demand price that buyers are willing to pay for an additional unit at the margin falls.

Supply

Supply in product markets is a reflection of the opportunity cost of resource inputs to production. Inputs may be drawn into a given use only if compensation is tendered for the sacrifice of their foregone contributions elsewhere. Labor must be paid a wage that attracts it from alternative endeavors. Investment funds must be raised through the payment of competitive interest rates. Material inputs to production command prices that reflect their value in the marketplace to competing users.

The essential premise behind the supply curve is that resources are differentially adaptable to various uses. Certain land is well-suited in soil and climate conditions to growing lychees, for example. The area under lychee cultivation can be expanded but only by diverting land from other crops at ever increasing sacrifice. Moreover, to coax decent yields out of lands that are less amenable to lychee production requires more of such complementary inputs as labor, fertilizer, and machinery. These other resources themselves must be drawn at ever higher sacrifice in terms of their alternative uses. Some people are inclined by aptitude and training to be good lychee farmers. As those whose talents are better suited to other activities are pulled increasingly into lychee cultivation, the costs in terms of foregone contributions elsewhere rise. All in all, this means the cost of lychee production increases at the margin as output expands, and hence so must the supply price of lychees increase.

Figure 3.2 Market supply for lychees

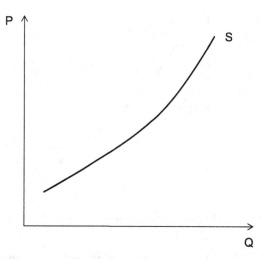

The upward slope of the supply curve
reflects increasing marginal cost of production.

The principle of *increasing marginal cost* is captured in the upward slope of the supply curve shown in Figure 3.2. Quantity is again plotted on the horizontal axis, and the price producers will accept to cover marginal cost on the vertical axis. As quantity increases, the supply price too increases in order to cover the rising marginal cost of production.

B   Equilibrium in Competitive Product Markets

Bringing the demand and supply curves together in the same graph allows us to examine their interaction. It is useful to distinguish between *demand* as a curve or schedule relating a continuum of quantities and prices and *quantity demanded* as a particular point on a given demand curve corresponding to a particular price, and similarly between *supply* as a curve or schedule and *quantity supplied* as a point on a given supply curve corresponding to a particular price. The idea of "supply increasing" or "demand decreasing" refers to a shift in an entire curve. In contrast, the idea of "quantity supplied increasing" or "quantity demanded decreasing" refers to a movement along a given curve. (This distinction is not adhered to outside the classroom, but for pedagogical purposes it works well.)

Demand and supply jointly determine the price and the quantity traded in a market. Price and quantity are the endogenous variables of the model, meaning they are determined within the model. An outcome is arrived at through a process of equilibration. When the market is not in equilibrium, forces will drive it in that direction. Once an equilibrium is reached, there is no tendency for further change. When factors exogenous to the model impact supply or demand, the result is captured as a shift in an entire curve. In the wake of such a shift, a new equilibrium price and quantity are arrived at.

The mechanics of market equilibration can be interpreted by reading from either the price axis or the quantity axis. Reading from the price axis, the story is one of decentralized market activity achieving order. The notion of the "invisible hand" of the market dates back to Adam Smith and the *Wealth of Nations* published in 1776. Smith wrote of self-interest as the great motivator of "the butcher, the brewer, or the baker" to provide the goods society desires with the market acting as arbiter. But competitive markets achieve something more profound and compelling than order as is revealed when the graph is interpreted from the quantity axis. The story told from this perspective is one of markets achieving efficiency in the allocation of scarce resources.

From the Price Axis: An Orderly Outcome

Trade in lychees in a Bangkok street market is depicted in Figure 3.3. In the version of the graph shown on the left we interpret equilibration from the price axis. At the relatively high price of 34 baht per kilo, sellers supply a plentiful 300 kilos of lychees. Buyers, on the other hand, are reluctant to purchase such expensive fruit demanding only 140 kilos. An excess supply of 160 kilos languishes on the market. Sellers find they must compete among themselves to attract customers and in so doing bid the price down. When the price reaches 24 baht per kilo, the intentions of sellers and the wishes of buyers coincide such that 240 kilos of lychees are bought and sold. If the price were to sink below 24 baht per kilo, the opposite scenario would play out. An initial excess demand would prompt buyers to bid the price up. Thus from any position other than 24 baht per kilo the price tends to move to this point, and

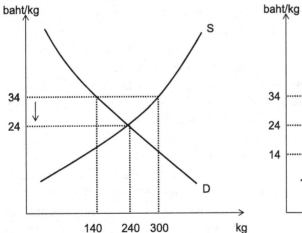
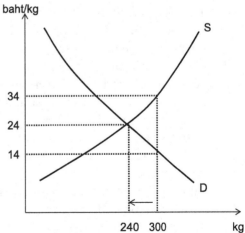

At a price of 34 baht/kg, quantity supplied is 300 kg but quantity demanded is only 140 kg. Price must fall for the market to clear.

At a quantity traded of 300 kg, marginal cost of supply is 34 baht/kg but marginal value to users is only 14 baht/kg. Quantity must fall for resource allocation to be efficient.

Figure 3.3 Market equilibration: Lychees in a Bangkok street market

when at 24 baht per kilo it tends to remain there. Twenty-four baht per kilo is a stable equilibrium price. It clears the market leaving no tendency for change.

Price competition pushes markets to clear. Buyers and sellers enter markets with certain intentions at prevailing prices, and if their intentions are not realized prices adjust until a resolution is achieved. In actuality, the process of adjustment is ongoing. Markets are buffeted relentlessly by forces that shift demands and supplies, in response to which equilibrium prices and quantities must be arrived at anew. That a market economy can constantly redirect resources in such a way that consumer demands are met is what inspired Adam Smith to conjure up the "Invisible Hand". Without a central plan, without a grand auctioneer, without a feudal order or a caste system or the strictures of tradition to direct resource use, an orderly outcome is nonetheless achieved, "tumult resolved into a chord" in the words of Robert Heilbroner in *The Worldly Philosophers*.

From the Quantity Axis: An Optimal Outcome

That free markets bring order to economic activity is no mean feat. But there is more to the story. In the version of the graph shown on the right of Figure 3.3 we interpret the equilibration process from the quantity axis. At a hefty quantity of 300 kilos of lychees in our Bangkok street market, the marginal cost of supply is 34 baht per kilo. In the short term this high supply price on a particular street market reflects the opportunity cost of diverting existing produce from other markets including the logistics costs involved. In the longer term, it reflects the foregone opportunities of farmers to produce other crops, or more generally of resource inputs, including farmers, to be allocated from other uses. As it turns out, such abundance of lychees in the market is not commensurately appreciated by the market's customers. The marginal utility of 300 kilos of lychees to local consumers is reflected in a willingness to pay just 14 baht per kilo. The marginal opportunity cost to suppliers exceeds the marginal value to users to the tune of 20 baht per kilo. Resources have been over allocated to supplying lychees to this market. Better uses are to be had for the resources involved. With buyers unwilling to pay the price sellers must receive to cover costs, quantity will be cut back. A sustainable equilibrium is ultimately reached at 240 baht per kilo. At this quantity the marginal cost to supply lychees to the market is just equal to the marginal value to consumers at 24 baht per kilo.

Alfred Marshall placed quantity on the horizontal axis of his original demand and supply graph so as to tell the story of market equilibration from the standpoint of allocative efficiency. Marshall's own rendering is reproduced in Box 3.1. The quantities of goods produced and consumed under competitive market conditions are such that at the margin the opportunity cost of supply just equals value in use. To allocate any more resources to a given purpose would push the marginal supply cost above the marginal value to users. To allocate any less would leave the marginal value to users above the marginal supply cost. The resource allocation achieved by competitive markets is thus optimal. Marshall's framework lies at the heart of neoclassical economics, which is discussed in Box 3.2.

Box 3.1 Alfred Marshall's rendering of market equilibrium

STABLE EQUILIBRIUM. 425

When demand and supply are in stable equilibrium, if any accident should move the scale of production from its equilibrium position, there will be instantly brought into play forces tending to bring it back to that position; just as, if a stone hanging by a string is displaced from its equilibrium position, the force of gravity will at once tend to bring it back to its equilibrium position. The movements of the scale of production about its position of equilibrium will be of a somewhat similar kind[1].

But in real life such oscillations are seldom as rhythmical as those of a stone hanging freely from a string; the comparison would be more exact if the string were supposed to hang in the troubled waters of a mill-race, whose stream was at one time allowed to flow freely, and at another partially cut off. The demand and supply schedules do not in practice remain unchanged for a long time together, but are constantly being changed; and every change in them alters the equilibrium amount and the equilibrium price, and thus gives new positions to the centres about which the amount and the price tend to oscillate.

These considerations point to the great importance of the element of time in relation to demand and supply, to the study of which we now proceed. We shall gradually discover a great many different limitations of the doctrine

BOOK V. CH. III.
Oscillations about a position of stable equilibrium.
are seldom rhythmical.
Looseness of the connection between the supply price of a commodity

[1] To represent the equilibrium of demand and supply geometrically we may draw the demand and supply curves together as in Fig. 19. If then *OR* represents the rate at which production is being actually carried on, and *Rd* the demand price is greater than *Rs* the supply price, the production is exceptionally profitable, and will be increased. *R*, the *amount-index*, as we may call it, will move to the right. On the other hand, if *Rd* is less than *Rs*, *R* will move to the left. If *Rd* is equal to *Rs*, that is, if *R* is vertically under a point of intersection of the curves, demand and supply are in equilibrium.

This may be taken as the typical diagram for stable equilibrium for a commodity that obeys the law of diminishing return. But if we had made *SS'* a horizontal straight line, we should have represented the case of "constant return," in which the supply price is the same for all amounts of the commodity. And if we had made *SS'* inclined negatively, but less steeply than *DD'* (the necessity for this condition will appear more fully later on), we should have got a case of stable equilibrium for a commodity which obeys the law of increasing return. In either case the above reasoning remains unchanged without the alteration of a word or a letter; but the last case introduces difficulties which we have arranged to postpone.

The fundamentals of demand and supply as set forth by Alfred Marshall in 1890 hold up to this day. Because Marshall did not want technical material to weigh down the narrative, he relegated the graphs to footnotes as shown in this page image from the third edition of *Principles of Economics* (1895).

Box 3.2 What is neoclassical economics?

Neoclassical economics is rooted in a theory of value based on marginal utility and marginal cost. Alfred Marshall is its leading light. Historian of thought David Colander places the origins of the neoclassical school in the period that began around 1870 and ended with a transition to "modern economics" in the 1930s and 1940s. Colander argues, however, that the term has evolved to encompass such a mishmash of meanings that in his view the best course may be to retire it from use altogether.

The classical precursor to the neoclassical school is represented by such luminaries as Adam Smith, Thomas Malthus, David Ricardo, and John Stuart Mill. Neoclassical continuity with these thinkers is evident in the focus on understanding the process of exchange and in the *laissez faire* bent of the conclusions. The classical notion of value, however, is limited to the cost side of the market with the basis for cost vested fully in labor. The demand side of the market and the opportunity cost of inputs to production other than labor were absent from the analysis.

Advances in neoclassical economics culminated in 1947 with Paul Samuelson's *Foundations of Economics*. Samuelson formulated formal models of household and firm behavior as the basis for generating demand and supply curves. Households are posited to maximize utility subject to a budget constraint and firms to maximize profits subject to given technology for converting inputs to outputs. The marginal utility and marginal cost interpretations of demand and supply are formally derived from these premises.

Against the neoclassical orthodoxy, heterodox approaches to economics have vied for recognition. The term "neoclassical" was coined in 1900 by institutionalist Thorstein Veblen who saw a need, in counterpoint to the rarefied abstractions of Marshall's households and firms, for more thoroughgoing analysis of the complexities of human "habits, propensities, aptitudes, and conventions." Other institutionalists, along with Marxists and their radical offshoots who emphasize social class and early macroeconomists who were concerned with the failure of labor markets to eliminate unemployment, took issue in diverse ways with the neoclassical focus on competitive market equilibrium. Over time, the moniker "neoclassical" came to be applied gener- ally – and usually pejoratively – to mainstream economics by any group identifying as outside the mainstream even as the mainstream itself expanded in content and evolved in analytical approach. Of note, in microeconomics game theory came into promin- ence and macroeconomics came to account for phenomena such as unemployment and the business cycle that lay beyond the scope of a standard market equilibrium framework. To absorb all of the modern mainstream under the neoclassical banner would move us far from the original conception.

Finally, adding one more complication, the term "neoclassical synthesis" has found application within macroeconomics. We will go into detail in Chapter 9. For now,

Box 3.2 (cont.)

suffice to say that the neoclassical synthesis holds that while classical principles of market equilibration apply as a long-run tendency, the process can get sufficiently bogged down in the short run – in particular with respect to labor markets achieving full employment – as to justify a role for government in expediting it.

Colander's wish for the term "neoclassical economics" to be expunged from the language will probably not be realized. At best, we can hope to understand the different ways in which the term is used and to discern by context the intent of the user. In this text, "neoclassical economics" is used to refer to the marginalist approach to understanding the allocation of resources and the distribution of income.

The sense in which the competitive market outcome is optimal is examined more closely in Figure 3.4. At the competitive equilibrium output, Q^* (read "Q-star"), marginal cost of supply and marginal value to users are equated. Inside the margin, however, for all units of output less than Q^*, marginal value exceeds marginal cost. For these infra-marginal units, the market price that must be paid, P^*, is less than the marginal value to users. The area above P^* and below the demand curve is known as "consumers' surplus". Further, the market price received by sellers for all units less than Q^* exceeds the marginal cost of supply. The area below P^* and above the supply curve is known as "producers' surplus". The combined area of consumers' and producers' surplus is maximized when output is at Q^*.

The concepts of consumers' and producers' surplus are applied by economists to analyze the impact of government policy measures that distort markets. Price controls, taxes and subsidies, and regulatory interventions all divert resources from their theoretically optimal allocations under competitive market assumptions. The degree to which such policies impact social welfare can be assessed through estimation of the effects on consumers' and producers' surplus.

Comparative Statics

Real world markets are in a constant state of flux, supplies and demands ever buffeted by myriad forces. Comparative static analysis provides a way of examining the impact on market equilibrium of changes in variables exogenous to the model. We isolate the market impact of a particular shock under the assumption of *ceteris paribus*, which translated from the Latin means "all else equal".

As an example, suppose that, *ceteris paribus*, an advance in technology reduces the cost to produce a good. Graphically, this is represented as a rightward shift of the supply curve, as shown in Figure 3.5. For any given quantity along the horizontal axis, the supply price at which sellers can cover marginal cost is lowered. Or reading from the vertical axis, at any

Figure 3.4 Consumers' and producers' surplus

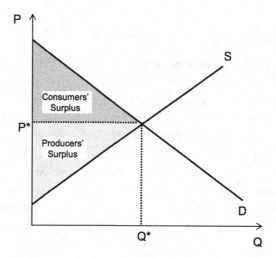

Consumers' surplus is the excess of the marginal value to users over the market price.
Producers' surplus is the excess of the market price over the marginal cost of production.

Figure 3.5 An increase in supply

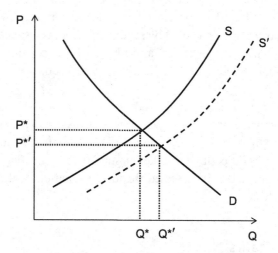

An increase in supply results in a lower equilibrium price and a higher equilibrium quantity traded.

given price more resources can be drawn into production so that a greater quantity is supplied. The shift in the supply curve yields a new market equilibrium. The equilibrium price falls from P^* to $P^{*\prime}$ (read "P-star-prime") and the equilibrium quantity rises from Q^* to $Q^{*\prime}$. The rightward shift in the supply curve results in a movement along the existing demand curve to the new equilibrium. Stated differently, an increase in supply results in an increase in quantity demanded following from the drop in equilibrium price.

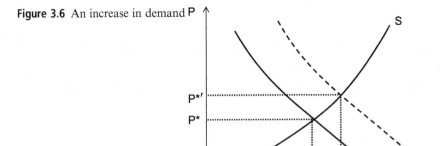

Figure 3.6 An increase in demand

An increase in demand results in a higher price and
a higher quantity traded.

Consider another example, this time affecting the demand side of the market. Suppose that, *ceteris paribus*, incomes rise broadly due to a generally strong economy. For a normal good this results in an increase in demand, or a rightward shift in the demand curve, as shown in Figure 3.6. The new demand curve reflects higher demand for the good at all prices. The equilibrium price rises from P^* to $P^{*\prime}$ and the equilibrium quantity from Q^* to $Q^{*\prime}$. The rightward shift in the demand curve results in a movement along the existing supply curve to the new equilibrium. Put another way, the shift in demand results in an increase in quantity supplied following from the increase in equilibrium price.

Exogenous factors other than income, changes in which can cause the demand curve to shift, include: consumer tastes and preferences; prices of goods that are substitutes for or complements to the good in question; expectations about the future; and government policy measures. And on the supply side, changes in exogenous factors, besides the technology example given, that can cause a shift, include: prices of inputs to production; prices of related products; expectations about the future; and government policy measures.

How the expectation of future price changes influences prices in the present is worth elaborating on for its importance in macroeconomics. On the demand side, the expectation of higher prices in the future motivates buying sooner rather than later to beat the increase. Consequently, the demand curve in the present shifts to the right. For sellers, the expectation of higher prices in the future provides the incentive to withhold output to take advantage of higher returns later. The supply curve in the present thus shifts to the left. These dynamics reinforce each other to accelerate the expected price increases making for a self-fulfilling prophecy. On an economy-wide scale, expectations of rising prices tend to be similarly self-fulfilling. This can make it difficult for authorities to rein in inflation.

C   Elasticity

The demand and supply framework holds that quantities respond in given direction to price changes. Elasticity provides a measure of the degree of this response. Elasticity is calculated as the percentage change in quantity demanded or supplied divided by the percentage change in price. If a 1 percent change in price yields more than a 1 percent change in quantity (in absolute value) the demand or supply curve is said to be *elastic*; if the response is less than 1 percent, it is said to be *inelastic*. Figure 3.7 illustrates. In both panels an increase in supply results in a movement along the demand curve to a lower equilibrium price and a higher equilibrium quantity. In the case represented on the left, the demand curve is inelastic so the supply increase drives the price down steeply to generate only a modest increase in quantity demanded. By contrast in the case represented on the right, the demand curve is elastic so that just a slight drop in price delivers a large increase in quantity demanded.

The *price elasticity of demand or supply* is generally sensitive to the time frame under consideration. Quantity responses tend to be greater the longer the passage of time. On the demand side, changes in household patterns of consumption rest on adjustments in habit and lifestyle that do not tend to play out quickly. On the supply side, for firms to make significant changes in production requires expanding or closing plants, hiring or laying off workers, or adopting alternative technologies. The oil price shocks of the 1970s presented a vivid illustration of long-run versus short-run responses to price. Oil price increases

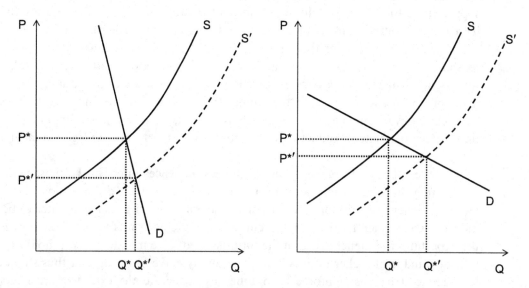

When demand is inelastic, an increase in supply results in a large decline in price and a small increase in quantity traded.

When demand is elastic, an increase in supply results in a small drop in price and a large increase in quantity traded.

Figure 3.7 Effect of demand elasticity under a supply shift

were forced by a cartel of oil producing nations that agreed to collectively restrict output. With only modest supply cutbacks, the price of oil quadrupled in 1974, and doubled again with renewed tightening of supply in 1979. After each initial shock, however, oil prices went into a long downward slide. This was because over time on the demand side, consumers cut back use by switching to smaller, more fuel-efficient vehicles and installing better insulation in their homes, among other things. And on the supply side, countries that did not belong to the cartel developed additional sources of production. In the long run then, both demand and supply proved quite elastic, and price increases moderated significantly.

The response of demand and supply to factors other than price is captured by various other measures of elasticity. The *cross-price elasticity of demand* measures the percentage change in quantity demanded of one good relative to a percentage change in price of another good. To continue the fuel oil example, we might expect the cross-price elasticity of demand for oil with respect to the price of natural gas to be fairly high, at least in the long run since oil and gas are close substitutes. The *income elasticity of demand* captures the responsiveness of demand to changes in income. For example, above a certain threshold of sustenance, the income elasticity of demand for food is low. The *elasticity of substitution* between two inputs to production is defined as the percentage change in the ratio of the input quantities to a percentage change in the ratio of their prices. Agriculture, for example, exhibits a fairly high elasticity of substitution between capital and labor inputs as illuminated by the widely differing approaches to farming seen across countries at different stages of economic development.

D   Relaxing the Perfect Competition Assumption

The model of perfect competition assumes that all buyers and sellers are price takers. In many markets, this assumption clearly does not apply to any reasonable approximation. Sometimes sellers or buyers are sufficiently dominant that they can wield influence over market price. As opposed to being price takers, they have *market power*. In the extreme case, a monopolist exercises total control over price – but not over both price and quantity simultaneously. In setting a higher price, the monopolist or any seller with market power must accept a reduction in sales.

Market power results from market concentration among a small number of sellers or buyers. Market concentration among sellers may come about for a variety of reasons. Some industries exhibit substantial economies of scale. This means that as output increases, the cost of production falls, which gives larger producers an advantage over smaller ones. Examples of industries where economies of scale limit the market to one or a small number of producers include the manufacture of jet planes and the local distribution of electric power. In other industries, barriers to entry may impede competition. Sometimes these barriers to entry are created by government conferring licenses or awarding patents and copyrights, and with good reason. Licenses ensure that standards are met while patents and copyrights are intended to incentivize innovation and creative endeavor. In still other industries market power derives from branding and product differentiation. Consumers become loyal to a particular make of car or brand of ice cream, for example. While the car manufacturer or the ice cream maker still faces competition from other brands, it nevertheless has some latitude for setting price beyond the iron dictates of a perfectly competitive market.

Under pure competition an individual firm effectively faces a perfectly elastic demand curve: at the market price the firm can sell any feasible level of output; but at any price above the market price it can sell nothing. By contrast, a firm with market power faces a downward sloping demand curve: it can increase sales only by lowering price. In choosing a price/quantity combination, the firm with market power will consider the impact on total revenue of its pricing decisions. Total revenue is equal to price times quantity, represented graphically as the area of a rectangle as captured in Figure 3.8. When the firm lowers price from P′ to P″ (read "P double prime") it gains additional sales but that does not make up for revenue lost on existing sales. The elasticity of the demand curve determines whether lowering price will increase or decrease revenue. If demand is inelastic, lowering price will decrease total revenue, as in Figure 3.8, because the revenue lost on a per unit basis exceeds the revenue gained from greater sales. Conversely, if demand is elastic, lowering price will increase revenue because a strong increase in sales more than offsets the lower per unit price. How elastic an individual firm's demand curve is depends importantly on the availability of close substitutes. Businesses look to branding and product differentiation to carve out a niche in the marketplace so as to reduce the elasticity of demand for their products. Monopolies created by significant economies of scale or barriers to entry may have a great deal of pricing power if left unregulated.

Figure 3.8 Total revenue of a firm with market power

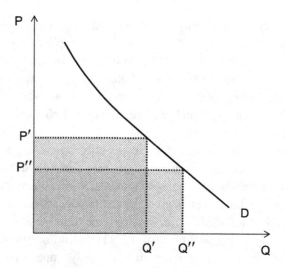

A firm with market power sets price in view of the effect on total revenue.

In the model of perfect competition, the assumption that buyers and sellers are price takers yields the appealing result that markets will allocate resources efficiently. Just the right amount of a good will be produced and consumed so that at the margin the value to consumers is equal to the cost to producers. In markets where firms are not price takers, however, this result does not hold. Competition among firms is essential to drive price down to meet marginal cost. Without competition a firm can raise price above marginal cost by limiting output. The wedge between the price, which aligns with the marginal willingness to pay by users expressed in the demand curve, and the marginal cost of production implies that resources are under-allocated to production of the good. The case for free markets is thus not so compelling when perfect competition does not prevail.

When market conditions are not conducive to perfect competition, governments sometimes get involved. In some cases this means government taking ownership, particularly in industries that are natural monopolies due to their economies of scale. Public utilities are a prime example. In other cases, private ownership may be permitted but with government stepping in to regulate investment and pricing decisions. Even for industries that lend themselves to competition, government has a role to play in safeguarding against collusion or blocking mergers and acquisitions that would concentrate market share unduly. Of course, government intervention in markets often leads to less than ideal outcomes in other ways. In practice, finding the best mix of public and private, regulation and free market, is an ongoing exploratory process.

E Factor Markets

Factor markets pertain to land, labor, capital, and entrepreneurship. These factors of production are remunerated, respectively, in the form of rent, wages, interest, and profits. The notion of profit in economics refers to an above normal rate of return to capital where the normal rate of return is indicated by the market rate of interest. Positive economic profits act as the reward to innovation and risk taking – the essence of the entrepreneurial contribution to an economy. The presence of economic profits in an industry acts as a magnet to new investment. The expansion of output that results drives prices down until returns in the industry are aligned with those elsewhere in the economy and economic profits disappear. Conversely, when economic profits are negative, businesses are pushed to close down or cut back production which causes prices to rise until economic profits are restored to zero. Sustained economic profits are a sign of barriers to entry and the existence of market power.

For the other three factors of production, demand and supply function under competitive market conditions to determine rates of compensation and levels of utilization. As in product markets, buyers and sellers in competitive factor markets are price takers and the neoclassical logic of the margin applies. Let us reason through the process with respect to labor. An individual firm takes the market wage for labor as given and makes the hiring decision based on the marginal productivity of labor relative to the wage. In the short-run, the firm's plant and equipment are fixed. As the firm adds more workers to its existing physical capacity, at some point the productivity of additional workers begins to decline. As long as an additional worker generates an increment to output that exceeds the wage the worker commands, the worker is worth hiring. Once the value of the marginal product of labor is just equal to the wage, employment has reached an optimal level. Adding further workers with marginal productivity falling short of the wage would decrease the firm's net revenue.

On the supply side of the labor market, devoting more workers to a particular use requires that they forego alternative pursuits. Workers differ in their skills, aptitudes, and preferences. Allocating people to a particular activity involves repurposing them at ever increasing opportunity cost from other things they like doing and are good at. A given market wage will attract a supply of labor into an activity until at the margin the foregone return in alternatives is just matched.

The market for a particular kind of work reaches equilibrium at a wage that equates the quantity of labor demanded with the quantity supplied. The level of employment at this equilibrium wage is such that the value of the marginal product of labor on the demand side is equal to the marginal opportunity cost of labor on the supply side. This outcome represents an efficient allocation of labor to a given use. To apply any less labor to such use would mean that the contribution of an additional worker at the margin would exceed the opportunity cost of that worker, while to apply any more would mean the worker's contribution at the margin would fall short of his opportunity cost.

Markets will arrive at an efficient allocation of labor among uses provided that the buyers and sellers of labor compete as wage takers. If either buyers or sellers of labor are able to exert market power over the wage rate, the outcome will deviate from optimality. On the demand side, large firms that dominate employment for particular skills or in particular geographic locations may be able to exercise market power over the wage. And on the supply side, workers have sometimes succeeded in forming unions to exert market power.

The demand for labor is derived from the demand for the final goods and services produced. Changes in product markets feed back to changes in the demand for labor through their impact on the value of labor's marginal product. A decrease in demand in a product market lowers the equilibrium price of the product which in turn reduces the value of the marginal product of the labor that produces it. Figure 3.9 captures this as a leftward shift of the labor demand curve and a movement along the labor supply curve to a lower equilibrium wage, $w^{*\prime}$, from the initial wage, w^*. Equilibrium employment drops from L^* to $L^{*\prime}$. Labor is released to other uses because the wage rate in this particular use no longer covers the opportunity cost of worker time.

An important determinant of the elasticity of demand for labor is the degree to which capital can be substituted for labor in the production process. In some industries capital is readily substituted for labor making the demand for labor quite elastic. In other industries,

Figure 3.9 A decrease in labor demand

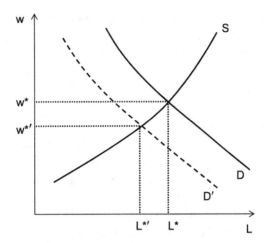

A decrease in labor demand results in a lower wage and a lower quantity of labor employed.

Figure 3.10 The market for land

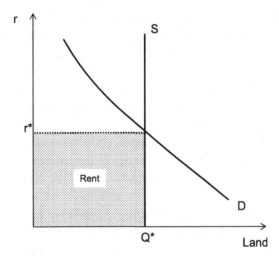

The rent paid to land reflects its scarcity value.

available technologies prescribe more rigid capital-to-labor proportions and the demand for labor consequently tends to be more inelastic.

Land is unlike other factors of production in being completely immobile. The market for land in a given location is thus characterized by a perfectly inelastic supply curve. Land defined by location has no opportunity cost as it cannot but be available precisely where it is. Regardless of the rental rate, r, the supply is fixed, as depicted in Figure 3.10. As a result, the rental price for land is determined entirely by the demand side of the market. Those desiring to make use of land in a particular location must compete against each other to obtain rights to it. The land's value thus reflects its scarcity, not the opportunity cost of its use elsewhere.

A more general concept of *economic rent* follows from the properties of land rent. Broadly speaking, economic rent refers to a return above supply cost. Often economic rents arise out of government policies that limit market competition. Governments grant monopolies, confer licenses, engage contractors, and impose regulations that can potentially generate returns to factors in excess of their opportunity costs. To gain advantage from such preferential opportunities, enterprising individuals engage in "rent seeking" behavior. Often, this is perfectly legal. But sometimes, rent seeking crosses the line into corruption – government officials extracting kickbacks, say, for awarding generous construction contracts. Legal or otherwise, rent seeking is generally not economically productive but rather draws its rewards from the redistribution of economic benefits. Good policy design thus aims at minimizing the existence of opportunities for rent seeking.

Capital inputs to production (buildings, equipment, land improvements) are distinguished by their long lives. New capital assets are mobile with respect to how and where they are to be utilized. Once assets have been situated into production facilities, however, they can lose much of this mobility. On the supply side, the price of new assets reflects their costs of production. On the demand side, firms will acquire new assets to the point where at the margin the expected rate of return covers the interest cost of investment funds. As time passes, however, expectations are not necessarily realized. Once established in use, plant and equipment take on something of the fixity of land. The sunk costs associated with the initial production of the assets then lose relevance in the decision to continue to employ them. The value of assets in place is determined more narrowly by the returns they are expected to generate in their current or any alternate uses. Existing assets in place will be engaged as long as the rate of return covers the variable costs of maintenance and operation.

For factors of production of all types, demand is derived from the markets for end products. Supply, on the other hand, varies in nature depending on the factor. Land being fixed by location, cost of production vanishes from the calculus. Price is determined solely by demand-driven scarcity. Of course, if we think of land supply by form of usage within a locality much fungibility exists, and supply of land to one use will reflect opportunity cost in other uses. Labor, on the other hand, is for the most part highly mobile by location, by industry, and by function. The wage at which labor will be supplied to any particular use or location thus reflects its opportunity cost in other uses or locations. Capital is a hybrid, mobile *ex ante* but largely fixed *ex post*. The initial supply of a capital asset into any given use reflects the opportunity cost of resources absorbed in its production. Once in place, however, the sunk costs of the initial outlay do not matter. What is relevant to utilization decisions for an asset in place is the cost of continued maintenance and operation versus any liquidation value it may have. Under competitive market conditions, factor inputs will in general be allocated to alternative uses to the point where marginal product is aligned with marginal opportunity cost. Market determination of wages, interest rates, and rents drive this equilibration process.

Entrepreneurial talent is not traded on such well-organized markets as the other factors of production. It is too hard to quantify and price. Rather, entrepreneurs act as the residual claimants of the returns to productive activity. After the other factors have received their due, entrepreneurs claim the economic profits or bear the economic losses. It is up to them to allocate their abilities to the highest return uses. That is what makes them entrepreneurs.

F Micro Fundamentals for the Study of Macro

Microeconomic tools will prove useful in two ways for our study of macroeconomics. For one, we will invoke them, in a very stylized way, to thinking of the economy as a whole as one big demand and supply system. More pointedly, we will apply them to analyzing key markets that function at the level of the economy as a whole.

The basic concepts of demand and supply can be extended to an economy-wide level. Generalizing to an aggregate notion of output and an overall price level, we can conceive of aggregate demand and supply functions that yield an equilibrium outcome. Following the lessons of micro, when aggregate demand increases (that is, the aggregate demand curve shifts right), the price level and aggregate output will rise. When aggregate demand decreases (or the aggregate demand curve shifts left), the opposite happens. When aggregate supply increases (or the aggregate supply curve shifts right), aggregate output rises and the price level falls, and vice versa. This model will take us some distance in interpreting macroeconomic phenomena and analyzing government policies that affect demand or supply in broad terms. The aggregate demand / aggregate supply framework will be laid out fully in Chapter 9.

The model of equilibrium in the aggregate is ultimately unsatisfying, however, in view of the all too obvious tendency for economies to function at less than full capacity for extended periods. The equilibration process clearly does not work in a timely or fulsome manner to eliminate unemployment and keep plant and equipment operating at full steam. Moreover, economies tend to cycle through periods of slump – with unemployment high and growth sluggish – and overheating – with inflation mounting and growth hitting unsustainable levels. A theory centered on equilibrium is at odds with observed cyclicality involving sustained periods of underperformance. Indeed it effectively denies the very processes of core interest to macroeconomists. While the neoclassical theory of the market may function satisfactorily to explain activity at the micro level for the vast majority of labor force participants who are employed even in bad times, its inability to explain a significant minority of workers being jobless for long stretches is an untenable failing from a macro standpoint. Macro theory must then consist of more than an aggregate demand and supply framework rooted in the principles of micro.

Microeconomic theory comes into its own in the analysis of two particular markets of special relevance for the economy as a whole. These are the markets that set the prices for loanable funds and foreign exchange. The price of loanable funds is the interest rate. The interest rate is key to guiding credit growth, which in turn acts as a catalyst for economic growth broadly. The exchange rate at which foreign currency trades for domestic currency is pivotal in determining exports and imports, again with significant consequences for overall economic growth. Demand and supply will prove essential tools for understanding these markets in the macroeconomic context.

Bibliographic Note

Alfred Marshall's *Principles of Economics* is the primordial source for the demand and supply graphs that remain at the heart of today's microeconomic textbooks. First appearing in 1890, Marshall's volume went through eight editions over the ensuing 30 years. Marshall's nephew, C.W. Guillebaud, has done the great man's followers a service in tracing the roots of every passage contained in the eighth edition to its first appearance in a previous edition. Guillebaud's exegeses was published in 1961 as *Principles of Economics: Volume II – Notes*, in conjunction with a re-release of Marshall's eighth edition. Guillebaud's painstaking review led him to conclude that the third edition represented the expository peak of the *Principles*, subsequent revisions having served on balance to "devitalize" it.

Marshall's ideas had antecedents among the classical economists Adam Smith, Thomas Malthus, David Ricardo, and John Stuart Mill. The concept of utility that undergirds the principle of demand is due to Jeremy Bentham. A highly readable history of thought that traces the ideas of these pioneers in economic science is Robert Heilbroner's *The Worldly Philosophers* (the quote in this chapter being taken from page 5). A more deeply analytical treatment is provided by Joseph Schumpeter in his *History of Economic Analysis*.

BIBLIOGRAPHIC CITATIONS

Bentham, Jeremy, 1789. *An Introduction to the Principles of Morals and Legislation* (London: T. Payne, and Son).

Colander, David, 2000. "The Death of Neoclassical Economics," *Journal of the History of Economic Thought*, Vol. 22, No. 2, pp. 127–143.

Guillebaud, C. W., 1961. *Principles of Economics, 9th (Variorum) Edition with Annotations, Volume II Notes* (London: MacMillan).

Heilbroner, Robert L., 1962. *The Worldly Philosophers: The Lives, Times, and Ideas of the Great Economic Thinkers* (New York: Time Inc.).

Malthus, Thomas, 1803. *An Essay on the Principle of Population* (London: T. Bensley).

Marshall, Alfred, 1895. *Principles of Economics*, 3rd Edition (Cambridge: Cambridge University Press).

Mill, John Stuart, 1848. *Principles of Political Economy* (Boston: C.C. Little & J. Brown).

Ricardo, David, 1817. *Principles of Political Economy, and Taxation* (London: John Murray, Albemarle Street).

Samuelson, Paul, 1947. *Foundations of Economic Analysis* (Cambridge, MA: Harvard University Press).

Schumpeter, Joseph A., 1954. *History of Economic Analysis* (New York: Oxford University Press).

Smith, Adam, 1776. *An Inquiry into the Nature and Causes of the Wealth of Nations* (London: W. Strahan; and T. Cadell).

Veblen, Thorstein, 1900. "The Preconceptions of Economic Science. III," *The Quarterly Journal of Economics*, Vol. 14, No. 2 (Feb.), pp. 240–269.

4   National Income and Product Accounts

The National Income and Product Accounts provide a framework for measuring the size of an economy and its component parts. Breakdowns are made along lines of: (i) what is produced; (ii) who receives the income; and (iii) how the income is spent. In all aspects, the economies of Emerging East Asia show great diversity.

Gross domestic product (GDP) is the standard measure of the overall size of an economy. The first two chapters of this text have referenced this measure to characterize economic performance in the Emerging East Asia region. The breakdown of GDP along various dimensions sheds light on the workings of an economy, providing a window into development processes and macroeconomic balances.

In this chapter we lay out approaches to calculating GDP and related measures of aggregate economic activity as covered under the National Income and Product Accounts (NIPA). We take Taiwan as a case study showing how the make-up of its economy has changed through seven decades of successful development. And we draw comparisons across the economies of Emerging East Asia for the year 2020 to reveal the great diversity of the region.

Three different approaches have been formulated for compiling GDP: the product approach; the income approach; and the expenditures approach. The *product approach* involves adding up the value of all productive activity over a given period of time. Productive activity generates incomes, so the *income approach* comes at the same result by adding up different types of income over the period. Finally, the incomes earned are spent in assorted ways with the *expenditure approach* capturing spending in different forms. The three approaches to GDP measurement form the basis for the three sections of this chapter.

A   Product Approach

The product accounts are the starting point for national income accounting. Countries with only rudimentary NIPA systems maintain product accounts even when they have not developed the capacity to implement other approaches to GDP measurement.

Accounting Concepts

The product approach follows from the basic definition of GDP as the value of productive activity in an economy over an interval of time, either annually or quarterly. The time dimension indicates that GDP is a flow concept as opposed to a stock which is measured at an instant in time. To illustrate the distinction, capital assets are a stock while investment that adds to those assets over a period of time is a flow.

Measurement of production must be defined in value added terms to avoid double counting of the intermediate inputs to production. We want to avoid, for example, counting up the value of the bread produced plus the value of the flour produced plus the value of the wheat produced because the value of the bread incorporates the value of the flour used to make it, as in turn the value of the flour incorporates the value of the wheat. The value added measure of production nets out the consumption of intermediate inputs so that the magnitude entering the accounts in this simple example is: Grain + (Flour – Grain) + (Bread – Flour), where the elements are expressed in value terms per unit of time. In general then, GDP captures the value of output across sectors minus the value of intermediate inputs. Thus derived, value added reflects the contribution of factor inputs to production.

The production of long-lived capital goods – continuing the bread making example these would include ovens and bakery facilities – gets counted fully in GDP for the year the goods are produced. Over their lifespan these capital goods in turn contribute to the production of other goods and services counted in GDP year by year. With each passing year, some portion of an economy's capital stock wears out in the production process. The "gross" in gross domestic product means this capital consumption is subsumed in the output value measure. By deducting it we get a measure of output net of that part of newly produced capital that has served merely to replace assets that were depleted. This measure of output is referred to as net domestic product (NDP):

$$\text{NDP} = \text{GDP} - \text{capital consumption.} \tag{4.1}$$

Although conceptually important, in reality capital consumption, or depreciation, is difficult to formally specify and measure. So while a net measure might be preferable in principle for many purposes, the gross measure tends to predominate on practical grounds.

The boundary on what is considered production for GDP purposes is subject to certain limitations. To a large extent, production for own consumption is not counted even as production of the same goods or services for commercial purposes is. For example, home cooked meals are not counted whereas meals prepared in a restaurant are. Housekeeping activities of family members are not counted whereas the same functions performed by paid domestic helpers are. Do-it-yourself home repairs are not counted even though the paid services of a contractor are. Further, volunteer work for charity organizations is not counted whereas paid employment in the same organizations is. In all such cases, GDP captures activities when they are transacted in markets but not otherwise. This limitation of measurement has the effect of biasing downward the GDP valuation of less developed economies. This is because households tend to be more self-reliant when incomes are lower – eating at home, caring for young children within the family, and enjoying the company of family and friends as entertainment, for example, rather than purchasing such services in the market.

There are two areas of production in which the lack of market transactions necessitates an imputation of output values. The first is agricultural production for subsistence use. Clearly this is an important form of economic activity for societies at low levels of economic development. The second is the rental value of owner-occupied homes. In general, the stock of housing yields residential services that are appropriately included in GDP. For homes that are rented, a transaction occurs to register the value of these services. For homes that are occupied by their owners, the value of services is imputed as if the owners paid rent to themselves. Homeowners are thus treated as though they are in the business of property rental.

While transactions generally serve as the basis for valuing productive activity for GDP accounting purposes, note that not all transactions signify underlying productive activity. Rather, transactions often function merely to transfer ownership of existing assets, as in the sale of real property or of stocks and bonds. However, the services involved in facilitating such transactions, as rendered by an agent or broker for example, are counted in GDP. Changes in the market value of assets are not counted.

We must emphasize that GDP is not designed as a measure of welfare in any general sense. In fact, its connection to welfare can at times be anomalous. For example, an increase in crime clearly makes people worse off even as it generates work in security and policing services. Similarly a disease epidemic stimulates activity in the health care industry that raises GDP despite the suffering involved. War, natural disasters, environmental degradation – all have devastating consequences for humanity, yet often such calamities precipitate increases in measured productive activity. The upshot is that GDP must be kept in proper perspective as a measure of activity rather than an indicator of well-being or prosperity.

Sectoral Breakdown

The product measure of GDP allows for breakdown by sector. The three principal sectors are agriculture, industry, and services, with industry further decomposed into mining, manufacturing, and construction. The process of economic development rests fundamentally on the shift in economic activity from agriculture to industry to services. We document this shift with data from Taiwan spanning seven decades and for a cross section of Emerging East Asian economies in 2020.

Taiwan's structural transformation over the period 1951 to 2020 is illustrated in Chart 4.1. Agriculture's share in output fell from 32.4 percent in 1951 to just under 2 percent by 2001 where it has remained stable ever since. Industry's share expanded to fill the gap until the 1980s, rising from 19.9 percent of GDP to a peak of 46.0 percent in 1986, after which it gave way to services. By the 2000-aughts, the service sector had consolidated its predominance at about two-thirds of GDP. In the 2010s, industry saw a modest resurgence, reaching 36.9 percent of GDP in 2020, with services retrenching to 61.5 percent.

Chart 4.1 GDP by sector, Taiwan, 1951–2020

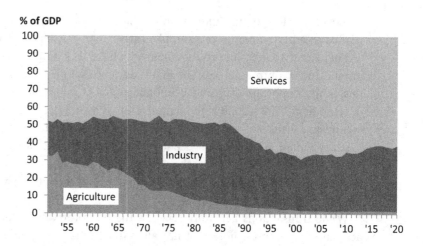

Chart 4.2 GDP by sector, select economies, 2020

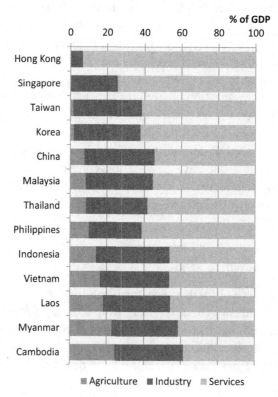

The process of structural change is portrayed in cross-section in Chart 4.2. As of 2020, the low income economies of Cambodia and Myanmar still depended on agriculture for more than 20 percent of their GDP. With rising income, agriculture's share drops steadily to virtually zero for Singapore and Hong Kong. By contrast, industry's share is strikingly similar across much of the income spectrum within a range of 33–40 percent of GDP for Taiwan, Korea, China, Malaysia, Thailand, Indonesia, Vietnam, Laos, and even Myanmar and Cambodia. The Philippines joins Hong Kong and Singapore as an outlier to the downside with an industry share of just 28.4 percent. Commensurately, the service sector dominates in Hong Kong and Singapore, and takes an outsized position in the Philippines with a share of more than 60 percent to put the country on par with Korea and Taiwan. We may infer from this that while structural change is highly correlated with per capita GDP, other factors such as resource endowments and government policy are also involved.

B   Income Approach

Economic activity yields income in conjunction with producing output, so in principle, measuring income offers an alternative route to arriving at the same result. Relatively sophisticated statistical systems are required to compile GDP by this approach. Time series data are available for Taiwan to a limited degree. However, cross-section data are not adequate for a comparison by economy.

Accounting Concepts

A number of adjustments are required to transform a product measure into an income measure suited to breaking down income by type of recipient. GDP is based on the location of production, regardless of whether it generates income to foreign or domestic parties. By contrast, Gross National Income (GNI) captures the income of domestic parties regardless of whether the income is earned at home or abroad. To convert GDP to GNI the foreign-sourced income of domestic parties must be added and the domestic-sourced income of foreign parties must be subtracted. Consolidating these two adjustments into a single net measure, we have:

$$\text{GNI} = \text{GDP} + \text{net foreign factor income.} \qquad (4.2)$$

Foreign factor income includes wages and salaries of workers employed abroad as well as returns on foreign investment. GNI may be greater than, less than, or equal to GDP depending on the balance on net foreign factor income.

Distribution of income is tracked along lines defined by institutional unit and factor of production. Institutional units are classified into five broad types: households, including unincorporated businesses owned by households; non-financial corporations; financial corporations; government; and non-profit institutions serving households. Because income initially received from productive activity by one type of institutional unit may in turn be transferred to another type of unit, the national accounts represent income flows in two stages: the primary distribution of income account; and the redistribution of income account. Redistribution involves unilateral transfers where no good or service is provided in exchange. Examples include income taxes, pensions, and social assistance.

The redistribution of income account reflects receipts subsequent to all unilateral transfers. Domestically, these mainly involve government exercising its powers of taxation and social welfare support. Internationally, remittances of family members resident abroad figures importantly for some economies (e.g., the Philippines). The addition of net foreign transfers to GNI yields gross national disposable income (GNDI):

$$GNDI = GNI + \text{net foreign transfers}. \tag{4.3}$$

GNDI may be greater than, less than, or equal to GNI depending on the balance on net foreign transfers.

Institutional units differ in the forms of factor income they receive. Households alone receive returns to labor. Labor income comprises wages and salaries, both in cash and in kind, as well as social insurance contributions made by employers for the benefit of employees. Households also receive returns to property, the principle forms of which are interest, rent, and distributed income from corporations (e.g., dividends paid to shareholders). Household income from unincorporated businesses is regarded as a mix of returns to labor and property that cannot be easily disentangled. All household income receipts are recorded on a pre-tax basis in the primary distribution of income account.

Primary income of government is derived from sources other than taxes applied to incomes of households or enterprises. Most notably, these sources include value added taxes, sales taxes, import duties, and earnings of government enterprises. Subsidies paid by government to farms or enterprises for productive activities are deducted from government primary income.

The income of enterprises is equal to pre-tax earnings not distributed to shareholders and is regarded as income from property. By its nature, this income is saved as retained earnings rather than consumed. Only households and government engage in consumption. This consumption versus saving distinction is expanded on in the next section.

Technically, national income should be defined net of capital consumption (depreciation) which is properly viewed as a cost of production rather than a component of income. Realistically, however, the difficulty of measuring capital consumption inclines statistical authorities to use of the gross measure. The NIPA guidelines allow for either method to be adopted. Net national disposable income (NNDI) is defined as GNDI minus capital consumption:

$$NNDI = GNDI - \text{capital consumption}. \tag{4.4}$$

To sum up, getting from GDP to NNDI requires the following steps: (i) adding net foreign factor income; (ii) adding net foreign transfer income; and (iii) subtracting capital consumption.

The Taiwan Case

Table 4.1 walks through the conversion of GDP to NNDI for Taiwan for the year 2020. Taiwan's GDP in that year was NT$19.77 trillion (which at an exchange rate of NT$29.6 to US$1 was equal to US$668 billion). Net foreign factor income added NT$0.55 trillion to

Table 4.1 Taiwan GDP to NNDI conversion, 2020

in NT$ trillion

Gross Domestic Product		19.77
Net Foreign Factor Income	+	0.55
Gross National Income		20.32
Net Foreign Transfers	+	–0.09
Gross National Disposable Income		20.23
Capital Consumption Allowance	–	3.15
Net National Disposable Income		17.08

Chart 4.3 Labor share in income, Taiwan, 1955–2015

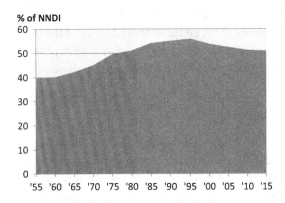

that amount to yield GNI of NT$20.32 trillion. Foreign transfers were on balance outbound in the amount of NT$0.09 trillion leaving GNDI of NT$20.23 trillion. Finally, netting out a capital consumption allowance of NT$3.15 trillion yields NNDI of NT$17.08 trillion.

NNDI represents all income, including net transfers, received by domestic parties. NNDI is distributed as primary income to households, corporations, and government, with redistribution then taking place through taxes and subsidies. The distribution presented in the Taiwan accounts is a hybrid of primary income and redistributed income. Household incomes are taken as pre-tax, corporate incomes as post-tax. The corporate income figure thus represents retained earnings after taxes which constitutes corporate saving. Government income then comprises business profit taxes as well as indirect taxes less subsidies, net income from government property and enterprises, and compulsory fees, fines, and penalties. Household income is divided between compensation of employees and private income from property.

Changes in measurement over time impede a full compilation of time series for income shares. Limiting the focus to labor's share though, we can look at Taiwan's history dating back to 1955, shown in Chart 4.3. Through the early decades up to 1995, the share of income going to labor rose steadily. Recall from Figure 4.1 that this was a period of rapid industrialization. Workers were being drawn out of agriculture into more productive urban jobs.

The combination of expanding urban employment and rising wages as labor markets tightened drove the increase in employee compensation. Once this process had run its course and the service sector began to take on greater weight, labor's share fell off somewhat then stabilized at a little over 50 percent of income.

C   Expenditures Approach

The third approach to GDP measurement closes the loop to tally expenditures of income on the purchase of final goods and services. Spending generates demand, and demand is critical in determining how close an economy gets to reaching its potential. Producers will not long continue to produce if their wares do not sell. Production may generate incomes, but if those incomes are not channeled into spending, the circle is broken and the engine of economic growth stalls. The expenditures approach to GDP thus forms the basis for analyzing economic performance through the ebbs and flows of the business cycle. We lay foundations for thinking about this by examining the relationship between saving – or not consuming – and the investment that channels that saving into demand for products.

Accounting Concepts

Expenditures on final goods and services are categorized as follows: consumption by households; investment by households and businesses; consumption and investment by government; and exports less imports. Expenditures by businesses on goods and services for intermediate use are not included because these costs are absorbed in the ultimate spending on final goods and services. Spending on imports must be subtracted because such spending is implicitly counted in the other components of spending, yet has no domestic production counterpart. Formally:

$$GDP = C + I + G + X - M \tag{4.5}$$

where C = consumption by households;

I = investment by households and businesses;

G = government consumption and investment;

X = exports;

M = imports.

A consumption good or service is defined as yielding direct satisfaction of human wants or needs. Private consumption is undertaken by households at their own expense. Public consumption occurs when government bears the cost.

Investment has two components – formation of fixed capital and changes in inventories. Fixed capital refers to produced assets with a useful life of more than one year. Housing is included in fixed capital although consumer durables such as motor vehicles and appliances are not, even when identical items if purchased by businesses do get treated as investment.

Improvements to existing assets are included when the improvements go beyond routine maintenance. Research and development expenditures are included insofar as they represent investment that is expected to yield economic returns in the future. Fixed investment is measured gross of capital consumption in the context of GDP, net of capital consumption in the context of NDP.

Inventories are stocks of products held either for use as inputs to production or in readiness to be sold to final users. An increase in inventories over a period represents a positive contribution to investment, a decrease a negative contribution. Changes in inventories are small relative to other components of final demand, and indeed may be negative. Yet the magnitude of such changes tends to be volatile and the effect on the GDP growth rate can thus be quite significant.

Government spending includes both consumption and investment components. The investment component reflects spending on physical assets. Although government spending on education and health care contributes to the formation of human capital, for purposes of the national accounts such spending is treated as the consumption of services rather than as investment.

Exports and imports involve trade in goods and non-factor services to conform with the product measure of GDP. As applied to exports then, that means the scope includes spending by foreigners on goods and services produced by the home economy but does not include spending of foreigners on the services of home-economy labor and capital mobilized overseas.

$S - I = X - M$

Income not spent on consumption is by definition saved. In an accounting sense, this saving must balance with the non-consumption elements of GDP expenditures. In the most primitive scenario, imagine a subsistence agricultural economy where the harvest is either eaten or preserved as seed to be planted the following year. Under such circumstances saving is transformed into investment in a straightforward way. In a modern economy saving on the part of some units is intermediated by the financial system to provide funds for other units to undertake investment. The equilibration between saving and investment thus becomes more complex. Consider first an economy with no foreign trade. Saving in this case must be exactly absorbed in domestic investment. Either it is channeled through the financial system to support fixed capital formation and desired inventory accumulation, or failing that, undesired inventories will accumulate as goods that remain unsold. The *ex ante* intentions of businesses may not be realized in the sense that inventory changes do not necessarily emerge as planned. Yet *ex post*, foregone consumption is fully transformed into investment in some form, whether it be fixed capital formation or the unintended build up of inventories.

In an open economy, exports can provide an outlet when domestic demand (or *domestic absorption*) is insufficient to prevent undesired inventories from accumulating. Let us simplify the analysis of the connection between domestic saving and investment and the foreign trade sector by subsuming government spending into our measures of consumption and investment. We redefine these components of demand to include government such that:

$$GDP = \hat{C} + \hat{I} + X - M,\tag{4.6}$$

where $\hat{C}$ = consumption by households and government;

$\hat{I}$ = investment by households, businesses, and government.

The difference between $\hat{C}$ and $\hat{I}$ (read *C*-hat and *I*-hat) as used here and C and I as used previously is the inclusion of government spending in the hat versions.

Framing the analysis in terms of GDP means the external account is defined by trade in goods and services exclusive of factor services and transfer payments. Alternatively we could specify GNDI as the aggregate and would then need to incorporate foreign factor income and transfers into our measure of the external account. The broader measure of external flows reflected in GNDI comprises the current account of the balance of payments. Balance of payments accounting is the subject of Chapter 5. For present purposes, we keep the focus on trade in goods and services as associated with GDP.

Saving with respect to GDP is defined as the difference between income generated by domestic production and final consumption. Thus:

$$GDP = \hat{C} + S.\tag{4.7}$$

It is worth emphasizing that saving is a flow as opposed to savings (with a final "s") which is a stock. Savings may take the form of deposits in commercial banks or cash stuffed into mattresses. That is not the way to think about national saving though. National saving is a residual in the National Income and Product Accounts, its value being inferred from other magnitudes. Simply put, it is income not spent on consumption.

Setting equal the two foregoing expressions for GDP (Equations 4.6 and 4.7), the consumption terms drop out and with some rearranging we obtain:

$$S - \hat{I} = X - M.\tag{4.8}$$

The left hand side of the expression represents the excess of saving over domestic investment. This excess flows out in acquisition of foreign assets. The right hand side represents an excess of exports over imports. Export revenues not spent on imports – a trade surplus – provide the foreign exchange to support acquisition of foreign assets. A trade surplus is thus matched by a capital outflow.

The reverse set of flows may also materialize. When domestic investment exceeds saving, an inflow of foreign capital is implied. On the trade account this means imports exceed exports. This trade deficit is financed by the capital inflow. That an economy is running a trade deficit therefore tells us it is borrowing from abroad to support domestic investment not covered by saving generated at home.

The expenditures approach to compiling GDP figures importantly in the analysis of business cycles. While supply side forces as embodied in labor, capital, and technology determine an economy's long-run productive potential, demand side forces as reflected in the elements of expenditures are important in driving fluctuations relative to potential from year to year. The export and investment components of expenditures in particular tend to be volatile and vulnerable to shock. The ramifications will be explored in later chapters of this text.

Saving and Investment Rates in Emerging East Asia

Taiwan's saving and investment rates for 1951 to 2020 are presented in Chart 4.4. Taiwan's trade balance can be inferred as the difference between its saving and investment rates. In the early years the saving rate was low, falling well short of the investment rate. This means that Taiwan was importing capital from the rest of the world and concomitantly running trade deficits, using borrowed funds to finance imports in excess of exports. As is common in an economy's development take-off phase, Taiwan's saving rate shot up during the 1960s rising from 11.1 percent in 1959 to 35.0 percent in 1973 for an average annual increase of about 2.0 percentage points of GDP. While the investment rate increased too, the pace was not as rapid so that by the 1970s the saving and investment rates were in rough equivalence. The trade account was consequently more or less in balance. A turning point was reached around 1980. Since then, Taiwan's saving rate has consistently exceeded its investment rate meaning that capital has flowed outward and the trade account has been in surplus with exports exceeding imports. Through the 2010s, the gap rose steadily. By 2020 a saving rate of 37.4 percent exceeded a domestic investment rate of 23.7 percent to yield a net outflow of capital of 13.7 percent of GDP. The trade account was thus in surplus by this same magnitude.

Saving and investment rates for the economies of Emerging East Asia in 2020 are presented in Chart 4.5. Singapore led with a saving rate of 53.2 percent of GDP followed by China at 46.4 percent. To benchmark, the world average is remarkably stable over time at about 25 percent. Also far exceeding this norm are Taiwan and Korea at 37.9 percent and 35.4 percent, respectively. Well below the norm at the bottom of the chart is the Philippines

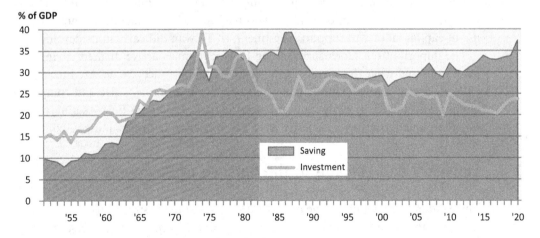

Chart 4.4 Saving and investment rates, Taiwan, 1951–2020

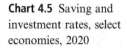

Chart 4.5 Saving and investment rates, select economies, 2020

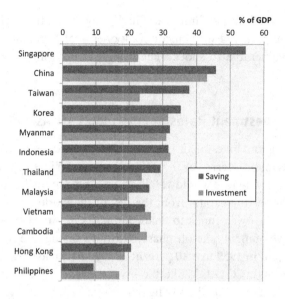

with a saving rate of 9.6 percent. The Philippines suffered a particularly sharp drop in income in 2020 with the pandemic which hit its saving rate hard. The 2019 figure of 14.3 percent is more characteristic. But even this is low, and the numbers merit further interpretation. The picture for the Philippines is distorted by the omission from GDP of income from foreign factors which is especially high in its case and supports domestic consumption through remittances. The saving residual calculated with respect to a fuller measure of income that includes foreign earnings is significantly higher.

The economies with the higher saving rates saw saving outstrip domestic investment, with the flip side of that being trade surpluses. Singapore's imbalance was the most extreme at 32.0 percent of GDP meaning the country was offering nearly a third of its income as investment to the rest of the world. At the lower income end of the scale, saving fell short of domestic investment for Vietnam, Cambodia, and the Philippines with these countries running corresponding trade deficits. This means the lowest income economies are making use of capital inflows to support investment, as Taiwan did early in its development.

The important questions surrounding how economies arrive at their saving and investment rates and what this means for macroeconomic balance are deferred to later chapters. Here we are concerned with defining measures of an economy's size and composition. Our glimpse into the range of circumstances manifest in Emerging East Asia may serve at this stage to pique the reader's curiosity as to macroeconomic causes and consequences.

D   Summary and Linkage to the Balance of Payments

Three different approaches have been devised to measure the size of an economy, all in theory capturing the same volume of activity but from different perspectives. First and most fundamental is the measuring of value added in production. Second is the summing up of factor incomes derived from the production process. And third is the tabulating of expenditures on final goods and services. Under the product approach the aggregate may be decomposed by industrial sector (agriculture, industry, and services). Under the income approach the decomposition is by institutional recipient (households, corporations, and government) and by factor of production (labor and property). And under the expenditures approach the breakdown is by uses of income (consumption, investment, government, and net exports).

Examination of national accounts data for Taiwan historically and for the economies of Emerging East Asia in contemporary cross section reveal systematic patterns of development along some lines but more idiosyncratic diversity along others. The pattern synonymous with economic development is a declining share of output from agriculture as per capita income rises, to be supplanted initially by industry and later by services. Concurrent with this structural transformation of the economy, the share of income attributable to employee compensation tends to rise with an expanding industrial sector with gains moderating under the further shift to services. Finally, during sustained periods of exceptionally rapid development, the saving rate tends to rise as in the Taiwan case, and although the investment rate rises as well, its pace does not match that of saving. Taiwan, as a result, went from importing capital and running trade deficits to exporting capital and running trade surpluses. A pattern of the lowest income economies generating relatively little saving domestically and relying instead on capital from abroad carries through in our cross-section sample. But at mid to higher levels of income, saving and investment rates do not show a clear correlation with income level.

In outlining the National Income and Product Accounts, connections between the domestic economy and the outside world have come to light. These involve exports and imports, foreign factor income and transfers, and cross-border capital movements. For a systematic accounting of an economy's external relations we turn attention in Chapter 5 to the international balance of payments. The economies of Emerging East Asia are for the most part highly open. Study of their macroeconomic performance thus requires a firm grasp of balance of payments accounting.

Data Note

Cross-country data for 2020 are from the World Bank's World Development Indicators database.

Data for Taiwan are generally from the Republic of China (Taiwan) Statistical Bureau with pre-1985 data on labor's share in income for Chart 4.3 from the Republic of China Council for Economic Planning and Development.

Bibliographic Note

The definitive reference for national income accounting is the *System of National Accounts,* the 2008 edition being the latest. The volume bears the imprimatur of five multilateral organizations: the United Nations; the European Commission; the Organization for Economic Co-operation and Development; the International Monetary Fund; and the World Bank. The first edition of the SNA was launched in 1953. The immediate motive was to standardize national accounting systems as a basis for apportioning shares in then formative international organizations in the aftermath of World War II. Subsequent editions in 1968 and 1993 sought to better accommodate the circumstances of developing and command economies and to keep up with changes in the nature of economic activity. In view of the rapid pace of economic change, it is perhaps surprising that updates in the SNA have not been more frequent. But the need to meet changing circumstances must be balanced against the merits of preserving continuity in measurement over time.

A post on the Asia Economics Blog of July 15, 2020, makes the case that interludes of rapid growth have been accompanied by sharp increases in saving rates across the East Asia region. The piece focuses on China and the eruption of its macro imbalances in the 2000-aughts, with the point made that China is not unusual.

BIBLIOGRAPHIC CITATIONS

European Community, International Monetary Fund, Organization for Economic Cooperation and Development, United Nations, and World Bank, 2009. System of National Accounts, 2008 (New York: EC, et al.). http://unstats.un.org/unsd/nationalaccount/docs/SNA2008.pdf (accessed November 14, 2018).

Republic of China Council for Economic Planning and Development, 2002. Taiwan Statistical Data Book 2002, p51. https://ws.ndc.gov.tw/Download.ashx?u=LzAwMS9hZG1pbmlzdHJhdG9 yLzEwL3JlbGGZpbGUvNTYwNi83MTgvMDAwMTMxOS5wZGY%3D&n= MjAwMkRhdGFCb29rQDk5MzUwNy44NDI5MjMxNDkyQC5wZGY%3D&icon=..pdf (accessed November 7, 2021).

Republic of China (Taiwan), Statistical Bureau, 2021. National Statistics. https://statdb.dgbas.gov.tw/pxweb/dialog/statfile1L.asp (accessed November 7, 2021).

Wiemer, Calla, 2020. "The Real Reason for China's Unbalanced Growth (Orlik Review Addendum)," Asia Economics Blog, July 15. http://acaes.us/blog/reason-for-china-s-unbalanced-growth (accessed December 28, 2021).

World Bank, World Development Indicators database. http://databank.worldbank.org/data/source/world-development-indicators# (accessed November 13, 2021).

5 Balance of Payments Accounts

Transactions between residents of one economy and residents of the rest of the world are captured in the economy's balance of payments accounts. The balance of payments must balance. If an economy buys more than it sells in one category, it must sell more than it buys by the same amount elsewhere.

Exports, imports, interest on foreign reserves, wages of expatriate workers, foreign investment, borrowing from abroad – all are transactions that enter an economy's balance of payments. The main division in the balance of payments is between the current account and the capital and financial account. The current account encompasses transactions involving the sale of goods and services, payments to labor and capital, and unilateral transfers. The capital and financial account pertains to the acquisition and disposal of assets and liabilities.

An economy's balance of payments can reveal strengths and vulnerabilities in its external position, and hint at potential macroeconomic risks. Foreign trade can be a boon to growth for many reasons: It allows an economy to specialize in production, following its comparative advantage in the use of resources; it permits the exploitation of scale economies through access to a broader market; it intensifies competition and promotes adoption of best practices; and it facilitates technology transfer and learning from the rest of the world. At the same time, however, reliance on trade exposes an economy to global market fluctuations and creates vulnerability to external shocks. Similarly, participation in international financial markets yields benefits but also carries risks. Foreign capital can facilitate business expansion and the transmission of new technologies and ideas. But it also creates obligations set in foreign currencies that may become difficult to meet.

We begin this chapter by laying foundations in basic accounting principles. We characterize credits and debits within the balance of payments context and explain how the practice of double-entry bookkeeping ensures that the balance of payments will balance. We then outline the structure of the accounts, first in broad overview, then filling in the details. China serves as the case study for this chapter. China is of interest because the large imbalances in its payments over recent decades have redounded throughout the global economy. We follow the China case study with an overview of balances in the main accounts for the economies of Emerging East Asia. Finally, we relate the balance of payments to the macroeconomic aggregates introduced in Chapter 4 and briefly preview the connection to domestic money creation, the subject taken up in Chapter 6.

A   Accounting Principles

The balance of payments records international flows over a period of time, typically a year or a quarter. In contrast, stocks of foreign assets and liabilities are measured at an instant in time and are recorded under a separate framework – the international investment position. Balance of payments transactions for assets and liabilities register as changes in an economy's international investment position.

Transactions recorded under the balance of payments take place between residents of an economy and non-residents. Residents include persons and institutional units such as corporations or government agencies whose predominant economic interests lie within the economy's territory. For persons, residency is usually established on the basis of the principal dwelling place, although other criteria may also figure in. Students, for example, are usually treated as residents of their home countries. It is possible for individuals to claim residence in the territory of one economy while being employed in the territory of another. Corporations are regarded as resident in the jurisdiction where they are registered. For other types of enterprises, residency is generally determined by the principal locus of activity.

Every transaction enters the balance of payments twice, once as a credit and once as a debit such that the two entries cancel out. The sum of all credits and debits should therefore equal zero, at least in principle. Statistical procedures being incomplete and imperfect, however, a non-zero residual tends to emerge. This residual is assigned to the balancing item "net errors and omissions."

Credits and Debits

Credits are associated with payment inflows, debits with payment outflows. Thus a credit generally involves the sale of something, a debit the purchase of something. The sale or purchase may pertain to goods and services or to assets and liabilities.

For goods and services, exports result in a credit, imports a debit.

Asset transactions are more complicated because an asset can be bought and later resold. When a foreign entity makes an investment in an economy, it acquires an asset from a domestic entity, thus yielding a credit for the domestic economy. If the foreign entity later disposes of the asset by transfering it back to a domestic entity, that registers as a debit. Conversely, if a domestic entity makes an investment abroad, that results in a debit, and when the asset is liquidated and the funds repatriated, that is a credit.

Income payments may be made across borders to pay for the services of capital and labor. Payments for capital services take the form of interest and dividends, payments for labor services the form of wages and salaries. Such factor payments are credits when received by residents of the domestic economy and debits when made to non-residents.

Sometimes payments are made unilaterally with no quid pro quo. Such payments are often made in the form of remittances from family members resident abroad.

To sum up, credits (+) are associated with payment inflows pertaining to:

- exports of goods and produced services;
- interest and dividend receipts from abroad;
- compensation of domestic residents from foreign sources;
- inbound unilateral transfers;
- inbound investment;
- sale of foreign assets held by domestic residents, including . . .
- decumulation of official reserve assets by the monetary authority.

Debits (–) are associated with payment outflows pertaining to:

- imports of goods and produced services;
- interest and dividend payments made to foreign residents;
- compensation paid to foreign residents from domestic sources;
- outbound unilateral transfers;
- sale of domestic assets held by foreigners;
- outbound investment, including . . .
- accumulation of official reserve assets by the monetary authority.

Double-Entry Bookkeeping

Every transaction involves both credit and debit sides. To illustrate, we work through three examples, proposing an initiating credit or debit flow, then considering alternative possibilities for the offsetting flow. We use T-accounts to delineate credits and debits (following the balance of payments convention of placing credits on the left and debits on the right in reverse of the standard business accounting format).

Case 1: An agribusiness firm in the home economy exports a shipment of tangerines. The export of goods generates a payment receipt that appears as a credit on the balance of payments. The debit that results will depend on how the foreign exchange earnings are utilized. Perhaps the exporting firm acquires a deposit in a foreign bank. Perhaps it pays off a foreign loan. We could even allow for the exporter to take payment in cash, and this too would be treated as the acquisition of a foreign asset. (While cash payment may seem unlikely for tangerines, there are certainly instances of transactions for which cash is used.) In some guise then, the foreign exchange earnings from exports are directed toward the acquisition of an asset or the liquidation of a liability, and this constitutes the debit side of the transaction.

CASE 1

Credits (payment inflow)		Debits (payment outflow)
export of tangerines	⇒	deposit acquired in foreign bank (OR foreign currency loan repaid) (OR cash hauled off in a briefcase)

Case 2: A bank from the home economy extends a loan to a foreign firm. The loan itself is a payment outflow that registers as a debit on the balance of payments of the home economy. The form of the associated credit depends on how the foreign firm uses the loan proceeds. Perhaps it buys goods from the home economy which then appears as an export credit. Or perhaps it acquires deposits in the lending bank. Either way, the result manifests as a credit on the balance of payments.

CASE 2

Credits (payment inflow)	Debits (payment outflow)
export sales financed (OR deposits acquired in lending bank)	⇐ loan to foreign firm

Case 3: A remittance is made by a family member working overseas to her relatives back home. The remittance itself is a credit on the home economy's balance of payments. The matching debit may take the form of foreign currency assets acquired by the receiving household. Or the remittance may be structured such that the household receives local currency and a financial intermediary acquires the foreign currency asset. Either way, a debit is registered on the balance of payments. That the remittance is a one-way transfer rather than a two-way transaction does not matter for purposes of double-entry accounting on the balance of payments. It is not the real movement of goods and services that enters the balance of payments in any case, but rather the associated payment flows.

CASE 3

Credits (payment inflow)		Debits (payment outflow)
remittance	⇒	foreign assets acquired by recipient (OR assets acquired by intermediary)

B   Structure of the Accounts

The accounts within the balance of payments are differentiated by the type of item for which payment is being made. We outline the main accounts first, then explore the elements of the main accounts in more detail.

Main Accounts

The main division in the balance of payments is between the current account and the capital and financial account. The current account covers payments for goods and services, including the services of labor and capital, and also absorbs unilateral transfers. The capital and financial account captures payments for assets, ownership of which can potentially revert back across the border at a later date. The capital and financial account is often loosely referred to as simply the capital account. Technically, this designation pre-dates the 1993 revision to the accounting system. Under this revision what had previously been referred to as the capital account was renamed the financial account with the newly named capital account absorbing certain transactions previously subsumed under the current account. The capital account as now formally defined is very small in size. We adhere to official terminology in this text, referring to the capital and financial account by its full name or shortening to just "financial account." Note, however, that common parlance generally goes with "capital account." Further muddying the waters, we typically refer to flows on the financial account as "capital flows." The terminology, then, is somewhat loose.

For analytical purposes, the activity of the central bank is separated by a line from the remainder of the capital and financial account, as represented in Table 5.1. The combined balance on items "above the line" is known as the *overall balance*. Central bank transactions appear "below the line." Table 5.1 identifies transactions of the central bank as the *official settlement balance*. This item may also be referred to as *reserve assets*. The final element in Table 5.1 picks up net errors and omissions. In principle, if all transactions between domestic residents and the rest of the world were fully and properly measured, this item would be zero. Because accounting systems are imperfect, however, this entry deviates from zero in practice, sometimes substantially so.

The official settlement balance is positive when the central bank is a net seller of foreign assets since this involves a payment inflow. Conversely, the official settlement balance is negative when the central bank is a net buyer of foreign assets since this involves a payment

Table 5.1 Balance of payments main accounts

	Credits	Debits	Balance
Current Account	..	..	..
Capital & Financial Account	..	..	..
Official Settlement Balance	..	..	..
Net Errors & Omissions	..	..	..

outflow. Within our sample of Emerging East Asian economies, the market interventions of central banks can be large and consequential for macroeconomic outcomes.

Items above the line involve autonomous transactions of economic agents undertaken for their own sake. By contrast, central bank activity below the line is generally motivated by the desire to accommodate above-the-line transactions. For example, central banks often buy up foreign exchange earnings in support of a trade surplus to keep export industries going strong. They also respond to buy or sell when large capital flows in or out threaten to be disruptive.

Under the terms of a dual-entry bookkeeping regimen, the elements of Table 5.1 must sum to zero. Abstracting from net errors and omissions, we have:

$$CA + CFA + OSB = 0, \tag{5.1}$$

where: CA = current account balance;

CFA = capital and financial account balance excluding central bank activity;

OSB = official settlement balance.

The balance on any of these three items taken on its own can be positive, negative, or zero. If the combined balance on items above the line is positive, the official settlement balance must be negative. That is, if the current account and the capital and financial account together are in surplus, the central bank must be a net buyer of foreign assets. Conversely, if the current account and the capital and financial account together are in deficit, the central bank must be a net seller of foreign assets. In short, the central bank finances a deficit or surplus position in the overall balance.

Account Details

The current account contains three principle elements: trade in products, further divided between goods and services; income payments for trade in factor services (primary income); and current transfers (secondary income). Goods are distinguished from services by their physical presence. They exist separately from the act of production whereas services generally exist only in the act of production. Included in services trade are transport, communication, construction, insurance, finance, and information services.

Under the trade account, both goods and services are the output of a production process. In contrast, the services of primary factors are utilized directly and generate income payments for their contributions. The income item of the current account contains sub-components for labor and capital identified respectively as compensation of employees and investment income. Investment income includes interest, dividends, rent, and reinvested earnings. Reinvested earnings are in principle counted in the host country as both a debit in the current account and a credit in the capital and financial account.

Finally, current transfers are unilateral payments in exchange for which nothing is received in return. Counted within this item are both personal transfers, often in the form of remittances from family members working abroad, and public transfers, mainly income taxes and social welfare contributions and benefits.

The capital and financial account is divided in the first instance according to the elements in its name. The capital account itself amounts to so little quantitatively that for practical purposes the financial account is virtually synonymous with the capital and financial account. Transactions covered in the capital account involve "non-produced non-financial assets." Put in positive terms, this embodies claims on natural resources, such as land and mineral rights; marketable rights and entitlements, such as the right to operate a port or the entitlement to purchase a product on an exclusive basis; and marketing assets such as brand names, trademarks, and logos.

The financial account contains four functional asset classes: direct investment; portfolio investment; financial derivatives; and other investment. Separately identified are the official reserve assets of the monetary authority which span various functional asset classes. For each asset class both inbound and outbound flows are registered. An inbound investment counts as a credit when a domestic asset is acquired by a foreign resident and a debit when the asset is disposed of. Conversely, an outbound investment counts as a debit when an overseas asset is acquired by a domestic resident and a credit when the asset is disposed of.

Direct investment involves a significant ownership stake in a firm and connotes a high degree of control over its operations. Portfolio investment in stocks and bonds is conducted through an economy's financial markets and allows quicker liquidation of positions than direct investment but affords little or no influence over business operations. Derivatives are instruments that derive their value from underlying assets with the aim of transferring risk. "Other investment" captures primarily loans, deposits, trade credits and advances, and accounts receivable and payable. (Chapter 7 on finance goes into depth on these asset classes.) The functional classification of assets differentiates along lines pertinent to macro-economic and financial stability concerns. Sudden movement of funds in and out of an economy can be highly disruptive. Direct investment usually entails a long-term commitment whereas portfolio investment and short-term lending can be highly volatile. Emerging economies typically adopt regulations to try to contain the potential for volatility.

If the overall balance on the capital and financial account plus official reserves is positive, the economy is a net borrower from the rest of the world. If it is negative, the economy is a net creditor to the rest of the world. An economy's net international creditor or debtor position is integrally related to domestic saving and investment behavior, as will be elaborated in Section E.

C   The China Case

China ran sizable payments imbalances during its period of rapid growth in the 2000-aughts, to be followed by jarring volatility in the 2010s. Given its size, the rest of the world – and most pointedly the USA – struggled to contend with China's economic emergence, as China itself learned to contend with the destabilizing forces of greater openness. China's experience offers a case study of what the balance of payments accounts can tell us, not only about a particular economy but about the world it interfaces with. We examine China's balance of payments for 2014 in some detail, going back in time because in more recent years less detail has been publicly reported. We then consider movement in the country's net positions on the broad accounts over the period 2002–2020.

A Close Look at 2014

China's balance of payments accounts for 2014 are presented in Table 5.2. Both the current account and the capital and financial account were in surplus, the former by $220 billion, the latter by a much smaller $38 billion. The net payments inflows on these accounts were partially offset by a payments outflow in the reserve assets account meaning the central bank was acquiring foreign reserves. The net debit in reserve assets was $118 billion. The difference between this and the overall balance above the line of $258 billion falls to net errors and omissions.

Within the current account, the bulk of activity emanated from goods trade. This item exhibited a much larger surplus than the current account overall, with China's services trade generating the major countervailing deficit. Income payments, too, showed a small deficit. Most of the activity underlying the incomes item traced to investment income whereas

Table 5.2 Balance of payments, China, 2014

in US$ billion

	Credit	Debit	Balance
Current Account	**2,799**	**2,579**	**220**
Goods Trade	2,354	1,878	476
Services Trade	191	383	−192
Incomes	213	247	−34
Current Transfers	41	71	−30
Capital & Financial Account	**2,573**	**2,535**	**38**
Capital Account	2	2	0
Financial Account	2,571	2,533	38
Direct Investment	*435*	*227*	*209*
Outbound	56	136	−80
Inbound	380	91	289
Portfolio Investment	*166*	*84*	*82*
Assets	29	40	−11
Liabilities	137	44	93
Other Investment	*1,969*	*2,222*	*−253*
Assets	99	402	−303
Liabilities	1,870	1,820	50
Reserve Assets	**31**	**149**	**−118**
Net Errors & Omissions	**0**	**140**	**−140**

employee compensation played a much smaller role. Although China received substantial interest income on the reserve assets held by its central bank, the amount fell short of outgoing returns paid on foreign investments hosted by China. Finally, a small deficit on current transfers also contributed to offsetting the surplus on goods trade.

Within the capital and financial account, capital account flows are minuscule such that the financial account amounts to virtually the whole. Within the financial account in turn, the "other investment" category exhibits the largest volume of flows, and within this most of the activity is on the liabilities side. These liabilities mainly constitute Chinese borrowing from foreign sources, with credits representing the initial receipt of funds and debits the repayment. This borrowing is largely short-term, aimed at supporting trade transactions and other working capital needs rather than financing long-term investment. Because of this, credits and debits tend to cancel out within a year's time leaving only a small balance. The balance of US$50 billion against credits of US$1,870 billion is consistent with this pattern. Against this, however, on the assets side of "other investment" a deficit erupted in 2014 of exceptionally large proportions by historical standards. A deeper delve into the balance of payments accounts shows this to have been largely associated with Chinese residents acquiring deposits abroad. This activity will be placed in context in the next sub-section which traces China's balance of payments over time.

The deficit in "other investment" was more than offset by surpluses for direct investment and portfolio investment to result in a modest overall surplus on the financial account. Within both these categories, large inflows of foreign funds predominate as seen by credits on inbound direct investment and on liabilities in portfolio investment. The inflows on direct investment represent long-term commitments that do not pivot quickly toward an exit. Nor under China's capital controls do portfolio flows respond readily to changing sentiments about the investment environment. We will see in the next sub-section, however, how the forces of market perception can play out with more time.

Above the line in the combined current and capital and financial accounts, a surplus of US$258 billion materialized. This was balanced below the line in part by central bank acquisition of reserves at US$118 billion. When the central bank acquires reserves it must buy foreign currency by selling renminbi in the foreign exchange market which puts downward pressure on the value of the renminbi. The lower value of the renminbi makes China's exports cheaper and its imports more expensive. Reserve accumulation and the trade surplus thus represent two sides of the same coin, so to speak.

Finally, the US$140 billion outflow under errors and omissions is the measure of our ignorance. On balance, much money moved out without leaving a trace.

Main Accounts over Time

Net magnitudes over time on China's main accounts are captured in Chart 5.1. The story is one of surging imbalances in one direction during the 2000-aughts followed by a great deal of volatility thereafter.

China joined the World Trade Organization in 2001 after a 15-year stretch of negotiations. With that, its exports soared and its economic growth accelerated well into double

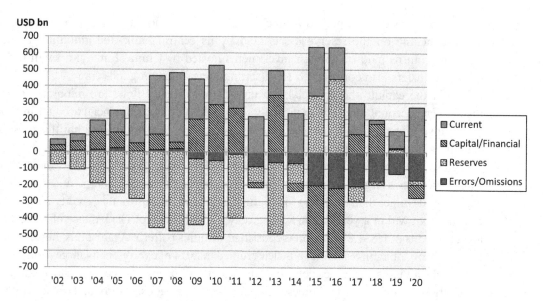

Chart 5.1 Balance of payments, China, 2002–2020

digit rates. As is common for developing countries during a period of sustained take-off (illustrated by Taiwan in Chart 4.4), China's saving rate rose sharply against an investment rate that, already exceptionally high by world standards, did not keep pace. Per the relationship developed in Equation (4.7), $S - \hat{I} = X - M$, slower growth in investment than in saving meant that imports did not keep pace with exports either. The central bank did its part to keep the growth engine running in the face of lagging domestic consumption by purchasing the export earnings not going toward import purchases. In effect, China was lending to the USA to support American consumption of Chinese goods. Chart 5.1 reflects these dynamics in a ballooning current account surplus, up from US$35 billion in 2002 to US$421 billion in 2008, accompanied by rising reserve accumulation. Year by year central bank buildup of foreign reserves mounted to reach nearly US$2 trillion in 2008, which at the time seemed quite stunning (although it was not over yet).

Relative to GDP, China's current account surplus peaked in 2008 at a ratio that exceeded 10 percent, much to the ire of trade partners who took this as a sign of unfair practices. In the following few years, however, not only was the surplus to fall in absolute terms but given China's rapid GDP growth, the ratio to GDP shrank to just 2.8 percent by 2011. This is not an outsized figure by world standards.

The contraction in China's current account surplus in 2009 was brought on by the collapse in world trade that followed the Great Financial Crisis. The investment climate in China nevertheless remained vibrant, aided by a government stimulus program that fed credit into infrastructure development. At the same time, relaxation of capital controls opened the floodgates to foreign funds pouring in. What was lost in the way of a current account surplus was thus made up by burgeoning surpluses on the financial account. Reserve accumulation continued apace, and the US$3 trillion threshold was surpassed in 2011.

In a foretaste of what was to come, the financial account balance reversed in 2012 when investors grew worried about a slowdown in China's economic growth and the potential for renminbi depreciation. But sentiment soon rebounded, and strong capital inflows resumed in 2013. The next bout of investor skittishness was not so easily overcome, however. By 2014,[1] maintenance of a renminbi tie to the US dollar as the dollar was appreciating relative to other currencies conveyed a sense of increasing overvaluation of the renminbi. Once the central bank finally succumbed to pressure to engineer a tentative devaluation, panic set in. Investors unloaded renminbi assets and moved their money to other shores while borrowers hastened to repay foreign currency loans and shift new borrowing into domestic currency. In each of 2015 and 2016, net outflows on the financial account exceeded US$400 billion in additon to which outflows of more than US$200 billion a year appeared as errors and omissions. In the face of this capital flight, the central bank sought to allay fears by liquidating reserve assets and selling foreign currency to meet the demand in the foreign exchange market. Between mid 2014 and late 2016, central bank reserves plummeted from US$4 trillion to US$3 trillion. To observers who had judged China's reserves to be excessive, the speed at which they could slip away was eye popping.

Eventually, the market stabilized. By 2017, the balance showing on the capital and financial account had returned to positive territory. However, errors and omissions continued to register net outflows that more than offset the net inflows on the capital and financial account. As part of the government's strategy to stabilize the market, it tightened controls on the cross-border movement of funds. The continued large volume of uncategorized outflows suggests ingenuity on the part of economic agents in circumventing these controls.

D   Emerging East Asian Economies, 2020

China is far from alone in the region in running current account surpluses, as Chart 5.2 bears out for 2020. The surplus for the region stood at US$307 billion in addition to China's US$274 billion. These figures were higher with the pandemic relative to 2019 values of US$225 for the region plus US$103 billion for China. Korea, Singapore, and Taiwan all ran surpluses in the US$60–100 billion range. Relative to GDP, these magnitudes outstripped China's 2008 peak for Singapore at 17.6 percent and Taiwan at 14.2 percent. While Korea's surplus was comparable in absolute terms, relative to its GDP the figure was not a standout at 4.6 percent.

The economies running current account surpluses balanced the inflows with differing mixes of central bank and non-central bank capital outflows. For Singapore, net inflows on the financial account were positive which added to the overall surplus the monetary

---

[1] Magnitudes for 2014 in Chart 5.1 do not conform with those in Table 5.2. The data for the chart are from a 2020 database whereas those for the table are from a 2015 release that was later subject to updating. Detail at the level of the 2015 release is no longer publicly reported.

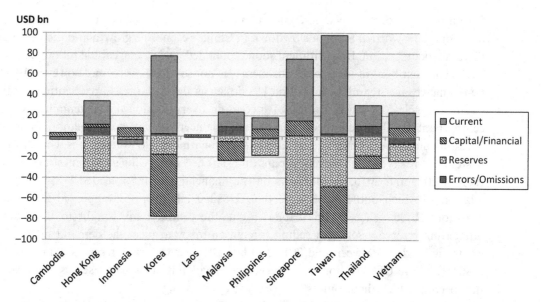

Chart 5.2 Balance of payments, select economies, 2020

authority absorbed. For Korea and Malaysia the central bank played a relatively minor role in balancing current account surpluses whereas for Hong Kong, the Philippines, Thailand, and Vietnam the central bank's role was dominant. Cambodia, Indonesia, and Laos ran current account deficits that were small in all cases relative to surpluses elsewhere in the region but in Cambodia's case large relative to its GDP at 8.7 percent. This pattern continues a history of large capital inflows to Cambodia as reflected in the stock measure of its foreign direct investment shown in Chart 2.4. Balancing this capital inflow, Cambodia not only ran a current account deficit but was also able to increase its official reserves.

The Hong Kong case is distinctive in that the monetary authority is obliged to maintain a fixed exchange rate relative to the US dollar, buying dollars to absorb a surplus on the overall balance of payments and selling to fill a deficit. In 2020, all major elements of Hong Kong's balance of payments were in surplus with the inflows duly purchased by the monetary authority in exchange for equivalent issue of Hong Kong dollars.

Large current account surpluses for Emerging East Asia have been the norm ever since the Asian Financial Crisis. Of course, for one part of the world to run a current account surplus, another part must run a deficit. That role has fallen largely to the US, as Box 5.1 recounts.

Box 5.1 Global current account imbalances

Globally, economies that sell more products than they buy must square off against counterparts that buy more than they sell. The USA has assumed the net buyer position in a major way through recent decades as the figure below shows. At its peak

Box 5.1 (cont.)

in 2006, the US current account deficit reached nearly 6 percent of its GDP. This gap was so enormous that the surplus of all of East Asia, inclusive of Japan, filled only 2/3 of it.

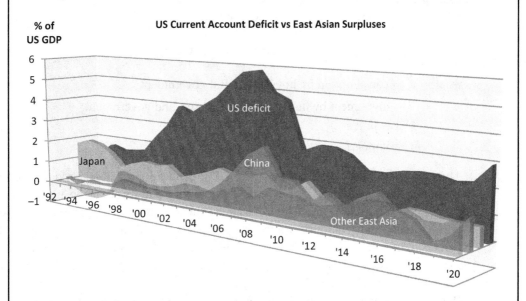

The year 1998 was pivotal for global current account imbalances. The Asian Financial Crisis precipitated capital flight not only from much of Emerging East Asia, but from the broader developing world as well. The resulting deficits in emerging market financial accounts had to be met with surpluses in their current accounts. Meanwhile, investors seeking safe haven were drawn to US dollar assets, and capital movements into the USA were of necessity balanced by current account deficits there.

The shift in China's current account balance came later with gradual upward creep in the early 2000s followed by sharp ascendance later in the decade even as the US deficit started to narrow. The Great Financial Crisis brought a retrenchment in US trade, and with it a sharp contraction in the country's role in absorbing Asian surpluses. Indeed, from 2009 onward, the collective surpluses of East Asia, including Japan and China, exceeded the US deficit, meaning that other countries became more of an outlet for Asia's net exports.

With the pandemic in 2020, China's surplus rose sharply in tandem with the US deficit. Both countries responded to the crisis with government stimulus programs, the difference being that support in China went mainly to businesses to sustain production whereas support in the US went mainly to households to sustain consumption. Resulting changes in trade balances were predictably complementary.

E   Linkage to the National Income and Product Accounts

The main elements of the current account of the balance of payments enter directly into national income and product aggregates. Recall that GDP as defined under the expenditures approach incorporates exports minus imports along with consumption and investment (both consumption and investment being specified here to include government spending as signified by the hat, following the notation of Chapter 4):

$$GDP = \hat{C} + \hat{I} + X - M, \tag{4.5}$$

where: $\hat{C}$ = consumption by households and government;

$\hat{I}$ = investment by households, businesses, and government;

X = exports;

M = imports.

Through inclusion of the trade balance, GDP captures goods and services produced in the home economy and sold for export while netting out spending on imports of goods and services which are implicitly subsumed in the other components of spending. Mathematically, the relationship appears to suggest that if an economy can increase its exports and/or reduce its imports, it will increase its domestic output. With respect to reducing imports, this is strictly an illusion since lower imports necessarily correspond to lower expenditures elsewhere for no net gain.

With respect more generally to exports net of imports there is a more indirect catch. Balance of payments accounting requires that a surplus on the trade account be met with a countervailing deficit elsewhere. Non-trade items in the current account typically being small, as a practical matter this implies net capital outflows, either through the official settlement balance or through other channels. In other words, an economy must serve as a net lender to the rest of the world to sustain a trade surplus. This comes at a cost in that domestic saving is being channeled abroad rather than invested at home where it might find application in projects that would contribute to higher output in the future. In particular, rather than accumulating assets abroad, an economy might instead use its export revenues to purchase capital equipment that would boost its future productive capacity. Much of the capital outflow from Emerging East Asia has resulted from a deliberate policy choice to accumulate official reserve assets, the merits of which choice can be debated. Does the stimulus to growth from policies that expand exports in conjunction with reserve accumulation outweigh the mitigation to growth from channeling saving abroad? An understanding of the balance of payments accounts does not answer this question, but it does help frame the analysis.

Let us elaborate on the connection between the domestic saving-investment balance and the external balance. Besides the trade balance, the current account balance also captures net foreign factor income and net foreign transfer income:

$$CA = X - M + Y_f \qquad (5.2)$$

where: CA = current account balance;

Y_f = net foreign factor and transfer income.

Recall from Equations (4.1) and (4.2) that adding net foreign factor and transfer income to GDP yields gross national disposable income, GNDI, which we can now express incorporating the current account balance:

$$GNDI = \hat{C} + \hat{I} + CA. \qquad (5.3)$$

In Chapter 4 we defined a notion of saving, S, as that part of GDP which was not consumed. Setting $\hat{C} + S$ equal to the expression for expenditures GDP, we derived a relationship between saving net of domestic investment and the trade balance:

$$S - \hat{I} = X - M. \qquad (4.7)$$

This notion of saving rests on output produced in an economy rather than income earned by an economy's residents. The income basis is more useful for reckoning saving if we wish to decompose saving behavior along institutional lines (households, enterprises, and government) or factor lines (labor and capital) regardless of country of residence. Let us define an income-based notion of saving as the difference between GNDI and consumption so that:

$$GNDI = \hat{C} + S' \qquad (5.4)$$

where: S' = saving out of GNDI.

Note that the value of consumption is treated as the same regardless of which income measure we use. It is the saving residual that absorbs the difference between GDP and GNDI.

With GNDI as our notion of income and S' our notion of saving, the current account balance now reflects the difference between saving and investment:

$$S' - \hat{I} = CA. \qquad (5.5)$$

The saving-investment gap defined in this way is in turn equal to the negative of the balance on the combined capital and financial account and official settlement balance. That is to say, saving taken as S' net of domestic investment captures the full net outflow of capital to the rest of the world.

In practice, the difference between the two notions of saving is usually small relative to the size of an economy because net foreign factor and transfer income is usually small relative to the size of an economy. For some economies, however, the difference is material. The Philippines with its large contingent of overseas workers is a case in point. Net foreign factor and transfer income raised Philippine GNDI by nearly 9 percent over GDP in 2019. This has critical implications for how we interpret the country's saving behavior. Subtracting consumption from GDP yields a saving rate of just 14.3 percent whereas subtracting the same consumption figure from GNDI brings the rate up to a more normal 22.1 percent (versus a global average of 25 percent). The saving shortfall relative to investment as implied by the trade balance was 9.6 percent of GDP but as implied by the current account balance was just 0.8 percent GNDI.

To conclude, drawing from the expenditures approach to GDP measurement, the trade balance is often taken as the measure of an economy's saving-investment gap. This measure is misleading for economies that have large net foreign factor incomes, however. For such economies, the current account balance better captures saving with respect to the full measure of income and more accurately reflects net international capital flows.[2]

F   Summary and Linkage to the Money Supply

Transactions between residents of one economy and the rest of the world are recorded in the economy's balance of payments. By virtue of double-entry bookkeeping, the balance of payments must balance. If an economy shows a surplus in one segment of the accounts, it must show a matching deficit elsewhere. For the major economies of Emerging East Asia in recent decades, this has meant trade surpluses (net credits) largely being met through foreign reserve acquisition by monetary authorities (net debits). Many economies in the region have accumulated enormous foreign reserve caches by following this routine through sustained periods of years.

The acquisition of reserves by a monetary authority has important ramifications for the domestic money supply and hence for economic activity. Money is the subject of Chapter 6. We outline the connection briefly here. If a monetary authority buys foreign exchange, it issues domestic currency to support the purchase. Conversely, if the authority sells foreign exchange, it withdraws domestic currency from circulation. Changes in the money supply in turn affect credit availability and the level of economic activity. An economy's balance of payments position is therefore integrally related to its macroeconomic performance.

Data Note

China's balance of payments data for Table 5.2 are from the State Administration of Foreign Exchange of the People's Bank of China.

---

[2] As a matter of accounting precision, when the current account balance is the measure of the saving-investment gap, the appropriate income basis is GNDI. Alternatively, when the trade account balance is the measure of the gap, the appropriate income basis is GDP. In fact, it is common practice to compare current account balances with GDP – and we did so in discussing Chart 5.2 – but technically, doing so mismatches notions of income between numerator and denominator. Even in the Philippine case though, the quantitative difference does not amount to much. The country's current account balance relative to GDP was 0.8 percent in 2019 versus a current account balance relative to GNDI of 0.7 percent.

Balance of payments data for 2020 for the broad sample of Emerging East Asian economies and the USA and for the China time series of Chart 5.1 are from the IMF International Financial Statistics database.

Taiwan's balance of payments data are from the Central Bank of the Republic of China (Taiwan).

Bibliographic Note

The standard reference on balance of payments accounting is the IMF's *Balance of Payments and International Investment Position Manual, Sixth Edition*, published in 2009. The first edition of this manual dates back to 1948. The current edition embodies major revisions to its predecessor which had served since 1993. Significant advances include: extending coverage to encompass the international investment position in view of the importance of understanding an economy's balance sheet in assessing macroeconomic vulnerabilities; addressing the demands of globalization through more elaborate treatment of multinational corporations, labor migration, and cross-border production processes; and dealing with developments in finance such as derivatives and securitization. Nevertheless, the overall structure of the accounts remained the same.

A separate manual – *The Balance of Payments Compilation Guide* – provides advice on the practical aspects of compiling balance of payments statistics. Other guides exist to cover balance of payments compilation in such specific areas as direct investment, portfolio investment, international reserves, trade in services, external debt, international banking, and remittances.

BIBLIOGRAPHIC CITATIONS

Central Bank of the Republic of China (Taiwan), 2018. Balance of Payments & International Investmet Position databae. https://cpx.cbc.gov.tw/Tree/TreeSelect?mp=2 (accessed November 12, 2021).

International Monetary Fund, 2012. *Balance of Payments and International Investment Position Manual*, 6th edition (Washington, DC: IMF, 2009). www.imf.org/external/pubs/ft/bop/2007/pdf/bpm6.pdf (accessed November 15, 2018).

International Monetary Fund, 2021. International Financial Statistics database. http://data.imf.org/?sk=4C514D48-B6BA-49ED-8AB9-52B0C1A0179B&sId=1390030341854 (accessed November 12, 2021).

State Administration of Foreign Exchange, People's Bank of China, 2015. "中国国际收支平衡表时间序列数据1982–2014 (BPM5)" [In Chinese.] www.safe.gov.cn/safe/2015/0630/3269.html (accessed November 15, 2018).

6   Money

The spending of money acts as fuel to an economy: not enough, and the economy will stall; too much, and it will overheat. Money is supplied to prospective spenders through a process that begins with the central bank and is amplified by the commercial banking system. Central banks have a delicate balancing act to manage in getting this supply right.

Money represents claims on an economy. Bearers may obtain these claims by contributing to economic production, by selling assets, by borrowing, or by receiving transfers from others. They exercise the claims by making purchases.

The quantity of money in circulation and the velocity with which it moves from bearer to bearer in support of transactions jointly determine the total value of transactions over an interval of time. To narrow the focus from total transactions to GDP, it is useful to define velocity as the rate at which a unit of money is spent on final goods and services. Velocity so defined multiplied by the money supply yields nominal GDP. For given velocity, an increase in the money supply must be absorbed in nominal GDP either as an increase in real output or as higher prices, or as some combination of the two.

In this chapter we explore the relationship between money and the economy, theoretically and empirically for Emerging East Asia. The case of Myanmar provides a particularly vivid illustration of the connection between money and inflation due to the pronounced fluctuations in money supply growth that have occurred there.

First, though, we examine what money is and where it comes from. Money creation is integrally related to the expansion of credit. Commercial banks play a vital role in the process by making loans through the creation of deposits which are themselves a form of money. Monetary policy aims to guide the creation of deposit money through levers that work indirectly and with time lags. This makes for a challenge in keeping an economy on course, operating at its full potential but not straining beyond potential to rev up inflation.

A   What Money Is

We consider the nature of money as to form and function first. We then abstract to treat money as a concept.

Form

Historically, money took the form of commodities of intrinsic value, most recognizably precious metals although a wide variety of other materials has also been used. Bolts of silk cloth, for example, served as money along the ancient Silk Road. A major drawback to metal coins in support of more than minor purchases is the inconvenience of lugging their weight around. A further problem is that coins lend themselves to debasement, at the minting stage through the blending in of baser metals and once in circulation through shaving or clipping or sweating (shaking in a bag to yield precious dust).

Paper money was a great innovation in overcoming these problems – notwithstanding the vulnerability of paper, too, to debasement through excessive printing of notes, officially or in counterfeit. The advent of paper money dates to the turn of the 11th century in Song Dynasty China. Box 6.1 offers insight into why the innovation came about at the time and place it did and how these paper notes later fell into dissolution.

Box 6.1 The advent of paper money

Paper money got its start in the early 11th century during China's Song Dynasty (960–1279). What turned mere slips of paper into money was their negotiability. Earlier, under the Tang Dynasty 618–907), paper remittances came into use, but these claims are not believed to have passed from hand to hand. A merchant from the provinces would sell his wares in the capital and be issued a note, known as *feiqian* (flying cash), to be redeemed in coin at his local bureau. The innovation under the Song was for a claim to pass from the original payee to any bearer. Initially the notes were issued by private merchants to be redeemed for bronze coin in variable amounts as stipulated on their faces. Later, government took over issuance, printing notes in standard denominations. For four centuries, paper currency circulated in China, finally meeting its demise under the Ming Dynasty (1368–1644). At times over the course of this history, notes were redeemable in metal or in commodities monopolized by the state such as salt. At other times, though, notes circulated as fiat money, their value resting purely on state decree and the confidence of each in others to accept them in turn.

A number of factors contributed to paper money emerging at the time and place that it did. Technology played a part. More durable paper was fashioned from mulberry bark, and higher quality printing was achieved with metal plates. Further, China's traditional reliance on base metals for coinage lent itself to surrogates. The

Box 6.1 (cont.)

large masses of bronze and iron tokens needed to support purchases came to be represented by abbreviated strings hung together through holes in their centers. From this shorthand, representation by paper was a natural step. Ultimately, the backing of a strong state was essential to sustain confidence in paper money as legal tender. Tax liabilities could be met with the paper currency while government payments were executed with it. The ruler's stamp itself conferred value absent any intrinsic worth to the medium.

That paper money lasted for four centuries through a succession of dynasties is a wonder given paper's vulnerability to easy replication, both official and unofficial. A variety of safeguards kept counterfeiters at bay. Sophisticated production processes involving multiple printing plates in different colors impeded copying. Notes were stamped with official seals and identified with serial numbers. Beyond the technical barriers, forgery was subject to penalty of death, a warning to that effect being inscribed on some notes along with an offer of reward to informants. None of this, however, could prevent government profligacy. Lack of restraint in running the presses led to periods of inflation hinted at through ever larger denominations of notes. New issues sometimes replaced old ones at a fraction of their face value. But there were also remarkably long periods of restraint. Most of the 12th century was characterized by a stable currency despite the pure fiat nature of the notes.

Poor fiscal management under the waning Ming Dynasty brought the demise of paper money. Ming emperors undertook grandiose imperial projects, funded the seafaring expeditions of Admiral Zheng He, and bore the enormous cost of relocating the capital from Nanjing to Beijing, all by printing money. The paper money became worthless and was ultimately supplanted in the marketplace by silver, infusions of which arrived from Japan and the Americas. Meanwhile, the Europeans finally caught on to the wonders of paper money along about the 1600s, even as China had given it up. Not until the 20th century did paper money make a return to China.

Song Dynasty currency plate.

Source: Goetzmann and Rouwenhorst (2005).

Through much of the history of paper money, notes were redeemable for specie at a given rate. Paper money backed in this way by commodities is known as *representative* or *fiduciary money*. The global monetary system remained, in principle, on a fiduciary standard until 1971 when US President Nixon revoked the convertibility of the dollar into gold. In the wake of this break with gold, the world's currencies carried on as *fiat money* – meaning money because we say so, or by fiat. With no specie backing, fiat money rests on collective faith. We accept it in payment from others in the belief that others will in turn accept it from us.

Today's money consists largely of entries in electronic ledgers. We spend this money by writing checks, sliding debit cards, and submitting online payments. It passes from account to account without ever passing from hand to hand.

Function

Its form having proven so malleable, money is typically defined instead by its function. The standard list of three functions is given as follows: (1) medium of exchange; (2) unit of account; (3) store of value.

Most fundamental is the medium of exchange function. Without money, transactions would depend on barter. An exchange would require a match between two parties who could each offer items the other wished to acquire. Transactions would thus rest on a double coincidence of wants. Money allows for the act of offering to be divorced from the act of acquiring. This opens up tremendously the scope for economic activity.

Once the separation is drawn between offering and acquiring, the other two functions of money readily follow. Money provides a common unit of measurement on the basis of which to integrate distinct transactions into a coherent system. And money serving as a store of value allows selling and buying to be separated in time. Of course, if prices are rising significantly during this time lapse, the store of value function is compromised.

Concept

At its essence, money is debt. The bearer is owed, and claims his due by making purchases. The instrument of debt is issued by the banking system, then passes from one claimant to another with effect that society as a whole takes on the liability. There are many ways to obtain monetary claims on society: selling one's labor or capital services in exchange for them; accepting them in return for some other asset; borrowing them; or receiving them as gifts. We as members of society accept these monetary claims in good faith that others will do so in turn. Under a fiat money system, there is no other recourse.

B   How Money Is Created

Economist Milton Friedman famously explained the impact of a money supply increase by supposing that money were dropped from a helicopter. While an effective storytelling device, this is not what really happens. And yet, what really happens is very much akin to money appearing out of thin air. For the creation of money, occurring as it does through expansion of the balance sheet of the banking system, is an ethereal process indeed.

In the Old Days

To get a grasp on that process, let us consider how money creation worked in an earlier era when paper notes were backed by gold. Gold itself served as the unit of account, and to some extent a medium of exchange and a store of value. But gold is a hassle to carry around, to weigh and measure, to check for purity. So bankers found business opportunity in taking gold on deposit and issuing notes redeemable in gold by the bearer. As long as the holders of the notes believed they could redeem them in principle, there was no cause to actually exercise this prerogative. Only if a panic took hold that a bank was unsound would people run to collect their gold. Under normal circumstances, bankers could rest easy knowing their notes would circulate and the gold would sit idle in their vaults.

Now, bankers could not make money simply by taking in gold and issuing equivalent notes to depositors. Profits were to be had in lending at interest against the gold on deposit. Provided redemption of notes was a rare occurrence, notes could be issued in multiple against the gold on deposit leaving bankers safely able to make good on any claims that might be presented. With this, a given amount of base money embodied in gold could support a much larger amount of bank money conveyed in paper.

Bank balance sheets showed gold and loans outstanding on the asset side against bank notes issued on the liability side. A balance sheet of this form could expand through the making of additional loans and the corresponding issuance of bank notes subject only to the limits of public faith in the bank to honor any claims on demand. The system would remain viable as long as the public believed in it, and the public would believe in it as long as it appeared viable ... as it would right up until the moment some confidence shattering incident caused the whole thing to collapse.

Today no economy relies on precious metals or private bank notes as the basis for its monetary system. For more on those days and how confusing things sometimes became, see Box 6.2. Under the modern system, central bank liabilities take the place of gold, and deposits at commercial banks take the place of private bank notes. But the principle of an expansion in the balance sheet of the banking system acting to increase the supply of money applies just the same.

Box 6.2 Before there were central banks

Nowadays, we take for granted a system of national currencies based on notes issued by central banks. But it wasn't always so. Before there were central banks, all manner of coins comingled while currencies were spawned by a plethora of banks and other sundry agents. Monetary systems could be quite chaotic.

Box 6.2 (cont.)

The economy of colonial Southeast Asia rested on a profusion of foreign and domestic coins. Dutch guilders, British trade dollars minted in India, silver dollars from the Americas, coins struck by trading companies, and later on Japanese silver yen and US dollars, all vied for use. Private tokens and counterfeit coins flowed in from China. A number of banks chartered by the British issued notes that gained regional circulation. But much tender remained localized.

In China by the early 20th century, the Nationalist government had granted an ostensible monopoly on national currency issuance to the mixed state/private Bank of China. But the similarly mixed state/private Bank of Communications nevertheless continued to issue money as well. Further complicating matters, both banks issued notes by province even as provincial banks were issuing their own notes. Over-issue of national bank notes in Beijing to fund government spending led to their debasement and a preference within the capital for notes from other provinces or from foreign countries.

As chaotic as the East Asian milieu of yore may seem, worse existed across the Pacific. According to economist John Kenneth Galbraith, "by the time of the Civil War, the American monetary system was, without rival, the most confusing in the long history of commerce and associated cupidity." Some 1600 different banks, many defunct, had put into circulation roughly 7000 different types of notes in varying denominations. Counterfeiting thrived, as did periodicals that reported status updates on the trading value of these notes.

Early central banking took shape with formation of the Bank of England. Established with a large loan by private parties to the government in 1694, the Bank proceeded over the next century to finance wars, first against the revolting American colonies and then against an expanding Napoleonic empire. Not until 1844, however, was the Bank of England granted a monopoly over currency issuance. On this foundation, it consolidated central bank functions of taking deposits from and making loans to other commercial banks, manipulating interest rates through the trading of securities, and acting as lender of last resort to banks temporarily unable to meet depositor demands for withdrawals.

Central bank monopoly over currency issuance arrived in the USA in 1914. In China, a unified and stable currency was achieved in 1949 with the founding of the People's Bank. Following Indonesia's independence, the Dutch-chartered Java Bank was reconstituted in 1953 as a central bank under the moniker Bank Indonesia. Bank Negara Malaysia was established as a central bank in 1959, although currency issuance was left to Singapore's Currency Board until 1967. The Singapore Currency Board dated to 1897, with the Monetary Authority of Singapore being established as a de facto central bank in 1971.

Sources: Galbraith (1973); Hamilton-Hart (2002); Sheehan(2003).

In Modern Times

Under a modern fiat money system, the gold of olden times is replaced by claims against the central bank. The central bank issues these liabilities against itself in the form of currency notes or deposits credited to commercial banks in exchange for the purchase of assets. Let us consider this process with reference to the Central Bank of Myanmar. The balance sheet for the Central Bank of Myanmar for 2020, in kyats, is shown in Table 6.1.

On the asset side of the balance sheet the first item is foreign assets net of foreign liabilities. As recently as 2011, this entry had a negative sign showing the Central Bank of Myanmar to be a net debtor internationally. In the intervening years, it managed to accumulate 9.3 billion kyat (US$7.0 billion) in net foreign assets. It did this by entering into the foreign exchange market to sell kyats of its own issuance and buy foreign currency, which it then used either to pay down foreign debt or to invest in foreign securities.

The second item under assets is claims on commercial banks, which refers to central bank loans to commercial banks. A central bank lends to commercial banks by creating deposits in their names that appear as liabilities on the other side of its balance sheet. Claims on commercial banks represent a relatively small portion of assets for the Central Bank of Myanmar.

The third item, claims on the central government, accounts for the bulk of the central bank's assets. These claims arise from the purchase of government debt instruments. Indirectly, the central bank has printed money to pay for government expenditures.

On the liabilities side, the first and largest item is currency in circulation. This refers to notes issued by the Central Bank of Myanmar for use as legal tender. These notes have been printed by the central bank for the purpose of acquiring assets.

Next under liabilities is deposits of commercial banks held at the central bank. As explained above, these liabilities may be created in connection with loans extended to commercial banks. For the most part though, they are created when the central bank purchases an asset either directly from a commercial bank (say, a government bond that the bank holds) or indirectly from a customer of the commercial bank who then deposits payment in an account at that bank. In most countries, commercial banks are required to maintain deposits with the central bank as reserves according to some ratio relative to the deposits they hold of the banking public. But even where reserves are not required (the United Kingdom, for example), commercial banks must as a practical matter maintain a

Table 6.1 Balance sheet of the Central Bank of Myanmar, 2020

in kyats billion

Assets		Liabilities	
Net Foreign Assets	9,282	Currency In Circulation	18,267
Claims on Commercial Banks	705	Deposits of Commercial Banks	3,712
Net Claims on Central Government	17,351	Other (Net)	5,361
TOTAL	**27,339**	**TOTAL**	**27,339**

prudent level of working balances with the central bank for clearing purposes. A given commercial bank may, after all, find that on any particular day its own depositors draw on their funds to make payments to the depositors of other banks that exceed the payments received by the bank's own depositors from outside the bank. As a consequence, the bank will be obliged to transfer reserves from its own account at the central bank to the accounts of its counterparts to make up the difference.

Finally under liabilities, items of lesser importance are subsumed in the residual "other."

The central bank balance sheet is contrived for making money, not just in the literal sense already outlined of issuing currency notes and creating commercial bank deposits, but in the colloquial sense of making a profit. On the asset side, all claims yield interest while on the liabilities side no interest is paid on currency and little if any (depending on the economy) on commercial bank deposits that it holds. To be sure, costs are incurred in the physical printing of money and the conduct of central bank operations. Nevertheless, central banking is a highly lucrative endeavor, with the benefits redounding ultimately to the government. For the very revenues central banks collect from the government in debt service in large part revert back to it in central bank profits. Government debt is, in effect, wiped out when it is converted by the central bank into money. One form of government liability embodied in a bond that commands interest and must be repaid is transformed into another form as currency notes that bear no interest and need never be repaid.

The returns derived from printing money are known as *seigniorage*. Governments benefit from the power of seigniorage. But it is all too tempting to over-exercise that power. We examine the consequences of excessive money creation in the next section of this chapter.

The liabilities the central bank issues against itself as currency and commercial bank deposits constitute central bank money. This money goes by a variety of names, all referring to precisely the same thing:

- base money (or monetary base);
- reserve money;
- high-powered money;
- outside money;
- central bank money;
- M0.

The central bank balance sheet points to the channels for central bank money creation. The central bank issues base money when it purchases assets from among the three classes specified in Table 6.1. Hence a change in the monetary base (M0) is equal to the sum of changes in net foreign assets (FA), loans to banks (LB), and loans to government (LG). Letting Δ represent the change operator we have:

$$\Delta M0 = \Delta FA + \Delta LB + \Delta LG. \tag{6.1}$$

This equation makes clear that the central bank may take action that expands the monetary base on one front – for example buying foreign currency in the foreign exchange market – and offset this with action that contracts the monetary base on another – for example, selling government bonds. In the situation just described, the central bank is said to *sterilize* its foreign exchange market intervention. No net increase in the monetary base has ultimately taken place. This process will come under further discussion in our analysis of monetary policy in Chapter 11.

An increase in the monetary base precipitates expansion in the money supply on a broader scale via the commercial banking system. Under a fiat money system, an increase in base money plays the same role that an increase in gold played under the system of private bank note issuance described in the preceding subsection. Under the gold-based system, commercial banks issued notes at a multiple of the gold reserves held in their vaults. In an analogous process, under a fiat money system, commercial banks issue customer deposits at a multiple of their combined central bank reserves plus the currency in their vaults. Modern commercial banks must be prepared to meet the demand of depositors for currency or payments to customers of other banks in the same way that commercial banks in days of old had to be prepared to meet the demand of their note holders for gold. This then limits the extent to which their balance sheets can be expanded.

The Money Multiplier

A money multiplier captures the effect of an increase in the monetary base, represented by M0, on some broader money aggregate. Money aggregates are specified according to their degree of liquidity. The most liquid form, M1, is currency in circulation (i.e., outside bank vaults) plus demand (checking) deposits. M2, also known as "broad money," adds time (savings) deposits to M1. M3 is more expansive still, bringing in less liquid assets such as commercial paper and shares in mutual funds.

These categories used to be well delineated, but technological advance has now blurred the lines. With online banking and ubiquitous automatic teller machines, funds may be moved easily and instantaneously from one type of account to another such that liquidity does not vary much along the spectrum. Indeed, classification standards differ across economies making comparison among them as to the size of monetary aggregates not very meaningful. For a given economy over time, however, we can still glean important relationships between money and the economy.

Money multipliers for a particular economy over a given period of time are calculated as the ratio of the change in a monetary aggregate to a change in the monetary base. The central bank can directly initiate an increase in the monetary base by purchasing assets and issuing liabilities against itself. What happens from there is up to commercial banks and the banking public. At the core of their business model, commercial banks create deposit money in association with making loans. Regulatory provisions particular to each economy constrain this lending and deposit creation process, as does the tolerance of economic agents for risk and their desire for liquidity.

Formally, the size of the multiplier depends on two ratios: (i) how much the public holds in currency (as opposed to deposits) against an increase in base money, call this ratio c; and (ii) how much commercial banks hold in reserves (as opposed to making loans) against an increase in deposit money, call this ratio r. Letting C represent currency in circulation, R

commercial bank reserves with the central bank, and D broad deposit money (demand plus savings deposits), the key ratios are expressed as follows:

$$c = \Delta C / \Delta M0; \tag{6.2}$$

$$r = \Delta R / \Delta D. \tag{6.3}$$

To compute the M2 multiplier, given as $\Delta M2 / \Delta M0$, we start from definitions:

$$\Delta M0 = \Delta C + \Delta R; \tag{6.4}$$

$$\Delta M2 = \Delta C + \Delta D. \tag{6.5}$$

By substitution, and rearranging terms:

$$\begin{aligned}
\Delta M2 &= c \Delta M0 + (1/r)\Delta R \\
&= c \Delta M0 + (1/r)(\Delta M0 - c \Delta M0) \\
&= [c + (1/r)(1 - c)]\Delta M0.
\end{aligned} \tag{6.6}$$

The M2 multiplier is then the expression in square brackets. The bounds on c, as the share of an increase in base money held in currency, are zero at the minimum and one at the maximum. If c is one, the multiplier is also one because any increase in base money is fully absorbed in currency with no increase in deposit money. The commercial banking system simply has no role to play in money creation. This represents a lower bound on the multiplier. At the opposite extreme, if c is zero, the full increase in base money is deposited by the public in commercial banks and the multiplier then depends on r.

Given that commercial banks are in the business of lending money, the ratio of their reserves with the central bank to customer deposits, r, must be less than one, and hence $1/r$ is greater than one. The smaller the value of r, the more deposit money is created from given reserves and the larger is the multiplier. As r approaches zero, the multiplier approaches infinity. The banking system becomes more unstable the lower the value of r since meeting the demands of deposit holders to convert their deposits into cash rests more precariously on a smaller reserve base.

For Myanmar, the M2 multiplier during recent years has taken a value close to 4. This is in line with other economies at its stage of development which remain largely cash-based. More advanced economies in the region, such as Korea, Malaysia, and Thailand, have M2 multipliers in the range of 8–10.

The money multiplier is a critical magnitude for the conduct of monetary policy. Why this is so will become clear as we turn our attention to the relationship between money and the economy.

C   Money and the Economy: Theory

A connection between rapid money supply growth and rising prices was easily recognized at least as far back as the decline of the Roman empire. The connection was similarly obvious with the fall of every dynasty in China from the Song to the Yuan to the Ming (recall Box 6.1). Under stress of survival, Roman emperors debased the coin of the realm by thinning down its silver content while Chinese rulers printed notes without restraint. The result was "too much money chasing too few goods" as the adage goes. Rampant inflation accompanied the end of empire, from one continent to another.

In this section we formalize the relationship between money and prices. The upshot is that while major episodes of inflation are invariably rooted in excessive money creation, the short-term effects of modest increases in money are more complicated.

The Equation of Exchange

The amount of money in an economy is related to the nominal value of output produced over a period of time through the *velocity* of circulation, or the number of times a unit of money is spent on final goods and services during the period. This is purely definitional: velocity is defined as nominal output divided by the money supply. Rearranging terms yields the *Equation of Exchange*:

$$MV = PQ \tag{6.7}$$

where M is the money supply, V is the velocity of money circulation, P is the price level, and Q is real GDP. The Equation of Exchange says that spending on output is equal to the value of output produced, or nominal GDP.

The Equation of Exchange is a tautology and as such engenders no controversy. To develop a theory of money and the economy, however, we need to posit a story of how velocity is influenced by economic phenomena and how equilibrium is re-established following disruptions to an economic system. Such a modeling exercise rests on the specification of a variety of different types of relationships. These are outlined in Box 6.3. Imbuing the Equation of Exchange with theories of human behavior and equilibration processes has involved much controversy indeed.

Box 6.3 Equation forms for macro modeling

Three types of equations are used to construct macroeconomic models. They are characterized as follows:

1) **Accounting Identities**

These hold precisely and without exception by virtue of the way variables are defined. They are tautologies. The Equation of Exchange is an example:

$$MV = PQ$$

where M is the money supply, V is velocity of money circulation, P is the price level, and Q is aggregate real output. Velocity is herein *defined* as the value of output (PQ)

Box 6.3 (cont.)

divided by the money supply. V captures how many times each unit of money changes hands for a given total volume of transactions. The equality cannot but hold.

2) Behavioral Expressions

These hold as approximations subject to a margin of error. They focus attention on key behavioral patterns suppressing less important or less relevant considerations. An example is the consumption function (foreshadowed in Chapter 4 and studied in Chapter 9):

$$C = C_0 + \beta \cdot Y$$

where C is consumption, Y is income, and C_0 and β are parameters. Income is highlighted here as a determinant of consumption although certainly a plethora of other factors must have an influence as well. The consumption function abstracts from all such noise to isolate a core feature of behavior for a particular analytical purpose. Deviations around this core behavior are to be expected.

3) Equilibrium Conditions

These hold as theoretical tendencies given the passage of sufficient time for all adjustments to given circumstances to be completed. An example is the equating of aggregate demand (AD) and aggregate supply (AS) (concepts foreshadowed in Chapter 4 and elaborated in Chapter 9):

$$AD = AS$$

where AD and AS are respectively demands and supplies across all markets for final goods and services. Of course, the circumstances to which markets respond come under a constant barrage of changing forces, and that puts the target equilibrium in a constant state of flux. Equilibrium is thus more theoretical construct than observable outcome.

The Quantity Theory of Money

Certain long-run patterns are well-established with respect to the variables that enter the Equation of Exchange. In general, real output has shown a gradual secular increase and velocity a gradual secular decrease over time, apart from what may have been happening with money and prices. The increase in real output is attributed to growth in factor inputs and advances in technology (as discussed in Chapter 1). The decline in velocity means people hold rising money balances relative to income, and for that a variety of explanations may be posited. Economic development involves specialization and the division of labor. As the supply chain lengthens, given output is undergirded by an expanding web of transactions which must be supported by money. Development also involves a faster rise in wealth broadly speaking than in income, with money being one form that wealth takes. Finally, money in the form of demand deposits has become more attractive to hold versus other less liquid assets with advances in finance such as interest bearing checking accounts and debit cards.

Taking long-run trends in real output and velocity as exogenous leaves the remaining variables of money and the price level to be co-determined within the Equation of Exchange. The record shows they tend to move together: both may increase steeply; both may hold fairly stable; both may even decline. Nowhere in the realm of experience, however, do we find protracted divergence between money and prices. Sustained increases in the price level are invariably linked to growth in the money supply. In the oft-quoted words of Milton Friedman, "Inflation is always and everywhere a monetary phenomenon."

This quote conveys the thrust of the *Quantity Theory of Money*. The theory says in essence that the value of money – in other words, its purchasing power – depends on its quantity. The Quantity Theory was quintessentially articulated in 1911 by Irving Fisher, although the precept was by that time well ensconced in economic thinking. The theory came under disparagement in the 1930s, however, eclipsed by Keynesianism with its shift in attention to shorter-term variations in the money/price relationship. Milton Friedman then led a comeback in the 1950s and remained a staunch defender of the faith throughout his long lifetime which extended into the next century.

To a large extent, the two sides actually agree on the basics. Keynes accepts, however grudgingly, that "the total quantity of money remains, if not an overruling factor [in price fluctuations], at least in the long run a dominant one – and of exceptional practical significance because it is the most *controllable* factor." But Keynes's most famous line may well be: "In the long run we are all dead." A time frame of less than the long run thus commanded his attention. For their part, Fisher and Friedman recognized that in the short run velocity could be volatile, with the connection between money and prices therefore unstable. Despite this scope for agreement, the two schools arrive at sharply opposing positions on government policy.

We take up the policy discussion later in the chapter; first, we must flesh out the theory. Friedman is on record that "In the short run, which may be as long as three to ten years, monetary changes affect primarily output" while "[o]ver decades, on the other hand, the rate of monetary growth affects primarily prices." The dynamics work through the interest rate. Faster growth in the money supply drives an easing of credit that initially depresses the interest rate. Real output expands as a result, led by strong investment demand and associated job growth. But as bottlenecks in supply develop and labor markets tighten, prices begin to rise. Over time, expectations of continued inflation take hold. Nominal interest rates must rise to preserve the real rate of return on lending. With that, investment is discouraged, employment slackens, and real output growth eventually returns to its trend path.

A remnant of the elevated rate of money supply growth remains, however. Once inflationary expectations have been established, higher interest rates persist. This means the initial increase in the rate of growth of the money supply must be maintained if real output is to stay at trend. Inflation is locked in. The only way to quell it is to slow money growth. But this would mean tightening credit and pushing the interest rate even higher than its already inflation-adjusted level. With that, output growth will drop below trend and inflation will then gradually subside under slack demand. Eventually, expectations of continued high price increases will fade, and the nominal interest rate will drop back to its non-inflation baseline. Output growth will ultimately recover to its trend path.

Velocity is not presumed by quantity theorists to remain constant over the course of this cycle. On the contrary, there is good reason for velocity to increase as inflation heats up. The increase follows from a desire on the part of wealth holders to shift out of money balances and into assets that will hold their value or generate a return to offset the impact of inflation on money's purchasing power. But the very process of the broad public seeking to spend away its money balances only adds to inflationary pressure. Thus the initial impetus to inflation from an increase in money supply growth is accentuated by a feedback loop that involves rising velocity. Changes in velocity can thus introduce considerable variability into the relationship between money and prices in the short run.

As Friedman sums up the Quantity Theory: "Money matters." It matters for prices in the long run, but also for real output in the short run. Too much money ultimately results in inflation, and inflationary episodes are difficult and costly to unwind. But too little money can be harmful as well. In Friedman's assessment: "There is strong evidence that a monetary crisis involving a substantial decline in the quantity of money is a necessary and sufficient condition for a major depression." Why money matters is discernible from the Equation of Exchange. The scope for variation in velocity is limited. That means M feeds through systematically to PQ.

The Keynesian Challenge

Keynes discounts the long run heavily since none of us now incarnate will be there to see it. Within the more immediate time horizon of his concern, the main drivers of economic activity are other than money. Money may or may not matter in the Keynesian context as a policy instrument.

While concurring with the quantity theorists on the long-run relationship between money and prices, Keynes maintained that in the short run the price level and real output depend primarily on aggregate demand. The argument hinges on the relationship between saving and investment. Income not spent on consumption is saved. In order to keep an economy operating at its potential within a closed setting, this saving must be channeled into investment. If desired investment spending does not materialize to absorb available saving, aggregate demand comes up short of aggregate supply and output prices weaken. Businesses find they are unable to cover costs so they cut back on production. The economy goes into a downturn.

The decision to invest is the key to the Keynesian business cycle. Investment involves a commitment to the future, and that makes it vulnerable to the vagaries of expectations. When investors are bullish, it follows that spending is strong, prices rise, and output expands. When investors turn bearish, the opposite transpires. Once the economy falls into a slump, there is no automatic tendency for it to recover in any timely fashion in the Keynesian milieu. Pessimism is self-reinforcing, and an economy can remain mired in it for a long while. A detailed exposition of the Keynesian model must wait until Chapter 9. In the present context we turn our focus to the monetary implications.

Money's impact on the economy is dubious under the Keynesian view. Fisher took velocity to be quite rigid so that an increase in the money supply was transmitted directly to nominal output. Friedman allowed for greater variability in velocity, but in a systematic way based on identifiable factors. The transmission mechanism between money and nominal output worked, if not as mechanistically as Fisher believed. By contrast, Keynes saw velocity as very pliant. Money balances, in Keynes's framework, are held not just for the purpose of supporting transactions, but with an eye to managing an asset portfolio. If wealth holders expect bond prices to fall, they will absorb expanding money balances until investment prospects improve. Conversely, if they expect bond prices to rise, they will shift their portfolios out of cash and into bonds. In Keynes's world of fickle human sentiment and malleable expectations, the willingness to hold money balances can be quite unstable.

Moreover, money as a policy instrument is beset by a further problem for Keynes, and that is that money supply is endogenous. Monetary authorities are seen to have limited influence over money creation. Their command is confined to the monetary base. Commercial bankers then determine the degree to which they will extend loans and expand deposit money. In boom times, bankers will be eager to fuel economic expansion with credit while in hard times they will be reticent to do so. The money multiplier can drop so low as to make monetary policy ineffectual. Rather than serving as a lever of policy to actively manage the economy then, money becomes endogenous to the business cycle and accentuates it. The money supply contracts when times are bad, and expands when times are good. The central bank will be hard pressed to override this tendency which is inherent in the commercial bank incentive structure.

Their differing interpretations of how the economy works lead quantity theorists and Keynesians to opposing views on policy. Before we take up the policy debate, however, let us examine the empirical record on money and prices for Emerging East Asia.

D   Money and the Economy: Empirics

Empirical validation of the positive relationship between money and prices is to be found both in cross-section analysis of the economies of Emerging East Asia and in movement over time with respect to our featured economy for this chapter, Myanmar, where fluctuations have been quite dramatic.

Cross-Economy Comparisons

Chart 6.1 plots money growth versus inflation for our sample of economies measured during two different decades. Economy labels are attached to the 1990s data point with the matching symbol by economy representing the 2000-aughts data point. In general, over time and across economies a positive relationship is visible such that higher money growth is associated with higher inflation. At the upper extreme, Myanmar and Laos both had inflation rates above 20 percent during the 1990s with money growth rates above 30 percent. At the lower extreme, Hong Kong experienced deflation in the 2000-aughts and a low rate of money growth at about 8 percent.

The 1990s was in general a much higher inflation era than the 2000-aughts. Economies that endured very high inflation in the 1990s all saw the rates come down in conjunction with slowing rates of money growth. Vivid examples are to be seen in Laos, Myanmar, Thailand, and Indonesia. Economies with more moderate inflation in the 1990s, such as the Philippines, China, and Korea, achieved reductions on a more modest scale. By the 2010s, low inflation had become such the norm throughout the region that graphing it would reveal no pattern as all points would be clustered at the lower left. By this time, the lessons of money growth and inflation seemed to have been well learned and taken to heart, at least until some future day when they are forgotten.

While a general pattern exists between money growth and inflation, significant variation around this pattern is nevertheless apparent. Some economies managed to combine fairly

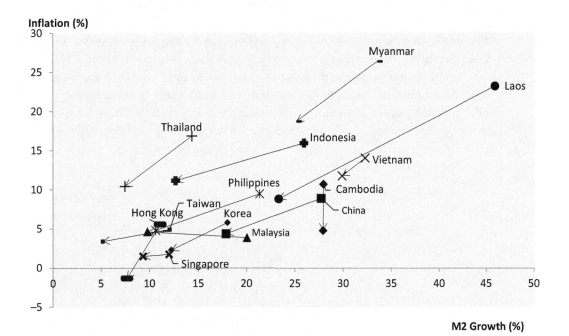

Chart 6.1 Inflation and M2 growth, select economies, 1990s and 2000-aughts

rapid money growth with moderate to low inflation – China, Cambodia, and Malaysia being cases in point. Certainly, other factors enter into the nexus. Importantly, higher rates of money growth can be absorbed with less inflationary pressure when real growth in output is rapid and when economic development brings rising monetization of productive activity. Leaning in the opposite direction, Thailand in the 1990s experienced high inflation even with modest money growth. Note that Thailand went through a crisis in the 1990s that was disruptive to normal economic outcomes in many ways.

The Case of Myanmar

Chart 6.2 tracks inflation and money growth for Myanmar for the period 1995–2010. Extremely sharp movements in both indicators bring the connection into stark relief. Peaks and troughs in money growth were followed at a one year lag by peaks and troughs in inflation. Money growth spiked to as high as 51 percent in 2001, with inflation following to hit more than 40 percent a year later. Money growth then plummeted to 17.4 percent and inflation dropped to 3.5 percent. Up again, down again, the pattern repeated until finally the decade ended with a spurt in money growth, leaving inflation seemingly poised for yet another take-off.

Such extreme gyrations beg an explanation. An IMF review of 2012 noted that the Central Bank of Myanmar was subordinate to the Finance Ministry and took as its primary function the monetization of fiscal deficits. The government, rather than issuing bonds to borrow in financial markets, enlisted the central bank to simply print money in support of public expenditures. Under such easy spending terms, discipline tends to lapse. For the central bank to gain independence in managing the money supply, financial markets must develop in Myanmar so that the government can rely on bond issuance to cover its deficits. While progress in that direction seemed on the horizon in the late 2010s, a coup d'état in early 2021 against the backdrop of the global pandemic does not bode well for progress in economic management.

The Myanmar case illustrates a clear short-run relationship between money and inflation under circumstances of pronounced fluctuation in money growth. The more subdued money growth patterns exhibited by other economies in our sample would not tend to yield such an

Chart 6.2 Inflation and money growth, Myanmar, 1995–2010

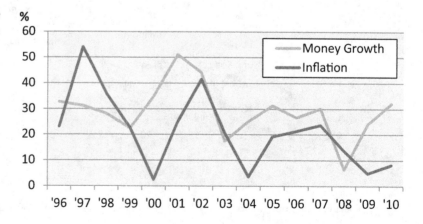

obvious short-run connection, other factors taking on greater relative importance. Overall then, the empirical picture from our sample of Emerging East Asian economies is one of a generally supported relationship between money growth and inflation in the long run with money growth having the potential to take on decisive influence over the price level even in the short run if the growth is turbulent enough.

E   Money Supply as a Policy Target

Historically, debate raged over the role the money supply should play in policy formulation. Quantity theorists believe in a direct relationship between money and prices. As articulated by Friedman, the theory takes velocity as subject to identifiable and contained influences, if not treating it as strictly fixed. Keynes, on the other hand, regarded the link between money and prices as more tenuous and the behavior of velocity as less coherent. The Keynesian view lends itself to a more activist approach to money management even as it implies reservations about the potential effectiveness of monetary policy. Quantity theorists by contrast advocate steady growth in the money supply as a means of achieving steady growth in the real economy at stable prices. This policy school is known as *Monetarism*.

Monetarists emphasize the pernicious effects of excessive price increases and advocate monetary restraint to prevent inflation from getting out of hand. When inflation catches people off guard, its disruptive consequences can discourage risk taking for years to come. Lenders find the purchasing power of their repayment receipts is undermined. For retirees who depend on investment income and watch their life savings being dissipated, this may be particularly unsettling. Workers suffer as well insofar as their wages lag behind increases in the prices of things they buy. Borrowers, on the other hand, receive a windfall. The lesson taken by savers may be that it is safer to hold wealth in gold or real property than in the financial assets that fund business investment.

When inflation sets in and is fully anticipated, some of the costs can be mitigated. Nominal interest rates rise to compensate for rising prices and preserve real rates of return while cost of living adjustments are built into employment contracts and pension agreements. Yet unavoidable costs remain. Inflation acts as a tax on cash balances and thus distorts the decision to hold cash as opposed to other assets at a sacrifice of convenience. Because price adjustments as a practical matter occur in lurches at discrete intervals, distortions ripple through the economy. Business planning is subject to greater uncertainty, and cost management commands more effort. The communication of price changes to customers also takes effort, as summed up in the term "menu costs."

Keynesians for their part emphasize the hardship of recession and see monetary stimulus as a potential, if not entirely reliable, remedy. They regard high unemployment in the here and now as far more damaging than some vague threat of inflation in the future trusting that any inflationary tendencies can be monitored and addressed in a timely fashion. For Keynes, the principal source of economic malaise is inadequate investment demand. Expansionary monetary policy through its impact on interest rates addresses this investment reticence directly. The key in Keynes's view is to use monetary policy strategically to bring about balance between investment and saving.

The Keynesians and the Monetarists are diametrically opposed in their views on the conduct of monetary policy. Keynesians see a critical role for active intervention, the authorities stimulating the economy or reining it in as warranted to counter the vicissitudes of public sentiment. Monetarists believe such intervention does more to destabilize than to stabilize. They oppose the use of discretion, preferring a rules-based system that targets a steady course for money supply growth. Discretionary policy, in their view, introduces one more element of uncertainty into economic life, compounding the difficulty of businesses and households to form valid expectations on the basis of which to make sound decisions.

Historically, money supply targeting of the sort favored by Monetarists has been been implemented in both Germany and the USA. Germany's Bundesbank initiated money targeting in 1974 and kept inflation in check under this modus operandi for more than two decades until transition to the euro intervened. In the USA, the impetus for money targeting was the escalation of inflation in the 1970s. Federal Reserve chairman Paul Volcker committed to conquering inflation by strictly restraining money growth and succeeded, seeing his mission through despite the hardship imposed by soaring interest rates as credit tightened. Even today, in the Japanese environment of deflation and interest rates going to zero or below, a given increase in the monetary base is specified as a target.

The economies of Emerging East Asia for the most part focus on targets other than the money supply in the conduct of monetary policy. For China, though, references to M2 and other quantitative measures of money and credit figure prominently in the quarterly policy reports of the central bank. This approach to policy is rooted in the legacy of a planned economy and a banking system that continues to be dominated by state-owned banks. In this setting, market-based targets for policy such as interest rates or exchange rates are less amenable to use in manipulating the economy. While the target for M2 growth in China is not hard and fast, it nevertheless remains important for steering policy.

In a broader sense, the distinction between Monetarists and Keynesians turns on the preference for a rule to determine policy versus discretion. For the most part, monetary authorities in Emerging East Asia have opted for discretion. Hong Kong is an exception with its exchange rate peg to the US dollar serving to anchor monetary policy. Advocates for a rule-based system argue that by taking discretion out of the mix, one important source of economic uncertainty is eliminated. In Hong Kong's case, that argument has been compelling. More on the Hong Kong model follows in Chapter 7.

F   Summary and Linkage to Finance

In a modern economy, money takes the form of currency and deposits in commercial banks. Currency notes are issued as liabilities of the central bank in exchange for the acquisition of assets such as domestic government securities or foreign exchange. Deposit money is issued as the liabilities of commercial banks against loans made to the public on the asset side. Deposit money can be converted into currency at commercial banks conditional on the demand for conversion remaining circumscribed in the aggregate. But under a modern fiat money system, that currency cannot in turn be converted into anything at the central bank. Currency does not take its value from being backed by precious metal or any other commodity of intrinsic worth. It takes its value by functioning as a claim on the economy at large. Thus, claims on the central bank in effect become claims on the economic system.

Commercial banks are limited in their deposit money creation by the need to convert deposits to currency on demand. In readiness, they hold reserves in the form of vault cash and deposits with the central bank. Regulatory requirements on the ratio of commercial bank reserves to customer deposits are generally imposed by governments. By controlling the level of reserves, the central bank is able to indirectly influence deposit money creation.

Central bank manipulation of commercial bank reserves is at the foundation of monetary policy. Central banks generally exercise discretion over how monetary policy is conducted, though not always. In some cases, Hong Kong being an example, discretion is eliminated under a rules-based system that automates money supply growth. In other cases, as with Myanmar, the central bank becomes an arm of the finance ministry, printing money perforce to fund government deficits. More typically though, monetary policy is undertaken deliberately with the aim of pursuing macroeconomic balance. When growth slips below its potential, a monetary stimulus is mobilized. Conversely, when growth goes into overdrive and inflation rears up, monetary restraint is imposed.

The conduct of monetary policy involves a great deal of judgment and finesse. Why that is so will become clear in later chapters. One of the extenuating factors, to be examined in Chapter 7, is that much credit creation takes place outside the confines of the commercial bank deposit-money realm. Broadly speaking, any promise to pay may in principle function as money if others are willing to accept it in payment. Financial innovation is often a force behind the credit proliferation that generally accompanies economic booms. Conventional monetary policy holds little sway over such credit expansion.

Data Note

Central bank balance sheet data for Myanmar in Table 6.1 are from the IMF International Financial Statistics database as are data used to calculate money multipliers. The 1990–2005 time series data on money and inflation for Myanmar in Chart 6.2 are also from this source. These early data for Myanmar must be regarded as subject to a high margin of error, and this example should thus be taken as merely illustrative.

For the cross-economy comparisons of Chart 6.1, the data are from the World Bank World Development Indicators database with data for Taiwan from the Republic of China (Taiwan) Statistical Bureau. Growth rates are derived from regression estimation of exponential curves based on annual magnitudes. This approach avoids undue influence of any endpoint outliers.

Bibliographic Note

Milton Friedman's helicopter story of money creation is recounted in the 1994 volume *Money Mischief* (Chapter 2). For invoking this story in a speech in 2002, US Federal Reserve chairman Ben Bernanke gained the nickname "Helicopter Ben."

Perhaps the most quoted statement in all of economics is Friedman's "Inflation is always and everywhere a monetary phenomenon." Friedman uttered these words in a lecture given in India in 1963, which was then published as a slim volume that might otherwise have passed into obscurity. The volume is *Inflation: Causes and Consequences*, the passage appearing on page 17.

The seminal work on the Quantity Theory of Money is due to Irving Fisher. Fisher's 1911 *Purchasing Power of Money* was the jumping off point for Friedman's "Restatement" of 1956. Both authors convey a strong sense of the adversarial nature of their positions.

The opposing view is due to John Maynard Keynes. Keynes's *Treatise on Money* published in 1930 anticipates the Great Depression in describing how excessive saving relative to investment demand can cause an economy to underperform. As an antidote, Keynes supported an activist monetary policy. His concession on the long-run inflationary tendencies of money growth is articulated in the *Treatise on Money* (Volume II, p. 49). His famous dismissal of the long run is from the *Tract on Monetary Reform* (p. 80), and reads in full:

But this *long run* is a misleading guide to current affairs. *In the long run* we are all dead. Economists set themselves too easy, too useless a task if in tempestuous seasons they can only tell us that when the storm is long past the ocean is flat again.

Friedman, for his part, concurs that money affects primarily output in the short run and primarily prices in the long run, the quote presented in the text coming from *Money Mischief* (p. 48). The same source provides the quote on a substantial decline in the quantity of money being necessary and sufficient for a depression. Friedman's last word on the subject of money was published posthumously in 2006 in the *Wall Street Journal* under the fitting title "Why Money Matters."

The examination of money and inflation for Myanmar draws on two sources. The first is Article IV consultations of the International Monetary Fund for 2011 and 2017. Article IV refers to an item under the IMF Articles of Agreement that authorizes surveillance over the exchange rate policies of member countries. This surveillance broadly pertains to member obligations to direct their "economic and financial policies toward the objective of fostering orderly economic growth with reasonable price stability." Article IV consultations generally take place once a year. IMF economists meet with government officials and other stakeholders, then prepare a staff report to be published conditional on member approval. About four out of five countries agree to publication of their Article IV staff reports.

The second source on Myanmar is a report published by the South East Asian Central Banks (SEACEN) Research and Training Centre (www.seacen.org). Established in 1982 in Kuala Lumpur, this organization has grown to 19 members from the Asia-Pacific region as of 2021. Its purpose is to foster learning, research, networking, and capacity building within the region and to represent regional interests within the global multilateral institutions. The report consulted is a multi-country study of monetary policy led by Nephil Matangi Maskay (2010), the chapter on Myanmar having been contributed by Tin Maung Htike, Research Officer of the Central Bank of Myanmar.

Analysis of China's monetary policy with evidence on the ineffectiveness of the interest rate as a policy instrument and the need to emphasize quantitative targets may be found in Berkelmans, et al. (2016).

BIBLIOGRAPHIC CITATIONS

Berkelmans, Leon, Gerard Kelly, and Dena Sadeghian, 2016. "Chinese Monetary Policy and the Banking System," *Journal of Asian Economics*, 46(C).

Fisher, Irving, [1911] 1922. *The Purchasing Power of Money*, 2nd edition (New York: The Macmillan Co.). www.econlib.org/library/YPDBooks/Fisher/fshPPM.html (accessed November 4, 2012).

Friedman, Milton, 1956. "The Quantity Theory of Money: A Restatement," in Milton Friedman (ed.), *Studies in the Quantity Theory of Money* (Chicago, IL: University of Chicago Press), pp. 3–24.

Friedman, Milton. 1963. *Inflation: Causes and Consequences* (New York: Asia Publishing House).

Friedman, Milton, 1994. *Money Mischief: Episodes in Monetary History* (New York: Harcourt Brace).

Friedman, Milton, 2006. "Why Money Matters," *Wall Street Journal*, November 17, 2006.

Galbraith, John Kenneth, 1973. *Money: Whence It Came, Where It Went* (Boston, MA: Bantam).

Goetzmann, William N. and K. Geert Rouwenhorst (eds.), 2005. *The Origins of Value: The Financial Innovations that Created Modern Capital Markets* (New York: Oxford University Press). In particular: Goetzmann and Rouwenhorst, "Introduction: Financial Innovations in History," pp. 3–16; Valerie Hansen, Part I, and Valerie Hansen and Ana Mat-Fink, Part II, "How Business Was Conducted on the Chinese Silk Road during the Tang Dynasty, 618–907," pp. 43–64; Richard von Glahn, "The Origins of Paper Money in China," pp. 65–90.

Hamilton-Hart, Natasha, 2002. *Asian States, Asian Bankers: Central Banking in Southeast Asia* (Ithaca, NY: Cornell University Press).

International Monetary Fund, 2020. Articles of Agreement of the International Monetary Fund (Washington D.C: IMF). www.imf.org/external/pubs/ft/aa/index.htm.

International Monetary Fund, 2000. Monetary and Financial Statistics Manual (Washington, DC: IMF). www.imf.org/external/pubs/ft/mfs/manual/index.htm (accessed December 6, 2021).

International Monetary Fund, 2021. International Financial Statistics database. http://data.imf.org/?sk=4C514D48-B6BA-49ED-8AB9–52B0C1A0179B&sId=1390030341854 (accessed November 20, 2021).

International Monetary Fund, 2012. Myanmar 2011 Article IV Consultation (Washington, DC: IMF).

International Monetary Fund, 2017. Myanmar 2017 Article IV Consultation (Washington, DC: IMF).

Keynes, John Maynard, 1923. *A Tract on Monetary Reform* (London: Macmillan).

Keynes, John Maynard, [1930] 2011. *A Treatise on Money* (Mansfield Centre, CT: Martino Publishing).

Maskay, Nephil Matangi (Project Leader), 2010. *Macro-Financial Links and Monetary Policy* (Kuala Lumpur, Malaysia: The Southeast Asian Central Banks (SEACEN) Research and Training Centre). Of note: Chapter 5 on Myanmar by Tin Maung Htike, pp. 129–148.

Minsky, Hyman P., [1986] 2008. *Stabilizing an Unstable Economy* (New York: McGraw Hill).

Republic of China (Taiwan) Statistical Bureau, 2021. National Statistics. https://eng.stat.gov.tw/ct.asp?xItem=37408&CtNode=5347&mp=5 (accessed November 19, 2021).

Sheehan, Brett, 2003. *Trust in Troubled Times: Money, Banks, and State-Society Relations in Republican Tianjin* (Cambridge, MA: Harvard University Press).

World Bank, 2021. World Development Indicators database. http://databank.worldbank.org/data/source/world-development-indicators# (accessed November 19, 2021).

7   Finance

A financial system channels funds from net savers to net spenders. But it does more than that, for the pie need not be fixed in size. Through its power of credit creation, the financial system can fuel economic expansion. The process is prone to fragility, however, and overshoot can end in crisis.

The Great Financial Crisis of 2008 brought attention to the role of finance in macroeconomic fluctuations. The economics profession was caught off guard by such an event emanating from the USA. Financial crises had come to be regarded as a malady of the developing world. In retrospect, the US financial system clearly succumbed to excess. But the clarity of that hindsight has not made foresight and prevention any more assured, in the USA or elsewhere.

We begin this chapter by outlining the basic elements of a financial system, then go on to examine the dynamics of financial deepening and financial innovation. Through the course of this discussion, we develop notions of risk and consider mechanisms for dealing with it. We flesh out the concepts with an empirical overview of the economies of Emerging East Asia to reveal widely differing states of financial development across the region. Hong Kong is featured for in depth discussion in view of its position as a globally important financial hub. Foundations laid, we develop the link between the financial system and the macroeconomy by explaining how the market for loanable funds determines a key macroeconomic price, the interest rate, and then we delve into the implications of interest rate movements for asset valuation. We end with a brief statement foreshadowing later chapters on how the vital function of the financial system to support growth is prone to instability.

A   Elements of a Financial System

The essential function of a financial system is to bridge the gap between those operating in surplus as net providers of funds and those operating in deficit as net users of funds. The efficiency of a system is judged by how well it allocates funds among competing uses to generate the highest return adjusted for risk. Risk is inherent in the financing of undertakings that incur costs up front in exchange for payoffs to be realized in the future. Will investment in a new business generate a profit? Will research in product development yield a breakthrough? Will pursuing a college degree lead to a good job? Will a public infrastructure project boost growth and expand a community's tax base to enable debt servicing? All such endeavors involve risk and uncertainty for both users and suppliers of funds. For those on the supply side, the risks are compounded by the difficulty of discerning the reliability of potential users of funds and the worthiness of their projects, and of monitoring those projects once they are underway.

A financial system embodies an array of mechanisms to contain and package risk to suit the varied characteristics and preferences of market participants. In this section, we consider how the elements of a financial system are designed to handle risk at the micro level, reserving for the next section attention to risk at the macro, or systemic, level. Risk at the micro level pertains to individual parties, whereas *systemic risk* extends to the economy as a whole. Financing arrangements that appear to carry only moderate risk at the individual level may nonetheless combine to heighten systemic risk when the arrangements are pursued in sufficient numbers. For example, a home loan to an individual of low credit standing may not seem terribly risky in itself provided the lender has recourse to repossess the home and sell it to recover the loan amount. However, if a great many such loans are made and default occurs on a wide scale, property values can fall broadly such that the debts become unrecoverable collectively. Guarding against systemic risk of this sort is no easy task.

In categorizing the elements of a financial system, a basic distinction is made between financial intermediaries, which issue claims against themselves in order to provide funds to users, and financial markets, which facilitate the direct exchange of claims between suppliers of funds and users of funds. We discuss financial intermediaries and financial markets in turn.

Financial Intermediaries

Commercial banks are the quintessential financial intermediary. Their core business has traditionally involved taking deposits and making loans. By intermediating between lenders and borrowers, banks mitigate and spread risk. There are two forms of risk that banks specialize in managing. One is the adverse selection process that tends to make less credit-worthy candidates more eager to seek loans. This is sometimes known as the "lemons" problem, taking terminology from the used car trade. Lemons refer to the defective vehicles that are particularly likely to end up on used car lots because their owners want to get rid of them. The problem arises in credit transactions due to asymmetric information between borrowers and lenders. Lenders generally do not know as much about borrowers as borrowers know about themselves regarding the likelihood of repayment. To overcome this problem, banks develop screening methods to assess creditworthiness and are able to apply these methods systematically across a large pool of prospective borrowers to select those of highest quality.

Financial intermediaries
• commercial banks
• other deposit taking institutions
• fiduciaries

The other form of risk that banks are in a position to ameliorate is moral hazard. Borrowers are spending other people's money and, left unsupervised, may not be as prudent as if the money were their own. Banks typically develop multi-faceted relationships with their clients, providing them with a range of financial services and keeping tabs on their affairs. This allows bankers to monitor their borrowers' activity and enforce compliance with the terms of the loan.

Financial intermediaries that are similar to banks in taking deposits and making loans vary in specifics across countries reflecting diverse paths of coevolution between business organization and regulatory system. These *other deposit taking institutions* often develop to cater to niche markets. For example, credit unions serve a particular organizational clientele, such as a university, while rural credit cooperatives focus on providing loans to farmers.

For the protection of depositors – and in turn the economy broadly – banks are favored with government support in various guises but are at the same time subject to a high degree of regulation. Support takes the form of governments insuring bank deposits to ward off any sudden losses of confidence that would tend to be self-fulfilling if depositors in large numbers sought withdrawals simultaneously. Further, central banks stand ready to act as lenders of last resort to commercial banks should they become stressed for liquidity in meeting demand for withdrawals. In turn, banks are subject to prudential regulation to contain risk. Specifically, they are required to hold reserves against customer deposits and to maintain capital (owners' equity) at a prescribed threshold relative to assets. In addition, banks must meet extensive disclosure requirements. The upshot is that holding wealth in the form of bank deposits carries very little risk, but commensurately, yields relatively low returns.

Types of financial intermediaries that do not rely on deposit taking, known as *fiduciaries*, include mutual funds, pension funds, hedge funds, private equity funds, insurance companies, and finance companies. This is the realm of "shadow banking," broadly conceived. The Financial Stability Board, an intergovernmental body housed at the Bank for International Settlements, defines shadow banking as "credit intermediation involving entities and activities outside the regular banking system." The nature of such entities and how their activities can contribute to the build up of systemic risk will be fleshed out in the next section which deals with financial innovation.

The various non-deposit-taking intermediaries are differentiated by the forms of assets and liabilities they hold. Assorted types of investment funds obtain resources from shareholders for the purchase of asset types that differ by risk and expected return. Specifically, mutual funds and pension funds invest mainly in tradable securities of the sort described in the next subsection. Hedge funds, in original concept, were meant to pursue investment strategies that would result in gains whether securities markets rose or fell, meaning they could hold short positions (commitments to sell or repay instruments they do not own). As the construct has evolved, however, hedge funds have turned to supporting all manner of bets on market outcomes. These funds are highly leveraged (indebted) and lightly regulated, but impose investment thresholds that limit access to high net worth individuals who are presumed able to assess and tolerate the risks involved. Private equity funds take full ownership of corporations with the intent of reorganizing them and selling at a profit, either as a whole or broken into parts. Finance companies lend to certain kinds of borrowers or for certain kinds of purchases, for example, automobiles. Insurance companies obtain funds from policy holders who collect on condition of specific untoward contingencies.

Financial intermediaries contribute positively to the economy in a number of ways. They aggregate funds to spread risk and achieve economies of scale in investment. They mitigate risk by screening and monitoring borrowers. And they provide liquidity to their depositors, who may withdraw funds on short notice, even as they offer long-term credit to borrowers. Such liquidity transformation is possible because routine withdrawals and deposits occur in large numbers that tend to be offsetting thereby allowing long-term loans to rest on a base of liquid funding that remains stable in the aggregate.

Financial Markets

Financial markets place claims on users of funds directly into the hands of providers of funds without intermediation by banks or fiduciaries. These claims are broadly distinguished between equities (stocks) and debt. Debt instruments with terms of less than one year trade on *money markets*. Bonds, which carry terms of a year or more, along with stocks trade on *capital markets*. Resting on these asset markets are markets in *derivatives*, which are instruments that derive their value from the assets, the purpose being to allow hedging against, or profiting from, risk. Finally, *offshore markets* offer trading of securities denominated in foreign currencies to effectively move transactions beyond the reach of national government regulation.

Financial markets
• money market
• capital market
○ stocks (equities)
○ bonds
• derivatives market
• offshore market

Equities represent ownership shares in corporations. Shareholders are the residual claimants of corporate earnings after all debt obligations have been met. The price of a stock, in principle, reflects the present value of the expected stream of a company's future earnings. Given the uncertainties surrounding future earnings, stock prices tend to fluctuate a great deal, and stock ownership thus involves considerable risk.

Money market instruments include commercial paper, letters of credit, bank acceptances, and short-term government securities such as US treasury bills. Commercial paper is generally backed by a bank loan commitment which effectively guarantees the paper to the bearer thus shifting the risk of loss to the bank. Letters of credit and bank acceptances also involve bank commitments.

Bonds are referred to as "fixed income securities" since they generally pay interest at a fixed rate relative to the face value to be paid at maturity, although bonds with variable interest rates do exist. Bond holders face two types of risk: credit risk that the issuer of the bond will default; and market risk that prevailing interest rates will rise and prices of bonds outstanding will consequently fall to realign their returns with the new higher yielding bonds available in the marketplace.

While investing in securities is inherently risky, government regulation aims at ensuring transparency and fairness. Issuers of stocks and bonds are required to follow standardized accounting procedures and to provide regular disclosure of financial data. For stocks, insider trading involving those with privileged access to information is prohibited. For bonds, private agencies evaluate risk and report ratings. The investing public is thus aided in assessing risk under rules of the game that level the playing field.

Derivatives offer a hedge against risk for holders of underlying assets or, in effect, a way to place bets on changes in asset values for those who do not hold the assets. Derivative contracts derive their value from that of other assets – stocks, bonds, loans, commodities, or foreign currencies. Swaps, options, and forwards are important types of derivatives. Interest rate swaps involve the exchange of interest obligations between two parties, a fixed rate commonly being swapped for a floating rate. Currency swaps involve an exchange of payment obligations across currencies. Options entitle the holder to buy (call option) or sell (put option) a given amount of a financial asset at a fixed price within some period of time. Forwards are more constrained, requiring the exchange of a given amount of a financial asset at a fixed price at a specified point in time. Normally with derivatives, the assets themselves are not transacted; rather, only the difference between the value of the asset at the contracted price and its realized market value changes hands. As investments, derivatives are highly risky since their value is extremely sensitive to market price fluctuations, although as hedges, this risk is structured to offset the risk of holding the underlying assets. In the Great Financial Crisis, losses on derivatives brought down major financial institutions.

Offshore markets operate in one country for securities denominated in the currency of another country. The practice took off with "Eurodollars" in the 1970s as accumulation of US dollars in the hands of oil-exporting nations motivated a demand for investment opportunities beyond the control of US regulatory and taxing authorities. Dollar bank deposits and dollar bonds held in Europe met this demand. The practice of offshoring banking and securities trading has proliferated to a variety of currencies and markets. The Hong Kong bond market, for example, shows listings as of October 2021 for, Malaysian petroleum company Petronas in US dollars, the Province of Ontario in Canadian dollars,; and Hong Kong and Shanghai Banking Corporation in Singapore dollars, to name a few.

Transactions in financial markets are facilitated by brokers and dealers under the umbrella of investment banking, also known as merchant banking. *Dealers* take ownership of assets temporarily on their own accounts while *brokers* manage the transfer of assets between other parties. By standing ready to buy or sell at announced bid/ask prices, dealers, also known as market makers, help to supply liquidity to markets. A vital function of investment banks is the launch of new corporate share issues. Investment banks underwrite the new shares, purchasing them on their own account, then selling them through their client networks to raise funds for corporate expansion. For a company selling shares to the public for the first time, the issuance is known as an initial public offering (IPO). Established public companies may also issue new shares to raise capital. Once issued, public shares trade on secondary markets.

B   Financial Deepening and Innovation

In the course of economic development, financial systems grow in size relative to GDP and become more complex. Up to a point, this secular process of financial deepening is a positive force. Evidence suggests, however, that the beneficial effects reach a plateau, and moreover, that excessively rapid growth in credit can be destabilizing. Episodes of very rapid credit growth can spring from innovations in financial products or organizational forms. That such innovations have overshot their usefulness is too often revealed only in the aftermath. In this section, we take up the topics of financial deepening and financial innovation, then apply the concepts to interpreting the credit boom in the USA that led to the Great Financial Crisis.

Financial Deepening

In the early stages of economic development, saving and investment rates are typically low, with the mobilization of saving for investment purposes taking place largely through internal or informal means. Small business investment and major household purchases are generally funded by family and friends or by local money lenders. Bigger businesses may have access to bank credit, but still tend to rely heavily on retained earnings to support expansion.

As economic development takes off, national saving rates rise while at the same time production becomes more capital intensive creating a need for greater concentration of funds. The resulting opportunities for financial intermediation between savers and investors stimulate growth of the banking industry. For businesses to grow larger still and for savers to reap higher returns in conjunction with taking on more risk, direct forms of financing via capital markets must come into play. Capital market development requires significant advances in legal and regulatory capacity to ensure investor protections and foster competition. This involves structures for enforcing contracts and property rights, for implementing accounting and disclosure standards, and for promoting effective corporate governance. In many emerging market economies, stock markets have been jump started by share issuance of state enterprises. Similarly, bond markets have been launched through government debt offerings. Thus kindled, these formative capital markets in time come into their own to take on mobilization of funds for private sector investment. The ultimate in financial maturity is marked by the emergence of derivatives markets for hedging risk.

At its best, a financial system serves economic development by allocating funds to their highest valued uses adjusted for risk. It does this by aggregating diffuse savings to support large projects and broaden risk sharing; by affording borrowers access to long-term funding while preserving liquidity to lenders through short-term deposits and active secondary markets in securities; by identifying and packaging risk, and subjecting it to market pricing and exchange; and by providing oversight of managerial performance and exposing laxity. These many benefits of a strong financial system notwithstanding, empirical work indicates that a positive correlation between financial depth and economic development exists only to a point. Beyond some threshold, further financial deepening fails to yield discernible increments to growth. Explanations proposed for a disappearing or even negative relationship are that a bloated financial sector may divert resources, especially human talent, from more productive uses, and that taken to excess, financing becomes fragile and inclined toward feeding speculation rather than supporting productive investment.

The concern that financial depth leads to increased speculative activity and thus macroeconomic fragility is not supported empirically, however. Indeed, to the contrary, the evidence suggests that greater financial depth affords more resilience and better capacity for shock absorption. Simple bank dominated systems in less developed countries have a storied history of susceptibility to crisis. Nevertheless, complex financial systems in advanced countries can spill into crisis as well, the USA offering a notable example in 2008. Rather than the level of depth, the rapidity with which credit expands seems to be the more telling predictor of instability. Rapid expansion of credit often follows from innovations in financial instruments or financial organization. Let us proceed to explore the nature of financial innovation, with particular attention to the origins of the Great Financial Crisis.

Financial Innovation

Recall from Chapter 6 that money, in effect, represents claims on an economy. Creating money seems easy enough. Central banks do it by issuing liabilities against themselves in exchange for government debt securities or other assets. Commercial banks do it by recording deposits in support of new lending. In principle, the capacity to create money is even broader than this. As Hyman Minsky put it, "Everyone can create money ..." How that is so is described in Box 7.1.

Box 7.1 "Everyone can create money ..."

The quote in the header is from Hyman Minsky, known for his work on business cycles. In full it reads:

Everyone can create money; the problem is to get it accepted.
Minsky (2008), p. 255.

Here's how it works: Suppose the author of this text writes an IOU (I owe you) as depicted at left. Perhaps the payee has lent $50 in cash to the author or maybe he has rendered some service to be met with delayed compensation. This IOU note captures what Minsky means by creating money. The problem getting such a thing accepted is obvious. Even if

Box 7.1 (cont.)

Wiemer's credit is good with the original payee, for that individual to find someone else who will likewise accept this note as payment will not be easy.

In principle, the inking of this note is no different than what a bank does when it creates money. In granting a loan, the bank issues debt (an IOU) in the form of a deposit liability. This deposit can then be spent – through the writing of a check or the use of a debit card – moving on to become someone else's deposit at some other bank. The money supply would expand in the same way if Wiemer's IOU were to pass from hand to hand in support of purchases.

Money issued as debt of the banking system supports spending. Banks grow their business by increasing the amount of this debt in tandem with corresponding loan assets. For the economy as a whole, however, excessive infusions of debt-fueled purchasing power can be inflationary, as explained in Chapter 6. When channeled into asset markets, increases in purchasing power can give rise to bubbles, sowing the seeds of later collapse. Governments therefore impose regulations to limit growth in the financial sector's balance sheet. Inevitably, however, entrepreneurial financiers devise ways around such regulation with new and creative ways to expand bank lending. Box 7.2 demonstrates how the process can work.

The loan securitization process described in Box 7.2 increases credit in the economy in circumvention of the power of the central bank to control the amount of deposit money. This new credit supports growth in spending. The increase in credit is associated with an increase in debt of a short-term, highly liquid nature even as the lending it supports may be long term. The commercial paper issued by the shadow banks is indeed so liquid that it is included in broad definitions of the money supply. Expansion of the financial sector balance sheet in this way has a stimulatory effect on the economy.

Box 7.2 Securitization: Liquidity is generated, debt is piled on

Commercial banks generate revenue by charging interest on loans. The more they lend, the better for their business (provided of course the loans are repaid). Bank lending is constrained, however, by regulation requiring that reserves be held against deposits and that capital be held against assets. Banks naturally look for ways around these impediments to "making money." One ploy is to securitize loans and move them off bank balances sheets with the aid of the shadow banking system. The process is outlined in the T-accounts below.

Box 7.2 (cont.)

COMMERCIAL BANK				SHADOW BANK			
Round 1				**Round 1**			
Assets		Liabilities		Assets		Liabilities	
Loans	120	Deposits	180				0
Reserves	30						
Other	50	Capital	20				
Round 2				**Round 2**			
Loans	20	Deposits	180	Securities	100	Commercial Paper	90
Reserves	130					Capital	10
Other	50	Capital	20				
Off Balance Sheet Vehicle							
Loans	100	Securities	100				
Round 3				**Round 3**			
Loans	120	Deposits	180	Securities	100	Commercial Paper	90
Reserves	30					Capital	10
Other	50	Capital	20				
Off Balance Sheet Vehicle							
Loans	100	Securities	100				

In Round 1 the commercial bank holds capital at 10 percent of assets, and reserves at about 17 percent of deposits. Let us suppose these ratios are pressing up against regulatory limits.

In Round 2, the commercial bank finds a way to unleash new lending potential. It bundles together $100 in loans and sells claims on the income streams from the loans in the form of tradable securities. Since the new holders of these asset-backed securities bear the risk exposure to the loans, and bank owners and depositors do not, the bank is able to move the package of loans and securities into a special purpose vehicle off its balance sheet. The asset backed securities are purchased by a shadow bank providing the commercial bank with a $100 increment to its reserves. To obtain the necessary funds to make the purchase, the shadow bank is established with $10 in capital and issues $90 in commercial paper.

Finally in Round 3, the commercial bank lends out the $100 it raised by selling securities in Round 2. Since this brings it back up against its lending limit, the bank may wish to repeat the securitization exercise all over again.

Box 7.2 (cont.)

To sum up the results: the financial system expanded with the establishment of a shadow bank and a special purpose vehicle off the balance sheet of the commercial bank; liquidity increased through the transformation of illiquid loans into tradable securities; and the overall level of debt rose through multiple channels involving asset-backed securities, commercial paper, and new loans. All this occurred despite regulation on bank reserves intended to keep lending in check.

Historically, entrepreneurs have proven adept at devising all manner of new methods for expanding the financial sector balance sheet. Important innovations in this spirit that have become established elements of today's financial landscape include checking accounts, credit cards, and mutual funds. Regulatory authorities strive to keep pace with new developments. The trick is to facilitate financial innovation that is supportive of economic growth yet to impose enough restraint on the process to prevent asset bubbles from inflating and unsustainable debt loads from accumulating.

US Credit Boom of the 2000-Aughts

The US credit boom of the 2000-aughts had its basis in the model of Box 7.2 – securitization of loans supported by a shadow banking system that was itself funded by short-term debt. Securitization of loans per se was nothing new. The basic concept is that income streams, most notably in the form of interest paid on loans (with other possibilities ranging from real property rents to credit card receivables to student loan repayments) are bundled and used as collateral to back the issue of tradable debt instruments. The innovation of the 2000s started from the premise that even in a high risk bundle of loans, not all would go bad even if all the borrowers as individuals were poor credit risks. Mortgage-backed securities were structured into tranches such that the bottom tranche would be exposed to losses from default first while the top tranche would bear exposure only if the entire pool fell into default. The top tranches were granted high AAA ratings and were much in demand. The less desired lower tranches were submitted to a further round of bundling and structuring with the top tranches again emerging as AAA rated products. In this way, mortgage loans made to borrowers of poor "subprime" credit standing were transformed into ostensibly low risk investment vehicles.

The delusion the marketplace succumbed to was that complicated financial products had diversified risk and transferred it to willing bearers for a higher expected return. In fact, however, all sight of risk had been lost in an opaque piling on of complicated debt instruments. The forgotten reality was that subprime mortgages were widely configured for interest rate resets that would hit fragile borrowers in a nationwide wave. Meanwhile, property values had been bid up to unsustainable levels which stimulated an oversupply of new construction. Collapse was in the cards. By 2007, hedge funds and investment banks were taking sizeable losses on subprime mortgage securities as mortgage debt went into default. The bankruptcy of investment bank Lehman Brothers in September 2008 sent the financial sector into full-on panic. The next year would see a series of financial giants fail or succumb to acquisition. All told, bank losses in the USA are estimated by the IMF to have reached $855 billion with total global losses put at $2.28 trillion.

C Finance in Emerging East Asia

Variation among the economies of Emerging East Asia is nowhere more stark than in the realm of finance. Hong Kong is home to the highest ratio of financial assets to GDP in the world while in the least developed economies of the region banking systems are rudimentary and capital markets little more than an idea. In this section we compare measures of financial sector development and performance and consider the implications. With respect to standard indicators of depth, liquidity, volatility, and fragility, the range of outcomes runs the gamut.

Depth

The Asian Financial Crisis of 1997 sounded a warning on the pressing need for local capital market development. In the run up to the crisis, domestic saving had been diverted outward through both official reserve accumulation and private acquisition of foreign assets. Meanwhile capital flowed inward in the form of foreign direct investment and loans, the latter being mostly short term yet applied to the funding of long-term projects. This resulted in a double mismatch on domestic corporate balance sheets: long-term, illiquid assets against short-term liabilities in need of constant rollover; and domestic currency assets against foreign currency liabilities. When local currencies depreciated sharply, many borrowers found themselves unable to pay back or refinance their debts. The conclusion drawn from the crisis was that domestic capital markets were needed to provide better local investment opportunities for savers and to generate long-term domestic currency funding for capital formation.

From a small base, capital markets have developed impressively since the crisis in much of Emerging East Asia, although bank finance still predominates in Cambodia, Laos, Myanmar, and Vietnam. Chart 7.1 presents asset to GDP ratios in 2020 for four asset categories: private bank credit; stock market capitalization; private debt securities; and public debt securities. Debt securities include both local and foreign currency issues.

The ratio of private bank credit to GDP lies in a fairly tight range of 125–180 percent for Thailand, Singapore, Malaysia, Vietnam, Taiwan, Korea, and China. For Hong Kong the ratio lies well above this band while for the Philippines and Indonesia, it is somewhat lower.

Stock market capitalizations (total market value of all shares) in Emerging East Asia have received a major boost from the listing of state-owned enterprises. Given the high degree of market capitalization accounted for not just by state shares sold to the public but also by shares still held by the state, market capitalization figures overstate the role of the stock

Chart 7.1 Financial asset-to-GDP ratios, select economies, 2020

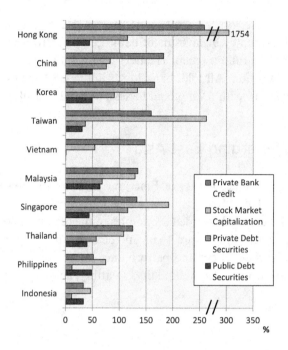

market in raising capital for investment. At over 1700 percent, Hong Kong's ratio of stock market capitalization to GDP speaks to its role as a financial center for China. Taiwan's stock market, too, bears Mainland Chinese influence with major listed firms (TSEC, Acer, ASUS) basing their manufacturing operations across the straits, and Singapore as well serves a broader hinterland. Ratios around 110–130 percent for Korea, Malaysia, and Thailand indicate well-developed stock markets serving domestic corporations.

Ratios of private debt securities to GDP lie in the range of about 60–120 percent for Hong Kong, China, Korea, Singapore, Malaysia, and Thailand, and fall well below this level for Taiwan, the Philippines, and Indonesia while for Vietnam the ratio is minuscule. For public debt securities, the ratio to GDP is led by Malaysia at 64 percent with Hong Kong, China, Korea, Singapore, Thailand, and the Philippines following at 40–50 percent.

Although in broad terms financial deepening is readily seen to accompany economic development, the structure of financial systems varies greatly even among the world's most advanced economies. The USA in 2020 had a ratio of private bank credit to GDP of only 52 percent in contrast to Japan's 122 percent and Britain's 94 percent. Conversely, the US ratio of stock market capitalization to GDP stood at 194 percent versus 149 percent for the UK and 71 percent for Japan. Europe and Japan in general rely more on bank financing, the USA more on capital markets. Many factors influence these outcomes, important among them regulatory environment and tax provisions. Over time, though, a common trend is apparent for a broad cross section of economies in an expanding role for capital markets relative to bank finance. This is a result of stock and bond markets becoming increasingly accessible to savers, both directly and through fiduciaries, to offer the liquidity of banks but with higher expected returns for those prepared to bear the risk.

Liquidity

Liquidity is vital for effective functioning of financial markets. Without active trading, meaningful asset prices cannot be arrived at. In debt markets, pricing involves the determination of interest rates and the assessment of risk. In equity markets, pricing is a vital tool of corporate governance, serving as a mechanism to assess manager performance.

The size and liquidity of an asset pool tend to be related. More liquid assets attract more investors because the assets can be readily converted back to cash, and consequently the asset pool grows. In turn, the bigger an asset pool and the greater the number of investors, the more transactions tend to be generated. A greater volume of transactions lowers transactions costs. In debt markets this results in lower spreads between the interest rate paid by borrowers and that received by lenders. The importance of scale economies in financial markets is evident from the high degree of concentration of assets among a small number of global financial centers.

Securities markets in Emerging East Asia remain generally small in size by global standards, which inhibits liquidity. The value of bonds outstanding for the region's economies in both local and foreign currencies is shown in Chart 7.2. Because China's economy is so large, even a relatively small ratio of bonds to GDP implies a large asset pool, at nearly US$17 trillion in 2020, of which renminbi denominated bonds reached an equivalent US$15.5 trillion with US dollar denominated bonds accounting for the remaining US$1.4 trillion. Korea was a distant second in bonds outstanding, with other economies positioned much further down at only a few hundred billion in US dollar equivalent.

A key indicator of liquidity is the *turnover ratio*, measured as transactions value during a given period of time relative to the stock of an asset. Equities exhibit turnover of close to two in the Chinese and Korean markets. This is on par with rates seen in mature financial markets,

Chart 7.2 Bonds outstanding, select economies, 2020

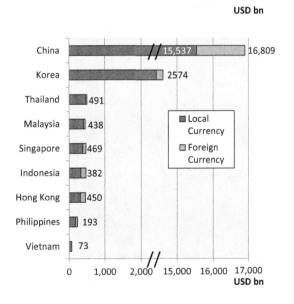

although equity turnover is prone to high variability from year to year with the numbers shooting up in times of stress. Equity turnover ratios are well below this level in other Asian markets. Markets for government bonds are generally more liquid than those for corporate bonds. For benchmarking purposes, it is worth noting that annual turnover for US corporate bonds stands around one and for US treasury bonds reaches a very liquid 30. In the Emerging East Asia setting, bonds are more often bought and held to maturity which depresses liquidity.

Volatility and Fragility

Stock prices are closely monitored in real time as the readiest barometer of economic sentiment. In troubled times, stock markets can become highly volatile reflecting increased uncertainty about the future. Chart 7.3 depicts market volatility as measured by the standard deviation of stock returns. The impact of the Great Financial Crisis comes through clearly with the spike in volatility in 2009. Hong Kong, with its openness to global capital, saw a particularly sharp increase in volatility, the standard deviation on returns rising from 17 in 2007 to peak at 47 in 2009. Further back in time, volatility during the Asian Financial Crisis was similarly high. A spike in volatility is evident for China in 2015–2016 in connection with a stock market boom and bust. At stake, characteristically for China, was not so much changing assessment of corporate fundamentals but skittish expectations about the long reach of government in influencing stock market behavior. Ripple effects from instability in China are visible across the region.

Stock market movement serves a function in registering economic shocks and communicating their consequences. Investors in equities understand that the greater risk associated with these fluctuations is tied to higher expected returns. Holders of bank deposits, on the other hand, need to feel secure in the knowledge their money is safe. A measure of fragility in the banking sector, known as the Z-score, is constructed as the sum of the return on assets

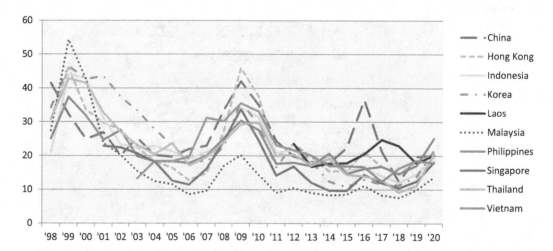

Chart 7.3 Stock return standard deviation, select economies, 1998–2020

plus the capitalization ratio divided by the standard deviation of the return on assets. A high capitalization ratio ensures owners bear the brunt of any losses in asset value thus shielding depositors. High returns and capitalization relative to volatility provide a buffer against shock. Z-scores in Emerging East Asia have shown fairly low volatility over time. Even the Great Financial Crisis caused no serious perturbations as the region's banks had little exposure to troubled US debt securities.

A diversified financial system presents a multiplicity of channels for absorbing shock. Provided diverse components of the system respond differently to various stressors, the overall effect of diversification is to increase resilience. The economies of Emerging East Asia bore the Great Financial Crisis through increased stock price volatility but no loss of security in their banking systems. A stable footing for banking facilitated recovery even as stock price fluctuations may have hindered the raising of equity capital. Under other circumstances, another kind of a shock could well have the opposite effect of destabilizing banking systems but leaving capital markets functioning effectively to support economic activity.

D The Special Case of Hong Kong

Hong Kong is unique in having its own currency and its own customs and immigration authorities despite being a city subsumed under a sovereign state. It functions as a distinct economy even as it interacts symbiotically with Mainland China. While Hong Kong has long served as an international financial hub, its capital markets exploded after the handover from Britain to the People's Republic in 1997. Between then and 2020, the number of listed companies on the Hong Kong Stock Exchange rose from 658 to 2,538. Bond listings took off later, rising from just 69 in 2010 to 1,574 in 2020.

In this section, we first look at Hong Kong's monetary institutions and their tailoring to the territory's distinctive circumstances. We then expand on the territory's role as a global financial hub and more particularly a platform for the internationalization of the renminbi.

Hong Kong Monetary Institutions

Hong Kong's monetary system rests on an exchange rate peg. The peg at HK$7.8 to the US dollar was established in 1983 to halt a downward spiral in the value of the Hong Kong currency precipitated by concerns about Hong Kong's future upon the expiry of the British lease on the New Territories. The fixing was intended to restore confidence, and succeeded in doing so. Hong Kong has stood by its peg through the handover to Chinese sovereignty, the swirling of financial crises, and much currency volatility in the region at large, with the credibility of the peg consequently well established.

With discretion removed from currency issuance, responsibility for this function is delegated to commercial banks. To issue Hong Kong dollar notes, the authorized banks must submit US dollars to the Exchange Fund of the monetary authority for which they obtain "Certificates of

Indebtedness" that serve as backing for currency issuance. Conversely, to redeem US dollars banks must relinquish the Certificates of Indebtedness back to the monetary authority. In this way, the Hong Kong monetary base is entirely backed by US dollars.

This system has the advantage of being free of the intrusion of politics into monetary affairs. The Hong Kong money supply expands or contracts in response to market forces. The process is simple, transparent, and predictable, at least insofar as market forces themselves are so. A further advantage is that exchange rate risk is eliminated vis-à-vis the US dollar. Trade in goods and services and the transfer of financial claims can thus proceed without worry about exchange rate fluctuations with regard to the world's foremost reserve currency.

The main disadvantage of the peg is that exchange rate adjustment cannot serve as a buffer in absorbing shock. Shocks may occur, for example, in the form of movement in the US dollar relative to other currencies, fluctuations in world commodity prices, or changes in US interest rates. Adjustment must take place through domestic prices, extending to wages, interest rates, and asset values as well as product prices. Hong Kong's highly agile market economy generally allows for fairly quick and effective responses to maintain competitiveness. And the strong position of government fiscal affairs means repercussions for public debt are not a concern. Yet in times of broad-based and steep depreciation in regional currencies, such as occurred during the Asian Financial Crisis, the burden to absorb economic adjustment without recourse to the exchange rate has been hard to bear. Nevertheless, the commitment to the peg has held.

Hong Kong as a Global Financial Hub

Hong Kong is an entrepot for finance just as it is for trade in goods and services. Financial institutions from all over the world have set up shop in the territory with minimal barriers to entry. Banks take deposits and make loans not only in Hong Kong dollars but in other currencies as well, serving customers from near and far. Foreign companies list on the Hong Kong stock exchange, raising funds from investors worldwide. Business thrives in the managing of wealth for global private clients and the raising of venture capital for far-flung start-up firms. In 2019, Hong Kong's foreign exchange market turnover ranked fourth globally, behind the UK and the USA, and roughly tied with Singapore.

Referring to Chart 7.1, the asset class in which Hong Kong stands out most dramatically is equities. Early in the reform and opening of Mainland China in the 1980s, state enterprises began to tap funding indirectly in Hong Kong dollars. So-called red chip stocks were issued by firms incorporated in Hong Kong but with controlling share ownership tracing to the Mainland. Later on, firms incorporated on the Mainland began listing "H-shares" in Hong Kong, the first instance of this occurring with Tsingtao Brewery in 1993. Typically H-share listings involve parallel listings on Mainland exchanges in "A-shares" that are denominated in renminbi.

Historically, the debt market figured little in Hong Kong finance. An important reason for this is that the strong fiscal position of the Hong Kong government left it with no need to borrow. And without active trading in government debt, the market lacked benchmark interest rates to signal a baseline low-risk cost of funds. To fill this void, the Hong Kong Exchange Fund initiated an aggressive program of debt issuance beginning in 2009. The Exchange Fund bills and notes sold under the program present a range of maturities from three months to 10 years in order to generate a yield curve for market reference. Once the public debt market was established, growth in the corporate debt market accelerated. This market includes issuance of renminbi denominated bonds, known as "dim sum" bonds, the first being issued by McDonald's in 2010.

Banks in Hong Kong began taking retail deposits in renminbi as early as 2003. However, not until cross-border settlement of payments was established in 2010 did holding renminbi deposits find wide appeal. The banking and bond developments of 2010 set the renminbi on a path to internationalization even as capital controls continued to limit the currency's flow across the Mainland border and to restrict access by foreign investors to markets onshore. China's trade has increasingly been invoiced in renminbi, with Hong Kong meeting related demand for payment processing and credit.

Even as the Mainland has driven growth in Hong Kong's financial markets, its own onshore markets have overtaken those of Hong Kong in absolute terms. Indeed, by the end of 2020, the combined market capitalization of the Shanghai and Shenzhen exchanges was double that of the Hong Kong exchange. As for bond markets, Hong Kong's is minuscule relative to China's, as shown in Chart 7.2.

Against the backdrop of the Mainland's own mammoth financial markets, the question of just how much China needs Hong Kong as a financial entrepot has drawn attention as the political ground has shifted. Editorials in western publications have argued that despite the size of the Mainland financial system, Hong Kong's role remains vital, a headline in the *Wall Street Journal* reading "Hong Kong is the Lung through Which Chinese Banks Breathe" (September 11, 2019). Critically, what Hong Kong has had that the Mainland lacks is the rule of law. This is the foundation for a system of property rights, dispute adjudication, and corporate governance that permits fluid financial engagement with the rest of the world.

E   Interest Rates and Asset Prices

Financial systems channel funds from savers to spenders. Savers seek to earn a return on the funds they supply, with that return meant to be higher the greater the risk and the longer the time commitment. Thus, users of funds must be prepared to pay back more than they borrowed. Generally, then, borrowed funds are directed toward investment – in plant and equipment, in education, in research and development, in infrastructure, or in assets that will appreciate in value over time.

The interest rate represents the price that lenders receive and borrowers pay for funds. In this section we first consider how the interest rate is determined in the market for loanable funds. We then examine the relationship between the interest rate and asset prices.

Interest Rate Determination

Macroeconomics routinely references "the" interest rate. "The" interest rate is pivotal for an economy due to its effect on investment and in turn GDP growth. The notion of a singular interest rate is an abstraction, of course, for in actuality, the market for loanable funds generates a wide spectrum of interest rates reflecting differences in risk and term to maturity. Nevertheless, in normal times interest rates as a whole tend to move in sync so that as an analytic construct "the" interest rate serves to capture the macroeconomic dynamic.

Analysis of the response of savers and investors to changes in the interest rate rests on a rate expressed in real terms, that is, the nominal rate minus the rate of inflation. In practice, loan contracts are generally specified in nominal terms with the real interest rate revealed after the fact once the inflation rate becomes known. If inflation surprises on the high side, the real interest rate *ex post* will be lower than was anticipated *ex ante*, and vice versa. When inflation accelerates unexpectedly, the real interest rate can turn negative if the nominal rate has been set low enough. This amounts to a boon for borrowers, but a setback for lenders.

The market for loanable funds determines the interest rate, as represented in Figure 7.1. Savers enter the market on the supply side, investors on the demand side. In the microeconomic analysis of markets, studied in Chapter 3, the general representation of the supply curve as upward sloping rests on the argument that a rising price permits resources to be drawn at increasing opportunity cost from competing uses. Such an argument does not fit in this situation for we are looking at the choice to save in the aggregate rather than the choice to absorb saving in one use as opposed to others. To assess whether the supply of saving in the aggregate increases with the interest rate, we must inquire as to why people save. Saving

Figure 7.1 Market for loanable funds

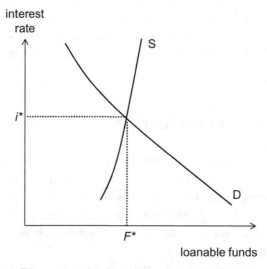

The market clearing interest rate equates the supply of loanable funds with the demand for loanable funds.

represents the sacrifice of current consumption for future consumption. A higher interest rate yields a higher payoff for deferred consumption, and that may well be enticing to some savers. For others, however, if saving is motivated by a desire to reach a particular goal – a comfortable retirement, the purchase of a big ticket item, a basic sense of security against the unknown – a higher interest rate would make the goal more easily attainable with lower saving. In principle, then, the supply curve could slope backward. Given the ambiguity, Figure 7.1 shows the aggregate saving function as highly inelastic, as supported by empirical evidence.

The demand for loanable funds reflects borrower expectations about the prospects for making a return on various investment opportunities. As the interest rate falls, more potential projects are seen as viable and the quantity of funds demanded increases. A given demand relationship rests on the assumption that all factors other than the interest rate remain constant. Any change in an exogenous factor causes the entire demand curve to shift. The demand for loanable funds is in fact prone to pronounced volatility. This is because the decision to borrow money and commit to an investment project hinges on expectations about the future. Crowd psychology tends to take over such expectations. During boom times, optimism prevails and the demand to borrow runs high. Graphically, the demand curve shifts to the right and the interest rate rises. But booms are prone to overreaching. In the retrenchment that ensues, investor sentiment succumbs to pessimism and the demand curve shifts left dragging the interest rate down. Even as interest rates approach a lower bound of zero, investors may feel limited desire to borrow.

While the notion of a single interest rate is analytically useful for some purposes in macroeconomics, the contours of the spectrum of rates can be telling for other purposes. The range of interest rates reflects differences in maturity and risk. The profile of interest rates associated with different maturities, which can extend from overnight to thirty years, is known as the *term structure* or *yield curve*. Normally, the yield curve rises as terms lengthen to reflect a premium paid to tie up funds and take on the greater uncertainty associated with a more distant future. Any expectation that inflation will increase will tilt the yield curve, as expressed in nominal terms, more steeply upward. In rare circumstances, the yield curve can become inverted meaning that short-term loans command higher interest rates than long-term loans. This pattern usually indicates fear of impending recession, which will increase the risk of loan default, perhaps combined with expectations of softening inflation.

The range of interest rates associated with perceived risk of borrower default is known as the *credit spread*. Credit spreads are prone to the psychology of boom and bust. In times of optimism and robust economic expansion, risk sensitivity relaxes and credit spreads narrow. Conversely, when the economy is in the doldrums and hopelessness prevails, risk sensitivity intensifies and credit spreads widen.

In emerging economies with immature financial systems, markets are not very effective in pricing risk. Nor do they generate a meaningful yield curve if trading across the range of maturities is not highly liquid. In such situations, financial markets show limited resonance with macroeconomic conditions. The dissociation is often compounded by government intervention in setting interest rates, sometimes coupled with outright assumption of bank ownership. Typically in such cases, governments repress interest rates and get involved in allocation of the resulting short supply of funds. This strategy is motivated by a possibly well-intentioned desire to lower the cost of public investment projects. The outcome, however, is that interest rates are neither fully responsive to macroeconomic conditions nor readily manipulated as policy instruments in macroeconomic management.

Relationship between Interest Rates and Asset Prices

The interest rate provides the link between present and future value. In the simplest application of this link, an asset currently valued at A that yields a rate of return i will be worth $A(1 + i)$ a year from now. Two years from now, it will be worth $A(1 + i)^2$, allowing for the compounding of interest.

In the reverse calculation, the *present value* of the stream of returns on an asset is derived by *discounting*. Letting R_1 represent a return on an asset to be yielded one year hence, the present value of the return is $A = R_1/(1 + i)$. A return to be yielded after two years, R_2, has a present value of $A = R_2/(1 + i)^2$. For a stream of annual returns extending to year t, where the final sum, R_t, includes the redemption value of the asset, the present value of the asset is given as:

$$A = \frac{R_1}{(1 + i)} + \frac{R_2}{(1 + i)^2} + \ldots + \frac{R_t}{(1 + i)^t}. \tag{7.1}$$

The interest rate in the above formula serves to discount, or capitalize, future receipts. The higher the interest rate, the steeper the trade-off between present and future. Discounting a given stream of future returns at a higher interest rate will result in a lower present value for the asset. Conversely, applying a lower interest rate means less differentiation between present and future resulting in a higher present value for given returns.

The relationship between interest rates and asset values may be illustrated with a bond. The face value of a bond is the amount to be paid at maturity, the coupon its annual interest payment. Consider a zero-coupon bond (meaning no payments are made until maturity) with a face value of $100 maturing in 10 years. At the time of issue, let the risk-appropriate market rate of interest be 6.0 percent. The current price of the bond is then $100/(1.06)^{10}$, or $55.84. If over the ensuing year the market interest rate remains constant, the price of the bond will rise to $59.19 = $100/(1.06)^9$ reflecting the shorter time to maturity. But suppose instead that the market interest rate rises to 7.5 percent. The price of the bond then drops to $52.16 = $100/(1.075)^9$. The increase in the interest rate results in steeper discounting to keep the price of the bond competitive with new bonds being issued with higher yields. In our example, this effect dominates the shortening of time till maturity. If the market interest rate had instead fallen, an existing bond issued at the previously higher interest rate would see its price rise. The risk that the price of a bond will fluctuate due to changes in market interest rates is known as *interest rate risk*.

Asset classes other than bonds are similarly subject to valuation changes in response to interest rate movements. In times of falling interest rates, asset values become generally buoyant. The couple of decades leading up to the Great Financial Crisis was such a time. This period saw real interest rates drop to unprecedented lows worldwide. Driving this, in the view of many observers including former chairman of the US Federal Reserve Alan Greenspan, was an abundance of global saving. Low inflation in economically important nations, and expectations that that would be sustained, also had a damping effect on interest rates in nominal terms. This stimulated a broad-based increase in asset values. Feeling wealthier, people in turn spent with enthusiasm. This powered a great economic boom. The concern must be, however, that when the inevitable return to more normal interest rates arrives, events will play out in reverse with asset values falling and spending contracting to the detriment of economic growth. Some analysts argue that with the passing of another decade of low interest rates subsequent to the Great Financial Crisis, asset prices have again become inflated and are destined for a fall.

F   Finance and the Macroeconomy

The financial system supports economic growth by channeling saving to investment. But beyond the static transfer of funds, the system generates new debt to drive dynamic increases in spending. This is achieved by banks making loans through the creation of new deposit money. Managing the pace of debt creation is a challenge. If debt grows too quickly, the additional spending can drive inflation. Inflation in product prices is readily monitored and gauged against a stable course. Increases in asset prices, however, are trickier to benchmark. The value of assets represents the discounted value of expected returns stretching into the distant future. Real factors, such as technological advance and globalization, can boost productivity to justify sustained increases in asset prices. But speculative fervor too can lift asset prices. And fueled by debt, a bubble can inflate, where a bubble by its nature must burst.

Finance is a pillar of growth but also a driver of volatility. Expansions are supported by new lending. Contractions are aggravated by a dearth of lending. Fluctuations up and down are amplified by the fickle nature of risk perception – that is, in booms the wildest gambles are imagined to pay off while in busts risk is seen as a danger to be avoided altogether. Monetary authorities attempt to rein in volatility through a combination of adjusting the monetary base and manipulating the ratio of deposit money to the monetary base. Nevertheless, financiers have proven adept at circumventing regulation when the boom is on and steadfast in hunkering down when boom turns to bust.

The economies of Emerging East Asia present particular vulnerabilities to financial instability. The Asian Financial Crisis demonstrated how quickly a crisis in one economy can spread across the region. The economies hit hardest showed similar weaknesses in their external debt profiles. But beyond the specifics of balance sheets, public perception is important in the timing and severity of a crisis, and perception is sensitive to circumstantial triggers. Changes in perception surrounding one economy can have a contagion effect. Greater openness to financial flows increases exposure to external shock even as it brings much in the way of benefit for economic development. Some economies in the region are already highly open to international capital flows, while others are moving in the direction of greater openness. The chapters that follow address the use of government policy to steer an economy along a steady course even when financial systems are open and impressionable.

We end this chapter with a take on finance in the broad sweep of human history. Box 7.3 presents the case that the innovations of paper money in the East and bonds in the West set the course for a fundamental divergence in the evolution of social structures and economic progress.

Box 7.3 The great divergence in finance

By one read of history, the great divergence in economic development between East and West traces to an early divergence in finance. Both regions gave rise to major financial innovations around the same time. In China the innovation was paper money in the 11th century, as detailed in Box 6.1. In Europe, it was bonds in the 12th century. For each region, the new financial instrument provided crucial support for waging war on a grand scale, and rebuilding in the aftermath. With that need met, the impetus to develop redundant mechanisms to serve the same purpose was seemingly forestalled. In neither region did the innovation of the other arrive until centuries later.

China under the Song Dynasty (960–1279) incurred a heavy financial burden defending its northern frontiers. Merchants who provisioned the garrisons were paid in government-issued paper notes, initially redeemable for coin by the cash-rich monopoly bureau. The northern region of the Song empire was eventually overrun by Jin invaders from the northeast, who themselves finally succumbed to the Mongols from the northwest. Holding its border cost the Song empire dearly. Wanton printing of money through the Song's waning decades resulted in severe debasement of the currency, leaving the conquering Mongols to start anew with their own currency upon consolidating the Yuan Dynasty (1272–1368). But the Mongols fell victim to the same temptation to pay their bills with excessive note issuance, until finally paper currency in China was debased to the point that it fell into obsolescence.

The Europeans took a different tack to finance their wars and reconstructions. In the 12th century, Italian city-states began borrowing from their citizenry. Initially the loans were voluntary, the wealthy being lured in by attractive interest rates. But as the need grew to fund wars against the Byzantines, the Turks, and each other, the city-states imposed bond purchase mandates on a broader populace at less compensatory rates of interest. The need thus arose for a secondary market for the unloading of bonds by unwilling buyers. The Venetians led the way in institutionalizing a system of negotiable bonds. Bond prices fluctuated with the state of war and peace, and the general degree of market confidence that obligations would be met.

Over the following few centuries bond financing became established routine for governments throughout Europe, although until the early 1800s the routine was

Box 7.3 (cont.)

limited to raising funds domestically in local currency. A new era was ushered in when the Rothschilds took the bond market international. With five brothers positioned each in a different country, the family was ideally situated to conduct financial business across borders. In the wake of the Napoleonic wars, European governments were in dire need of funds to pay off war debts in foreign currencies and recover from sovereign bankruptcy. The Rothschilds came to the rescue by launching an Austrian government bond in London that raised capital in British currency. In the years that followed, bonds would come to be issued simultaneously in multiple countries with interest payments collectible in a city of the bearer's convenience.

The development of bonds vs paper money may arguably have had far-reaching consequences. The bond finance of Europe significantly broadened access to capital and enabled the pricing and spreading of risk. This reoriented the nature of wealth and power away from a landed aristocracy to a much more mobile – geographically and socially – capitalist class. And this in turn put Europe on the road to industrial development. Economic life in China, meanwhile, was dominated by a landed gentry that held firmly to localized power. This kept it mired in subsistence agriculture.

Reference: Goetzmann and Rouwenhorst (2005).

Data Note

Data on financial assets in Chart 7.1 come from a variety of sources: for bank credit, the IMF International Financial Statistics database with Taiwan data from the Central Bank of the Republic of China (Taiwan); for stock market capitalization, the World Federation of Exchanges; and for debt securities, the Bank for International Settlements. Historical data on these and many other financial indicators have been aggregated by the World Bank in its Global Financial Development Database. Comparison figures for advanced economies reported in the text are from the Bank for International Settlements.

In support of bond market development in Asia, the Asian Development Bank offers a wealth of data and analysis through its website Asian Bonds Online. The data for bonds outstanding in Chart 7.2 and bond turnover in Chart 7.3 are drawn from this source.

Hong Kong stock and bond magnitudes referenced in Section D are from the World Federation of Exchanges.

The IMF has put out a *Global Financial Stability Report* since 2002, now semi-annually, that is also a useful source of data and insight. The estimates of bank losses associated with the Great Financial Crisis of 2008 are drawn from the report of April 2010 (p. 12).

Bibliographic Note

The claim that financial deepening supports economic development only up to a point finds support in an IMF study by Arcand et al. (2012). Also from the IMF, Goyal et al. (2011) argue that greater financial depth increases resilience against shocks. Taylor (2012) makes the case that excessively rapid growth in credit can be destabilizing.

An accessible account of how the USA spawned the Great Financial Crisis of 2008 and a few shrewd investors profited enormously from it may be found in Lewis (2010). A more technical analysis of the crisis is offered in Smith, Walter, and Delong (2012).

On Hong Kong finance, Ho, Scott, and Wong (2005) is of historical value while the website of the Hong Kong Monetary Authority provides contemporary information.

The role of finance in driving business cycles has been incisively articulated by Hyman Minsky (1986), whose argument is laid out more fully in Chapter 10.

BIBLIOGRAPHIC CITATIONS

Arcand, Jean-Louis, Enrico Berkes, and Ugo Panizza, 2012. *"Too Much Finance?" IMF Working Paper WP/12/161* (Washington, DC: International Monetary Fund).

Asian Development Bank, 2021. Asian Bonds Online. https://asianbondsonline.adb.org/data-portal/ (accessed August 20, 2021).

Bank for International Settlements, 2021. BIS Statistics Explorer. https://stats.bis.org/statx/srs/table/c1 (accessed August 14, 2021).

Central Bank of the Republic of China (Taiwan), 2021. Loans & Investments of Monetary Financial Institutions (by Property). www.cbc.gov.tw/public/data/Ebanking/ELOAN-N.xls (accessed August 13, 2021).

Financial Stability Board, Global Shadow Banking Monitoring Report 2012 (Basel, Switzerland: FSB).

Goetzmann, William N. and K. Geert Rouwenhorst (eds.), 2005. *The Origins of Value: The Financial Innovations That Created Modern Capital Markets* (New York: Oxford University Press). Of special note: Goetzmann and Rouwenhorst, "Introduction: Financial Innovations in History," pp. 3–16; Richard von Glahn, "The Origins of Paper Money in China," pp. 65–89; Luciano Pezzolo, "Bonds and Government Debt in Italian City-States," pp. 145–163; Niall Ferguson, "The First 'Eurobonds'," pp. 313–325.

Goyal, Rishi, Chris Marsh, Narayanan Raman, Shengzu Wang, and Swarnali Ahmed, 2011. "Financial Deepening and International Monetary Stability," IMF Staff Discussion Note, SDN/11/16.

Financial Stability Board, 2011. Shadow Banking: Scoping the Issues. www.fsb.org/2011/04/shadow-banking-scoping-the-issues/ (accessed January 25, 2022).

Greenspan, Alan, 2010. "The Crisis" (Washington, DC: Brookings). www.brookings.edu/~/media/Projects/BPEA/Spring%202010/2010a_bpea_greenspan.PDF (accessed November 20, 2013).

Ho, Simon S., Robert Haney Scott, and Kie Ann Wong, 2005. *The Hong Kong Financial System: A New Age*, 2nd edition (Hong Kong: Oxford University Press (China)).

Hong Kong Exchanges and Clearing Limited, 2021. Debt Securities. www.hkex.com.hk/Market-Data/Securities-Prices/Debt-Securities?sc_lang=en (accessed October 3, 2021).

Hong Kong Monetary Authority, 2012. Half-Yearly Monetary and Financial Stability Report, September 2012 (Hong Kong: Hong Kong Monetary Authority).

International Monetary Fund, 2004. Are Credit Booms in Emerging Markets a Concern? In *World Economic Outlook* (Washington, DC: IMF).

International Monetary Fund, 2010. Global Financial Stability Report, April 2010 (Washington, DC: IMF).

International Monetary Fund, 2021. International Financial Statistics database. https://data.imf.org/?sk=4C514D48-B6BA-49ED-8AB9–52B0C1A0179B&sId=1390030341854 (accessed August 13, 2021).

Lewis, Michael, 2010. *The Big Short: Inside the Doomsday Machine* (New York: W. W. Norton).

Minsky, Hyman, [1986] 2008. *Stabilizing an Unstable Economy* (New York: McGraw Hill).

Sheng, Andrew, 2012. "How to Develop Capital Markets in East Asia," in Masahiro Kawai and Andrew Sheng (eds.), *Capital Market Reform in Asia: Towards Developed and Integrated Markets in Times of Change* (New Delhi, India: SAGE Publications).

Taylor, Alan M., 2012. "The Great Leveraging," *NBER Working Paper 18290* (Cambridge, MA: National Bureau of Economic Research).

World Bank, 2012. Global Financial Development Report, 2013: Rethinking the Role of the State in Finance (Washington, DC: World Bank).

World Bank, 2021. Global Financial Development databank. https://databank.worldbank.org/reports.aspx?source=global-financial-development (accessed August 14, 2021).

World Economic Forum, 2012. The Financial Development Report, 2012 (New York: World Economic Forum USA).

World Federation of Exchanges, 2021. Statistics Portal. www.world-exchanges.org/ (accessed August 14, 2021).

8 Exchange Rates

Exchange rate management is a salient feature of the economies of Emerging East Asia. to varying degrees. At one extreme, Hong Kong maintains a hard peg to the US dollar. At the other, exchange rate regimes classified by the International Monetary Fund as "floating," but not "free floating," are followed by Indonesia, Korea, Malaysia, the Philippines, and Thailand. One way or another, however, market forces hold ultimate sway.

An exchange rate is the price of one currency expressed in terms of another. Left entirely to market forces, exchange rates can be highly volatile. The US dollar, the euro, and the yen – the world's most highly traded free floating currencies – can move relative to one another by as much as a couple of percent in a single day. With the onset of the Great Financial Crisis in October 2008, the dollar appreciated by 12 percent relative to the euro in one month. Such volatility creates great uncertainty for conducting international business and seriously increases the risk of borrowing in a foreign currency for any entity that must rely on local currency earnings to fund repayment. To damp down volatility and manage the movement of exchange rates, central banks in Emerging East Asia intervene in foreign exchange markets by buying and selling currencies.

To lay a foundation for understanding this market intervention, we devote most of this chapter to developing the extreme cases of floating and fixed (or pegged) exchange rates. With a grasp of these polar cases, we can make sense of how and why a hybrid approach may be implemented. We begin the chapter with a basic lesson in foreign exchange market mechanics wherein demand and supply emanate from underlying balance of payments flows. The basics in place, we look at measures of market activity and exchange rate movement. From there, we lay out a scheme for classifying the degree of central bank intervention and consider the placement of our 13 economies within this scheme. Regardless of the type of exchange rate regime adopted, market forces will tend to bring about balance in international payments. Under a free floating regime, the adjustment mechanism works directly through the market clearing behavior of the exchange rate. Under a fixed rate regime, the process is indirect, driven by central bank purchases and sales of foreign currency in turn affecting real output and the price level such that the entire economy moves to maintain balance. The core of the chapter lays out this process. Indonesia provides the case study, the exchange rate offering a lens through which to view the country's experiences with global capital flows. We conclude by advancing general principles for the management of intermediate exchange rate regimes and foreshadowing implications for the conduct of monetary policy, a line of discussion to be resumed in Chapter 11.

A   Foreign Exchange Market Mechanics

An exchange rate is a price in the market for a currency. Let us focus in this chapter on the market for US dollars, and consider the pricing of US dollars in a variety of other currencies as the purpose suits. The basic mechanics of supply and demand apply as in any other market. Of particular note in the trading of currencies is the relationship of supply and demand to underlying balance of payments flows. We walk through the principles, first in the case of a floating exchange rate, for which we will use the Japanese yen as the pricing currency, then in the case of a fixed exchange rate, for which we will use the Chinese renminbi as the pricing currency.

Floating Rates

The US dollar and the Japanese yen are both free floating currencies with the exchange rate between them determined entirely by market forces. Figure 8.1 depicts the market for dollars priced in yen. The market clearing equilibrium exchange rate is given by e^*. The supply of

Figure 8.1 Market for dollars priced in yen

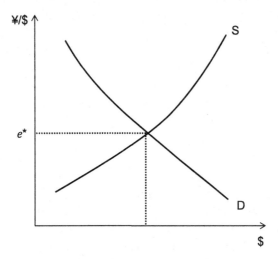

The yen to dollar exchange rate is determined in the market for dollars priced in yen.

and demand for dollars in terms of yen rest on underlying purchases and sales as captured in Japan's balance of payments.

Specifically, the supply of dollars into Japan's foreign exchange market derives from:

- Japanese exports to the USA;
- purchase of Japanese assets by Americans;
- sale of assets held in the USA by Japanese.

When a Japanese exporter sells a product to the USA, payment is received in dollars which the exporter supplies to the foreign exchange market to obtain yen. Similarly, to acquire Japanese assets, an American supplies dollars on the foreign exchange market to obtain the yen needed to carry out the purchase. Finally, when a Japanese sells a US asset, they convert the dollars back into yen by supplying them on the foreign exchange market. All of these transactions involve credits (or money inflows) on Japan's balance of payments. (For completeness, let us subsume in exports the services of labor and capital and note further than inbound unilateral transfers also enter the supply of dollars.)

Symmetrically, the demand for dollars derives from:

- Japanese imports from the USA;
- purchases of US assets by Japanese;
- sale of assets held in Japan by Americans.

When a Japanese importer purchases products from the USA, payment is made in US dollars which the importer demands on the foreign exchange market. Similarly, to purchase US assets, a Japanese demands dollars on the foreign exchange market to support the transaction. Finally, the sale of Japanese assets by an American results in a demand for dollars to repatriate the funds. All these transactions involve debits (or money outflows) on Japan's balance of payments. (Again for completeness, imports subsume factor services and outbound unilateral transfers.)

An increase in any of the exogenous determinants of the supply of dollars will shift the supply curve to the right, as shown in Figure 8.2. This increase in supply results in a depreciation of the dollar, meaning a dollar will purchase fewer yen. Conversely, the yen appreciates in that fewer yen are required to buy a dollar. The depreciation of the dollar brings about a rightward movement along the demand curve. This is because as dollars become cheaper, Japanese are induced to buy more dollars in order to take advantage of better deals on imports and US assets, and Americans are motivated to sell off Japanese assets and repatriate the returns. Thus, at the new lower price of a dollar, the quantity of dollars demanded increases to meet the increase in supply.

An increase in any of the exogenous determinants of demand will shift the demand curve to the right, as shown in Figure 8.3. The shift in demand results in an appreciation of the dollar (depreciation of the yen), which induces a rightward movement along the supply curve. Thus in response to the increase in demand for dollars, a rising value of the dollar brings more dollars into the market as Japanese exports rise, more Americans buy

Figure 8.2 Increase in supply of dollars

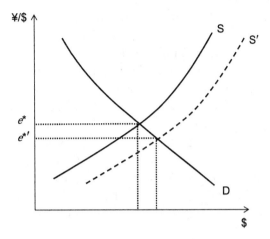

An increase in the supply of dollars results in a depreciation of the dollar (appreciation of the yen).

Figure 8.3 Increase in demand for dollars

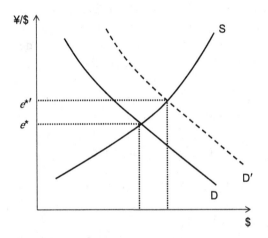

An increase in the demand for dollars results in an appreciation of the dollar (depreciation of the yen).

Japanese assets, and more Japanese sell off American assets which are now more valuable relative to Japanese assets. The quantity of dollars supplied thus rises to meet the increase in demand.

This analysis of market mechanics could be carried out inversely with respect to the market for yen priced in dollars, and the same conclusions about currency appreciation or depreciation would follow. In the market for yen priced in dollars, the demand for yen reflects the supply of dollars while the supply of yen reflects the demand for dollars. ·Determinants of the demand and supply of yen then trace to underlying flows on the US balance of payments. An increase in the supply of dollars that causes depreciation of the dollar relative to the yen now becomes an increase in the demand for yen that causes appreciation in the yen relative to the dollar. These are two different ways of expressing the same thing.

An important insight to be emphasized in this analysis is that a shock to one element of the balance of payments will work through the exchange rate to bring about offsetting adjustments elsewhere in the balance of payments. Under a floating exchange rate (meaning the central bank does not intervene in the market) the balance of payments must balance, with equilibration in the foreign exchange market at the heart of this balancing process. An exogenous increase in a credit entry in an economy's balance of payments will put upward pressure on the value of its currency inducing domestic residents to spend more on foreign goods or assets (or foreign residents to withdraw their investment funds) for a matching increase in debits. This principle is nicely illustrated by the phenomenon of "Dutch disease" as explained in Box 8.1 with an application to the Philippines.

Box 8.1 Dutch disease, Philippine style

The term "Dutch disease" was coined in reference to a decline in manufacturing in the Netherlands brought on by a boom in natural gas exports that followed a new discovery of offshore reserves in 1959. The increased demand for Dutch guilders to support foreign purchases of natural gas drove up the guilder's value. This undermined the competitiveness of the Netherlands' manufacturing sector causing the country's exports of manufactures to decline and its imports to rise. In effect, the Dutch could export natural gas in exchange for manufactured goods more cheaply than they could produce such goods domestically given the opportunity cost of economic resources drawn into production of natural gas as well as non-traded goods and services.

"Dutch disease" has come to be applied to any situation in which a particularly robust export crowds out domestic production of other traded goods. For the Philippines, the term has been invoked in connection with the deployment of vast numbers of overseas Filipino workers. By 2019, 2.2 million Filipinos – more than 5 percent of the labor force – were working overseas. These overseas workers send home remittances that generate a demand for Philippine pesos, driving up the currency's value. This in turn makes imports of manufactured goods cheap for Filipinos relative to the cost of domestic production. The Philippines has an exceptionally small manufacturing sector for its level of per capita income, with Dutch disease, resulting from the strong export of labor services, being one reason why.

The phenomenon of Dutch disease illustrates the broader principle of the role of the exchange rate in bringing about balance in international payments. For a country to export more of something, an offsetting adjustment must occur. Either the country must export less of something else or import more of something, or see realignments on the financial account. These adjustments happen automatically through the price mechanism, resting on the exchange rate.

Fixed Rates

Under a fixed exchange rate, the central bank intervenes in the foreign exchange market to block the exchange rate from responding to market forces, thereby forcing a deficit or surplus in the balance of payments. The exchange rate of the renminbi relative to the US dollar has been maintained for periods of varying duration at both overvalued and undervalued levels, so let us use this currency for illustration purposes.

Consider first the case of renminbi undervaluation, shown in Figure 8.4. The exchange rate is pegged at $\bar{e}$ such that more renminbi are required to buy a dollar than at the market clearing level. This undervaluation of the renminbi means the price of a dollar is inflated. Under such circumstances, the quantity of dollars supplied exceeds the quantity demanded. The resulting surplus of dollars must be purchased by the Chinese central bank for $\bar{e}$ to be sustained. The central bank consequently accumulates foreign reserves with associated purchase of foreign assets showing up on the Chinese balance of payments as outflows, or debits. Elsewhere in the balance of payments, accommodation occurs to preserve overall balance of payments surplus. The most obvious and politically sensitive accommodation has taken the form of large surpluses on the Chinese trade account (discussed in Chapter 5) as the undervalued renminbi boosted exports and diminished imports.

In late 2014, market conditions changed radically so as to transform the former surplus on the foreign exchange market at $\bar{e}$ into a shortage. The situation is depicted as renminbi overvaluation at the peg in Figure 8.5. Under the new conditions, the quantity of dollars demanded exceeded the quantity supplied, with the central bank thus having to sell dollars into the foreign exchange market to maintain the peg. The change in circumstances resulted from a turn in the preferences of creditors and debtors that induced sizable net outflows on the financial account. Graphically, this is represented as some combination of a leftward shift in the supply of dollars and a rightward shift in the demand relative to the positions

Figure 8.4 Undervaluation of the renminbi

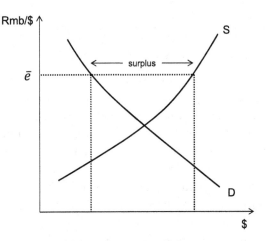

Undervaluation of the Rmb under an exchange rate peg results in foreign exchange surpluses and Chinese accumulation of official reserves.

Figure 8.5 Overvaluation of the renminbi

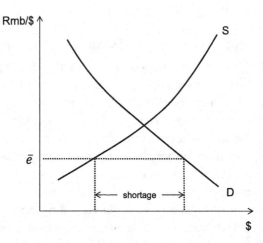

Overvaluation of the Rmb under an exchange rate peg results in foreign exchange shortages and Chinese decumulation of official reserves.

shown in Figure 8.4. The resulting balance of payments deficit at $\bar{e}$ was met with an offsetting credit in the form of central bank decumulation of reserve assets. More simply put, money wanted to move out of China at a faster rate than it was moving in, so the central bank had to satisfy this excess demand for dollars.

The 2014 experience was not China's first time contending with an overvalued renminbi. The era of reform and opening began on just such a footing in the 1980s. Under the relatively closed command economy of that time, however, the method for managing the overvaluation involved administrative means rather than central bank intervention. As generally tends to be the case under administered price controls, however, the market had a way of reasserting itself. Box 8.2 tells the story.

Box 8.2 Foreign currency black markets

The management of currency overvaluation discussed in connection with Figure 8.5 pertains to an economy with reasonably open trade flows. The case of contemporary China fits the bill. The China of the 1980s, however, was quite a different place. Back then, the government maintained tight controls on foreign trade. Exporters were required to remit their foreign exchange earnings which planners then allocated to chosen import uses, all at an exchange rate that left dollars in short supply. Yet there was no need for the central bank to step in and sell reserves to meet the excess demand at the peg. Prospective importers who were not in the government's favor simply had to do without.

The advantage of the system was that the government could make foreign exchange available for its priority uses – such as capital goods imports to serve state

Box 8.2 (cont.)

development objectives – at very low cost. The justification for this arrangement was that the government knew better than private agents which imports were good for society. An argument along these lines was particularly compelling for a country just emerging from decades of isolation and charting a gradual course of reintegration with global markets.

A disadvantage of the system, however, was that incentives to generate foreign exchange through exports were quashed by government expropriation of earnings on unfavorable terms. A further disadvantage was that the system could only remain viable as long as tight controls on market activity were maintained. Otherwise, those with access to foreign exchange would find that they could do much better selling through private channels than to the government. Indeed, in the Chinese case a very active black market in US dollars developed by the late 1980s. Shopkeepers in Beijing eagerly offered twice the official rate to passing foreigners and could without batting an eye change thousands of dollars at a pop. These transactions, however, involved counting huge wads of small denomination renminbi notes, so woe to the unwitting foreigner who might be duped by a sleight of hand.

China's gradual approach to reform was hastened along by the problems unleashed by black markets in foreign currency and other rationed goods. Those with privileged access at below market prices were very often government officials whom the public perceived to be making out like bandits from arbitraging the partially reformed economy. The situation ultimately became untenable. In January 1994, the Rmb was officially devalued by 33 percent, and the black market largely disappeared.

B   Measuring Market Activity and Exchange Rate Movement

Foreign exchange trading, at the wholesale level, takes place on electronic platforms among banks and other dealers scattered around the world. The size and structure of the foreign exchange market is gauged by the Bank for International Settlements (BIS) through a survey conducted every three years, the most recent round taking place in 2019 with nearly 1300 dealers covered. We begin this section with a look at the magnitudes of trading by instrument, location, and currency. We then introduce measures of exchange rate movement over time to be applied in Section E with the case study of Indonesia.

Market Turnover

Most foreign exchange trading involves three traditional types of instruments with newer derivative products occupying a small space. The traditional instruments are: spot trades;

outright forwards; and forex swaps. A spot trade between two currencies takes place at the current market price and is settled within two business days. An outright forward involves agreement to trade at a specified rate with settlement to be completed at a given date in the future. A forex (or FX) swap combines a spot trade with a forward trade such that each party obtains funds in the other's currency temporarily, but ultimately reverts back to holding the original currency. Derivatives are instruments that derive value from an underlying asset. They involve agreement to make payment based on future valuations without any actual trading of currencies taking place. Types of derivatives include futures, currency swaps, currency options, and non-deliverable forwards.

Daily turnover magnitudes by type of instrument are shown in Chart 8.1 for the period 2001–2019 at the three year intervals of the BIS survey. By 2019, total turnover on foreign exchange markets exceeded US$6 trillion **per day**. To appreciate the enormity of this figure, let us draw some comparisons. The total value of transactions on all the world's stock markets in 2016 was US$61 trillion for the **full year**. In other words, in just 10 trading days the turnover in foreign exchange markets surpassed annual trading volume on global stock markets. As another comparison, world merchandise trade for the full year of 2019 amounted to about US$19 trillion, equivalent to about three days worth of foreign exchange turnover. Clearly a lot more is involved in foreign exchange trading than support of international trade transactions.

Total market turnover is seen in the chart to have risen sharply over time through 2013, with a decline then visible in 2016. This seeming decline may be an artifact of the April timing of the survey, which in 2013 coincided with a surge in trading due to monetary policy developments in Japan. Abstracting from a likely non-representative observation for 2013, foreign exchange trading has followed a strong upward trajectory over time.

The largest share of foreign exchange market turnover has been associated with FX swaps, with this pattern consistent over time. In essence, an FX swap allows each transacting

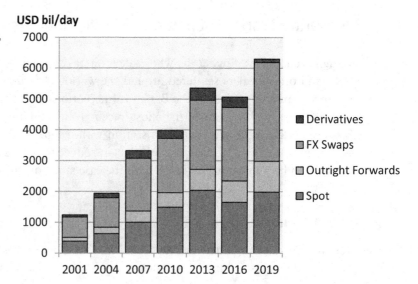

Chart 8.1 Foreign exchange market turnover by instrument, 2001–2019

party to borrow in a foreign currency while simultaneously lending in the home currency. This facilitates conducting business in a foreign currency or taking a short-term investment position in that foreign currency while hedging against the risk of exchange rate fluctuations. At an agreed upon date in the future, the parties will convert their funds back to their respective home currencies at a predetermined exchange rate. The next largest share of foreign exchange market turnover is associated with spot transactions, with outright forwards accounting for a much smaller share.

Foreign exchange turnover is highly skewed by both location and currency, as Table 8.1 shows. The UK had a dominant position in foreign exchange trading with 43.1 percent of turnover booked there in 2019. The US share was a big step down from that at 16.5 percent. The next three largest markets were in Asia – Singapore, Hong Kong, and Japan. Combined, their share reached 19.8 percent. Other Asian economies had much smaller forex markets.

Among currencies, the US dollar dominated, entering 88.3 percent of all trades (where since two currencies enter each trade, the share total comes to 200 percent). The euro was next with a 32.3 percent share, followed by the yen with 16.8 percent. The next Asian currency in the ranking was the renminbi in eighth place with a 4.3 percent share, which while still small was nearly double the 2.2 percent share shown in the 2013 survey. The Hong Kong dollar followed close behind at 3.5 percent. Other Asian currencies had shares of less than two percent.

Table 8.1 Foreign exchange market ranking and shares, select economies, 2019

By Location			By Currency		
1	United Kingdom	43.1%	1	US dollar	88.3%
2	United States	16.5	2	euro	32.3
3	Singapore	7.7	3	Japanese yen	16.8
4	Hong Kong	7.6	4	British pound	12.8
5	Japan	4.5	5	Australian dollar	6.8
6	Switzerland	2.8	6	Canadian dollar	5.0
7	France	2.0	7	Swiss franc	5.0
8	China	1.6	8	Chinese renminbi	4.3
9	Germany	1.5	9	Hong Kong dollar	3.5
10	Australia	1.4	12	Korean won	2.0
15	Korea	0.7	13	Singapore dollar	1.8
23	Taiwan	0.4	21	Taiwan dollar	0.9
30	Thailand	0.2	24	Thai baht	0.5
31	Malaysia	0.1	25	Indonesian rupiah	0.4
38	Indonesia	0.1	30	Philippine peso	0.3
43	Philippines	<0.1	34	Malaysian ringgit	0.1

Note: Includes spot, forward, and swap markets. Shares by currency sum to 200% since two currencies are involved in each trade.

The outsized share of the US dollar is due to its role in intermediating exchanges between other currencies given the high degree of liquidity in US dollar trades for most currencies. For example, a trade of Thai baht for Korean won would generally proceed with a trade of baht for dollars followed by a trade of dollars for won. Relative to 2013, the US dollar gained market share as did many emerging market currencies, while the euro and the yen lost share.

Real and Nominal Effective Exchange Rates

Thus far our attention has been limited to bilateral exchange rates. This is a narrow measure of the value of a currency against one other currency. A broader measure that captures the value of a currency against a basket of other currencies is known as an *effective exchange rate*. For a currency that is tightly managed relative to the US dollar, a bilateral exchange rate with respect to the dollar would give the appearance of being very stable over time. However, since the dollar itself can fluctuate greatly relative to other currencies, such appearance of stability would be misleading in a broader sense.

The nominal effective exchange rate (NEER) is calculated as the weighted sum of any number of bilateral exchange rates between one currency and the others. The weights are typically taken as shares in trade between the reference economy and the economies represented by the other currencies. The NEER is measured as an index with respect to a baseline year which is assigned a value of 100. A rising value of the NEER indicates nominal appreciation of a currency, a declining value, depreciation.

A currency can be stable in nominal terms and still move relative to other currencies in real terms if inflation in the home country differs from that in economies in the basket. Suppose, for example, that Indonesia's inflation rate were higher than the norm among its basket partners. Given a constant NEER and rising domestic prices, a rupiah would buy more in real terms in the international market than on the domestic market. In real terms, then, the rupiah would have appreciated given its rising relative purchasing power internationally. To construct a real effective exchange rate (REER), the value of each currency is deflated by the domestic price index. A rising value of the REER indicates appreciation of a currency in real terms, a declining value, depreciation.

C   Exchange Rate Determination

We have established that under floating exchange rate regimes, market forces determine exchange rates and that market supply and demand in turn derive from underlying balance of payments flows. But what drives those underlying balance of payments flows? For the trade account, the guiding principle is purchasing power parity. For the financial account, it is interest parity, where forward looking rates of return hinge on expectations – with all their subjectivity and caprice. In this section we discuss these market-based determinants of exchange rates, then consider the role of exchange rate regime in the outcome.

Market Factors

The cornerstone of exchange rate theory historically was the principle of *purchasing power parity* (PPP). The PPP principle rests on the law of one price, which holds that an item must sell for the same price on all markets. The logic is that arbitrage will eliminate any price differentials: as arbitrageurs buy on the cheaper market to sell on the more expensive market, the price is driven up on the former and down on the latter until prices in the two markets converge. The PPP principle applies this argument across different currencies to hold that a given currency must have the same purchasing power as in the home market when converted to another currency to be spent in a foreign market. For the Indonesian case, the price of a basket of goods domestically given in rupiah, P_{IDR}, should equal the price of the same basket of goods on international markets given in US dollars, P_{USD}, times the exchange rate of rupiah to dollars, $e_{IDR/USD}$, or equivalently, the exchange rate should equal the ratio of the basket prices:

$$e_{IDR/USD} = \frac{P_{IDR}}{P_{USD}}. \tag{8.1}$$

How well is the PPP principle supported in practice? Clearly the principle is meant to abstract from transportation and other transaction costs, which can be appreciable internationally, not to mention the impact of tariffs, quotas, and other administrative barriers to trade. These qualifications leave room for substantial divergence between the domestic and foreign purchasing power of a currency at market exchange rates. Broadly speaking though, we do observe that domestic price inflation higher than that in the USA tends to raise an economy's exchange rate relative to the US dollar such that purchasing power parity is preserved. In other words, as more units of a currency are needed to buy goods domestically, more units are also needed to buy the dollars needed to purchase goods on foreign markets, consistent with the PPP principle. Even so, the volatility of exchange rates far exceeds the volatility of relative price levels across economies, and the PPP principle does not account for this. Something else must be at work.

The PPP principle confines attention to trade flows on the balance of payments, which was a reasonable focus historically for understanding exchange rate determination. In modern times, however, financial flows play a major role in driving demands and supplies in foreign exchange markets. The principle that applies to explaining the effect of financial flows on exchange rates is *interest parity*. To develop a theory of interest parity, we must consider not simply a one-time flow of funds in the present, but prospective rates of return in two different currencies and the repatriation of funds in the future. Achieving parity through arbitrage will therefore depend on the simultaneous joint equilibration of the current exchange rate, the expected rate of return in the home currency, the expected rate of return in the foreign currency, and the expected future exchange rate. With expectations on so many variables involved in a world fraught with uncertainty, the potential for exchange rate volatility is obvious.

Investors pursuing a higher expected rate of return in a foreign currency may guarantee the future exchange rate at which they convert funds back to the home currency by purchasing a forex swap. Market expectations about the future movement of one currency relative to another will be formally priced into the swap contract. Arbitrage will drive markets to a joint equilibrium for the spot rate, the forward rate, and rates of return in the two currencies such that parity is achieved. The outcome when a forex swap is incorporated into the process is known as *covered interest parity*. *Uncovered interest parity* involves a spot conversion of funds that is not hedged by a forward contract. In the uncovered context, the expected future exchange rate is an implicit element of the equilibration process. Either way, whether the future exchange rate is explicitly or implicitly reflected, the actions of investors will push rates of return into alignment across currencies.

Let us consider an example involving covered interest arbitrage between the Japanese yen and the US dollar. Assume rates of return are in real terms and compensation for any market risk differential is netted out. Take a situation where the expected rate of return from purchasing a forex swap of JPY for USD and holding a USD bond exceeds the expected rate of return from holding a JPY bond. Specifically, suppose the interest rate is 4.0 percent a year on the USD bond versus 1.0 percent on the JPY bond and that the forward discount on the USD with respect to the JPY is 2.0 percent a year (meaning the USD is expected to depreciate by 2.0 percent relative to the JPY). The covered interest arbitrage margin is then $4\% - 1\% - 2\% = 1\% > 0$. There is money to be made by converting JPY to USD and investing in USD. As investors take advantage of this opportunity, markets respond. The ramifications are as follows:

spot selling of JPY, buying of USD $\Rightarrow$ JPY depreciates, USD appreciates;
funds move from JPY to USD bonds $\Rightarrow$ interest rates rise on JPY bonds, fall on USD bonds;
buying of JPY forwards in USD $\Rightarrow$ USD forward discount widens.

On all counts then, the arbitrage opportunity is diminished: the USD becomes more costly in JPY terms; the rate of return falls on USD bonds relative to that on JPY bonds; and future conversion of USD to JPY becomes less favorable. These forces conspire to bring the spot exchange rate into equilibrium in conjunction with the forward exchange rate and rates of interest in the two economies.

Transactions costs and other market frictions impede the perfect equating of expected rates of return across markets. And a constant barrage of disturbances to expectations, and to a host of other market influences, ensures that equilibration is always a work in progress. These qualifications notwithstanding, a basic conclusion emerges from the principle of interest parity: an increase in domestic interest rates, *ceteris paribus*, tends to bring about appreciation of an economy's currency, and a decrease in interest rates, a depreciation.

A final point is worth noting. Independent of expectations about domestic rates of return, expectations about the future direction of exchange rate movements can themselves drive market valuations. If investors broadly get the notion that the value of a currency is going to rise, they will move to acquire that currency, and this will in and of itself drive up the currency's value. Expectations can be self-fulfilling, at least in the short run. Longer term, however, the fundamentals of parity in purchasing power and real rates of return tend to prevail.

Table 8.2 Exchange rate arrangement, select economies, 2020

Exchange Rate Arrangement		Economies	
Hard Peg	no separate legal tender	13	
	currency board	11	Hong Kong
Soft Peg	conventional peg	41	
	stabilized arrangement	23	Vietnam
	crawling peg	3	
	crawl-like arrangement	23	Cambodia Laos Singapore
	other managed	15	China Myanmar
Floating	floating	32	Indonesia Korea Malaysia Philippines [Taiwan] Thailand
	free floating	31	
Total		192	

Exchange Rate Regimes

A market-based exchange rate functions to reconcile trade and financial flows on an economy's balance of payments. Yet left to their own devices, market forces can produce a great deal of unwelcome volatility in exchange rates. For the 13 economies within our scope, central bank intervention in foreign exchange markets is geared toward moderating this volatility to varying degrees.

The International Monetary Fund conducts an annual review of member economies to classify their exchange rate arrangements according to the degree of government intervention in the foreign exchange market. The three broad categories are defined as: hard peg; soft peg; and floating. Within each of these categories, more refined sub-categories are specified. The classification of our economies of interest for 2020 is presented in Table 8.2. Hong Kong is the only one with a hard peg. Those with floating – but not free floating – arrangements are Indonesia, Korea, Malaysia, the Philippines, and Thailand. Taiwan is seemingly a fit for this category as well, although it does not come under IMF classification.[1] Our remaining six economies have soft pegs of various sorts.

[1] A statement on the website of the Central Bank of the Republic of China (Taiwan) describes exchange rate policy in this way: Since 1979, "the NT dollar exchange rate has been determined by the market. However, when the market is disrupted by seasonal or irregular factors, the Bank will step in."

Of note, the two most open economies with the most highly developed financial sectors – Hong Kong and Singapore – do not maintain floating exchange rates. Hence there should be no foregone conclusion that a more open, market-based economy must necessarily adhere to a floating exchange rate. Indeed, balance of payments adjustment does not require a floating exchange rate. An alternative mechanism exists for bringing about balance in international payments under a fixed exchange rate, as explained in Section D of this chapter.

Of the 192 economies classified in 2020, 31 adopted free floating exchange rates. The world's most traded currencies – the US dollar, the euro, and the yen – are all free floating. Indeed, the magnitudes of trading for these three currencies effectively preclude central bank influence over their valuations. Another 32 economies maintained floating (but not free floating) exchange rate regimes. Thus, close to a third of IMF member economies maintained floating exchange rates, broadly defined. At the opposite extreme, 24 economies adopted hard pegs, with 13 of these not issuing their own legal tender but rather making use of a currency issued elsewhere, most commonly by the USA, a phenomenon known as dollarization.

Many considerations – some idiosyncratic by economy – enter into the choice of an exchange rate regime. Hong Kong adopted its system in 1983 after a period of high inflation had seriously undermined confidence not only in the currency but in Hong Kong's economy generally. Pegging the Hong Kong dollar to the US dollar was a way to restore confidence and maintain it through the transition from British colonial rule to absorption into the People's Republic of China. Under its currency board system, the Hong Kong Monetary Authority commits to buying or selling currency at a fixed rate of 7.8 Hong Kong dollars to one US dollar. The Hong Kong monetary base is thereby fully backed by US dollar reserves, and monetary policy is entirely subordinated to maintaining the peg. In justifying this choice, the Hong Kong Monetary Authority explains that the system "plays an important role in supporting Hong Kong as a leading international trading, services and financial centre." There need be no worries on the part of market participants about discretion or political pressure entering into exchange rate determination or monetary policy. Transparency reigns.

By contrast, Singapore follows a model with full latitude for discretion and minimal disclosure. Nevertheless, market confidence in Singapore as a global financial center is solid. The Monetary Authority of Singapore manages the Singapore dollar exchange rate against a basket of currencies. In so doing, it pursues an objective "to promote price stability as a sound basis for sustainable economic growth." The Authority sets a band within which the basket exchange rate is allowed to fluctuate and a path along which that band is held to track. In normal times, the parameters of the system are revised every six months, but early reassessment may take place as needed. Public statements regarding basket composition and weights, boundaries on the band, and trajectory of the path are kept deliberately vague so as to deter speculation. If, for example, it were transparent to speculators that the Singapore dollar had breached the Authority's upper bound, they would rush to sell the currency short which could trigger an unduly sharp fall.

China's exchange rate management has come under fire from the USA and other western countries. In the mid-2000s, China's trade surplus ballooned to reach nearly nine percent of GDP (discussed in Chapter 5, Section C), yet the Chinese central bank resisted the renminbi appreciation needed to restrain exports and encourage imports. A case can be made that the central bank was steering a course of long-run exchange rate stability, holding the line against medium-term pressure to appreciate so as to guard against renminbi overvaluation and pressure for depreciation in the more distant future. Indeed, in 2014–2015 the renminbi did come under pressure to depreciate, to which the central bank responded with a massive sell-off of foreign currency to preserve stability. China's adaptive approach to exchange rate management has had it moving about within the IMF classification system, coming under "other managed arrangement" as of 2020, but at times in recent years bringing it under "crawl-like arrangement" or "stabilized arrangement."

Intervention in the foreign exchange market is practiced to some degree by all 13 of the economies within our purview. Indeed, it is practiced by the vast majority of economies in the world. Of the 192 economies categorized in 2020, 161, or 84 percent, followed exchange rate regimes other than "free floating." The choice of regime embodies a trade-off between containing exchange rate volatility and allowing flexibility for quick rebalancing of international payments in response to shocks. We analyze the alternative adjustment processes in the next section.

D Balance of Payments Adjustment

Exchange rate movement absorbs the impact of shocks to the balance of payments and induces offsetting adjustments elsewhere. Under floating exchange rates, the balancing of international payments is ensured through market equilibration – the demand for foreign exchange, associated with debits on the balance of payments, is matched with the supply of foreign exchange, associated with credits. Under fixed exchange rates as well, a balancing mechanism exists, but it involves adjustment of the entire macroeconomy. In this section, we begin by laying out the mechanics of balance of payments adjustment under a fixed exchange rate focusing first on forces that work through the trade account channel of the balance of payments. We then compare adjustment processes under fixed and floating exchange rates considering both trade and financial account channels.

Adjustment under a Fixed Rate: Trade Account Channel

To maintain a fixed exchange rate, a central bank intervenes in the foreign exchange market, buying foreign currency in the case of excess supply and selling it in the case of excess demand. In buying foreign currency the central bank issues domestic currency thus expanding the monetary base; and vice versa, in selling foreign currency the central bank buys up domestic currency and thus shrinks the monetary base. These changes in the monetary base set in motion impulses to credit availability in the commercial banking system that in turn impact real output and the price level for the economy. This ultimately feeds back into the balance of payments to bring about the adjustment necessary to eliminate excess supply or demand in the foreign exchange market.

Let us walk through the process using Indonesia as an example. The steps are outlined with graphical representation in Box 8.3. Consider first a shock that results in a surplus on the balance of payments. This could derive from any number of causes: an increase in foreign demand for Indonesia's exports; a slowdown in Indonesian growth that undermines domestic demand for imports; an increase in world oil prices that boosts Indonesia's revenues from exports; a decline in US interest rates that drives investors to search for return in emerging markets. Any of these would increase credits relative to debits and push the balance of payments toward surplus.

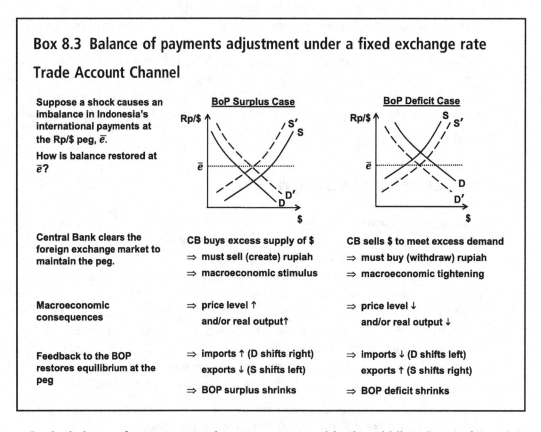

Box 8.3 Balance of payments adjustment under a fixed exchange rate

Trade Account Channel

Suppose a shock causes an imbalance in Indonesia's international payments at the Rp/$ peg, $\bar{e}$. How is balance restored at $\bar{e}$?	*BoP Surplus Case*	*BoP Deficit Case*
Central Bank clears the foreign exchange market to maintain the peg.	CB buys excess supply of $ ⇒ must sell (create) rupiah ⇒ macroeconomic stimulus	CB sells $ to meet excess demand ⇒ must buy (withdraw) rupiah ⇒ macroeconomic tightening
Macroeconomic consequences	⇒ price level ↑ and/or real output↑	⇒ price level ↓ and/or real output ↓
Feedback to the BOP restores equilibrium at the peg	⇒ imports ↑ (D shifts right) exports ↓ (S shifts left) ⇒ BOP surplus shrinks	⇒ imports ↓ (D shifts left) exports ↑ (S shifts right) ⇒ BOP deficit shrinks

In the balance of payments surplus case represented in the middle column of Box 8.3, the shock results in an excess supply of dollars in the foreign exchange market at the rupiah to dollar peg, $\bar{e}$, given initial supply, S, and demand, D, represented with solid curves. To maintain the peg, the central bank must purchase this excess supply of dollars. To do so, the central bank issues rupiah, which increases the monetary base in the form of reserves held by commercial banks at the central bank. Note that the central bank balance sheet expands by the amount of this transaction with an increase in official foreign reserves on the asset side and an increase in commercial bank deposits plus any currency leakages on the liability side. The increase in commercial bank reserves puts the commercial banks in a position to expand their lending. The increase in bank lending in turn supports growth in investment and consumption that boosts aggregate demand and stimulates the economy. This feeds into rising prices and growth in real output in some combination depending on the state of the output gap. (For a review of this process, see Chapter 6 on money.)

Both rising domestic prices and expanding real output have implications for the balance of payments. As domestic prices rise, foreign goods become cheaper relative to domestic goods at the pegged exchange rate. In real terms, the rupiah appreciates even as its value relative to the US dollar is fixed in nominal terms. This causes Indonesia's imports to rise and exports to fall, a phenomenon known as *expenditure switching* that pertains to a shift in demand between the home market and the foreign market. The increase in imports adds to debits on the balance of payments causing a shift in the demand for dollars to the right. At the same time, the decrease in exports reduces credits on the balance of payments causing a shift in the supply of dollars to the left. An expansion in real output has the same effect as an increase in the price level. Higher real output domestically leads to higher incomes which results in expenditure switching to the domestic economy. This means an increase in imports, with its associated rightward shift in the demand for dollars, and a decrease in exports, with its leftward shift in the supply. The resulting dashed supply, S', and demand, D', curves re-establish equilibrium in the foreign exchange market and balance in international payments at the pegged exchange rate.

In the case of a shock that results in a balance of payments deficit at the pegged exchange rate, the whole sequence of events runs in reverse. As outlined in the far right column of Box 8.3, an excess demand in the foreign exchange market prompts the central bank to sell dollars and withdraw rupiah. Commercial bank deposits with the central bank shrink as the central bank's balance sheet contracts. Commercial banks reduce their lending which has a negative impact on prices and real output. Under tightening domestic demand, imports fall and exports rise as expenditure switching to foreign markets takes place. Graphically, the demand for foreign currency shifts to the left, the supply to the right. This re-establishes foreign exchange market equilibrium at the $\bar{e}$ peg and eliminates the balance of payments deficit.

Floating and Fixed Rates Compared: Trade and Financial Account Channels

The adjustment process described in the preceding subsection was limited to the trade account channel of the balance of payments. The financial account channel enters into the adjustment process as well. Box 8.4 outlines the adjustment mechanism as it works through both the trade and financial account channels with comparison drawn between fixed and floating rate regimes. Attention is on the balance of payments surplus case. Under a floating rate, a surplus never actually becomes manifest. Once an impulse toward surplus is generated, the exchange rate moves to eliminate it thus triggering offsetting adjustments elsewhere in the balance of payments. We therefore refer to an "incipient surplus" under a floating rate. A manifest surplus must rest on central bank intervention which occurs only when an exchange rate is managed.

Box 8.4 Balance of payments adjustment under floating vs fixed rates

Surplus Case

Suppose a shock causes an imbalance in Indonesia's international payments at the prevailing exchange rate such that a surplus (or incipient surplus for a floating rate) emerges.

How is balance restored under floating vs fixed exchange rates?

<u>Floating exchange rate</u>

$ surplus at e^* ⇒ rupiah appreciates (Rp/$ ↓)

⇒ • imports ↑ ; financial outflows ↑
    ⇒ rightward movement along D

  • exports ↓ ; financial inflows ↓
    ⇒ leftward movement along S

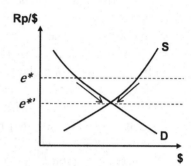

<u>Fixed exchange rate</u>

$ surplus at $\bar{e}$ ⇒ central bank buys $, sells rupiah

⇒ monetary base ↑ ⇒ bank lending ↑

⇒ • nominal GDP ↑ (PQ ↑)
    ⇒ • imports ↑ ⇒ D shifts right
      • exports ↓ ⇒ S shifts left

  • real interest rate ↓
    ⇒ • financial outflows ↑ ⇒ D shifts right
      • financial inflows ↓ ⇒ S shifts left

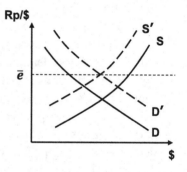

Again letting Indonesia serve for purposes of illustration, consider first the case of a floating exchange rate. From an initial position of equilibrium at exchange rate e^*, suppose impulses to the balance of payments increase credits and/or decrease debits such that at e^* an incipient excess supply of dollars emerges, as reflected in the figure. Under a floating rate, the rupiah price of the dollar is driven down (the rupiah appreciates) to pre-empt any actual surplus from emerging. Rupiah appreciation motivates an increase in imports, for a rightward movement along the demand curve for dollars, and a decrease in exports, for a leftward movement along the supply curve.

With similar effect, rupiah appreciation induces an increase in financial outflows and a decrease in financial inflows. The most straightforward way to think about this is that the stronger rupiah makes assets denominated in dollars cheaper in rupiah terms and those denominated in rupiah more valuable in dollar terms, hence investors sell rupiah assets and buy dollar assets. To isolate the impact of the current exchange rate movement, we assume expectations about rates of return on assets in both currencies and about the future exchange rate remain unchanged.

In sum, following a positive shock to the balance of payments, changes in flows on both trade and financial accounts will be stimulated so as to restore balance as the floating exchange rate finds a new equilibrium at $e^{*\prime}$.

Under a fixed exchange rate, adjustments in balance of payments flows in response to a surplus inducing shock are ultimately similar, even as the mechanism for achieving these adjustments is altogether different. The lower figure in Box 8.4 shows the same starting point of an excess supply of dollars in the foreign exchange market, with the exchange rate now given as $\bar{e}$. To maintain the exchange rate at $\bar{e}$, the central bank purchases the excess supply of dollars with newly issued rupiah. This increase in the monetary base supports new commercial bank lending to stimulate the economy. As the price level and real GDP increase in some combination, imports rise and exports fall. Rising imports shift the demand for dollars to the right (D′) while falling exports shift the supply to the left (S′). These forces work to close the balance of payments surplus and drive the foreign exchange market back to equilibrium at $\bar{e}$.

The central bank intervention on the foreign exchange market precipitates adjustments in financial flows as well as trade flows. As the monetary base increases and bank lending expands, the interest rate is pushed down. This reduces the attractiveness of rupiah assets relative to dollar assets. Consequently, financial outflows increase, shifting the demand for dollars to the right, and inflows decrease, shifting the supply of dollars to the left. Again, the effect is to rein in the balance of payments surplus and restore equilibrium in the foreign exchange market at the peg.

In essence, under a fixed exchange rate regime, the entire economy as measured by nominal GDP must move to bring about balance of payments adjustment in response to a shock. The economy realigns itself around the peg as the reference price against which all other prices and quantities in the economy must assume their relative positions. The adjustment is achieved through a domestic monetary response to an external shock. Under a floating exchange rate, by contrast, the exchange rate itself absorbs the external shock, and through its movement transmits a signal that brings about adjustment in trade and financial flows.

In the case exposited of a surplus inducing shock to the balance of payments, the central bank response is stimulatory. By contrast, for a shock that causes a balance of payments deficit, the central bank must sell foreign currency and withdraw domestic currency, which has a contractionary effect on the economy. If the economy is overheating and inflation is accelerating, this may provide needed restraint. However, if the economy is performing at or below potential, imposing a drag on it will be most unwelcome. Moreover, while in the balance of payments surplus case domestic currency can in principle be printed without limit to support intervention in the foreign exchange market, the same is not true for selling dollars in the deficit case. Foreign exchange reserves are finite, and their rapid depletion can be panic-inducing. For now, we must table these issues, to return in Chapter 11 to the complexities of conducting monetary policy under a managed exchange rate.

E   The Indonesian Experience

To flesh out the challenges of exchange rate management, we examine the historical experience of Indonesia. We consider first the phenomenal shock of the Asian Financial Crisis which caused the rupiah to lose 60 percent of its value relative to the US dollar within the space of two months. We then turn to the more recent period since the Great Financial Crisis during which the movement of global capital has buffeted the exchange rates of many emerging market economies, Indonesia among them.

The Asian Financial Crisis

For three decades preceding the Asian Financial Crisis, Indonesia had been one of the great success stories of the developing world, its real GDP growth averaging 6.6 percent a year. In early 1997, the country's macroeconomic fundamentals appeared strong: a fiscal surplus; a modest current account deficit; and high domestic saving and investment rates. Capital account liberalization had begun in the 1970s, but the underdeveloped financial system had attracted little foreign participation. By the 1990s, Indonesian corporations were taking on foreign debt to a degree that was not transparent. Moreover, this debt was to a large extent short term and was mostly unhedged due to confidence that historical stability in the exchange rate would be sustained. Although Indonesian banks had little direct exposure to foreign debt, they were exposed indirectly and unwittingly through their rupiah loans to domestic firms that were simultaneously borrowing internationally. This set the stage for disaster.

The rupiah was managed relative to the US dollar to allow for gradual depreciation through the mid-1990s, shown in Chart 8.2 as a steady decline in the USD exchange rate index. Meanwhile, however, from early 1995 the rupiah was appreciating modestly in nominal effective terms, and somewhat faster in real effective terms. The NEER

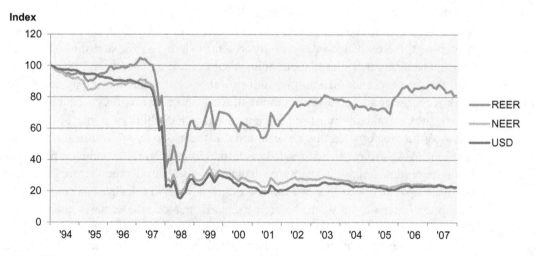

Chart 8.2 Exchange rate indexes, Indonesia, 1994–2007

appreciation means that the USD was appreciating relative to other currencies in the reference basket such that even though the rupiah was depreciating relative to the dollar, it was nevertheless appreciating relative to other currencies (particularly the yen). Moreover, the even faster appreciation of the REER means that inflation in Indonesia was higher than in the other basket countries generally. Thus the foreign purchasing power of the rupiah was rising relative to its domestic purchasing power which was being undermined by rising domestic prices. Between June of 1995 and February of 1997, the rupiah appreciated by 8.2 percent in nominal effective terms. This probably led market participants to suspect rupiah overvaluation that would eventually bring about a correction involving depreciation with respect to the US dollar. Still, the magnitudes involved do not suggest such severe misalignment in the exchange rate as to presage what was about to unfold.

The crisis began in Thailand. Once Thai borrowers started defaulting on foreign debt, borrowers elsewhere in the region came to be seen as suspect. Those who had borrowed short-term found they could not roll over their loans as they had been accustomed to doing. More generally, corporations that held a mismatch on their balance sheets of foreign currency debt against rupiah assets needed to convert rupiah into foreign currency as the rupiah began to depreciate in order to re-establish healthy balance sheets and maintain their creditworthiness. In short order, the rush to convert rupiah to dollars became a panic, and the rupiah collapsed. As businesses failed and the banking system came under stress, the real economy was also hit hard. In 1998, real GDP contracted by 13.7 percent.

How did a country that seemed so strong economically at the beginning of 1997 end up so devastated by the crisis? For Indonesia, "practically everything went wrong at once," according to Hill (2000), resulting in "a comprehensive collapse in confidence in its currency, its economy, its institutions, its social fabric and its political leadership." Ultimately, the Suharto regime was brought down by the crisis after more than 30 years in power, and the fundamental weaknesses of Indonesia's "crony capitalism" were laid bare. Whether such a drastic outcome might have been avoided by a more judicious response to early warning signs of trouble has been much debated. What is clear is that in exchange rates, as in finance more generally, confidence is crucial. Failure to shore up belief in the system as it began to falter made a full-on crisis hard to avert.

Eventually, even a collapsing currency will find its bottom. At some point, it begins to be attractive to buyers again and not so reviled by sellers.[2] Chart 8.2 shows 1999 bringing a modest recovery in Indonesia's USD and NEER exchange rates. The much greater rebound in the REER tells of high inflation. Indeed, Indonesia's inflation rate reached 80 percent in 1999. This resulted from generous credit support by the central bank aimed at keeping businesses and commercial banks afloat. Through the early 2000s, the USD and NEER rates remained fairly stable. Intervals of REER appreciation suggest bursts of inflation that were quickly brought in check.

---

[2] The author was in Indonesia as the rupiah collapsed and reacted with the question: "How much rupiah should I buy to be spent in my remaining one day in this country on items I can carry out in a suitcase?"

International Capital Flows in Recent Years

Much of the exchange rate volatility experienced by Indonesia in the decade beginning with the Great Financial Crisis was caused by international capital flows. Inflows of capital put upward pressure on the rupiah, which can be countered by central bank purchases of foreign currency. And vice versa, outflows of capital put downward pressure on the rupiah which can be countered by central bank sales of foreign currency. For most of the period between 2008 and 2020, the IMF classified Indonesia's exchange rate regime as "floating" (but not "free floating"), reflecting no steadfast effort to peg the value of the currency. However, during particular interludes the rupiah was managed more tightly, to be discussed.

To view the more recent period, we rebase the exchange rate indexes at January 2008 in Chart 8.3. The lower panel of the chart shows central bank foreign currency purchases (positive) and sales (negative) as captured in the reserve assets entry on the balance of payments. The chart shows vividly the impact of the Great Financial Crisis in late 2008. Despite its onset in the USA, the crisis triggered a retreat of global capital to the perceived safe haven of the US dollar. Commensurately, Indonesia experienced an outward rush of funds that cost the rupiah more than 20 percent of its value relative to the USD. The central bank moderated this drop by selling dollar reserves, committing more than $4 billion to the

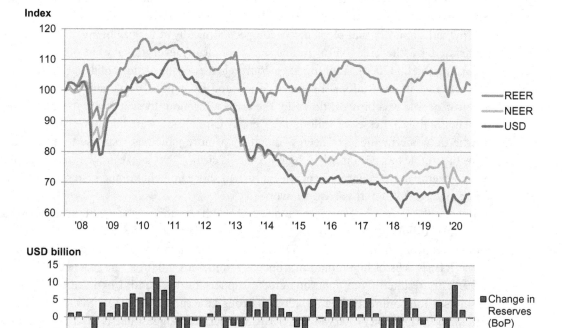

Chart 8.3 Exchange rate indexes and reserves, Indonesia, 2008–2020

purpose in the fourth quarter of 2008. This left reserves of about $52 billion, which benchmarking against such traditional indicators as imports and short-term debt holdings would have been deemed adequate. Within an environment of increasingly mobile global capital, however, such standards were being reassessed.

Thus when foreign capital came flowing back in over the next couple of years, upward pressure on the rupiah was met with reserve accumulation by the central bank. Further contributing to the balance of payments surpluses, export revenues were boosted by commodity price increases. By mid-2011, reserves reached nearly $120 billion. The enhanced stockpile of reserves would prove useful in the event of foreign capital again turning to exit. Strong purchases of foreign currency by the central bank served to stabilize the value of the rupiah relative to the USD. This led the IMF to reclassify Indonesia's exchange rate regime as "stabilized arrangement" for the period June 2010 to February 2011.

From February 2011, increased flexibility of the rupiah against the USD earned a redesignation of the regime as "floating." Even as the rupiah appreciated sharply relative to the USD through mid 2011, however, the NEER was trending downward. This indicates that the USD was depreciating relative to other currencies in the basket. The dollar's depreciation presumably provided the motivation to loosen the rupiah's tie to it and maintain more stable courses for the NEER and REER.

Later in 2011, foreign investors became spooked by financial developments in the eurozone as Greece headed toward default on its sovereign debt. With contagion fears looming, global capital again exited emerging markets, Indonesia's included. Compounding weakness in Indonesia's balance of payments going into 2012, global markets for its commodity exports softened. The rupiah consequently depreciated relative to the USD with the Indonesian central bank leaning against this by selling off reserves.

From June of 2012, the Indonesian central bank turned to managing depreciation against the USD along a gradual, steady course. In light of this systematic tracking, the IMF reclassified the regime as "crawl-like arrangement." This classification remained in place until August 2013 when the rupiah depreciated sharply against the USD. The break came under pressure from the "taper tantrum," which drew investment funds back to the USA in response to the Federal Reserve tapering back on bond purchases and steering interest rates upward.

Through 2014 and most of 2015, the rupiah continued to depreciate against the dollar. The NEER, however, tracked a more steady course. This divergence indicates that the dollar was appreciating in value relative to other basket currencies. Hence allowing depreciation relative to the dollar preserved the value of the rupiah more broadly. The years 2016 and 2017 saw tighter management of the rupiah relative to the USD through sustained foreign exchange purchases by the central bank. Such purchases warded off rupiah appreciation and built the reserve trove to more than $130 billion by the end of 2017.

Years 2018–2020 saw substantial volatility in the exchange rate but also volatility in central bank buying and selling to forestall even greater exchange rate volatility. This is the embodiment of the idea of floating but not free floating.

Over the period captured in Chart 8.3, the REER maintained a generally more stable course than the NEER or the USD rate. Higher inflation in Indonesia than in the basket countries meant that for the REER to remain stable, the NEER had to depreciate. Balance of payments pressures should tend to ensure nominal currency depreciation as an offset to relatively high inflation which would result in overvaluation at a given exchange rate, and this indeed is what happened for Indonesia.

F   A Middle Course of Exchange Rate Management

Indonesia's exchange rate story in the period since 2008 tells of the exercise of judgment in response to ever changing circumstances. In the regime space between fixed and free floating, the central bank authorities have veered in one direction or the other – stabilization or flexibility – as conditions, in their assessment, warranted. Against a currency appreciation inducing shock, such as a capital inflow or rising prices for exports, they intervened to buy foreign exchange and accumulate reserves. And vice versa, against a currency depreciation inducing shock, they intervened to sell foreign exchange, contingent on the availability of reserves. In this way, the central bank "leans against the wind," aiming to steer a steady course, yet bound ultimately by the dictates of the market.

Broadly speaking, in the post-Great Financial Crisis era the Indonesian central bank bought foreign exchange during periods of strong capital inflow and sold it during periods of net outflow, while on balance increasing its reserves substantially over the course of a decade. Amassing a large pool of reserves is crucial to a strategy that involves intervening when capital is flowing out. Indonesia and its neighbors learned the hard way during the Asian Financial Crisis that loss of public confidence in a currency can cause its value to plummet beyond all reason based on market fundamentals. Central bank capacity to intervene by selling foreign reserves could forestall such a crisis of confidence and thus foster a more stable environment in which to address the underlying domestic problems that might cause currency weakness.

Ultimately, foreign reserves are finite, so the capacity of a central bank to shore up a currency that is overvalued faces a limit. As explained in this chapter though, the intervention itself should in principle set in motion a chain of events to restore balance of payments equilibrium around the stabilized exchange rate. Selling foreign exchange and buying the domestic currency to prop up its value results in contraction of the domestic money supply which in turn raises interest rates and reduces aggregate demand. This then boosts net capital inflows and net exports, supporting the domestic currency on both counts. The central bank's intervention comes to a natural conclusion and reserves are conserved.

Relying on such macroeconomic forces to bring about balance of payments equilibrium around a stabilized exchange rate has its drawbacks, however. To lean against currency depreciation, the central bank must sell foreign currency and withdraw domestic currency which brings about a contraction in real output with all the pain of lost jobs and business failures that can entail. Letting the currency depreciate may be a more palatable way to go. For a real-world experiment in comparing the two approaches, consider the case of Hong Kong in the wake of the Asian Financial Crisis. As currency values were dropping in crisis-hit countries all around, Hong Kong maintained its peg and lost its competitiveness. Its economy contracted by 6.0 percent in 1998 despite a sound financial system that shielded it from the contagion effect. By contrast, Singapore, with its more flexible exchange rate, underwent a relatively modest 2.1 percent contraction followed by a much quicker rebound in the following year with growth of 6.2 percent versus Hong Kong's 2.6 percent. Hong Kong eventually re-established macroeconomic balance around its exchange rate peg, but only by realigning its real output and price level through a painful process.

In more general terms, the drawback of exchange rate stabilization is that it subordinates monetary policy – and its application toward achieving macroeconomic objectives involving real output and the price level – to managing the currency instead. We will return to this in Chapter 11 on monetary policy.

For purposes of this chapter, the upshot is that balance of payments equilibrium can be achieved under either floating or fixed exchange rates, and that a hybrid strategy that combines market determination and intervention to varying degrees depending on circumstances can endeavor to achieve the best of both worlds. Intervention is best aimed at ameliorating the impact of forces that are prone to reversal, such as capital flows or price fluctuations for traded commodities, or in the case of shocks with longer-term consequences, at diversifying the adjustment mechanisms such that the exchange rate, real output, and the price level all absorb some of the force. Such a strategy must rely on judgment, prediction of the future, and constant reassessment.

The first eight chapters of this text have laid foundations for understanding macroeconomic phenomena. In the next two chapters, we consider behavior of an economy in the aggregate, first in comparative static terms where the time dimension is abstracted to two points (before and after), then in fully dynamic terms that capture movement through a cyclical process.

Data Note

The Bank for International Settlements is the source for all foreign exchange data. Data on foreign exchange markets in Chart 8.1 and Table 8.1 are from the BIS Triennial Survey of 2019. This survey is conducted every three years during the month of April to collect data on the size and composition of foreign exchange trading by banks and other dealers. Data on exchange rates for Indonesia in Charts 8.2 and 8.3 are from the BIS Statistics Warehouse. The change in reserves indicator of Chart 8.3 is as measured from the balance of payments based on data from the IMF International Financial Statistics database.

Table 8.2 draws from classification of exchange rate arrangements by the International Monetary Fund as reported in its *Annual Report on Exchange Arrangements and Exchange Restrictions*.

Overseas Filipino worker counts are from the Philippine Statistics Authority.

The value of world stock trading comes from the World Bank Microdata Data Catalog, and the value of world trade comes from the World Trade Organization Statistics Database.

Bibliographic Note

The case of Dutch disease in the Philippines is discussed in Medalla, Fabella, and de Dios (2014).

The roiling of Indonesia by the Asian Financial Crisis is analyzed insightfully by Hill (2000). A post-mortem by Takagi (2004) assesses the role of the IMF in handling the crisis. The Indonesian experience since 2008 is described and evaluated year by year in the IMF's Article IV consultation reports.

BIBLIOGRAPHIC CITATIONS

Bank for International Settlements, 2021. Statistics Warehouse. www.bis.org/statistics/xrusd.htm?m= 6%7C381%7C675 (accessed December 7, 2021).

Bank for International Settlements, 2019. Triennial Central Bank Survey of Foreign Exchange and Over-the-Counter (OTC) Derivatives Markets in 2019. www.bis.org/statistics/rpfx19.htm (accessed December 7, 2021).

Central Bank of the Republic of China (Taiwan), Foreign Exchange Regime. www.cbc.gov.tw/ct.asp? xItem=856&CtNode=480&mp=2 (accessed February 28, 2018).

Hill, Hal, 2000. "Indonesia: The Strange and Sudden Death of a Tiger Economy," *Oxford Development Studies*, Vol. 28, No. 2: 117–139.

Hong Kong Monetary Authority, 2018. An Introduction to the Hong Kong Monetary Authority. www.hkma.gov.hk/media/eng/publication-and-research/reference-materials/intro_to_hkma.pdf (accessed February 28, 2018).

International Monetary Fund, 2008–2020. *Annual Report on Exchange Arrangements and Exchange Restrictions* (Washington, DC: International Monetary Fund).

International Monetary Fund, 2020. International Financial Statistics. http://data.imf.org/?sk= 4C514D48-B6BA-49ED-8AB9-52B0C1A0179B&sId=1390030341854 (accessed December 7, 2021).

Medalla, Felipe M., Raul V. Fabella, and Emmanuel S. de Dios, 2014. "Beyond the Remittance-Driven Economy: Notes As If the Long Run Mattered," University of the Philippines School of Economics Discussion Paper No. 2014–11.

Monetary Authority of Singapore, 2018. Singapore's Exchange Rate-Based Monetary Policy. www .mas.gov.sg/~/media/MAS/Monetary%20Policy%20and%20Economics/Monetary%20Policy/MP %20Framework/Singapores%20Exchange%20Ratebased%20Monetary%20Policy.pdf (accessed February 28, 2018).

Philippine Statistics Authority, 2019. Survey on Overseas Filipinos 2019. https://psa.gov.ph/content/ survey-overseas-filipinos-sof (accessed December 10, 2021).

Takagi, Shinji, 2004. "Responding to Currency Crises in Emerging Market Economies: The IMF in Indonesia, Korea, and Brazil," International Monetary Fund. www.imf.org/external/np/leg/sem/ 2004/cdmfl/eng/takagi.pdf (accessed April 18, 2018).

World Bank, 2021. Stocks traded, in Microdata Data Catalog. https://data.worldbank.org/indicator/ CM.MKT.TRAD.CD (accessed December 10, 2021).

World Trade Organization, 2021. WTO Stats. http://stat.wto.org/StatisticalProgram/ WSDBStatProgramHome.aspx?Language=E (accessed December 10, 2021).

9 Models of Equilibrium and Disequilibrium

Macroeconomic models provide a framework for relating key aggregate magnitudes: output; income; the price level; unemployment; the wage rate; consumption; investment; government spending and taxation; the money supply; the interest rate; international trade and capital flows; and the exchange rate. Classical and Keynesian models diverge on how quickly prices and wages adjust to eliminate the twin excess supplies characteristic of a downturn – a glut in product markets and unemployed workers in labor markets. With that, the two schools reach different conclusions on policy.

Schools of thought within macroeconomics diverge in how they regard the market clearing process. The classical school and its heirs view markets as well functioning and resilient in response to shocks. The constant hammering of shocks gives rise to fluctuations, to be sure, but these fluctuations are seen as healthy coping mechanisms in support of durable economic growth. Under the classical paradigm, macroeconomic policy intervention only adds to uncertainty and impedes the adjustment process. By contrast, the Keynesian school and its offshoots view economic slumps as serious, inexorable, and not self-correcting in any timely fashion. Keynesians favor an active government role in hastening recovery from downturns and maintaining stability more generally.

The comparative static models of this chapter rest on the theoretical construct of equilibrium. In the standard microeconomic application, a market in equilibrium at some price and quantity is subjected to an exogenous shock represented by the shift of a supply or demand curve that instantaneously resolves to a new equilibrium with a new price and quantity. The framework can be extended to macroeconomics, where the shocks jolt the economy as a whole away from growth at potential for it to then spontaneously rebound and resume that growth. This is macroeconomic modeling in the classical spirit. The Keynesian concern is that an economy will get stuck operating below its potential. The story is one of disequilibrium in the sense that markets for output and labor fail to clear in any timely fashion. The modeling exercise then involves pointing the way for government to bump the economy to its full-employment equilibrium. This, too, is a comparative static exercise in that the time dimension disappears. Dynamic models that expunge the notion of equilibrium will be taken up in Chapter 10.

The first section of this chapter reviews the basic tenets of the classical school. The second presents the Income–Expenditure Model inspired by Keynes. This is a disequilibrium model in the sense that excess capacity persists as prices and wages fail to adjust to clear markets within the time frame of the analysis. The Aggregate Demand / Aggregate Supply Model of the third section joins a short-run period in which wages are sticky with a long-run period in which wages and prices fully adjust. This model tracks the interplay of the price level and aggregate output as the response to shock plays out in the short and long runs. The fourth section introduces a more elaborate interpretation of Keynesian disequilibrium in the IS–LM model (the notation referring to investment, saving, liquidity, and money) and outlines its extension to an open-economy context with the Mundell–Fleming Model. Finally, the fifth section summarizes the evolution in classical versus Keynesian-based schools of thought as manifested in contemporary Dynamic Stochastic General Equilibrium Models.

A   Classical School

The first challenge for economics as a discipline is to explain how a market economy manages to achieve as much success as it does. Most people most of the time are put to work productively. Investment funds find their way into financing projects of a range of durations and risk profiles. Entrepreneurs develop new products and technologies and devise innovative ways of doing business. Economies grow and advance over time. The classical school offered insight into understanding this success. The story is one of prices equilibrating demands and supplies to allocate resources to the uses in which they are most highly valued.

The principle of equilibration that applies to individual markets can be extended to an economy as a whole. Adjustment of wages ensures full employment. Adjustment of interest rates matches saving with investment. An unbroken circle links production to income to spending on what has been produced. Say's Law, named for early 19th-century French economist Jean-Baptiste Say, captures this succinctly: Supply creates its own demand.

The full employment equilibrium of the classical paradigm is formulated in real terms. Money does not figure in. Only relative prices matter. Any good could be chosen as numeraire with the value of everything else expressed in terms of that referent. Introducing money provides a convenient unit of account, but its impact on resource utilization is held to be neutral. Doubling the supply of money simply reduces its value by half in terms of everything else as all prices double. No role is seen for credit expansion to boost real economic activity. When an economy operates inherently at full employment, credit infusions simply lead to higher prices.

Classical economic theory does well in explaining the impressive achievements of a market economy in yielding efficient utilization of resources and weathering shocks. The classical paradigm, however, was hard-pressed to explain the Great Depression of the 1930s. This terrible cataclysm sparked a revolution in economic thought.

B   Income–Expenditure Model

The Great Depression was a worldwide economic disaster of incomparable proportions. Although a number of other countries fell into recession sooner, the USA suffered the longest and deepest downturn. Unemployment reached 25 percent of the labor force. More than a third of all banks failed. Output declined by 30 percent, and by the end of the 1930s had still not recovered to the level of 1929. Globally, the contraction was compounded by the piling on of tariff barriers such that international trade plummeted by two-thirds.

John Maynard Keynes stepped up to meet the intellectual challenge of explaining, counter to classical doctrine, how an economy can become mired in recession. His *General Theory of Employment, Interest, and Money* was published in 1936. The Income–Expenditure Model is the simplest formalization of Keynes's argument. We first develop the key functional relationships of the model. We then apply the model to explaining persistent unemployment. In Keynes's view, the way to catalyze recovery is through government fiscal action. We proceed to examine the mechanics of such demand stimulus policies and the role of the Keynesian expenditures multiplier.

Consumption Function and Planned Expenditures

The Income–Expenditure Model turns on the relationship between consumption and income. Consumption by households is assumed to increase with income, but by less than the full measure of income. That part of income not spent on consumption is saved. Specifying the consumption function in linear form and expressing income as net of taxes, which for simplicity are assumed not to depend on income, we have:

$$C = C_0 + \beta(Y - \bar{T}), \tag{9.1}$$

where C = consumption by households;

C_0 = autonomous consumption (consumption when income is zero);

Y = income;

$\bar{T}$ = taxes (the bar indicates exogeneity);

β = marginal propensity to consume (MPC).

The marginal propensity to consume, β, is the slope of the consumption function, or the ratio of a change in consumption to a change in income, $\Delta C / \Delta Y$. Logically, β must take on a value between zero and one.

The Keynesian consumption function frames economic behavior in a fundamentally different way from Say's Law. Say's Law is premised on all income being spent. That part of income not directed toward consumption is expected to be absorbed by investment via the market for loanable funds. In the Keynesian scheme of things, by contrast, saving depends not on the interest rate but on income as the counterpart to consumption. Planned investment is treated as independent of current income, motivated rather by expectations about the future. Unplanned investment in the form of changes in inventories is, however, regarded as critically dependent on income as will be explained.

The specification of planned expenditures follows the expenditures approach to measuring GDP detailed in Chapter 4. All elements other than consumption are taken as exogenous as noted with an overbar. Inserting the consumption function specified above into the expenditures equation for GDP yields:

$$\text{Planned Expenditures} = C_0 + \beta(Y - \bar{T}) + \bar{I} + \bar{G} + \bar{X} - \bar{M}, \qquad (9.2)$$

where $\bar{I}$ = planned investment;
$\quad \bar{G}$ = government spending;
$\quad \bar{X}$ = exports;
$\quad \bar{M}$ = imports.

This expression for planned expenditures represents the aggregate demand side of the Income–Expenditure Model.

Persistence of Unemployment

The aggregate supply side of the model is given by the value of output produced which is identically equal to the income earned in the production process. The question to be examined by the model is: What happens when the income earned in production does not generate sufficient demand to purchase the output supplied?

Figure 9.1 captures the story as depicted by Samuelson (1948). The model is referred to as the "Keynesian Cross." Planned expenditures are an increasing function of income with slope given by the MPC at less than one. The 45-degree line, with slope of one, represents all income, absorbed as it must be in realized expenditures which are defined to include unplanned inventory accumulation or decumulation. Thus, realized expenditures are equal to output which is in turn equal to income. The level of output that provides full employment is given by an income of Y^{FE}. At Y^{FE} as depicted, planned expenditures fall short of output produced. The result is the unplanned accumulation of inventory. This inventory build-up prompts producers to lay off workers and cut back production. Only when income drops to Y^* does the economy generate planned expenditures sufficient to clear the market of output produced with any inventory changes matching producer intentions. At income of less than Y^*, inventories are drawn down motivating producers to expand output and income payments.

Alignment between saving and investment in this model (where saving, S, subsumes any cross-border inflows or outflows such that $S = I + X - M$ as explained in Chapter 5) is achieved not through interest rate equilibration as in the classical model but through unplanned inventory changes. Saving and planned investment may differ *ex ante*. But *ex*

Figure 9.1 Income–expenditure model

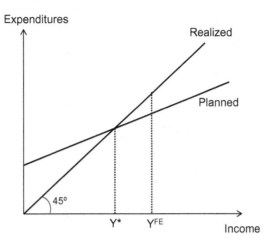

At Y*, planned expenditures are just sufficient to absorb all output produced such that inventory changes are neither more nor less than planned. Y* may fall short of full employment output, Y^FE.

post, any saving in excess of planned investment will find expression in the unplanned pile up of inventories.

An equilibrium of sorts is achieved at Y^* in that there is no tendency for change within the structure of the model. Yet this outcome is characterized by persistent unemployment. The labor market does not clear. In a broader sense, then, markets are in a state of disequilibrium. Classical theory holds that the wage rate should fall to eliminate the gap between those supplying labor and those demanding it. In the Keynesian world, however, wages are sticky. Workers resist cuts in pay and employers are loathe to impose them. The alternative of cutting jobs in the face of a slowdown in sales is more palatable. Moreover, Keynesians argue that any cut in wages would only exacerbate the deficiency of aggregate demand on product markets as with lower wages consumers have less income to spend. For Keynesians the solution to depressed economic conditions is to be found in government stimulus policies.

Demand Stimulus Policies

The Keynesian story of economic underperformance rests on insufficient aggregate demand. More spending would induce more production and higher employment. Government is able to provide the boost in spending an economy needs, either by increasing its outlays directly or by reducing taxes so that households take on the spending.

The mechanics of a fiscal stimulus are illustrated in Figure 9.2. An increase in government spending by ΔG shifts the planned expenditures line upward. At the original Y^*, planned expenditures now exceed realized expenditures by ΔG, with demand being met through unplanned disinvestment in inventories. Businesses respond to this unplanned drop in

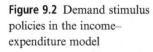

Figure 9.2 Demand stimulus policies in the income–expenditure model

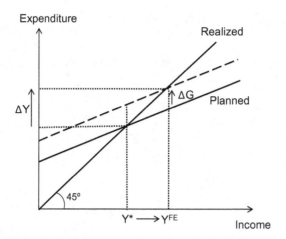

Increased government spending can stimulate
demand to move the economy to full employment.

inventories by increasing production, and income rises. With adequate government stimulus, the economy can be pushed to full employment.

A tax cut can similarly stimulate spending by leaving more discretionary income with households to support consumption. Other components of spending ($\bar{I}$ and $\bar{X} - \bar{M}$) are treated as exogenous in this model. Increases in planned investment and exports, were they to materialize, would stimulate economic activity, as would a reduction in imports that creates more opportunity for domestic substitutes.

Note in Figure 9.2 that the given increase in government spending gives rise to an increase in income, ΔY, that is substantially larger in magnitude than the initial spending increase. There is a multiplier effect, to be explained.

The Multiplier

Any initial impetus to planned expenditures is amplified in its effect on income through the expenditures multiplier. In the first instance, the increment to spending goes directly to stimulating new output and income. This new income in turn provides the basis for further consumption spending which creates yet further income and again further spending, and so on, ad infinitum. With each round, however, only a portion of income is consumed while the remainder is saved. Thus with each round the increment to spending gets smaller such that the total impact approaches a definable limit. The math is laid out in Box 9.1.

Box 9.1 Calculating the expenditures multiplier

Suppose a government undertakes a stimulus project involving an investment in public infrastructure launched with an outlay represented by ΔG. That ΔG in spending goes toward contracting work by engineering and construction firms, purchasing materials,

Box 9.1 (cont.)

and employing civil servants to engage in management and oversight. The spending feeds into incomes in all forms: wages, interest, rents, and profits. In turn, the recipients of these income streams will spend part on consumption and save part. The part spent on consumption then fuels a new round of income increases which generates more consumption and yet more income, and so on.

To trace the ultimate impact on income of the initial spending increase, let us formalize the series of spending increments round by round. At each round, a share of income from the last round equal to the marginal propensity to consume (MPC) becomes new spending.

$$
\begin{array}{ll}
\text{Round 1} & \Delta G \\
\text{Round 2} & \text{MPC} \cdot \Delta G \\
\text{Round 3} & \text{MPC}^2 \cdot \Delta G \\
\text{Round 4} & \text{MPC}^3 \cdot \Delta G \\
\quad\vdots & \quad\vdots
\end{array}
$$

Thus the increase in income that follows from an increase in government spending is given as:

$$\Delta Y = (1 + \text{MPC} + \text{MPC}^2 + \text{MPC}^3 + \dots) \cdot \Delta G$$

Because MPC takes on a value between zero and one, each time the ratio is raised to a higher power the resulting increment is diminished in magnitude. The elements of the series thus approach zero. Algebraically, the sum of the elements of the infinite series is equivalent to $1/(1\text{-MPC})$. The magnitude in the denominator, 1-MPC, is the marginal propensity to save.

The higher the MPC, the greater the impact of a fiscal stimulus. For an MPC of 0.8, for example, the multiplier is 5. For an MPC of 0.5, the multiplier is only 2.

A word of caution on the Keynesian remedy to a slump is in order. While increasing government spending and cutting taxes to stimulate an economy may find ready political appeal, the burden of the public debt can weigh against over reliance on Keynesian fiscal policies. Nevertheless, it is possible to raise spending and taxes by equal amounts and still deliver a stimulus within the framework of the Income–Expenditure Model. This is because some of the tax revenue diverted from private parties would have been saved and thus would not have contributed to aggregate demand whereas the government can act to spend all of it.

C   Aggregate Demand / Aggregate Supply Model

The Income–Expenditure Model discussed in the preceding section treats income and consumption as endogenous variables and explains how an economy can fall short of operating at its potential with no tendency for any timely recovery. All pricing variables, including the wage rate, the interest rate, and the exchange rate, are implicitly held fixed. In the long run, of course, prices are flexible and should function to resolve demand and supply mismatches. The model of aggregate demand and aggregate supply is an effort to bridge a short-run period when market response to shock is limited and the long-run time frame when an equilibrium is achieved.

Similar to the model of demand and supply in a particular market, the Aggregate Demand / Aggregate Supply Model focuses on the interaction between prices and quantities. We develop first the demand side, then the supply side. Once the model is formulated, we apply it to analyzing both a recessionary shock and the implementation of government stimulus policies.

Aggregate Demand

The aggregate demand function relates real demand for all final goods and services in an economy to the general price level. As with demand in a particular market, the relationship is inverse such that a rising price level is associated with a declining demand for real output. The reasons for a downward sloping demand curve on the aggregate level are different from those for a single market, however. First, the real balance effect (also known as the Pigou effect) holds that as prices rise, the purchasing power of given money holdings decreases to cause a decline in demand. Second, the interest rate effect rests on the Keynesian notion of a trade-off between holding liquid money balances to support transactions and tying up wealth in bonds. As prices rise, the need to keep more cash on hand diverts funds out of bonds causing the interest rate to rise which then restrains investment spending. Finally, the exchange rate effect notes that higher domestic prices act to increase the real exchange value of the local currency causing imports to rise and exports to fall which further undermines demand for home produced goods and services.

Changes in factors other than the price level that bear on the components of spending (consumption, investment, government, exports, and imports) cause the aggregate demand curve to shift. Important among these factors are expectations about the future, availability of credit, political forces, and global economic conditions.

Aggregate Supply

On the supply side, the short-run response to changes in the price level differs from the long-run response, as indicated in Figure 9.3. The economy depicted is in a state of both long-run and short-run equilibrium at Q^* and P^*.

In the long run, the supply curve is vertical. This is because in the long run production capacity is determined solely by real factor inputs and technology, not by the price level. With capacity given by Q^*, and the money supply set exogenously, prices, given time, will arrive at the level, P^*, that ensures full employment of resources.

In the short run, shocks can move the economy away from operation at potential. Product markets are on the front lines in absorbing shocks. The transmission of the impact to labor

Figure 9.3 Aggregate demand / aggregate supply model

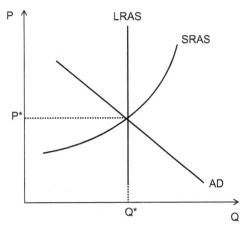

Aggregate demand (AD) is a negative function of the price level. Long run aggregate supply (LRAS) is determined by factors other than the price level. Short run aggregate supply (SRAS) is related positively to the price level.

markets takes time as terms of compensation are slow to be revisited and revised. Thus in the short run following a shock, real wages will diverge from their long-run equilibrium level. Following a shock that raises output prices, workers will only gradually realize that the purchasing power of their wages has been eroded. Seeking and securing wage increases is a protracted process. In the short run then, price increases result in lower real wages to workers and higher profits to producers. Producers respond by increasing output, which means drawing more people into paid labor and/or boosting worker hours. The economy moves upward along the short-run supply curve. With further passage of time, however, competition in the labor market as producers seek to expand hiring will drive up wages. Profits will then fall back to normal, and the economy will return to its long-run supply curve.

We proceed to apply the model, tracing the response in output and prices to changes in external forces.

Recession

The biggest source of macroeconomic volatility lies with investment demand. Investment is motivated by expectations of future profit, with time horizons that can run to decades. Willingness to take on risk is buffeted by sentiment about future prospects which can swing wildly between optimism and pessimism on a mass scale. Bad times tend to breed ever more doubt, good times ever more euphoria. When an economy overshoots on the upside, the downturn that follows can be sharp.

Figure 9.4 depicts the repercussions of a collapse in confidence. A drop in investment spending is reflected in a shift of the aggregate demand curve to the left. In the short run, the

Figure 9.4 Recession in the AD/AS model

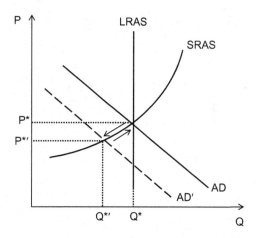

A drop in aggregate demand leads to recession. The economy moves along the short-run aggregate supply curve to temporarily lower equilibrium price and output levels. With recovery, demand rebounds to restore output to its long run potential.

price level falls to $P^{*\prime}$. Facing weak prices, producers scale back production to $Q^{*\prime}$, laying off workers and cutting hours. Even though real wages are actually rising as prices fall relative to nominal wages, cutting nominal wages can be fraught with impediments. Often long-term employment contracts are in place, and even when they are not, nominal wage reductions are bad for worker morale.

As time passes, durable goods wear out and need replacing and entrepreneurs at some point begin to recover their sense of opportunity. As sentiment turns more positive, spending regains steam. This is reflected in a shift in aggregate demand back to its former position to re-establish full-employment equilibrium at Q^* and P^*. The recession runs its natural course, and the economy recovers.

Demand Stimulus Policies

Governments seek to maintain economic stability through the application of monetary and fiscal policies. A monetary stimulus works through the injection of reserves into the banking system that drive new lending. The ramifications are shown in Figure 9.5. Let us take as a starting point an economy at long run equilibrium given by P^* and Q^*. The increase in spending stimulated by the expansion in credit shifts the aggregate demand curve to the right. The price level rises to $P^{*\prime}$ pushing the economy along its short-run aggregate supply curve. Rising prices relative to given wages drive profit growth motivating producers to expand production. Output increases to $Q^{*\prime}$. With time, however, workers react to rising prices with demands for higher nominal wages to preserve the real purchasing power of their pay. The increase in production costs is captured by a shift in the short-run supply curve to the left. As real wages regain their equilibrium level, the economy returns to its long-run aggregate supply

Figure 9.5 Monetary stimulus in the AD/AS model

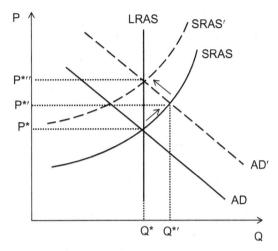

A monetary stimulus can increase output in the short run. But in the long run prices rise with no lasting effect on output.

curve with output at Q^* but with the price level now at $P^{*''}$. The monetary stimulus thus achieves only a temporary increase in output while the effect on prices is lasting.

A fiscal stimulus, involving increased government spending or reduced taxes, is represented with the same initial rightward shift in aggregate demand as in Figure 9.5. As the government competes with the private sector for goods and services, prices are bid up and profitable opportunities abound. The economy goes into overdrive. Once the spending spree runs its course, however, aggregate demand drops back and the economy reverts to its original equilibrium output and price level.

Stimulus action undertaken, as just outlined, when an economy is functioning at full capacity has only a fleeting effect on output. In the case of a monetary stimulus, the increase in prices is nevertheless enduring. In the case of a fiscal stimulus, any borrowing associated with spending increases or tax reductions results in a higher debt burden. This long-run consequence must be taken into account in assessing the merits of short-term stimulus gains. However, if the starting point is one of less than capacity operation, as in Figure 9.4 at $P^{*'}$ and $Q^{*'}$, and the recovery process, however foreordained, is protracted, stimulus policies may hold appeal for their catalytic power. Giving a stalled economy a jumpstart and shortening the time needed to regain full employment, if this can be achieved at tolerable cost to the fiscal budget and minimal impact on prices, represents the ultimate in successful macroeconomic policy.

D   IS–LM Model

In a Keynesian world, markets do not adjust quickly to reach equilibrium. Indeed, during the time frame addressed, a disequilibrium stasis can take hold. Unemployment persists, and production capacity sits idle. The crux of the problem is that aggregate demand at the full employment level of income is insufficient to induce that level of output and income to materialize. The Income–Expenditure Model suppresses prices and wages to cast demand purely as a function of income. By contrast, the Aggregate Demand / Aggregate Supply Model allows for quick adjustment of output prices in response to shocks but assumes stickiness in wages to describe a process of equilibration that plays out over time. The IS–LM model formulated by Hicks (1937) resembles the Income–Expenditure Model in that neither prices nor wages adjust quickly to clear markets leaving output short of potential and workers out of jobs.

The new element in the IS–LM model is an endogenous interest rate which serves as the fulcrum of macroeconomic adjustment to shock. The interest rate affects the economy through two channels. One is real investment spending. The other is the allocation of financial assets between liquid money balances and bonds. We consider each of these channels in turn, then bring them together to explain their joint determination of aggregate output. The model as originally conceived pertains to a closed economy. The Mundell–Fleming Model, which we outline briefly, extends the framework to an open economy.

Our treatment of the IS–LM and Mundell–Fleming Models is cursory. A thorough understanding would require working through comparative static exercises to trace the impact of external shocks, including, importantly, monetary and fiscal policy actions. For our purposes in developing a macroeconomics for Emerging East Asia, models that focus on a domestically determined market rate of interest are not the most suitable. A better fit is a model that incorporates managed exchange rates, which we develop in Chapter 13. Nevertheless, to varying degrees in the economies of Emerging East Asia, domestic interest rates do play a role in macroeconomic performance. Hence, we outline the structure of the arguments.

Marginal Efficiency of Capital and the IS Curve

The IS curve defines pairs of income (equal to output) and the interest rate that equate investment and saving. Investment is assumed to depend negatively on the interest rate. Simply put, this is because as the interest rate falls, more investment projects become viable. Keynes formalized the argument with his concept of a declining marginal efficiency of capital – the more extensive is investment at a given point in time, the lower is the return to the marginal unit of investment. This is due to diminishing marginal productivity of capital as capital becomes more abundant relative to other factors of production, given the state of technology. A lower interest rate increases the rate of return net of borrowing costs for the entire schedule of possible investment levels such that at the margin some projects that would not have been pursued at a higher rate of interest will be undertaken. Saving and consumption are assumed to depend on income in standard Keynesian fashion.

To capture the investment/saving side of the IS–LM Model, we rewrite the Keynesian expenditure equation expressing investment as a function of the interest rate and setting expenditures equal to income:

$$Y = C_0 + \beta(Y - \bar{T}) + I(r) + \bar{G} + \bar{X} - \bar{M}, \qquad (9.3)$$

where r = the interest rate.

To preserve the equality, an increase in I, following from a decrease in r, must be matched by an increase in Y sufficient to yield the necessary saving to support the higher I. Conversely, an increase in the interest rate inhibits investment which causes a decline in income sufficient to realign lower saving with the lower investment. Note that preservation of the saving/investment balance is implicitly ensured within the IS equation since Y minus all terms on the right hand side other than $I(r)$ is equal to saving (where government spending is subsumed under consumption for simplicity).

The IS equation traces an inverse relationship between the interest rate and the level of income, with investment and saving equated in the process. This inverse relationship is shown as the IS curve in Figure 9.6. To find that combination of interest rate and income level that will prevail in equilibrium, we need a second relationship defined on the two variables, Y and r.

Liquidity Preference and the LM Curve

The classical School posited that the interest rate is determined by a market for loanable funds in which saving on the supply side is equated with investment on the demand side. In the IS–LM framework, investment similarly depends on the interest rate, but saving depends strictly on income. Saving is not presumed to flow automatically into the loanable funds market. Rather, savers have a choice between holding non-interest-bearing money balances

Figure 9.6 IS–LM model

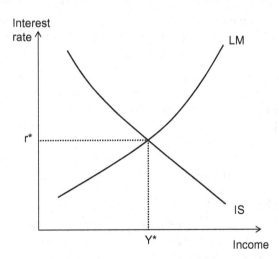

The IS curve reflects pairs of income and the interest rate that equate saving and investment. The LM curve captures pairs of the same variables that equate demand for money with given supply.

and interest-bearing bonds. The supply of loanable funds then arises not directly from saving but from the choice to allocate savings toward bond purchases as opposed to cash money balances.

Money balances have the advantage of being liquid. They are immediately available to support transactions. The demand for money for the purpose of supporting transactions increases as income rises.

To overcome the preference of wealth holders for liquidity, interest must be paid on bonds. The choice between money and bonds depends on the current rate of interest, but also on expectations about how the interest rate may change in the future. For when the interest rate rises, bond prices fall, as explained in Chapter 7. Therefore, if expectations are broadly held that the interest rate is likely to rise, holding cash will be seen as preferable so as to avoid the coming drop in bond prices. Keynes regarded this interest sensitivity as imparting a speculative demand for money balances. A low interest rate encourages a preference for liquidity due to the low current return on bonds as well as to the greater likelihood that the rate will rise in the future.

Combining the transactions demand and the speculative demand for liquidity (or money) gives us a function defined on the interest rate and income which we set equal to the exogenously given money supply,

$$\bar{M}^S = L(r, Y), \tag{9.4}$$

where $\bar{M}^S$ = exogenous money supply;
  L $(\cdot)$ = the liquidity preference function.

The function $L(r, Y)$ depends negatively on r and positively on Y. The LM equation yields pairs of r and Y at which the public is willing to hold the available supply of money.

For given $\bar{M}^S$, we can trace a relationship that must hold between r and Y. An increase in income will tend to increase the demand for liquidity for transactions purposes. To offset this, the interest rate must rise to induce the holding of bonds as an alternative to money. Thus the relationship between r and Y that preserves a given value for money demand, which will align it with money supply, is positive. This is represented by the upward sloping LM curve of Figure 9.6.

Equilibrium in Income and the Interest Rate

The IS and LM curves of Figure 9.6 jointly determine equilibrium values of income and the interest rate. Pairs of r and Y along the IS curve equate saving and investment. Pairs of the same variables along the LM curve preserve a given level of money demand set equal to an exogenously controlled money supply.

True to form in a model of Keynesian inspiration, the equilibrium income given by Y^* in Figure 9.6 need not represent a full-employment outcome. The economy can be operating at less than capacity with unemployment manifest at Y^* with no impetus for output and

D IS–LM Model   175

income to increase. In the IS–LM Model, both fiscal and monetary policy offer the potential to boost equilibrium output. A detailed exposition of the mechanics is beyond the scope of this text. In brief, expansionary fiscal policy involving government spending increases or tax cuts shifts the IS curve to the right pushing up the interest rate as income rises. The upward movement along the LM curve ensures equality between money demand and fixed money supply as the combination of higher income and higher interest rate have offsetting effects on money demand (higher income raising it, a higher interest rate lowering it). Expansionary monetary policy shifts the LM curve to the right driving the interest rate downward as income rises. The lower interest rate ensures that investment spending will pick up to match the increase in saving that follows from higher income.

External Balance and the Mundell–Fleming Extension

The basic IS–LM Model assumes a closed economy, or at least takes international trade and financial flows as fixed. The Mundell–Fleming Model incorporates an endogenous foreign sector into the analysis. The balance on the current account is assumed to be a function of income and on the financial account a function of the interest rate. As income increases, imports rise and exports decline in response to the increase in domestic demand. Hence the balance on the current account decreases (a surplus shrinks or a deficit expands). As the interest rate rises domestically, more capital flows in and less flows out. The balance on the financial account thus increases (a surplus expands or a deficit shrinks). An increased surplus on one account must be matched by an increased deficit on the other to preserve overall balance.

The BP curve of Figure 9.7 represents pairs of income and the interest rate that preserve balance in international payments. As income increases and the current account balance

Figure 9.7 Mundell–Fleming model

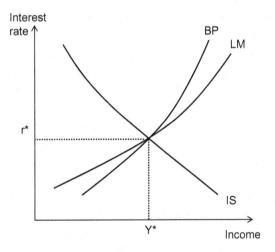

The BP curve extends the IS-LM model to introduce pairs of income and the interest rate that achieve balance in external payments.

declines, the interest rate must rise in order to bring about the necessary increase in the financial account balance to compensate. The positive slope of the BP curve indicates that income and the interest rate must move in the same direction to ensure balance in the balance of payments. A steep slope in the BP curve means that a large change in the interest rate is associated with a given change in income implying that barriers to capital flows allow the domestic interest rate to deviate readily from a global standard. If capital were perfectly mobile across the border, the global interest rate would prevail and the BP curve would be perfectly elastic at that interest rate.

A change in the exchange rate causes the BP curve to shift. A reduction in the value of the domestic currency in terms of foreign currency shifts the BP curve to the right as higher exports and lower imports support an increase in domestic output at any given interest rate. Assuming no intervention by the monetary authority, the exchange rate must adjust to bring about balance, meaning the BP curve must come to rest where all three curves intersect at the same value of Y. If the monetary authority intervenes to influence the exchange rate, the BP curve will diverge from this common point of intersection to create a wedge between the current account balance and the opposing financial account balance.

In the Mundell–Fleming open economy model, exchange rate management provides an additional macroeconomic policy lever for use in conjunction with monetary and fiscal policy, provided that capital is not perfectly mobile and the domestic interest rate may diverge from a global standard. If Y^* falls below full-employment income, a judicious use of monetary, fiscal, and exchange rate policies can push the system of IS, LM, and BP curves to the right to achieve balance along all dimensions at a level of income above the equilibrium.

E   Evolving Schools of Thought

The classical and Keynesian schools of thought have evolved over time in contention with one another. Classical theory provides an explanation for the demonstrated success of market economies in generating growth and creating jobs. Keynesian theory recognizes that economic performance fluctuates relative to potential and governments thus find scope to intervene. A compromise worldview involving classical foundations to explain long-run tendencies but allowing an ancillary role for stabilization measures in the short run to help an economy keep to its full-employment optimum came to predominate by the 1950s. Economist Paul Samuelson dubbed this the "neoclassical synthesis" in the third edition of his bestselling principles text.

The neoclassical synthesis represented a moderation of the more radical stand Keynes took in the *General Theory*. Keynes saw demand shortfall as a chronic and pernicious malady of the capitalist system. His concerns led him to argue "that the duty of ordering the current value of investment cannot safely be left in private hands" (p. 164), and consequently "that a somewhat comprehensive socialisation of investment will prove the only means of securing an approximation to full employment" (p. 375). For more on Keynes's not so prescient musings on the fate of private investment and the "euthanasia of the rentier," along with a digression into his more prophetic warnings on war reparations, see Box 9.2.

To be discussed in Chapter 10, macroeconomic models have become far more complex, running to hundreds, even thousands of equations. Yet the same tension between classical market clearing and Keynesian frictions and market imperfections has continued to play out in their evolution. The debate has yielded more sophisticated theories of how markets work and a better understanding of how to conduct stabilization policy. As the neoclassical synthesis emerged out of the Keynesian revolution that challenged the classic school that came before it, so a new synthesis has in more recent years bridged the gap between "new classicals" and "new Keynesians." The new classical econometric models that provided for general equilibrium across markets for goods, labor, and assets have been adapted to accept new Keynesian-style price stickiness. These models allow for labor to be unemployed and firms to operate at less than capacity without quick resolution.

The models presented in this chapter are static in nature. They characterize an economy in the moment, introduce a shock, then examine the outcome, with no cognizance of the passage of time. The Aggregate Demand / Aggregate Supply Model starts from full employment equilibrium, brings in a disturbance, then traces the return to equilibrium through two stages. The Income–Expenditure and IS–LM models take as their starting point a disequilibrium situation in which the economy is operating at less than capacity with no promise of timely recovery. The shocks of interest in the Keynesian context are policy measures that bring the economy up to full speed. In all these models, the analysis proceeds with no explicit time dimension. Yet business cycles are dynamic by nature. They involve movement of an economy over time, up and down, constantly in flux. In Chapter 10, we look at competing approaches to understanding this dynamism.

Box 9.2 What else Keynes said

Long before he wrote the *General Theory*, Keynes had achieved considerable stature not only as an economic theoretician but as a voice in world affairs. His *Economic Consequences of the Peace*, written in 1919, was a polemic against the spoliation of Germany by the victors of World War I. Keynes felt so strongly about this issue that he withdrew as an advisor to the peace negotiations in protest against a treaty he believed would "sow the decay of the whole of civilized Europe" (p. 225).

In his writing, Keynes developed the empirical case that Germany's capacity to pay reparations fell far short of the terms imposed by the Treaty of Versailles. He argued further that for Germany to make payments even on the order he was proposing, the country's exports would have to increase and imports decrease greatly to generate the necessary foreign exchange. This could happen only if Western Europe and the USA opened their own markets to German products and faced up to greater competition from German goods worldwide. Keynes advocated an alternative proposal whereby

Box 9.2 (cont.)

the USA would forgive the debts it was owed by Britain, France, and Italy, and these countries would in turn scale back greatly their demands on Germany.

Keynes wrote ardently:

I believe that the campaign for securing out of Germany the general costs of the war was one of the most serious acts of political unwisdom for which our statesmen have ever been responsible. To what a different future Europe might have looked forward if either [British Prime Minister] Mr. Lloyd George or [US President Mr. Woodrow] Wilson had apprehended that the most serious of the problems which claimed their attention were not political or territorial but financial and economic, and that the perils of the future lay not in frontiers or sovereignties but in food, coal, and transport. ... [T]he financial problems which were about to exercise Europe could not be solved by greed. The possibility of their cure lay in magnanimity." (pp. 146–147)

The book became an international bestseller – arriving too late, however, to alter history's harrowing course toward Nazism and another world war. Yet in the aftermath of World War II, the lessons had seemingly been absorbed. The USA dedicated enormous sums to the post-war reconstruction of Europe and Japan, launching an era of prosperity that redounded to all.

For all his brilliance, Keynes was not without ideas that failed to withstand the test of time. One of his odder notions in hindsight was that continued capital accumulation would lead to a day when the return on capital would fall to zero and result in the "euthanasia of the rentier" with profound implications for social organization. From the *General Theory*:

If I am right in supposing it to be comparatively easy to make capital-goods so abundant that the marginal efficiency of capital is zero, this may be the most sensible way of gradually getting rid of many of the objectionable features of capitalism. For a little reflection will show what enormous social changes would result from a gradual disappearance of a rate of return on accumulated wealth. A man would still be free to accumulate his earned income with a view to spending it at a later date. But his accumulation would not grow. He would simply be in the position of Pope's father, who, when he retired from business, carried a chest of guineas with him to his villa at Twickenham and met his household expenses from it as required." (p. 221)

Some 80 years on, society is no closer to the day when prospects for a positive return on investment have disappeared. Technological innovation seems to have provided escape from this fate, generating continuing opportunities for lucrative new undertakings.

Data Note

Information on the Great Depression is from Smiley (2008).

Bibliographic Note

Mankiw (2006) describes reading Keynes's *General Theory* as "both exhilarating and frustrating." A great mind applying itself to an enormous topic is much to be appreciated, in Mankiw's view, even as the outcome is amorphous and less than logically satisfying. Mankiw is similarly entertaining in his characterizations of the two sides of the new classical versus new Keynesian debates. Blanchard (2008) provides another fine summary of the tension between schools of thought and attempts at resolution.

The two models associated with Keynes in this chapter were not articulated graphically by Keynes himself. Rather, the graphical analyses were developed by others to interpret Keynes. The Income–Expenditure Model appeared in the first edition of Paul Samuelson's principles text (1948, p. 275). The IS–LM Model was devised by Hicks (1937), who was well on his way to formulating it before the *General Theory* was published. For a statement on the value of the IS–LM Model, see Krugman (2011). Debate has swirled around whether these models are valid representations of Keynes's thinking. Not only did Keynes never deign to react to Hicks's model, according to his biographer, Robert Skidelsky, he "tended to ignore anything which Hicks did." (interview in Snowden and Vane, 2005, p. 96). Perhaps Keynes accepted that Keynesian economics had taken on a life of its own.

Works by Mundell (1963) and Fleming (1962) laid the foundations for open economy macroeconomics. Salvatore (2013) offers a refined textbook treatment of the Mundell–Fleming Model.

BIBLIOGRAPHIC CITATIONS

Blanchard, Olivier, 2008. "Neoclassical Synthesis," in Steven N. Durlauf and Lawrence E. Blume, eds., *The New Palgrave Dictionary of Economics*, 2nd edition (Palgrave Macmillan). www .dictionaryofeconomics.com/article?id=pde2008_N000041 (accessed February 17, 2014); also, http://economics.mit.edu/files/677 (accessed February 17, 2014).

Fleming, J. Marcus, [1962] 1969. "Domestic Financial Policies under Fixed and Floating Exchange Rates," reprinted in Richard N. Cooper, ed., *International Finance* (New York: Penguin Books).

Hicks, John R., 1937. "Mr. Keynes and the 'Classics'; A Suggested Interpretation," *Econometrica*, Vol. 5, No. 2, pp. 147–159.

Hicks, John R., 1980. " 'IS–LM': An Explanation," *Journal of Post-Keynesian Economics*, Vol. 3, No. 2, pp. 139–154.

Keynes, John Maynard, [1920] 1995. *The Economic Consequences of the Peace* (New York: Penguin Books).

Keynes, John Maynard, [1936] 1964. *The General Theory of Employment, Interest, and Money* (New York: Harcourt, Brace & World).

Krugman, Paul, 2011. "There's Something about Macro," http://web.mit.edu/krugman/www/islm .html (accessed February 8, 2014). Linked from Paul Krugman, "Conscience of a Liberal," *New York Times*, October 5, 2011. http://krugman.blogs.nytimes.com/2011/10/05/tis-the-gift-to-be-simple/ (accessed February 8, 2014).

Mankiw, N. Gregory, 2006. "The Macroeconomist As Scientist and Engineer," Working Paper 12349 (Cambridge, MA: National Bureau of Economic Research).

Mundell, Robert, 1963. "Capital Mobility and Stabilization Policy under Fixed and Flexible Exchange Rates," *Canadian Journal of Economic and Political Science*, Vol. 29, No. 4, pp. 475–485.

Salvatore, Dominick, 2013. "Chapter 18," *International Economics*, 11th edition (Hoboken, NJ: John Wiley & Sons).

Samuelson, Paul, 1948. *Economics* (New York: McGraw-Hill), p. 275.

Samuelson, Paul, 1955. *Economics*, 3rd edition (New York: McGraw-Hill), p. 212.

Smiley, Gene, 2008. "Great Depression," in David R. Henderson, ed., *The Concise Encyclopedia of Economics* (Liberty Fund). www.econlib.org/library/Enc/GreatDepression.html (accessed January 28, 2014).

Snowdon, Brian and Howard R. Vane (eds.), 2005. *Modern Macroeconomics: Its Origins, Development and Current State* (Cheltenham, UK: Edward Elgar).

10 Business Cycles

The dominant paradigm for the analysis of business cycles takes full-employment equilibrium as the norm and attributes temporary and self-correcting deviations from this norm to exogenous shocks. There is, however, another way of thinking about business cycles to be found in the historical literature. This alternative paradigm takes the movement of an economy up and down through cycles as itself the norm and sees endogenous forces as driving the process.

For all the inevitability of the business cycle, the ups and downs prove difficult to predict in advance or even to interpret after the fact. A multitude of factors is seemingly involved. Some analysts place the emphasis on real influences, some on monetary influences. Some find efficacy in policy intervention to maintain stability; others regard policy activism as one more source of disruption. Finally – and this distinction will constitute a theme in this chapter – some adhere to a frame of reference that takes full-employment equilibrium as the norm and attributes deviations from this norm to exogenous shocks, while others tell a story of endogenous processes driving cycles such that cycles themselves become the norm.

We begin the chapter by tracing the roots of the distinction between endogenous and exogenous theories of the business cycle to early thinkers on the subject. We then go on to examine the mid-20th-century Keynesian consensus as to the power of policy to subdue the business cycle, and the subsequent pillorying of that consensus by events of the 1970s. That takes us to the new consensus that formed – among theorists if not policymakers – around the antithesis to Keynesianism which vested markets with primacy and derided the conceits of policy intervention. Through the decades since, the premise of market equilibrium has lain at the heart of increasingly sophisticated economic models based on shock-induced fluctuations, and we outline the form of these models. The failure of this approach, however, to even contemplate a crisis on the order of the one that struck the USA in 2008 led to a search for alternatives in which finance plays a more integral role. The long-sidelined endogenous cycle theory of Hyman Minsky fits the bill, as we explain. The Philippines serves as our case study for this chapter, offering a window on the interplay between endogenous credit cycles and exogenous shocks. We close by bridging the gap between the narratives of exogeneity and endogeneity by positing that an economy's vulnerability to or resilience against exogenous shocks is shaped by an endogenous cyclical process.

A   Early Thinking on Business Cycles

The recurring nature of booms and busts is apparent going at least as far back as the Roman Empire. Not until the mid-1800s, however, did observers draw a clear connection between the two as opposing phases of a cyclical process. Much intellectual effort had by that time been expended trying to explain the causes of crises and depressions as episodic events. A whole new way of thinking about the problem was encapsulated in a pithy assessment by Clement Juglar in 1862 that "the only cause of depression is prosperity."

The tension between the exogenous and endogenous views of the business cycle is deeply embedded in the history of economic thought. In this section we look to early exemplars, drawing the contrast between the seminal ideas of Mills (1868) and Pigou (1927) regarding what drives the business cycle. We then move forward through time to consider the opposing remedies proposed by John Maynard Keynes (1936) and the Austrian School as represented by Mises (1949). First though, we lay foundations by describing the features of the business cycle.

Features of the Business Cycle

As Chart 1.1 established, volatility in GDP growth is a scourge from which no economy is immune. Yet on occasion, relative calm can stretch on for a decade or more. This may then just as easily be followed by a flurry of gyrations striking hard and fast one upon another. Sometimes, too, growth rates can catapult from deeply negative to exuberantly positive, or do the opposite, while at other times movement follows gentle waves. In sum, both the frequency and the amplitude of ups and downs vary greatly.

The term "business cycle" should therefore not be construed to imply regularity, and indeed some economists prefer the term "business fluctuations" to avoid any such connotation. "Business fluctuations," however, suggests a lack of continuity between an upswing and the downturn that follows it whereas such continuity is the very focus of endogenous theories of the business cycle. To speak of "fluctuations" is then more in keeping with a notion of exogenous shocks as drivers. We will adhere to the term "cycle" because it invokes a continuum of phases and with that, is more amenable to the possibility of forecasting, an endeavor that occupies many in the economics profession.

The standard taxonomy of the business cycle identifies four phases: expansion or recovery; peak; contraction or recession; and trough. The expansion phase is characterized by high GDP growth and strong job creation but may give rise to accelerating inflation. Businesses are eager to borrow and creditors are happy to lend. At the peak of the cycle, an economy tends to overshoot its potential such that labor markets tighten, wages rise, and profits are squeezed. Debt loads increase to the point of unsustainability. Eventually, the run is exhausted and a downturn ensues, perhaps spurred by an exogenous trigger to which the economy has become vulnerable as an expansion depletes itself. The economy contracts (or in the case of a "growth recession" expands sluggishly relative to its potential), jobs are cut, businesses fail, and loans go into default. Then in the trough, bad debts are written off, excess inventories are liquidated at fire sale prices, and physical assets are put to new purpose. A trough that is extremely deep and long is known as a depression. The cleansing process that occurs in the trough lays the foundation for renewal.

Upsurges and downturns in the business cycle tend to be presaged by "leading indicators" and shadowed by "lagging indicators." Such indicators find use in forecasting efforts. Box 10.1 explains.

A final observation about business cycles is worth noting. The investment component of GDP fluctuates much more sharply over the course of the cycle than the consumption component. Any compelling theory of the cycle must be able to account for this pattern.

Box 10.1 Business cycle indicators

The forecasting of business cycles rests on a variety of indicators, some moving together with real output, some ahead of it, and some behind it. GDP as the ultimate embodiment of economic activity takes months to compile so coincident indicators that can be assembled in real time offer more ready insight into current conditions. Leading indicators tend to precede movements in GDP. But even lagging indicators have predictive power since within a cyclical process knowing where the economy has been reveals something about where it may be going.

Standard leading, coincident, and lagging indicators are shown in the table below.

Leading Indicators	Coincident Indicators	Lagging Indicators
expectations • consumer confidence • business sentiment economic activity • new business registration • construction permits • property transactions finance • stock market index • policy interest rate • exchange rates labor • average hours worked	economic activity • production • sales • exports and imports • electricity consumption • capacity utilitzation labor • employment	economic activity • inventories finance • debt level • loan rate of interest • consumer price index labor • unit labor costs

Survey responses about expectations make for good leading indicators since expectations guide action and thus tend to be self-fulfilling when broadly held. Consumer confidence and business sentiment are key expectations measures. New business

Box 10.1 (cont.)

registration, construction permits, and property transactions all signal major under-takings in the offing. Stock market valuations capture the beliefs of the investing public as to the discounted value of future earnings and, moreover, provide the basis for firms to raise capital. The interest rate targeted by policymakers reveals the government's stance on stimulating or restraining the credit flows that fuel future business activity. Exchange rate movements similarly impact businesses in ways that play out over time. In the labor realm, employers tend to adjust the hours of existing workers before undertaking more lasting moves to hire or fire.

Coincident indicators reflect current activity in the form of production, sales, and international trade. Measures of electricity consumption and capacity utilization offer immediate gauges of the state of economic affairs. Employment, too, is closely tied to current activity.

Lagging indicators signal that an economy has reached a late stage in an expansion or recession. As an expansion wears on, production ultimately outpaces sales and inventories begin to accumulate, while conversely late in a recession excess inventories at last begin to be drawn down. The late stage of expansion moreover brings rising debt levels, upward pressure on loan rates of interest, and accelerating inflation in consumer prices, whereas the opposite trends emerge late in a recession. Finally, labor markets tighten late in an expansion pushing up labor costs per unit of output, and they slacken late in a recession causing unit labor costs to fall. The panoply of forces that comes into play as an expansion runs its course has the effect of curbing growth. And vice versa, those forces that become manifest as a slowdown drags on pave the way for recovery.

Mills vs Pigou

Decisions to produce, and even more so decisions to invest, are forward looking. Well before any business revenue is generated, costs must be incurred. This means that credit is essential to business enterprise. The close association between business and credit explains why business cycles were referred to historically as "credit cycles." Credit is underpinned by faith in the future, and that makes it inherently sensitive to subjective perceptions and shifting expectations.

By 1867, John Mills discerned a periodicity in Britain's business fluctuations over the preceding half century and interpreted this as due to a self-perpetuating cycle that rested on the interplay of credit and "mental mood." In Mills' words: "As credit is a thing of moral essence, the external character of each stage of its development is traced to a parallel change of mental mood, and we find the whole subject embraced under the wider generalisation of a normal tendency of the human mind" (p. 17).

Mills's "tendency of the human mind" involves swings between the extremes of excitement and panic. In the excitement of the expansionary phase, easy credit fuels business start-ups and inflates profits. People assume that what is will always be, and confidence abounds. In time, however, credit and speculation begin to act upon each other. Prices are driven up. Investment becomes ever more reckless and goods are spilled onto the market faster than they can be absorbed. Eventually, prices must weaken. This eats into profits. Financing then becomes more difficult to renew and the sale of goods more imperative. Panic begins to take root. Price declines escalate and loans go past due. Ultimately, businesses fail and banks go under. In the wake of a panic, owners of capital retrench and banks push to strengthen reserves. Lenders and borrowers are reticent to engage … until at last, time heals wounds and new opportunities come to be perceived. Risk-taking is once again rewarded, and confidence regerminates. The cycle begins anew.

Mills did not find the remedy to ups and downs in averting panic. "Panics" he held, "do not destroy capital; they merely reveal the extent to which it has been previously destroyed by its betrayal into hopelessly unproductive works" (p. 18). Rather, his solution was aimed at the boom. "Is it a fatal necessity that credit must grow rank and rotten, and collapse in a spasm of terror?" (p. 38). Not necessarily. Mills believed that education was the key to forestalling the "liability to an ignorant speculative excitement, and a willingness to take immoral risks" (p. 39). Unfortunately, a century and a half on, humanity seems still not to have learned the lesson.

In contrast to Mills, Pigou (1927) looked to exogenous shocks for an explanation of the business cycle. He set forth three categories of shock: (i) real; (ii) monetary; and (iii) psychological. Sources of real shock run to harvests, technology, natural resource discoveries, labor disputes, tastes, and foreign demand. Impulses to any of these can reverberate across sectors of the economy with resources discharged from some activities reabsorbed only gradually elsewhere. Monetary shocks involve autonomous changes in the money supply, due, for example, to changes in government reliance on money creation to finance deficits. Pigou allows that monetary shocks can have real economic consequences, at least for a time, through their effect on interest rates and bank lending.

Psychological shocks pertain to errors of optimism and pessimism. Such errors can gain traction on a mass scale as business managers interact in "a quasi-hypnotic system of mutual suggestion" reinforced by the self-fulfilling nature of shared expectations (p. 79). Booms founded on errors of optimism can, Pigou concurs with Mills, turn to busts as errors rebound to the opposite extreme. Indeed, in such circumstances an error of pessimism can be "born, not an infant, but a giant. For an industrial boom has necessarily been a period of strong emotional excitement, and an excited man passes from one form of excitement to another more readily than he passes to quiescence" (p. 85). For Pigou though, the error pendulum is not a perpetual motion machine. Friction brings an economy's gyrations to rest, unless and until some new outside force acts upon the system.

Austrians vs Keynesians

For the Austrian School of economists, the business cycle is explained by a single form of exogenous shock: government mismanagement of the money supply. The Austrian focus on government misdeed fits into a broader world view that extols free markets and individual liberty, as outlined in Box 10.2. As the story goes, governments in capitalist societies routinely succumb to political pressure to stimulate the economy with expansionary monetary policy that acts to increase bank reserves and thus reduce interest rates. In the words of Mises (1949), a "boom is built on the sands of banknotes and deposits. It must collapse" (p. 559).

Box 10.2 The Austrian school of thought

The Austrian School is known for championing the free market. The School's formative thinkers contributed to our understanding of market pricing as a mechanism for achieving efficiency in the allocation of resources. They extended the basic argument by applying the notion of marginal utility to money and interest rates with ramifications for explaining business cycles. But their argument for free markets does not rest merely on efficiency. The ultimate value of free markets in the Austrian paradigm lies in their providing the essential foundation for a free society.

Seminal contributors to the Austrian School, all linked to the University of Vienna, include Carl Menger (1840–1921), Eugen von Boehm-Bawerk (1851–1914), Ludwig von Mises (1881–1973), and Friedrich Hayek (1899–1992).

The Austrian perspective took hold in counterpoint to the rise of socialist ideology in the late 19th and early 20th centuries. The vision of socialism was to organize society for the good of all by vesting ownership of the means of production with the state. The Austrians, by contrast, exalted the individual in the spirit of classical liberalism.

Hayek's *Road to Serfdom*, published in 1944, stands as the great manifesto for a market economy. Markets, Hayek argued, coordinate the activity of individuals, enabling entrepreneurs "to adjust their activities to those of their fellows" (p.56). Private property "is the most important guaranty of freedom, not only for those who own property, but scarcely less for those who do not. It is only because the control of the means of production is divided among many people acting independently that nobody has complete power over us" (p. 115). Wage differentials are the "yardstick" by which people "judge what they ought to do" (p.139). And the rule of law, as opposed to the rule of men, ensures predictability of state action so that individuals are "able to use their knowledge effectively in making plans" (p. 83).

The primacy of markets does not preclude a role for government in the economy. Hayek favored state guarantees of basic sustenance and public assistance in the face of "those common hazards of life against which, because of their uncertainty few individuals can make adequate provision" (p.133).

But any more general pursuit of central planning can only lead to tyranny in Hayek's reasoning. "[P]lanning leads to dictatorship because dictatorship is the most

> **Box 10.2 (cont.)**
>
> effective instrument of coercion and the enforcement of ideals and, as such, essential if central planning on a large scale is to be possible" (p. 79). Propaganda becomes imperative for mobilizing people to serve a socialist state. The full meaning of Hayek's invocation of "serfdom" in the title of his book becomes clear. "The skillful propagandist then has power to mold their minds in any direction he chooses, and even the most intelligent and independent of people cannot entirely escape that influence if they are long isolated from all other sources of information" (p. 169).

An artificially low interest rate distorts investment decisions. For sound investment to be motivated, the interest rate must convey information on the value of products to be yielded in the future relative to the value of resources diverted from consumption in the present. It falls to the interest rate to prevent the entrepreneur "from embarking upon projects the execution of which would not agree with the limited amount of capital goods provided by the saving of the public" (p. 544). The government, by driving down the interest rate, encourages investment that will not ultimately prove viable. The saving of the public is not increased by such a policy; rather, a given amount of saving is simply misallocated into applications with gestation periods too long to be economically justified.

To keep the boom going, money and credit must expand at an accelerating rate. Eventually this becomes unsustainable. The bust that follows exposes the malinvestment that has taken place. But the harm extends further. For as outstanding debts are not repaid, banks retrench and even sound businesses find they are unable to obtain credit. Recovery is a slow process that must rely on accumulation of new capital. But Mises advises against resorting to renewed credit expansion which "would at best only interrupt, disturb, and prolong the curative process of the depression, if not bring about a new boom with all its inevitable consequences" (p. 576).

The Austrian prescription for government to withdraw and allow a slump to run its course competed contemporaneously during the Great Depression with Keynesian advocacy for an active role of government in managing aggregate demand. Keynesians feared not just the periodic cyclical slowdown as an economy readjusted to changes in circumstances, but an endemic weakness in spending from which there would be no automatic tendency to rebound. Ideologically, the Keynesians won out, at least for a time.

B   The Neoclassical Synthesis and Its Demise

A theory stands or falls by its ability to explain observed reality. Keynesian theory was validated in the 1940s when massive government spending to fight World War II pulled the USA and Europe out of their prolonged depression. The conflict between Keynesian and classical views was reconciled under the neoclassical synthesis which held that while markets would in principle bring about full employment, government spending and tax policies could expedite an otherwise potentially protracted process. As explained in this section, however, there was believed to be a trade-off between reducing unemployment under Keynesian policies and ramping up inflation. Initially, experience seemed to verify the existence of such a trade-off. Ultimately, however, reality proved to be more complicated, and a new theory centered on the role of expectations in driving inflation was formulated to take its place.

The Phillips Curve

The argument for a trade-off between inflation and unemployment is easily understood: As unemployment declines, competition among businesses to hire workers intensifies thus putting upward pressure on wages. The lower the unemployment rate, the more an increase in demand for workers is channeled into higher wages. Conversely, when unemployment is high and labor markets are slack, jobless workers can be absorbed at the prevailing wage without much pressure to pay more. Increases in wages, to whatever degree, tend to be passed on in the form of higher prices for goods and services. Hence low unemployment gives rise to inflation.

Graphically, the relationship between unemployment and inflation was expected to look exactly like the line plotted in Chart 10.1 for the period limited to 1961–1969. At the relatively high unemployment rate of about 7 percent manifest in 1961, demand stimulus policies could achieve a reduction in joblessness with little impact on prices. With each further reduction in unemployment, however, the inflationary consequences were amplified. An arc relating unemployment and inflation in this fashion is known as the *Phillips curve* after the economist who mapped it out in 1958 using British data for the preceding century.

The US experience in the 1960s represented a deliberate experiment in applying Keynesian demand management techniques to exploit the Phillips curve relationship. Dissatisfied with unemployment rates holding in excess of 5 percent, President Kennedy

Chart 10.1 Inflation and unemployment rates, USA, 1961–1980

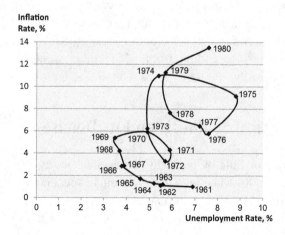

in 1963 proposed a tax cut to stimulate spending. The tax cut was implemented in 1964 and by 1965, unemployment had dropped to 4.6 percent with inflation remaining below 2 percent. The sense of triumph was captured by a headline in *Time* magazine declaring "We are all Keynesians now." The next few years under President Johnson saw big increases in government spending to support escalation of the war in Vietnam and an ambitious program to fight poverty. As predicted by economic theory, unemployment continued to drop while inflation shot up. At this point, the economy needed cooling down, so a tax increase was imposed. The result, however, was not to retrace the Phillips curve of the 1960s in reverse as had been anticipated. Rather, inflation remained high in 1970 and 1971 even as the unemployment rate climbed. Then just as inflation was finally being subdued, a cartel of oil-producing nations imposed an embargo in 1973–74 which sent oil prices soaring and pushed inflation to new heights. Rising unemployment followed as higher energy costs crimped business activity, yet high inflation was initially sustained. A tax cut in 1975 helped bring about recovery. But a second oil price shock in 1979 reignited inflation, and by 1980 it approached an unprecedented 14 percent even as unemployment stood at 7.6 percent.

This combination of high inflation and high unemployment was dubbed "stagflation" (stagnation + inflation). It defied the logic of the Phillips curve that high unemployment should have a restraining effect on wage and price increases. A new theory of unemployment and inflation was called for.

The Natural Rate of Unemployment

Already by the late 1960s, skepticism about the government's ability to manage the economy and choose at will from a menu of inflation and unemployment combinations was building among economists of a more classical bent. Milton Friedman (1968) and Edmund Phelps (1967) argued that the unemployment rate would tend to a natural equilibrium level determined by market frictions associated with matching people to jobs. The actual rate of unemployment fluctuates, and government policy can work to push it below the natural rate for a time. Doing so comes at a cost, however, in terms of higher inflation that is difficult to shake.

According to Friedman and Phelps, the natural rate of unemployment is consistent with any rate of inflation as long as that rate is foreseen by market participants. Workers build the anticipated rate of inflation into their wage demands and employers build it into their cost projections. Equilibrium in the labor market is then achieved on the basis of a real wage that is readily discernible to all as the difference between the nominal wage and inflation. Assuming expectations of inflation are based on past experience, any inflation rate that is sustained over a period of time will be fully anticipated and the labor market will function under such circumstances to arrive at the natural rate of unemployment.

Government policy can push the unemployment rate below its natural level only by engineering an inflation surprise. In the telling of Friedman and Phelps, a monetary stimulus drives down the rate of interest with businesses thus induced to take out loans and create new jobs. The economy is pushed to function above its sustainable potential. Before long, however, bottlenecks develop and prices are bid upward. For a time, this outcome is as the Phillips curve predicts. But workers come to realize the purchasing power of their wages has been eroded by inflation. They adjust their expectations of inflation and increase their wage demands to preserve the real value of their compensation. Employers respond by scaling back their hiring. The unemployment rate then returns to its natural level. The new inflation rate, however, has now become lodged in expectations. In order for those expectations to be realized, the government must continue its expansionary monetary policy. Should it instead seek to curtail inflation by tightening money growth, interest rates will rise and businesses will retrench. Unemployment will mount even as inflation maintains its momentum over some interim. The economy moves off its former Phillips curve, as the USA did in 1971 and 1975. Eventually, the slower money growth is translated into a lower rate of inflation, expectations adjust, and unemployment again returns to its natural rate.

An inflationary impetus once introduced by government tends to become entrenched. To sustain unemployment below its natural rate requires that inflation be accelerating. The natural rate of unemployment is therefore known also as the non-inflation-accelerating rate of unemployment, or NAIRU. Reining inflation back in once it has been unleashed causes unemployment to rise over the period of time required for expectations to readjust to lower inflation. In the classical spirit, the conclusion is that government intervention does more to disrupt the market equilibrating mechanism than to improve upon it, and that the Phillips curve, insofar as it may be said to exist at all, is highly unstable.

C   Exogenous Shock Theories

The demise of the Phillips curve as a menu of options and the neoclassical synthesis as the basis for policy choice among these options opened the way for a return to classical principles of market equilibrium centered on a natural rate of unemployment. The adaptive expectations of Friedman and Phelps that left economic agents forever a step behind in figuring out inflation were replaced by less inherently error-prone "rational expectations," to be discussed in this section.

Business cycle models built on rational expectations within a general equilibrium framework have evolved in stages over a period of decades. These models capture shocks as a stochastic process, and are known as *dynamic stochastic general equilibrium (DSGE) models*. A first generation of models exploited the classical dichotomy between the real economy and money to focus on real shocks as the drivers of cycles. A second generation incorporated money into the models with ramifications for the real economy. The limitations of these models were exposed by their failure to account for anything remotely resembling the financial crisis of 2008. This has inspired work on a third generation of models to overcome these limitations by, for example, recharacterizing the nature of equilibrium and its trajectory over time. We outline the structure of these three generations of models in turn.

Rational Expectations

Rational expectations theory assumes economic agents are able to predict the future as well as any economic model. This contrasts with the Friedman and Phelps assumption that workers systematically fail to predict an accelerating inflation and allow their real wages to slip behind even as the monetary authorities who institute the inflation and the economists who advise them comprehend what is to transpire. Rational expectations theory does not imply perfect foresight. That would be impossible in a world constantly buffeted by shocks. Rather, the idea is that the public is able to assess the likelihood of the range of possible future outcomes without systematic bias.

Even so, as Lucas (1972) originally set forth the argument, agents have difficulty sorting out in the moment the mix of real and nominal influences that act on prices. Suppose an entrepreneur experiences an increase in demand for her product. This will induce her to raise her selling price and expand production. If the increase in demand is specific to her particular product, the higher price will be sustained relative to the prices of other products, and the entrepreneur will enjoy higher real returns as the reward for her effort. On the other hand, if the demand increase is driven by an expansion in the money supply that impacts all markets, the entrepreneur will find her higher nominal returns eaten away in real terms as her costs rise along with the general price level. Realizing that the increase in demand is not special to her and that her increased activity is not supported by the marketplace, she will scale back production to its former level, although her higher output price will be sustained commensurate with higher prices in general. Lucas's model demonstrates how output and employment fluctuations can result even within a general equilibrium framework where all markets, including the labor market, clear, and thus unemployment does not exist other than in a voluntary sense. The aggregate fluctuations derive from agents misinterpreting general price shocks as being specific to their own markets. As with the story of Friedman and Phelps, then, agents are temporarily fooled.

The difference under rational expectations theory is that agents can only be fooled if a monetary stimulus comes as a surprise. But for it to come as a surprise, the stimulus cannot be predicated on the basis of economic conditions; it must be random. Yet if it is random, it cannot be undertaken purposefully to stabilize the economy, for if economic agents realize a money expansion is in play, they will neutralize any real impact by fully adjusting wages and prices without delay. The conclusion must be that monetary policy intervention is unjustifiable and that markets are best left to function on their own. Apropos of such market deference, the school of thought associated with a Lucas-type framework involving general equilibrium and rational expectations is known as new classical economics. In the narrow sense, this term applies to models in which only unforeseen monetary shocks can have an impact on real output. But the term is often applied more broadly to encompass real business cycle theory in which money is entirely absent.

Real Business Cycle Theory

Jumping off from Lucas, real business cycle theory incorporates rational expectations and assumes markets are always in equilibrium. In effect, Say's Law prevails: Supply creates its own demand. The theory further jettisons money. Business cycles are presumed to derive solely from supply-side shocks to productivity. Conceivable sources of such shocks include: advances in technology that while raising productivity in some activities are disruptive for others (think of word processors replacing typists or digital cameras driving film developers out of business); shifts in external trade or capital flows; changes in government fiscal, monetary, or regulatory policies; and revisions to broadly held expectations. Since the sources of shock are never treated explicitly in modeling exercises, they are often referred to simply as technology shocks. Box 10.3 explains how such shocks are formalized.

Box 10.3 Modeling productivity shocks

Trend growth in real output can be ascribed in part to increases in labor and capital inputs to production and in part to increases in the productivity of these inputs. Business cycles involve fluctuations around trend growth. In real business cycle theory, these fluctuations around trend are regarded as emanating from shocks to the productivity component of growth.

The process is formalized within a Solow (1957) growth model. Let output, Y, be related via a production function to inputs of labor, L, and capital, K, and a productivity factor, A. In a growth model, all variables are in turn functions of time, t. The Solow growth equation is then given as:

$$Y(t) = A(t)L(t)^{\alpha}K(t)^{1-\alpha}.$$

The parameter α reflects the elasticity of output with respect to the labor input. This elasticity is defined as the percent change in output associated with a 1 percent change in labor input. The value of α must reasonably lie between zero and one. Constraining the elasticities of labor and capital to sum to one implies constant returns to scale. In other words, if both labor and capital increase by 1 percent, output also increases by 1 percent.

A constant rate of trend productivity growth, r, implies A at time t may be expressed as an exponential function of A in the base year $t = 0$:

$$A(t) = A(0)e^{rt}.$$

The foregoing relationships are theoretical in nature. The observed value of output in year t, call it $Y'(t)$, will deviate from the theoretical value, $Y(t)$, by some disturbance term, call it $u(t)$ and allow it to enter the Solow growth equation multiplicatively. Productivity is then thought of as being enhanced or diminished by a factor $u(t)$ which is treated as random and therefore unpredictable. Formally, the observed value of productivity, $A'(t)$, is given as:

$$A'(t) = A(0)e^{rt}u(t).$$

Box 10.3 (cont.)

The disturbance term $u(t)$ captures the fluctuations of the business cycle relative to trend growth. To obtain values for $u(t)$ year by year, regression analysis is first used to estimate the model parameters α and r. Observed values of $L(t)$ and $K(t)$ are then entered into the Solow growth equation to obtain the theoretical value of trend output, $Y(t)$. Finally, the productivity shock $u(t)$ is inferred as the ratio $Y'(t)/Y(t)$.

The many equations of a DSGE model then trace the impact of productivity shocks on key macroeconomic variables such as employment, consumption, investment, trade, the price level, wages, profits, and so on.

Under real business cycle theory, shocks to productivity have ramifications for household labor supply. During periods of high productivity (and hence high remuneration) in market employment activities, households choose to supply a greater proportion of their time to paid work. Conversely, during periods of low productivity in market employment activities, households incline more toward non-market alternatives, for example, pursuing an education, taking on home repair projects, engaging in fitness and recreational activities, or spending time with family. The modeling exercise assumes households maximize utility over a long time horizon by substituting intertemporally between paid and non-paid activities. People work hard at paid jobs during some stages of life knowing they will be able to relax and attend to other aspects of living during other stages. The upshot for business cycles is that the effect of productivity shocks on output is amplified by a labor supply response: during periods of high productivity, more people choose to work more hours, and vice versa.

The production functions of firms and utility functions of households are at the core of the dynamic stochastic general equilibrium models of real business cycle theory. Production functions are typically specified for multiple sectors of the economy. Utility functions, in addition to framing household labor supply decisions, generate consumption and saving outcomes. The consequences of current choices are projected into the future through rules for capital construction and inventory management. The simplest models involve dozens of equations while the most elaborate run to thousands. DSGE models built on real business cycle theory perform well to reproduce normal cyclical patterns of movement in key aggregates. In accordance with observation, the models yield paths for an economy in which investment is more volatile than GDP which is in turn more volatile than consumption. By design, however, real business cycle DSGE models fail to convey anything about the effects of monetary policy or the role of finance in the business cycle. For that we must turn to a second generation of work.

New Keynesian Economics

New Keynesian models introduce money into the DSGE framework and, in Keynesian fashion, impose frictions in the movement of prices and wages. The result is that a money supply increase is transmitted first into real economic activity and only later into prices and wages. The price stickiness is achieved by assuming markets are not perfectly competitive. Firms have a degree of discretion in choosing price/quantity combinations, and in the face of a demand increase will react initially mainly by increasing output at given prices. Only later, as competition for labor and commodity inputs heats up, will wages and prices be adjusted.

Money further affects the economy in New Keynesian models through the interest rate acting on investment and saving. The relationship is complicated by the fact that investment decisions involve long-term commitments, hence not only current interest rates but expectations of future interest rates matter, as do expectations of future inflation.

Slow adjustment of prices and wages to productivity shocks means that economic outcomes can be less than optimal even within a market equilibrium framework. In particular, a negative productivity shock under sticky prices will mean that real output and employment bear the brunt of short-term adjustment. A monetary stimulus could in principle be used to offset such shocks and hold the economy to a stable course. DSGE modeling allows the effects of policy interventions along these lines to be assessed.

Proponents of DSGE modeling argue that their approach to macroeconomics is grounded in microeconomic foundations: households maximize utility and firms maximize profits; and rational expectations link current behavior to well-founded beliefs about the future. From these microeconomic premises, movements in aggregate magnitudes are derived. By contrast, traditional Keynesian economics lacks such foundations. Unemployment and the accumulation of excess inventories result from a failure of households and firms to adjust to changing market conditions. Why they fail, however, is not articulated from any first principles involving human motivation and rational choice.

Critics of DSGE models attack the assumption of no involuntary unemployment. The genuine hardship suffered by vast numbers of jobless people during recessions defies the benign characterization of their state as a voluntary pursuit of non-employment activities. Critics further charge that the Keynesian black box of household and firm behavior is replaced in DSGE models with the black box of productivity shocks. That shocks have occurred is only indirectly inferred through their impact on output and prices. The nature of the shocks and the process by which they affect productivity are never spelled out. The weakness of the DSGE approach was laid bare by the financial crisis of 2008. Whereas the models could be successfully manipulated to reproduce the moderate ups and downs of normal business cycles, a financial crisis the likes of which had not been witnessed in the USA in more than half a century was beyond their capacity to explain.

Self-Fulfilling Expectations and Path Indeterminacy

Although New Keynesian DSGE models incorporate a degree of stickiness in prices and wages, such models fail to do justice to Keynes's vision of a world plagued by chronic unemployment. Motivated by the financial crisis of 2008, a modeling program truer to

Keynes's spirit has since gained traction. The recent models incorporate two advances. First, labor markets are encumbered by significant costs on both the job search side and the employer recruitment side. Given the tremendous differentiation that exists among both jobs and workers, much information gathering and processing is required to achieve an employment match. Second, both confidence and wealth are treated as important determinants of consumption and investment demand. Confidence interacts with wealth in a mutually reinforcing dynamic within which feelings of exuberance lead to higher asset prices and higher asset prices in turn lead to even greater exuberance. Then too, the spiral can work in the opposite direction. Either way, expectations are prone to self-fulfillment.

Within this milieu, there is no single well-defined level of full-employment equilibrium output. A high degree of unemployment can persist with no tendency for correction. Sagging confidence intertwines with low asset values and stagnant demand for output so as to mire the economy in a slump. Large numbers of workers can lose their jobs with too few new jobs being created to absorb them even as other workers retain their jobs at wages that do not clear the market.

In a class of DSGE models reviewed by Farmer (2015), changes in beliefs act as the shock that drives economic fluctuations. In a radical twist on previous models, a shock can shift an economy to a permanently altered growth trajectory. This breaks with the classical tradition of an economy always tending back to a clearly articulated full-employment path. Growth may be limited within these models by sustained shortfalls in aggregate demand reminiscent of Keynes. Under imperfect functioning of labor markets, the economy will not move to a higher growth path unless confidence is revitalized. If more positive beliefs about the economy take hold, they will then be self-fulfilling. Self-fulfilling expectations and path indeterminacy provide a strong rationale for policy intervention. A stimulus that acts to boost confidence can be especially effective.

Models that allow for path indeterminacy seem particularly appealing for application to developing economies. Full-employment equilibrium does not, in this context, provide a very compelling benchmark against which to plot an economy's trajectory. Potential growth is more difficult to define, with growth rates in double digits known to occur for periods of years. Labor market imperfections must certainly account for even more of the story than in developed economies. And confidence may well have an even more powerful impact on outcomes.

D   Minsky's Endogenous Cycle Theory

Through several decades of evolution, DSGE models had by 2008 been fine tuned to replicate fairly closely the observed movement of macroeconomic variables in developed economies. But these models ultimately rely on vaguely articulated and unpredictable shocks from outside to keep fluctuations in motion. Formal models do not exist to fully endogenize the ups and downs of the business cycle. A story does exist, however, as laid out by Hyman Minsky (1986).

Minsky maintains that processes intrinsic to the nature of capitalist finance propogate instability. A financial system that is initially robust will transform itself into one that is fragile. Ultimately, the system will reach a crisis point. There will follow a protracted process of renewal to re-establish robustness, only for the cycle to repeat itself. We begin this section by defining Minsky's concepts of robust and fragile finance. We then lay out his argument for how the latter inevitably comes to dominate. We follow with an explanation of how government, in Minsky's view, by forestalling crisis and expediting recovery, imparts an inflationary bias to the economy. Finally, we look at the US crisis of 2008 as a "Minsky moment" of financial implosion.

Robust vs Fragile Finance

Financing the ownership of productive assets in a capitalist economy carries with it a fixed stream of future payment obligations juxtaposed against an uncertain stream of income receipts. Multiple layers of financial intermediation may separate the owners of productive assets from the ultimate providers of funds with each layer carrying its own conjoined streams of obligations and incomes. If debtors in substantial numbers are unable to meet their payment obligations due to unanticipated changes in economic conditions, financial markets will become distressed.

Minsky defines three categories of finance.

- Hedge finance: income > interest + principle obligations. The greater the share of equity finance relative to debt, the more secure this relationship since equity involves only a residual claim after interest and principle payments to other creditors have been met.
- Speculative finance: income > interest obligations only. New debt must be acquired to make principle payments that come due.
- Ponzi finance: income < interest obligations. New borrowing or selling of assets is required to meet interest obligations.

The name Ponzi comes from Charles Ponzi who ran a scheme in Boston in 1920 whereby money from new investors was used to pay returns to existing investors, and of course to Mr. Ponzi himself. When the scheme eventually collapsed for lack of new investors, he was charged with fraud and sent to prison. As bad as this sounds, finance on Ponzi terms plays a vital role in a dynamic economy. Major new undertakings in the initial investment stage typically generate little to no income against financing obligations. Continued infusions of money are needed to pay existing creditors and keep the venture going. Some endeavors may take years to generate sufficient income to produce a competitive return on capital, and some may ultimately fail altogether. Minsky notes that going too far in "lessening the possibility for disaster might very well take the spark of creativity out of the capitalist system" (p. 364).

Entities that depend on short-term borrowing to finance long-term asset positions are vulnerable to changing financial market conditions. When the time comes to roll over their debt, such entities may find themselves paying higher interest rates even as their revenue streams remain unchanged. Financial intermediaries routinely operate under such maturity mismatch conditions. Banks, for example, take in deposits payable on demand against which they make loans that take years to pay off. As interest rates rise, short-term obligations are hit first while long-term returns are fixed. Units that were operating in a hedge position may find themselves pushed into the speculative category as they roll over debt, and those in the speculative position may enter the Ponzi zone. Ponzi units will find their equity diminishing as they resort to liquidating assets to meet commitments, a situation that cannot long be sustained. Rising interest rates and tightening availability of credit can quickly threaten the viability of Ponzi and even speculative units. An economy that harbors widespread speculative and Ponzi finance is thus fragile in the face of shock. By contrast, an economy built on hedge finance is robust against shock as debt repayment is cushioned even if interest rates rise.

Financial Instability Hypothesis

Minsky's "financial instability hypothesis" holds that a robust and prosperous economy dominated by long-term hedge finance will move inexorably toward speculative and Ponzi finance. There are profits to be made in this transition so that the process will for a while be validated by the market. In normal times, short-term interest rates are lower than long-term rates. This reflects the greater degree of unknown associated with the more distant future, particularly with regard to inflation. Firms that borrow short term at lower interest rates will thus be more profitable than those that borrow long term at higher interest rates. And firms that borrow on an interest-only basis and defer principle repayment will have an even greater cash flow advantage.

On an economy wide basis, a shift to shorter-term borrowing will be a boon for growth. Rising profits will push up the value of productive assets. This will induce more capital goods production, which will create more jobs at better wages, and this will in turn fuel spending on consumer goods, thus generating even more jobs and more spending. People will come to believe that the good times will never end. Faith in the prospect of capital gains will encourage the build up of ever more leverage, as speculative or even Ponzi finance seems to make perfect sense. There is simply no need to rely on current income to pay down debt when you can count on selling assets at a profit later on.

Financial regulation is aimed at preventing risky behavior from getting out of hand. But regulation is oriented toward established financial instruments and institutions. Innovative ways of getting around regulation will always be found. At the time of his writing in 1986, Minsky observed that the USA since 1965 had experienced four serious runs on financial markets or institutions, with each incident following on the heels of a boom fueled by a financial innovation. The global financial crisis of 2008 fits the pattern, as will be discussed. Many observers are concerned that China in the wake of the global crisis has seen worrisome proliferation of innovative financing activity that has greatly increased leverage in the economy. For a description of the kinds of innovation involved, see Box 10.4.

Box 10.4 Chinese debt shenanigans

In the wake of the global financial crisis and collapse in world trade, China kept its economy growing with a massive infusion of bank credit. In 2009 alone, bank loans outstanding nearly doubled. The next year, the authorities tightened and loans contracted by 17 percent. Once the debt explosion had been unleashed, however, businesses became dependent on it to sustain new levels of activity. As lending by banks tightened, other sources of credit emerged to fill the gap. Total new lending held roughly constant in 2010 by the official measure.

A major form of credit growth in 2010 was in bankers' acceptances that did not come under government mandated credit quotas. The share of this form of credit leapt from 4.4 percent in 2009 to 23 percent the next year. A bankers' acceptance is issued by a bank in exchange for a letter of credit which is typically obtained by an exporter from its foreign buyer. The letter of credit represents a promise to pay at a future date upon delivery of goods. The bankers' acceptance obtained by the exporter in exchange for the letter of credit is a negotiable instrument that can be converted to cash, at a discount relative to its face value, at any time. In the Chinese case, it appears that use of letters of credit and bankers' acceptances expanded very suddenly into purposes well beyond their traditional scope in trade finance.

Since 2010, other financial innovations have fueled extensive debt creation beyond the readily visible balance sheets of banks. "Entrusted loans" are made under the arrangement of banks, for a fee, directly from one company to another. Nonbank "trust companies" pool the funds of individuals or small businesses by selling "wealth management products," often through banks, with the funds channeled into loans or other investments. The volume of these products has grown tremendously with most purchasers paying little attention to how their money is invested, taking solace in a belief that the Chinese government will not allow trust companies to fail.

Property developers with their vast borrowing requirements have come up with their own financing innovations. Units in residential complexes are often sold before construction even begins. Sometimes the sales take place with a promise by the developer to repurchase the units at a specified price that guarantees a hefty return. Or the developer may sell equity shares in the company and promise to repurchase the shares in the future. These arrangements are in fact thinly disguised debt. Companies can in essence be highly leveraged while obscuring this on their books.

Pundits began predicting collapse of the Chinese economy under a rising debt load as early as 2010. But debt and growth can propel a virtuous cycle for a long time. The precise moment at which it will end is hard to foresee. What Minsky tells us is that the end will certainly come.

Minsky argues that a boom bears the seeds of its own demise. The financial structure becomes fragile. Inflation heats up and authorities respond by tightening credit. With this, interest rates rise. Borrowers with speculative positions cannot refinance on terms they can afford. Businesses fail, jobs are lost, and the economy goes into recession.

A cleansing process will then follow. Borrowers and lenders find themselves chastened all around by the shake-out of bad debtors. New financing proceeds on far more cautionary terms. The economy is restored to a state in which hedge finance predominates. It is once again robust against shock and primed for stable growth.

Government Intervention Averts Disaster but Sows Inflation and Perpetuates Fragility

The widespread pain and economic loss associated with a shake-out of bad debtors creates the temptation for government to intervene. While government has the capacity to alleviate immediate suffering, Minsky argues that this comes at a cost of imparting inflation. Moreover, by validating risky financing maneuvers, government rescue efforts perpetuate underlying fragility and hasten the next run up to a crisis.

Governments make use of both fiscal and monetary measures to avert financial disaster and maintain economic stability. The standard view of fiscal stimulus is that increases in government spending and cuts in taxes boost aggregate demand to push an economy toward its potential. With his focus on finance, Minsky adds two elements to the picture. First, he emphasizes that debt carries with it payment commitments. When cash flows shrink in a recession, debtors become strained in meeting those commitments, and default on a wide scale can then loom. A fiscal stimulus helps to sustain cash flows and ensure that debt service payments continue to be made. Second, as government deficits mount, public debt instruments must be issued at an increased pace. These debt instruments offer a secure asset to fill the needs of financial institutions and other economic units for low risk holdings as faith in private debt is undermined and banks resist extending new loans.

Minsky's analysis of monetary policy similarly emphasizes the importance of finance in the economy. The quantity theory of money focuses narrowly on money's function as a medium of exchange in current transactions: $MV = PQ$ (recalling from Chapter 6, M is the money supply, V is velocity, P is the price level, and Q is aggregate real output). Quantity theorists treat money as exogenous and trace changes in the money supply through to changes in the price level and real output taking velocity as more or less constant. Minsky points out the importance of holding money as an asset when the value of other financial instruments becomes suspect. With reference to the quantity equation, the velocity of money falls as more money is held to bolster the security of portfolios rather than to support transactions. To meet the need for cash holdings, the central bank must stand ready to buy or accept as collateral assets that have become otherwise unmarketable. During times of financial distress, then, the central bank should provide infusions of liquidity. It must become the lender of last resort.

Through supportive fiscal and monetary actions, the government effectively validates debt that has become precarious and sustains the businesses that have incurred it. The economy is kept afloat, but on seas made prone to the roiling of future waves. Moreover, the policy response imparts an inflationary momentum. The central bank pumps liquidity into the economy to support spending during a time of weak aggregate demand and to satisfy the public's desire for cash balances. As confidence strengthens, however, spending recovers and portfolio preferences shift away from cash back toward riskier but more remunerative assets. The money that has been poured into deep coffers is then spent more freely. Minsky's concern is that recurring infusions of cash to rescue an economy from bouts of debt excess will propagate inflation and hasten the next setback. Absent the intervention of government, downturns would be deeper and unemployment more severe, but by the same token the restoration of healthy hedge finance would be more thoroughgoing and renewed growth of the economy would be more sustainable.

America's 2008 Minsky Moment

Minsky wrote his opus at a time when inflation in the USA was coming off double-digit levels. In the decades to follow, inflation would moderate even as government stabilization efforts would appear to be successful in subduing the business cycle. The illusion of the business cycle's demise was shattered, however, in 2008. Proclaimed a "Minsky moment," the crisis was fully in keeping with Minsky's narrative of prolonged periods of relative stability aided by government stabilization measures and regulatory oversight eventually giving way. For while government may be able to implement programs to keep the economy on track for quite some time, Minsky tells us that . . .

Such a restructuring will enjoy only transitory success. After an initial interval, the basic disequilibrating tendencies of capitalist finance will once again push the financial structure to the brink of fragility. When that occurs, a new era of reform will be needed. There is no possibility that we can ever set things right once and for all; instability, put to rest by one set of reforms will, after time, emerge in a new guise. (p. 370)

In hindsight, the fragility in US finance seemed all too obvious. Home mortgage loans to sub-prime borrowers had burgeoned, with the loans then securitized and marketed as AAA rated products (as explained in Chapter 7). The poor quality of the underlying assets was not recognized by holders of the securities. On the back of abundant financing, home prices were bid up to such a level that rental returns fell far short of mortgage financing costs, or anyway would fall short once contracted increases in interest rates or balloon payments kicked in. Nevertheless, buyers remained obliviously confident that continued appreciation in home values would cover all contingencies. In sum, Ponzi finance had taken hold.

Even before the scheme collapsed, some foresaw the day of reckoning to come. In July of 2007, former Chairman and Chief Executive of Citigroup Charles Prince gave the following oft-quoted statement to the *Financial Times*:

When the music stops, in terms of liquidity, things will be complicated. But as long as the music is playing, you've got to get up and dance. We're still dancing.

Yet, while some may indeed have predicted collapse, some are always predicting collapse. It's the timing that is hard to get right. And as long as the music plays, there is money to be made in dancing on.

E   The Philippine Experience

The Philippines has suffered the worst two-year contraction of any economy in our purview, while still faring better than most through crises that hit the region broadly. And it has enjoyed periods of solid expansion, even if these have not measured up to the most supercharged growth of the region. Chart 10.2 places Philippine GDP growth in the context of Emerging East Asia. Stretches of healthy growth are seen to alternate with periods of setback through four cycles prior to the pandemic shock of 2020. The worst crisis occurred in 1984–85 with the economy contracting more than 7 percent in each of two consecutive years. The next downturn in 1991 put the growth rate barely into negative territory. In both these cases, the Philippines was hit in isolation from the rest of the region. Then came the Asian Financial Crisis, pulling the country into its vortex yet leaving it not as badly pummeled as most of its neighbors. Similarly in 2009, the trade shock that followed the Great Financial Crisis took a relatively light toll on the Philippines.

We consider each cycle in turn.

Minsky Moment of the 1980s

The crisis of 1984–85 was tied to the fall of President Ferdinand Marcos who ruled the Philippines for two decades, the second of these under martial law. The trigger for the crisis

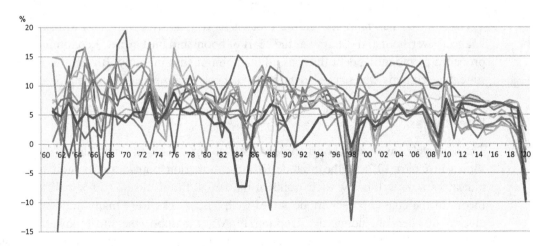

Chart 10.2 Philippine growth in regional context, 1977–2020

is commonly pinned on the assassination of opposition figure Benigno Aquino Jr. on August 21, 1983 as he arrived in the country from overseas and deplaned. After a three-year self-imposed exile in the USA, Aquino returned just as an anti-Marcos movement was beginning to coalesce, and his assassination galvanized that movement. However, according to de Dios (1984) and his colleagues at the University of the Philippines, the economy was by that time in such a state of fragility that "any major exogenous shock was bound to provoke a crisis" (p. 16). The Aquino assassination just happened to be that shock.

For indicators of the fragility of the Philippine economy, we take a cue from Minsky and look to the financial sector. The top panel of Chart 10.3 reveals a run-up in the ratio of bank assets to GDP from 25 percent in 1971 to 37 percent in 1983. The ratio of non-bank financial assets to GDP also increased, albeit more gradually. The picture becomes more radical with regard to foreign debt in the middle panel, the ratio to GNI catapulting from 33 percent in 1971 to 75 percent in 1983.

When the shock hit in 1983, a financial system primed for crisis went over the edge. Within three years assets of the banking system fell by half as loans went into default and banks failed. Meanwhile, foreign debt continued upward relative to declining GNI with the ratio topping out at nearly 100 percent in 1986. By then, the banking crisis had coursed to a resolution and an economic recovery took hold. Foreign debt was renegotiated and either paid down or written off.

How did the Philippines get into such a predicament in the first place? The government ran large fiscal deficits, financed in part by foreign borrowing, and encouraged government financial institutions, also relying on foreign borrowing, to lend to ill-conceived projects. While the borrowing frenzy fueled spending that boosted the economy for a time, ultimately the misdirection of funds into activities that did not generate returns sufficient to cover debt servicing doomed the system to failure. Underlying this misconduct, according to the University of the Philippines monograph, was a "concentration of power in the hands of the government, and the use of governmental functions to dispense economic privileges to some small factions in the private sector."

The story of the Philippines in the 1980s is in keeping with Mills and Minsky in putting financial overshoot and collapse at the heart of boom and bust cycles. Economic growth was propelled by mounting debt that passed the point of sustainability. Brought to a vulnerable state, the economy was struck down by such shock as happened to come along.

Later Cycles

The next cycle, involving a contraction in 1991, is not a ready fit for a Minsky-type story. As shown in Chart 10.3, in the prelude to the contraction both domestic and foreign debt indicators were well below their peaks of the 1980s. In this instance, a simple shock-based theory in the contemporary mode serves well. The shocks were many and serious: major natural disasters including the eruption of Mt. Pinatubo, the most powerful volcanic explosion of the 20th century; multiple coup attempts against the government of President Corazon Aquino; closure of US military bases that had accounted for 5 percent of GDP; and

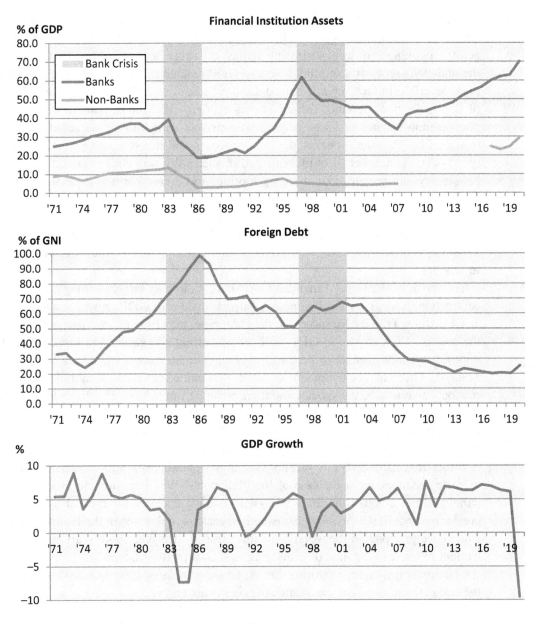

Chart 10.3 Debt indicators, Philippines, 1971–2020

disruptions to power supplies that caused widespread shortages of electricity. Per the standard contemporary paradigm, these shocks shifted the short-run aggregate supply curve to the left moving the economy temporarily below its long-run equilibrium growth path. A gradual recovery process then ensued as capital and labor resources were absorbed back into full employment.

The Asian Financial Crisis brought the next exogenous shock in 1998. Compared to its neighbors, the Philippines got off lightly with GDP growth barely dipping negative. This gentle reckoning may seem surprising against the surge in bank lending that took place in the mid-1990s, the ratio of bank assets to GDP reaching a much higher peak than in the previous crisis. In fact, a bank crisis did follow, and stretched on for five years. The cause of the 1990s bank lending run-up carries echos of the 1980s. Tan (2002) describes a phenomenon of "behest loans": "propose a project with little or no collateral upon the behest of the President, pocket the loan proceeds and invest a small fraction for show" (p. 5). Yet the number of banks engaged in such folly was circumscribed. Much of the banking system remained on a strong footing, and a credible free press was effective in communicating this to the public so that widespread bank runs were avoided. Nor was reliance on external borrowing excessive which would have created greater vulnerability to the capital flow reversals that hit other economies in the region. The minor contraction of 1998 thus represents a case of an external shock that the Philippines was well positioned to weather.

The shock of the Great Financial Crisis bore its impact largely through export market contraction. Here again, the Philippines outperformed with GDP growth remaining positive at 1.1 percent. The relative success of the Philippines may be explained in significant part by the country's low export-to-GDP ratio at 38 percent for goods and services in 2007 as opposed to ratios around 70 percent for Thailand and Vietnam and over 100 percent for Malaysia. One might be tempted to conclude that limited engagement in trade can shelter an economy against external shocks, and there is some truth to that. The downside, however, is slower trend growth as the advantages of trade are forfeited.

In interpreting the Philippine experience we have recognized a role for both exogenous shocks and endogenous vulnerability associated with the state of the financial system. A theory that focuses strictly on shocks within a paradigm of equilibrium may work well in some instances, as in the case of the Philippines' 1991 recession. In other instances, a paradigm that involves the financial system and its tendency for cyclical dynamics yields greater insight. That a political assassination, such as took place in the Philippines in 1983, could have precipitated the worst economic crisis in East Asia in 40 years strains credulity without recourse to the state of underlying financial conditions. Similarly, for understanding the Philippines' capacity to absorb the exogenous shocks of 1998 and 2008, recognition of the essential soundness of the financial system is instructive.

F   Interplay between Shocks and Fragility

An exogenous shock theory and an endogenous cycle theory of booms and busts need not be mutually exclusive. Indeed, Walter Bagehot (pronounced "badget") melded the two back in 1874:

It is of great importance to point out that our industrial organization is liable not only to irregular external accidents, but likewise to regular internal changes; that these changes make our credit system much more delicate at some times than others; and that it is the recurrence of these periodical seasons of delicacy which has given rise to the notion that panics come according to a fixed rule; – that every ten years or so we must have one of them. (p. 125)

According to Bagehot, there is a tendency in a time of economic expansion to perceive great opportunity in all manner of ventures. For a while, such perception is reinforced as success comes easy. Credit is readily extended and a virtuous cycle takes hold as new investment stimulates employment and incomes which in turn creates fertile ground for new investment. However, in Bagehot's words:

People are most credulous when they are most happy; and when much money has just been made, when some people are really making it, when most people think they are making it, there is a happy opportunity for ingenious mendacity. (p. 160)

Excessive risk taking and heavy leverage make an economic system vulnerable to shock. When the shock hits, some borrowers are unable to repay their loans. In turn, lenders become more cautious. Employment and spending contract, so that more businesses go under and more loans go bad. Society is then encumbered with a dearth of trust, and the economy stagnates. This malaise will have to run its course. In time, eyes will once again be opened to opportunity and new sprouts of activity will germinate. The cycle then begins anew.

Shocks are ongoing and ever present. What contemporarymodeling exercises miss is that at certain times an economy is highly resilient to them while at others it is brought down. Bagehot saw exogenous and endogenous forces working in concert. That perspective seems worthy of resurrection.

Data Note

US inflation and unemployment rates shown in the Phillips curve of Chart 10.1 are from the US Bureau of Labor Statistics.

Chart 10.2 is a repeat of Chart 1.2, data being from the World Bank World Development Indicators database. This is also the source for the external debt data in Chart 10.3 and the export ratios cited in the text. Data on Philippine financial assets in Chart 10.3 are from the World Bank Global Financial Development database.

Business cycles for a host of countries are tracked by The Conference Board, a non-profit business membership organization headquartered in New York City with offices worldwide. Since 1995, The Conference Board has been the official source of business cycle indicators for the United States, taking over this function from the US government. In Asia, the Conference Board produces indicators for China, India, Japan, and Korea. The Organization for Economic Cooperation and Development produces a database of leading economic indicators by country including China, India, Indonesia, Japan, and Korea.

Figures on Chinese debt are from the "Monetary Policy Reports" of the People's Bank of China.

Bibliographic Note

A 2011 interview of former US Treasury Secretary Lawrence Summers at the Institute for New Economic Thinking illustrates the recourse of modern economic policymakers to historic thinkers, Bagehot and Minsky included, in the wake of the 2008 financial crisis.

Besomi (2006) interprets the history of thought on business cycles along lines adopted in this chapter distinguishing between two views, one that holds equilibrium as the norm with fluctuations as aberrant and another that sees oscillations as the norm possessed of their own internal logic.

The Juglar quote from 1862 that "the only cause of depression is prosperity" is drawn from Joseph Schumpeter (1954, p. 1124). Schumpeter was himself in accord with this perspective. He regarded Juglar as "among the greatest economists of all times" (p. 1123), and took it as an "indictment" of "the vast majority of the economists" that "they treated cycles as a phenomenon that is superimposed upon the normal course of capitalist life and mostly as a pathological one; it never occurred to the majority to look to business cycles for material with which to build the fundamental theory of capitalist reality" (p. 1135).

In his 2007 memoir, Alan Greenspan provides a colorful insider account of US events during 1960–1980 as depicted in Chart 10.1.

The concept of rational expectations originated with Muth (1961) and was launched into the macro modeling mainstream by Lucas (1972). The pioneering work in real business cycle DSGE modeling is Kydland and Prescott (1982). King and Rebelo (1999) provide an overview and assessment of real business cycle theory. The standard reference on New Keynesian DSGE modeling is Woodford (2003). In cutting edge DSGE models, Farmer (2016) points to a key role for confidence. He refers to these models as "endogenous business cycle" models but means something different by this term than is meant in this chapter. His notion involves exogenous shocks being endogenously propagated, in contrast with standard models that require repeated shocks in the same direction to sustain a boom or a slump. Farmer's article provides a succinct outline of the structure of various classes of DSGE models.

The discussion of Chinese credit innovation draws on unpublished notes to clients from GaveKal Dragonomics and J Capital Research.

On the Philippines, a penetrating analysis of the causes of the crisis of 1984–85 was produced by the University of the Philippines School of Economics under the editorship of Emmanuel de Dios (1984). A good overview of the 1980s and 1990s is presented in Balisacan and Hill (2003). Tan (2002) provides an insightful analysis of the banking crisis of the early 2000s.

BIBLIOGRAPHIC CITATIONS

Bagehot, Walter, 1910[1874]. *Lombard Street: A Description of the Money Market* (New York: E.P. Dutton).

Balisacan, Arsenio M. and Hal Hill, 2003. "An Introduction to the Key Issues" in Balisacan and Hill (eds.), *The Philippine Economy: Development, Policies, and Challenges* (Oxford, UK: Oxford Scholarship Online).

Besomi, Daniele, 2006. "Tendency to Equilibrium, the Possibility of Crisis, and the History of Business Cycle Theories," *History of Economic Ideas*, XIV/2006/2.

The Conference Board, 2000. Business Cycle Indicators Handbook (New York: The Conference Board).

The Conference Board, 2021. Global Business Cycle Indicators. www.conference-board.org/data/bci .cfm (accessed December 16 2021).

de Dios, Emmanuel. ed., 1984. *An Analysis of the Philippine Economic Crisis* (Quezon City: University of the Philippines Press).

Farmer, Roger, 2016. "The Evolution of Endogenous Business Cycles," *Macroeconomic Dynamics*, Vol. 20, Issue 2, pp. 544–557.

Friedman, Milton, 1968. "The Role of Monetary Policy," *American Economic Review*, 58, pp. 1–17.

Greenspan, Alan, 2007. *The Age of Turbulence* (New York: Penguin Press).

Hayek, Friedrich, 1994 [1944]. *The Road to Serfdom* (Chicago: University of Chicago Press).

Keynes, John Maynard, 1964 [1936]. *The General Theory of Employment, Interest, and Money* (New York: Harcourt, Brace & World).

King, Robert G. and Sergio T. Rebelo, 1999. "Resuscitating Real Business Cycles," in John B. Taylor and Michael Woodford (eds.), *Handbook of Macroeconomics, Volume 1B* (Amsterdam: Elsevier), pp. 927–1007.

Kydland, Finn E. and Edward C. Prescott, 1982. "Time to Build and Aggregate Fluctuations," *Econometrica*, Vol. 50, No. 6 (November), pp. 1345–1370.

Lucas, Robert E. Jr., 1972. "Expectations and the Neutrality of Money," *Journal of Economic Theory*, 4, pp. 103–124.

Mills, John, 1867. "On Credit Cycles and the Origin of Commercial Panics," *Transactions of the Manchester Statistical Society, Session* 1867–68, pp. 5–40.

Minsky, Hyman, 2008[1986]. *Stabilizing an Unstable Economy* (New York: McGraw Hill).

Mises, Ludwig von, 1949. *Human Action* (New Haven: Yale University Press).

Muth, John F., 1961. "Rational Expectations and the Theory of Price Movements," *Econometrica*, Vol. 29, No. 3 (July), pp. 315–335.

Nakamoto, Michiyo and David Wighton), 2007. "Citigroup Chief Stays Bullish on Buy-Outs," *Financial Times*, July 10, 2007.

Organization for Economic Co-operation and Development, 2021. Composite Leading Indicators database. https://stats.oecd.org/Index.aspx?DataSetCode=MEI_CLI (accessed December 16 2021).

People's Bank of China, multiple years. Monetary Policy Reports. www.pbc.gov.cn/en/3688229/ 3688353/3688356/index.html (accessed December 16 2021).

Phelps, Edmund S., 1967. "Phillips Curves, Expectations of Inflation and Optimal Unemployment over Time," *Economica*, 34(135), pp. 254–281.

Phillips, A. W., 1958. "The Relation between Unemployment and the Rate of Change of MoneyWage Rates in the United Kingdom, 1861–1957," *Economica*, 25, pp. 283–299.

Pigou, A. C., 1927. *Industrial Fluctuations* (London: MacMillan).

Schumpeter, Joseph A., 1954. *History of Economic Analysis* (New York: Oxford University Press).

Solow, Robert, 1957. "Technical Change and the Aggregate Production Function," *Review of Economics and Statistics*, Vol. 39, No. 3 (August), pp. 312–320.

Summers, Larry, 2011. "Larry Summers and Martin Wolf: Keynote at INET's Bretton Woods Conference 2011," (New Hampshire: Institute for New Economic Thinking). www.youtube.com/ watch?v=Vgg5DoPkgYc (accessed January 29 2015).

Tan, Edita, 2002. "Bank Performance and Rate of Economic Recovery: The Philippine Case," University of the Philippines School of Economics Discussion Paper No. 0206. www.econ.upd.edu .ph/dp/index.php/dp/article/view/37/31 (accessed July 20, 2017)

Time, 1965. We Are All Keynesians Now, December 31, cover. https://web.archive.org/web/20070211210619/www.time.com/time/magazine/article/0,9171,842353,00.html (accessed January 25, 2022).

Woodford, Michael, 2003. *Interest and Prices: Foundations of a Theory of Monetary Policy* (Princeton, NJ: Princeton University Press).

World Bank, 2021. Global Financial Development database. https://databank.worldbank.org/reports.aspx?source=global-financial-development (accessed December 16, 2021).

World Bank, 2021. World Development Indicators database. https://databank.worldbank.org/source/world-development-indicators (accessed December 16, 2021).

US Bureau of Labor Statistics, 2014. Data Tools. http://data.bls.gov/cgi-bin/surveymost?bls (accessed October 29, 2014).

11 Monetary Policy

Monetary policy involves managing the supply of money for purposes of macroeconomic stabilization. The interest rate and the exchanges rate, as indicators of the value of money, serve to guide policy action. In the Emerging East Asian context, the interaction between interest rate and exchange rate calls for particular attention. The region offers a diversity of policy frameworks and experiences for comparative study.

All that has gone before in this book is pertinent for the study of monetary policy. Chapters 9 and 10 on macroeconomic behavior explain the tendencies toward volatility and underperformance that motivate policy intervention. The concepts of internal and external balance framed in Chapters 4 and 5 establish the goals of policy. Foundations for how money is created and how it affects the economy are laid out in Chapter 6. Chapter 7 connects money and credit to interest rates and asset prices. And Chapter 8 relates the exchange rate to internal and external balance. This chapter builds on all these pieces.

We begin by reviewing the money creation process and elaborating on how this process is managed by the authorities in the conduct of monetary policy. We then consider how central bank action may target the interest rate or the exchange rate, but in the context of open capital markets, not both independently of one another. This leads us to an exposition of the Trilemma which holds that an economy cannot have all three of: a fixed exchange rate; an independent monetary policy; and open capital markets. With that, we examine the choice of monetary policy framework adopted by the economies of Emerging East Asia, and then look empirically at how foreign exchange market intervention has figured in. The Singapore case is highlighted for its policy focus on exchange rate management under globally integrated capital markets. Apart from Singapore and Hong Kong, however, the choice between exchange rate management and interest rate targeting has not been drawn so starkly, and we consider how the trade-offs have been managed. Finally, we prepare to turn attention to fiscal policy as a second arm of stabilization policy.

A   Foundations

Monetary policy works through central bank management of the money supply. Recall from Chapter 6 that the money supply consists of currency plus demand deposits held by the public at commercial banks and, as such, is only indirectly controlled by the central bank. Further complicating the exercise of policy, central bank influence on the money supply feeds through to macroeconomic outcomes with long and variable lags. Thus, the conduct of monetary policy is a complicated business that involves a great deal of judgment in an ongoing process of trial and adjustment (the case of Hong Kong being an exception since the pegged exchange rate is entirely determinative of monetary policy as explained in Chapter 7).

We lay foundations for understanding monetary policy in this section.

Goals

The foremost goal of monetary policy for all central banks is low and stable inflation. What is meant by "low" varies among central banks, but the range is generally on the order of 2–5 percent. The target must be high enough to guard against deflation. Deflation is harmful to an economy for a number of reasons: it squeezes business profit margins due to the time lag between purchasing inputs in a higher price environment and selling products in a lower price environment; it incentivizes the delay of purchases since items will be cheaper in the future; and it inhibits lending because for borrowers repayment becomes more difficult while for lenders simply holding cash ensures rising purchasing power. On the other hand, if inflation gets too high it tends to be unstable and disruptive as price adjustments do not occur continuously and evenly across all goods and services but rather in discrete and spotty jumps that distort relative prices. Thus, there is a happy medium on inflation that central banks seek to maintain.

For some central banks, low and stable inflation is the only goal of monetary policy. This is the case, for example, by mandate, with the European Central Bank. More commonly, central banks are concerned with other aspects of macroeconomic performance, and this then sets up a tension in the face of trade-offs. Beyond inflation, many central banks take account of output growth relative to potential, or internal balance. For Emerging East Asian economies, external balance is also an important goal. International payments are highly vulnerable to external shocks acting on trade and capital flows. Such external shocks not only disturb external balance, but spillover onto domestic output, employment, and prices as well. Finally, financial stability, as reflected in asset prices and the health of financial institutions, can enter into the scope of central bank concerns. The Great Financial Crisis of 2008 brought a hard realization that financial markets can become fragile even when real output and prices are tracking a stable course. In sum, central

Goals
• low inflation
• GDP growth at potential
• external balance
• financial stability

banks can keep a watch on a variety of indicators and must reckon with competing claims on their limited power.

Transmission Mechanism

Monetary policy operates through expansion and contraction of the money supply. Recall from Chapter 6 that the central bank exercises direct control over the monetary base which consists of currency plus commercial bank reserves held at the central bank. These are liabilities on the central bank balance sheet. To expand the monetary base, the central bank acquires an asset – government debt securities, loans to commercial banks, or foreign assets – in exchange for issuing liabilities against itself. Conversely, to contract the monetary base, the central bank liquidates an asset and thus reduces its liabilities held by the public.

Expansion or contraction of the monetary base is just the first step of a change in the money supply. The resulting creation of new commercial bank deposits at the central bank lays a foundation for bank lending which leads to the creation of new deposit money held by the public. Thus, the increase in the monetary base results in an increase in the money supply by some multiple. The magnitude of that multiple depends on two factors. One is the choice on the part of the public to hold currency versus bank deposits. The other is the choice on the part of commercial banks to hold reserves at the central bank above some mandatory minimum versus lending. Similarly, a contraction in the monetary base reduces commercial bank reserves at the central bank so that less bank lending and deposit creation is supported and the money supply contracts.

Changes in the money supply act on economic output and the price level through aggregate demand. More money in people's hands means more spending which increases aggregate demand, thus putting upward pressure on output and/or prices. Further, as the supply of money increases, its value falls as reflected in the interest rate and the exchange value of the domestic currency against other currencies. The lower interest rate encourages investment while the lower value of the domestic currency encourages exports and discourages imports. Jointly, these forces conspire for a positive effect on internal balance (an increase in a positive output gap or a decrease in a negative output gap) and a negative effect on external balance (a widening current account deficit or a narrowing current account surplus). Note that the increase in the current account balance is met with an offsetting decrease in the financial account balance as the lower domestic interest rate prompts an increase in net capital outflows. Conversely, a decrease in the money supply drives all of these processes in reverse.

Transmission
• monetary base
• bank lending
• money supply
• prices & output
• trade & capital flows

Tools

Monetary policy tools are of two sorts: those that affect the monetary base; and those that affect the money multiplier. The monetary base is manipulated through transactions captured on the central bank balance sheet. Recall from Chapter 6 that the central bank balance sheet contains three main types of assets: government debt securities; foreign assets; and net loans to commercial banks. Each of these three asset types provides the central bank with an associated tool in the form of acquisition or disposal. In the first case, purchase or sale of government debt securities takes place through open market operations. As a variation on this, some central banks in Emerging East Asia that lack marketable government securities on their balance sheets instead issue their own securities, known as central bank bills, to withdraw base money. In the second case, purchase or sale of foreign assets takes place in conjunction with foreign exchange market intervention. And in the third case, lending to commercial banks operates through the discount window of the central bank with the rate of interest, or discount rate, set by the central bank. To influence the willingness of commercial banks to borrow, the central bank raises or lowers the discount rate. A transaction of given magnitude with respect to any of the three asset types has exactly the same impact on the monetary base.

Two further tools of monetary policy alter the money multiplier by affecting commercial bank behavior. First, the reserve requirement ratio determines how much commercial banks must hold in reserve at the central bank relative to deposits of their customers. Reducing the reserve requirement ratio increases the money multiplier, and vice versa. Second, central bank adjustment of the interest rate paid on reserves affects the willingness of commercial banks to hold reserves in excess of the requirement. A reduction in the rate of interest paid on reserves increases the money multiplier, and vice versa.

In sum, the central bank can pursue an expansionary monetary policy using any of the following tools: purchase of government securities; purchase of foreign assets; lowering of the discount rate; lowering of the reserve requirement ratio; or lowering of the rate of interest paid on reserves. A contractionary monetary policy involves the opposite use of these tools.

Tools (stimulus)
• government securities (buy)
• foreign assets (buy)
• discount rate (lower)
• reserve requirement ratio (lower)
• interest rate on reserves (lower)

Instruments

To chart its course, the central bank makes use of *instruments*, also known as *operating targets*, that track immediately with a change in monetary policy stance. There are three principal options. The most direct operating target is the monetary base, or relatedly bank reserves as a component of the monetary base. For a more expansionary policy, the central bank increases its target rate of growth in the monetary base while for a more contractionary policy it decreases this target. The second option is a policy rate of interest, typically an overnight rate on interbank lending. Through adjustment of a target interest rate, growth in the monetary base is determined indirectly. A lower interest rate target is achieved by supplying more base money relative to given demand, and vice versa. The third option is an exchange rate target.

As with an interest rate target, growth in the monetary base is determined indirectly. A lower value of the domestic currency relative to foreign currencies calls for a greater supply of base money relative to given demand for the domestic currency, and vice versa. Note that for both the interest rate target and the exchange rate target, demand-side forces will influence the rate of growth in base money at chosen levels of the operating targets.

In sum, a more expansionary policy course can be set by targeting a higher rate of growth in the monetary base, a lower policy rate of interest, or a lower exchange value of the domestic currency.

Conduct of Policy

The impact of monetary policy on prices is felt with long and variable lags of one to two years. That means policy choices of today must be made based on forecasts of economic conditions to come that derive from knowledge of the past combined with extrapolation and guesswork. This has been likened to driving while looking in the rear view mirror. Overly strong past growth that is projected into the future will call for a tightening of policy, and vice versa. As actual events unfold, however, constant adjustment will be needed.

Targets
Operating (Instruments)
• monetary base
• overnight interest rate
• exchange rate
Intermediate
• broader money aggregates
• longer-term interest rates
Final
• inflation
• output
• external balance

Intermediate targets can be helpful in lining up a path. A change in an operating target, such as an overnight interest rate or growth in the monetary base, can be monitored for its impact on longer term interest rates or broader monetary aggregates (e.g., M1 as currency plus demand deposits or M2 as M1 plus time deposits) which can in turn be projected onto future inflation and output growth. If a shift to more expansionary policy is seen to be lowering longer-term interest rates or raising money supply growth more than is consistent with achieving a desired inflation target, policy can be tightened before any overshooting on inflation is realized. Thus, targets can be identified at a range of time horizons: operating targets, which are immediate; intermediate targets, such as longer-term interest rates and growth in broader monetary aggregates, at a horizon of some months; and finally an inflation target at a horizon of one to two years. As outcomes are realized at the intermediate term, any deviations from objectives can then feed back into adjustment of operating targets to steer a return to the long-term course.

When goals other than inflation are given weight in monetary policy, authorities must nevertheless remain mindful of the ultimate consequences for inflation. It can be tempting to inject a quick boost to output and employment that will only later manifest in rising inflation. The political appeal of pursuing output growth now at a cost of inflation later is the reason that central banks are generally granted independence from political leaders in managing monetary policy. Politicians love to run for office on the back of a strong economy. Yet once inflation sets in, expectations tend to sustain its momentum so that quelling it with monetary tightening comes only by sacrificing growth down the line. To prevent the temptation of going after short-run output growth, central banks in democratic societies are typically insulated from politics and charged with meeting an inflation target first and foremost. As for countries in which leaders do not have to run for office and can act in the best long-term interest of society without regard for the next election, central bank independence is immaterial.

B   The Trilemma

While a diverse array of options exists in the tools and instruments of monetary policy, these tools and instruments do not function independently of one another. Open market operations aimed at targeting the interest rate have implications for the exchange rate, and conversely interventions in the foreign exchange market aimed at targeting the exchange rate have implications for the interest rate, although conditions apply. The Trilemma frames the options.

Interest Rate vs Exchange Rate Targeting

Consider first a monetary policy based on targeting the interest rate, and suppose the monetary authority adopts an expansionary stance in response to some negative shock. The expansionary stance implies the central bank must buy government securities to push down the interest rate to a new lower target. The lower interest rate in turn makes domestic bonds less attractive relative to foreign bonds. Consequently, capital outflows increase and capital inflows decrease. This then puts downward pressure on the exchange value of the domestic currency. The upshot is that the authorities cannot pursue a discretionary monetary policy based on interest rate targeting and at the same time stabilize the exchange rate under open capital markets.

Now consider a monetary policy anchored by an exchange rate peg, and suppose there is a positive shock to the credit side of the balance of payments. To stabilize the exchange rate, the central bank must buy foreign exchange and sell local currency. This increases the domestic money supply, which in turn pushes down the interest rate. This indeed is what must happen to restore balance in external payments in response to the initial positive shock, as explained in Chapter 8. The domestic stimulus from the money supply increase raises domestic demand causing net exports to fall and the lower interest rate causes net capital inflows to decline, both of which weigh on the debit side of the balance of payments. Thus, the expansionary monetary policy response to the initial positive shock drives countervailing debits to re-establish balance of payments equilibrium at the exchange rate peg.

Note that whether the interest rate or the exchange rate is the policy instrument, the mechanism by which the system responds to a policy action involves foreign capital flows. In the case of an interest rate target, a change in the target precipitates a capital flow response that moves the exchange rate. The exchange rate is thus at the mercy of interest rate targeting. In the case of an exchange rate target, pursuit of the target dictates monetary responses that act on the interest rate. That leads us to the Trilemma.

The Trilemma

The Trilemma, also known as the Impossible Trinity, holds that an economy cannot have all three of: a fixed exchange rate; an independent monetary policy; and open capital markets. Figure 11.1 presents a visualization of the Trilemma.

The combination along the bottom edge of the triangle involves monetary policy independence and open capital markets with a fully floating exchange rate. The world's major developed economies operate here. The combination along the right edge of the triangle involves a fixed exchange rate and open capital markets, but no monetary policy discretion. Hong Kong provides an example of this strategy. As an international financial center, Hong Kong must accede to global market determination of interest rates. Moreover, the territory's lack of sovereignty makes establishing credibility especially important. The US dollar peg achieves that credibility by putting money supply growth unassailably beyond the realm of human interference. Finally, the left side of the triangle captures the combination of a tightly managed exchange rate with space to pursue an independent monetary policy because

Figure 11.1 Trilemma visualization

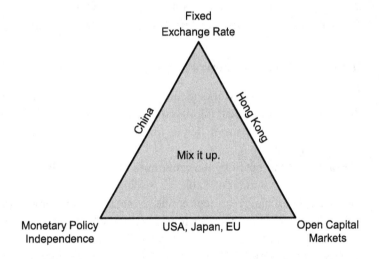

The Trilemma holds that policymakers may choose only two from among the following three aims: a fixed exchange rate; open capital markets; and monetary policy independence. Yet, there is some leeway to vary the degree of adherence to one or another and mix it up over time.

international capital movements are subject to controls. China provides an example of this strategy.

Where does that leave the rest of Emerging East Asia? The answer: mixing it up inside the triangle. To understand how this works, first note that for developing economies especially, frictions exist in international capital movements, meaning that while capital flows respond to some degree to changes in domestic versus global interest rates, the responses are not so sharp and strong as for a financial hub like Hong Kong, or for that matter Singapore which also relies on an exchange rate target for monetary policy but with discretion over the target's positioning. The frictions result from such market impediments as transactions costs, information asymmetries, risk factors, and of course, government regulation. This affords some leeway for authorities to pursue exchange rate management to a degree along with interest rate targeting to a degree.

Beyond the wiggle room afforded by market frictions, authorities have scope to shift emphasis between the interest rate and the exchange rate as instruments in light of circumstances. Leaning against movement in the exchange rate will imply allowing more flexibility in the interest rate and vice versa. Judgment and responsiveness are involved in handling this mixing of instruments, as with the exercise of monetary policy generally.

C   Emerging East Asia Record

As hinted in connection with Figure 11.1, the economies of Emerging East Asia have opted for a variety of different strategies in framing their monetary policies. In this section, we first present a broad categorization of these policies. We then focus in on the extent to which exchange rate management figures into monetary policy in practice for our sample of economies.

Monetary Policy Framework

Monetary policy frameworks identify the guideposts by which authorities anchor growth in the money supply. Specifying a framework helps to assure the public that authorities will keep inflation under control. This is important since public expectations about inflation are a big factor in driving it.

Frameworks adopted by the economies of Emerging East Asia are reported in Table 11.1. The table is an extension of Table 8.2, which shows exchange rate regimes, in recognition that the choices of exchange rate regime and monetary policy framework are related. The categorization is due to the International Monetary Fund which puts out an annual report on the subject.

Four of the economies in our sample base their monetary policies on an exchange rate anchor: Hong Kong; Vietnam; Cambodia; and Singapore. Hong Kong's exchange rate anchor takes the most extreme form of a hard peg to the US dollar, fixed since 1983. The monetary base of Hong Kong is fully backed by US dollars. Under a currency board system, the monetary authority buys or sells US dollars to whatever extent necessary to maintain the fixed rate of exchange. This leaves no discretion in the exercise of monetary policy. When the

Table 11.1 Exchange rate arrangement and monetary policy framework, select economies, 2020

Exchange Rate Arrangement		Economies	Monetary Policy Framework
Hard Peg	no separate legal tender	13		
	currency board	11	Hong Kong	exchange rate anchor (USD)
Soft Peg	conventional peg	41		
	stabilized arrangement	23	Vietnam	exchange rate anchor (composite)
	crawling peg	3		
	crawl-like arrangement	23	Cambodia	exchange rate anchor (USD)
			Laos	other
			Singapore	exchange rate anchor (composite)
	other managed	15	China	monetary aggregate target
			Myanmar	monetary aggregate target
Floating	floating	32	Indonesia	inflation targeting
			Korea	inflation targeting
			Malaysia	other
			Philippines	inflation targeting
			[Taiwan]	[other]
			Thailand	inflation targeting
	free floating	31		
Total		192		

value of the Hong Kong dollar pushes upward against the US dollar, the authority must sell Hong Kong dollars and buy US dollars, thus expanding the domestic money supply. And vice versa, when the value of the Hong Kong dollar presses downward against the value of the US dollar, the authority must buy Hong Kong dollars and sell US dollars thus shrinking the domestic money supply.

Cambodia also maintains a peg to the US dollar as the nominal basis for its monetary policy. However, in practice exchange rate management has little bearing on domestic monetary conditions given the high degree of dollarization in Cambodia. Indeed, with more than 90 percent of bank deposits in the country held in US dollars, the central bank has little effective control over the money supply.

In contrast to Hong Kong and Cambodia, Singapore and Vietnam peg their currencies to a composite, or basket, of foreign currencies as the basis for their monetary policies. Roughly speaking, this involves pegging to the nominal effective exchange rate (NEER), although weights assigned by currency may differ between the peg basket and the basket used to calculate the NEER. Pegging to a basket allows for flexibility relative to the US dollar with the advantage that when the dollar moves sharply against other currencies, volatility between the local currency and non-US dollar currencies is buffered.

Two economies in the sample – China and Myanmar – base their monetary policies on the targeting of a monetary aggregate. Direct targeting of a monetary aggregate is more effective for these economies than indirect management via an interest rate target due to heavy state ownership in the countries' banking systems that makes lending not very responsive to market forces.

The monetary policy frameworks of Laos and Malaysia are classified as "other." The IMF describes the framework in Laos as involving a mix of monetary targeting and an exchange rate anchor. In Malaysia, the central bank has a broad mandate that puts price stability first but extends beyond that to allow consideration of economic conditions more generally. The main policy instrument is an overnight interest rate. Similarly in Taiwan, the central bank mandate is broadly conceived to extend beyond inflation targeting (as indicated by information on the website of the Central Bank of the Republic of China).

That leaves four economies – Indonesia, Korea, the Philippines, and Thailand – for which the monetary policy framework is defined as "inflation targeting." This means the central bank follows a mandate to focus on maintaining price stability yet may use a variety of policy instruments to pursue that mandate. In all four cases, the exchange rate is floating but not free floating. This means that while the exchange rates of these economies are largely determined by market forces, central banks intervene as circumstances motivate. While all central banks are concerned with keeping inflation low and stable, a regime of inflation targeting involves the explicit statement of a target range of inflation that the central bank is committed to achieving with public accountability. This commitment does not strictly preclude monetary authorities from considering other aspects of economic performance in the formulation of policy as long as the inflation targeting goal is not compromised. In particular, there should be no exploiting of short-term output stimulus at the expense of longer-term price stability. The underlying principle is that there will be no succumbing to political pressures.

Foreign Exchange Market Intervention

The degree of central bank involvement in the foreign exchange market can be discerned from the magnitude of reserve asset flows on the balance of payments. Chart 11.1 presents this magnitude as a percentage of the stock of reserve assets held by the central bank by economy and by year for the period 2008–2020. Technically, central bank accumulation of foreign reserves is a debit on the balance of payments, and vice versa central bank decumulation of foreign reserves is a credit (as explained in Chapter 5, Section B). However, Chart 11.1 follows the reporting convention of the IMF database in treating a central bank purchase of foreign reserves as positive and a sale as negative.

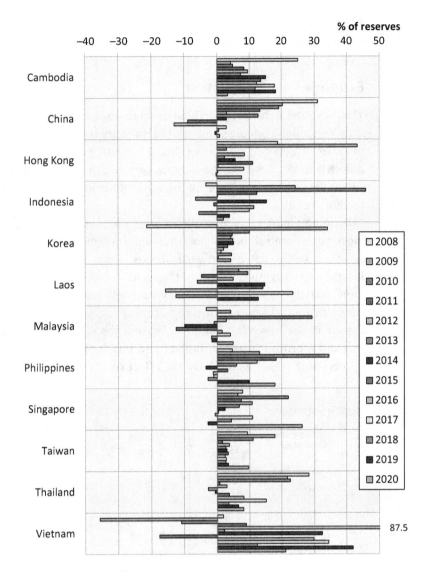

Chart 11.1 Balance of payments reserve asset flows, select economies, 2008–2020

Several patterns are notable. First, the vast majority of values are positive at 123 of 156 observations. That means for most of the sample economies in most years, central banks were net purchasers of foreign reserves. Second, year to year variability is very high. A spike in one year is often preceded or followed by a much lower value in adjacent years. Third, changes in the stock of reserves due to net flows on the balance of payments are frequently large. In 57 cases, the absolute value of the change is greater than 10 percent.

Taken together, these patterns suggest that central banks in Emerging East Asia engage purposefully in the foreign exchange markets. The degree of intervention varies greatly from year to year, and is sometimes quite large. This behavior is presumably not random.

Moreover, a strong preference is evident for net acquisitions to be positive, with decumulation of reserves being fairly rare yet large in some instances.

Exchange Rate Stabilization

The purposeful behavior behind foreign exchange market intervention is directed at stabilizing the exchange rate in the face of balance of payments shocks. Chart 11.2 provides evidence in support of this. The chart plots the percentage change in reserves as reflected in net flows on the balance of payments (from Chart 11.1) on the vertical axis versus the percentage change in the value of the local currency in terms of the US dollar on the horizontal axis.

Echoing Chart 11.1, most observations lie above the horizontal axis, meaning that in most years central banks accumulated foreign reserves. Accumulation of reserves is strongest to the left of the vertical axis where the change in the local currency to the US dollar is negative, meaning the local currency is appreciating. Hence central banks more heavily buy foreign currency and sell local currency when the local currency is strengthening. They are thereby leaning against the appreciation. No observations appear in the lower left quadrant beyond the edges. This means that in no appreciable way did a central bank sell dollars and buy local currency when the local currency was appreciating which would have the effect of amplifying the appreciation. Moving to the

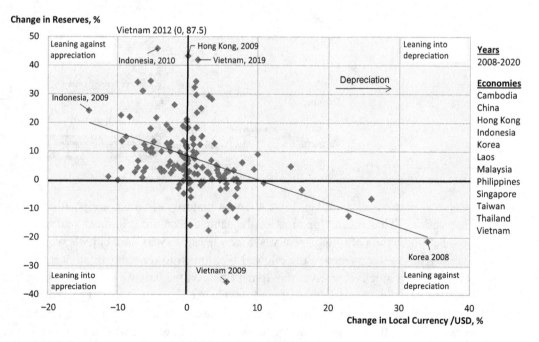

Chart 11.2 Reserves vs exchange rate, select economies, 2008–2020

right across the graph, the stronger the depreciation in the local currency, the greater the tendency for decumulation of foreign reserves. In the lower right quadrant, central banks are leaning against depreciation. In other words, when the local currency is losing value, central banks buy it and sell foreign currency.

Extreme cases captured in Chart 11.2 can be revealing as to policy principles. Hong Kong, with its hard peg, must always lie on the vertical axis. In 2009, to preserve the peg, the monetary authority was obliged to make massive purchases of foreign currency to the extent of increasing its reserves by more than 40 percent. Foreign currency inflows into Hong Kong were precipitated by a combination of factors: monetary easing in the USA that sent a wave of capital out into global markets; large stock issuances by mainland Chinese companies that attracted foreign investment capital; and mainland Chinese money pouring into Hong Kong real estate. Purchase of the foreign capital inflows by the monetary authority drove an expansion of the money supply which resulted in strong growth in real output but also put upward pressure on prices, especially property prices. Note that had the Hong Kong dollar been allowed to appreciate in value, the effective higher cost to foreigners of Hong Kong assets would have mitigated the foreign capital inflows to some extent.

Indonesia, too, was an outlier in 2009 and again in 2010. Like Hong Kong, it experienced massive capital inflows with global liquidity being a major driver. This push factor combined with pull side forces of strong domestic growth and heavy borrowing demand. At the same time, exports were burgeoning due to favorable global market conditions for Indonesia's commodity products. These positive shocks to both the financial account and the current account were absorbed in 2009 by a combination of rupiah appreciation and central bank purchases of foreign exchange. But after so much rupiah appreciation in 2009, the central bank intervened more heavily in 2010 to absorb continued money inflows. The potential danger of such sustained foreign currency purchase is excessive money supply growth that would push up inflation. Indonesia was successful in impeding this, however, as will be discussed in the next section on sterilization.

Korea was an outlier a year earlier in 2008, but in the opposite direction. With the onset of the Great Financial Crisis, heightened global risk aversion combined with Korea's high foreign indebtedness set off a bout of capital flight. At the same time, Korea's exports were hit hard amid plummeting global trade generally. To absorb these negative balance of payments shocks, the won was allowed to depreciate by nearly 35 percent even as the central bank intervened to forestall even greater depreciation. The intervention to sell US dollars and buy won cost the central bank roughly 20 percent of its foreign reserves. Central bank purchase of won had the effect of contracting the money supply with negative repercussions for prices and output growth. But the adverse shocks had to be absorbed, the only choice being in how to spread the pain.

The point is worth highlighting that Indonesia and Korea have both adopted monetary policy frameworks of inflation targeting, not exchange rate targeting. Yet their central banks intervened heavily in foreign exchange markets to stabilize their exchange rates in response to balance of payments shocks. There is not necessarily an inconsistency between such intervention and inflation targeting. The key is to understand how exchange rate stabilization affects the money supply and to coordinate with the use of other tools of monetary policy to stay the course on inflation.

For Vietnam, extremes are identified in 2009, 2012, and 2019. Further, Chart 11.1 shows that beyond these super extremes, other years saw changes in reserves that by the standards of the sample generally still exceeded norms. As its monetary policy framework, Vietnam has adopted an exchange rate peg. In 2012 and 2019, authorities held tightly to that peg in US dollar terms, accumulating reserves against heavy pressure for dong appreciation. Conversely in 2009, they held depreciation to around 6 percent by selling off 35 percent of reserve stocks. Vietnam's transition from a closed to an open economy has been recent and swift. It entered the World Trade Organization only in 2007, welcoming foreign direct investment and using it to leverage export growth. This development strategy has exposed the country to substantial external shocks even as it has driven impressive growth.

Reserve Assets

Charts 11.1 and 11.2 reveal that central banks in Emerging East Asia have generally inclined toward reserve accumulation, resorting to decumulation only when the domestic currency comes under strong downward pressure. Clearly, to be in a position to sell foreign currency in pushback against depreciation, a history of reserve accumulation must have gone before. And the stock of accumulated reserves must be substantial enough for any stance taken against depreciation to be convincing. Otherwise, speculators will bet against the currency making it that much harder to defend against the slide.

Accumulated reserve stocks as of 2020 are presented in Chart 11.3. The magnitudes are normalized on GDP making China's world beating trove in nominal terms appear relatively small against the size of its economy at 22.8 percent. Hong Kong ranks at the top of the chart under a system that requires its monetary base to be fully backed by US dollars. Vietnam's high annual rates of reserve accumulation through the 2011–2020 decade (Chart 11.1) have yielded only a modest reserve stock relative to GDP at 27.8 percent. Vietnam's recent entry into global engagement means the large rates of increase applied to a very small base. In this light, the country's exploitation of upward pressure on the dong to accumulate reserves seems sensible.

D   Monetary Policy in Singapore

Exchange rate targeting has served as the basis for Singapore's monetary policy since 1981. We begin this section by describing the framework, then look at exchange rate data over time to interpret policy implementation.

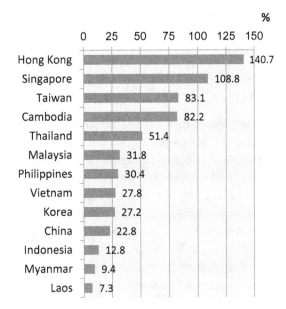

Chart 11.3 Official reserves/ GDP, select economies, 2020

Exchange Rate Targeting Framework
==================================

A monetary policy framework based on exchange rate targeting has proved a good fit for Singapore's circumstances. Notably, those circumstances involve extremely high degrees of openness to both trade and capital flows. Singapore's high trade ratio to GDP means that prices of traded goods feed heavily into domestic prices, intermediated by the exchange rate. The exchange rate is thus an effective instrument for managing inflation. At the same time, Singapore's open capital markets and position as a leading international financial center mean that global interest rates prevail with no latitude for independent management of domestic interest rates.

Singapore's exchange rate–based monetary policy involves three elements: a basket; a band; and a crawl. The basket is the mix of currencies to which the Singapore dollar is pegged with weights applied based on shares in Singapore trade. The band is a range in which the Singapore dollar is allowed to trade with respect to the basket before the monetary authority intervenes. And the crawl is a path of appreciation or depreciation relative to the basket that the nominal exchange rate is targeted to track. The monetary authority issues statements twice a year to vaguely indicate its monetary policy stance. The specific quantitative magnitudes of the basket, band, and crawl are not disclosed, although a bevy of analysts makes its living trying to uncover these mysteries, the better to predict the authority's actions and speculate accordingly.

The goal of monetary policy in Singapore is "to maintain price stability conducive to sustained growth of the economy," which suggests a degree of discretion in adjusting inflation goals as may be warranted to keep the economy on a solid growth trajectory. Between 1982 and 2020, annual inflation averaged 1.6 percent within a range of –1.4 percent to 6.6 percent. GDP growth averaged 5.8 percent within a range of –2.2 percent to 11.4 percent until 2020 when under the pandemic it dropped to –5.4 percent. This may be deemed a very successful record.

Policy Experience

Let us analyze the movement over time of Singapore exchange rates by various indexes to infer how the monetary authority has responded to changing circumstances. The US dollar exchange rate, the nominal effective exchange rate (NEER), and the real effective exchange rate (REER) for the period 1980 to 2020 are shown in Chart 11.4. Recall these exchange rate indexes were introduced in Chapter 8 with the Indonesian case used to illustrate in Chart 8.2.

Overall, the REER shows rolling movement over time, but no long-term directional trend. By contrast, the US dollar rate was generally rising over time indicating appreciation of the Singapore dollar relative to the US dollar. This is to be expected given higher inflation in the USA than in Singapore. Nominal appreciation of the Singapore dollar relative to the US dollar realigned purchasing power toward parity as the US dollar lost purchasing power due to inflation. More generally, this pattern shows up in the appreciation of the Singapore NEER as economies in the index basket generally had higher inflation than Singapore. Hence, as the nominal exchange rate appreciated relative to the basket, in real terms the Singapore dollar remained roughly stable relative to other currencies.

The NEER approximates the exchange rate relative to a basket of currencies the monetary authority uses as a policy instrument. The sharpest movement in the NEER was the drop in 1986. Singapore was hit hard by recession in late 1985 brought on by contraction in key export products, in part due to falling global demand although this was aggravated by rising

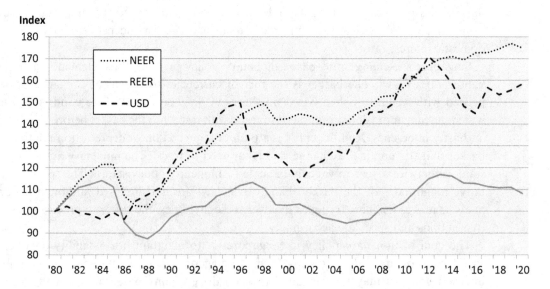

Chart 11.4 Exchange rate indexes, Singapore, 1980–2020

wages in Singapore relative to its newly emerging competitors. The monetary authority responded by reducing the exchange rate target to restore competitiveness and stimulate growth. Lowering the target meant selling Singapore dollars in exchange for foreign currency, thus expanding the domestic money supply to give the economy a boost.

The decade from 1988 to 1997 then saw steady appreciation in the NEER. During this period, Singapore sustained average GDP growth in excess of 9 percent a year. Appreciation of the currency restrained Singapore's global competitiveness and slowed growth of the money supply to keep inflation in check. The good times came to an end with the Asian Financial Crisis in 1997. The crisis was met with a steep reduction in the exchange rate target, reflected in the declining NEER, to increase competitiveness and provide monetary stimulus. Most recently, with the pandemic in 2020, the target has again been redirected downward.

A pattern has been revealed. In response to negative shocks, the monetary authority lowers the exchange rate target which simultaneously makes Singaporean goods and services more globally competitive and triggers expansion of the domestic money supply to provide credit stimulus. Conversely, strong economic growth is met with a rising exchange rate target which makes Singaporean products less competitive and induces a tightening of money growth to restrain the economy and inhibit inflation.

E Sterilization

Singapore's experience seems to have unfolded so very conveniently with exchange rate management meeting the dovetailing needs of both external and internal balance. Singapore is exceptional, however, in the degree to which the external sector dominates the economy. Under such conditions, it is perhaps not implausible that a single policy tool could address both external and internal pressures simultaneously. But for countries with larger, more autonomous domestic economies, what are authorities to do when a balance of payments shock seems to call for an intervention to the exchange rate that runs contrary to the goal of internal balance? Sterilization is a policy adaptation designed to contend with such exigencies. We first explain the mechanics of sterilization, then consider examples and discuss limitations.

Mechanics

Sterilization of a foreign exchange market intervention involves the central bank implementing an offsetting transaction elsewhere on its balance sheet. For example, suppose an economy is hit with a large capital inflow, which registers as a credit shock to its balance of payments. This will cause the value of the local currency to rise, which is precisely what is needed to bring about adjustments elsewhere in the balance of payments to restore equilibrium. Specifically, the higher value of the domestic currency will reduce exports, increase imports, and impact other capital flows so as to offset the credit shock. But, of course, these disruptions to the status quo will be painful to some parties.

To prevent such pain, the central bank can intervene to buy foreign currency and hold the line on the exchange rate. However, the foreign exchange purchase then sets up another sequence of events to re-establish balance in external payments through a different route. That process was outlined in Box 8.3, which is reproduced as Box 11.1 with modifications. Both credit and debit shocks to the balance of payments are considered, echoing Chapter 8 in taking Indonesia for purposes of example. The credit shock creates a surplus on the balance of payments. To maintain the exchange rate peg, the central bank must buy foreign currency and sell rupiah. This increases the domestic money supply causing the price level and/or real output to rise, and these macroeconomic consequences in turn feed back into the balance of payments. The upshot is that even under a fixed exchange rate, market processes have a way of restoring balance of payments equilibrium.

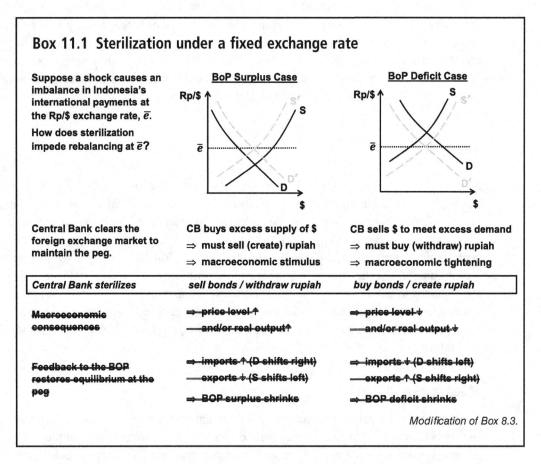

But what if these macroeconomic consequences aggravate domestic imbalances? Suppose the economy is already operating with a positive output gap such that real output growth is exceeding sustainable potential and inflation is accelerating. The foreign exchange market intervention involving sale of domestic currency will increase the money supply and make matters worse for internal imbalance.

Table 11.2 Central bank balance sheet

Assets	Liabilities
Net Foreign Assets	Currency In Circulation
Claims on Commercial Banks	Deposits of Commercial Banks
Net Claims on Central Government	Other (Net)

There is a possible way out, but it is subject to limitations. The central bank can sterilize its foreign asset purchase by implementing an offsetting transaction elsewhere on its balance sheet. The central bank balance sheet is shown in Table 11.2. In isolation, the increase in foreign assets resulting from the foreign exchange market intervention must be matched with central bank liabilities, in other words, base money (currency plus commercial bank deposits). This implies economic stimulus. The central bank can avert this simply by selling government securities or reducing net lending to commercial banks. This preserves the size of the central bank balance sheet and prevents the incipient increase in the money supply associated with the foreign exchange market intervention from transpiring.

The concern, however, is apparent from Box 11.1. Sterilization blocks the balance of payments equilibration process from carrying through. If the exchange rate the central bank is trying to preserve is out of line with economic fundamentals, the central bank will be bound to continue intervening perpetually to buy foreign currency and to sell government securities or reduce net lending to commercial banks with no resolution in sight. And this seems problematic. Let us consider two case studies to understand how circumstances matter in pulling off a sterilization operation.

Case Study 1: Indonesia, 2009–2010

The first case involves Indonesia in 2009–2010. Recall from Chart 11.2 that Indonesia was hit with large positive shocks to its balance of payments during this period. In 2009, these shocks were absorbed with a combination of rupiah appreciation relative to the US dollar of 14 percent and an increase in foreign reserves of 23 percent. By 2010, with the onslaught continuing, reticence to sustain currency appreciation is evident as the absorption mix shifted to a 4 percent appreciation against a 48 percent increase in foreign reserves.

Such large foreign reserve acquisitions by the central bank could have dire consequences for money supply growth and price stability. To avert this, Bank Indonesia sterilized its foreign exchange purchases. A standard vehicle for sterilization is the sale of government securities. This route was not available to Bank Indonesia because the government securities it held in substantial amount were not legally tradable and had to be retained until maturity. Instead, then, Bank Indonesia borrowed from the public by selling its own central bank bills to shrink the monetary base.

The drawback of this approach was that the central bank bills had to offer a market rate of interest on risky developing country terms in order to find buyers. Meanwhile, the foreign currency acquired by Bank Indonesia was mostly invested in US treasury securities that paid a lower rate of interest. Thus, the sterilization operations were a money losing proposition.

In addition to sterilization, Bank Indonesia made use of other standard tools to restrain money supply growth. These included raising its policy rate of interest and increasing the reserve requirement ratio. The combination of measures succeeded in keeping inflation within the target band of 4–6 percent.

An important consideration in Bank Indonesia relying heavily on sterilization to manage an imbalance in international payments was that the shock was understood to be largely temporary and ultimately reversible. Rapid capital inflows can turn around and become rapid capital outflows. By accumulating foreign reserves on the inflow side, Bank Indonesia stood ready to sell off reserves on the outflow side. Over time, these interventions would stabilize the exchange rate at a level consistent with underlying fundamentals. Thus, Bank Indonesia was not getting caught in a position of defending an exchange rate that was at odds with market forces over the long run.

Case Study 2: China, 2007–2008

China's central bank in 2007–2008 also relied heavily on sterilization of foreign currency purchases, but under very different circumstances from the Indonesian case. Recall from Chart 5.1 that in 2007 and 2008 China ran massive current account surpluses on the order of 400 billion US dollars a year. Absorbing these surpluses along with modest surpluses on the financial account ballooned the central bank's foreign reserves by nearly a trillion US dollars in just two years to create quite a stir among global onlookers.

Similar to Bank Indonesia, the People's Bank of China relied on issuance of central bank bills to sterilize its foreign exchange purchases. In the China case this was due to the rarity of fiscal deficits historically and thus a lack of government securities on the central bank balance sheet for it to sell. The People's Bank had an advantage over Bank Indonesia, however, in being able to sell its central bank bills to a captive market of state-owned commercial banks at very low interest rates. Thus, its cost of borrowing did not exceed the returns it was making on foreign exchange holdings invested in US treasury securities and it could therefore continue with its sterilization program without financial losses.

Similar to Bank Indonesia, the People's Bank of China augmented its sterilization operations with increases in the reserve requirement ratio to reduce the money multiplier. And it had a further tool not available to Bank Indonesia in the use of "moral suasion" to discourage commercial banks from lending under the continuing legacy of a command economy. Through use of an assortment of tools then, the People's Bank was successful in keeping money supply growth and inflation in check even as large balance of payments surpluses prevailed.

The saving grace of Bank Indonesia's sterilization program was that it responded to a temporary shock containing the seeds of its own reversal and was thus aimed at stabilizing an exchange rate consistent with medium term fundamentals. The Chinese case is very different in that regard. The People's Bank was absorbing surpluses on the current account rather than on the financial account, so there was no prospect of future flow reversals. Rather, China's sustained trade surpluses were taken by critics as a sign that the renminbi exchange rate was fundamentally misaligned with equilibrium in international payments. Yet China was able to preserve this misalignment through sterilized exchange market intervention seemingly without limit – or at least without economic limit, although politically the policy provoked an uproar from certain quarters. We revisit this issue in Chapter 16 to make the case that China was playing the long game in its macroeconomic stabilization policy. Eventually, its economic fundamentals did realign around a stabilized exchange rate to bring its trade surplus down to unobjectionable proportions.

Limitations

How did China manage to pull off such massive sterilization stretching over a period of years in contravention of economic fundamentals that we would expect to force a return to balance in international payments? One advantage China had has already been noted: it could borrow using central bank bills at a repressed rate of interest. Thus, unlike central banks operating in a market setting, China's central bank did not incur financial losses on sterilization due to a gap between high borrowing costs and low returns on foreign asset holdings.

But this is not the only protection China gained from its command and control economic system. A country with open capital markets and exposure to international trading in its currency would find any similar such persistent sterilization effort hitting up against the throes of speculation. China's renminbi was undervalued with respect to an exchange rate that would have brought about balance in international payments. This favored exports and penalized imports to generate a trade surplus of very large proportions. Normally, such a state of affairs would give rise to expectations of renminbi appreciation. And if a currency is expected to appreciate, the public will want to buy it en masse to reap the gains, and surging demand will then create even more pressure for appreciation such that eventually central bank efforts to hold the line will be overwhelmed. This could not happen in the Chinese case because the renminbi was not freely traded and speculators could not readily move money into China to buy renminbi assets. Hence, China's payments imbalances could be sustained and the sterilization could continue without speculative forces breaking the central bank's hold.

Indonesia did not face a speculative attack on its foreign exchange intervention and sterilization for a different reason: Investors were not skeptical about the fundamental alignment in the rupiah exchange rate. They accepted that the rupiah was under temporary upward pressure which the central bank was leaning against to moderate excessive fluctuation. Thus, there was no expectation of speculative gains to be had from betting on greater appreciation.

One other limitation of sterilization must be noted. Both the Indonesian and Chinese case studies involved balance of payments surpluses and associated central bank purchase of foreign exchange to block local currency appreciation. The opposite situation of a payments deficit and associated sale of foreign exchange can also manifest. Indeed, in the Indonesian case such a possibility was foreshadowed in connection with capital flows reversing to put downward pressure on the rupiah which the central bank would be prepared to moderate by selling its foreign reserve holdings. But the limitation in the more general situation of a central bank leaning against depreciation is easy to see. Whereas central banks in principle have open-ended capacity to buy foreign currency by creating liabilities against themselves, they face a hard finite limit on the amount of foreign currency they can sell. And speculators will thus move all the more aggressively knowing that a central bank will have to give up in fairly short order on an intervention to keep a currency from depreciating such that quick gains are assured.

F   The Juggling Act

Monetary policy is a juggling act. There are multiple goals, at least in principle. There are multiple tools, at least potentially. There are operating targets, intermediate targets, and final targets. There are trade-offs everywhere. Let us summarize and assess.

Frameworks Compared

Monetary policy involves the pursuit of stability in a world beset with constant disruption. The open economies of Emerging East Asia are particularly vulnerable to external shock transmitted through the balance of payments and exchange rates. Against this turbulence, the main focus of monetary policy is on achieving price stability, but more broadly this price stability is sought within a context of internal and external balance.

In pursuit of the same general end, the economies of Emerging East Asia have adopted differing monetary policy frameworks. Let us compare three alternative frameworks with respect to their responses to a common external shock in the form of a sudden capital outflow. The alternative frameworks are the pegged exchange rate of Hong Kong, the managed exchange rate of Singapore, and the inflation targeting frameworks of a number of other economies in the region.

In the Hong Kong case, the capital outflow under a pegged exchange rate creates a deficit on the balance of payments that requires sale of foreign currency by the monetary authority. The flip side of the sale of foreign currency is the authority's purchase of Hong Kong dollars which brings about a decrease in the domestic money supply. This has a contractionary effect on the economy expressed through some combination of declining output growth and disinflation. And in turn, this economic contraction brings about equilibration in the balance of payments as under reduced domestic demand, exports increase and imports decrease. Monetary policy in Hong Kong is fully subordinated to the exchange rate peg to the US dollar. In the long run, price stability in Hong Kong rests on price stability in the USA and the efficacy of purchasing power parity. In the short run, however, price and output volatility can be amplified by the need for monetary authorities to respond in full to balance of payments shocks without recourse to exchange rate adjustment.

In the Singapore case, the exchange rate relative to a basket of currencies is managed to track along a path set by the authorities. Subject to this preordained path, the sudden capital outflow would transmit a negative shock to the Singapore economy. The monetary authority, however, has discretion to adjust the path toward slower appreciation or faster depreciation to absorb some of the shock of the capital outflow. Thus, the outflow would have less impact on the money supply and more direct impact on the prices of traded goods. Adjustment involving higher exports and lower imports would take place in response to the currency depreciation rather than, as in the Hong Kong case, in response to slowing output growth and disinflation.

Under an inflation targeting regime, still more policy tools are available. To slow capital outflows, the authorities can raise the policy interest rate. This mitigates the original balance of payments shock and the associated currency depreciation. However, it still brings about slower growth in the money supply and imposes restraint on the domestic economy. The central bank can also intervene in the foreign exchange market to limit currency depreciation caused by the capital outflow. This similarly has a tightening effect on the money supply and a slowing effect on the economy, so either way that consequence is not avoided. Many factors will enter into the central bank's choice of actions: its capacity to draw down foreign reserves; the responsiveness of foreign capital to an increase in domestic interest rates; and the resilience of the domestic economy to the alternatives of higher interest rates and currency depreciation.

Negotiating the Trilemma

The Trilemma holds that an economy cannot have all three of: a fixed exchange rate; an independent monetary policy; and free capital mobility. Under open capital markets, management of the exchange rate determines the money supply. With sufficient barriers to capital mobility, as in the Chinese case, it is possible to maintain an exchange rate that yields sustained surpluses in international payments without generating unsustainable increases in the domestic money supply. Indeed, China was long able to keep domestic money growth in check by sterilizing its foreign exchange market intervention on a grand scale. Central bank borrowing to keep money tight did not result in rising interest rates because state-owned banks could be induced to lend to the central bank without regard for the interest rate. Further, speculators could not buy up renminbi in a bet on appreciation due to barriers to capital mobility. So, the combination of exchange rate management and an independent monetary policy against a backdrop of closed capital markets is an option, as the China case demonstrates.

Exchange rate management along with open capital markets is also an option, but requires giving up a monetary policy independent of the exchange rate. This does not mean giving up discretion in the use of an exchange rate target as the basis for monetary policy, as the Singapore case shows. The Singapore monetary authority exercises full discretion over monetary policy by realigning the projected path of its exchange rate in response to economic circumstances. It can pursue a tight monetary policy by charting a steep course of appreciation or a loose monetary policy by engineering a depreciation. By contrast, Hong Kong has given up discretion in its exchange rate and monetary policies by adopting a hard peg to the US dollar.

The reason for Hong Kong's choice of a hard peg is worth contemplating. Under a hard peg, external shocks must be fully absorbed in domestic output and prices to achieve balance of payments adjustment. Especially in response to negative shocks, this can be painful as output tends to decline first bringing employment down with it, while prices adjust downward with a longer lag as output then slowly recovers. Yet Hong Kong has not stuck to a hard peg since 1981 without good reason: the credibility of its currency and with that its position as a global financial hub rests on it. Credibility is important to all central banks. The public must believe the authorities are committed to holding the line against inflation despite the temptation to push for short-term output gains that will only later result in rising inflation. For Hong Kong, credibility is all the more fragile since it is not a sovereign state and ultimate authority lies in Beijing. For an international financial center, any loss of confidence in the soundness of the currency would have dire consequences. Hong Kong has found a framework that suits its circumstances, and has stuck with it.

Finally, we come to the inflation targeters who move around within the confines of the Trilemma. Their capital markets are fairly open, yet there are more frictions and regulations than for Hong Kong and Singapore, and thus more space for domestic interest rate targeting. For these economies a policy rate of interest is an important instrument of monetary policy. Nevertheless, interest rate manipulation by central banks is ultimately subject to limits imposed by global capital movements. Fortunately, these economies have another policy instrument of which to avail themselves, and that is the exchange rate. Foreign exchange market intervention is an especially valuable tool for dealing with external shocks. Nevertheless, the Trilemma holds, broadly speaking. Intervention in the foreign exchange market acts on the money supply and through that on the interest rate. And conversely, open market operations that affect the interest rate have repercussions for the exchange rate. Exchange rate targeting and interest rate targeting may both be pursued but subject to interdependence. Sterilization may even afford a degree of independence between the two instruments, but this, too, is subject to limitations. Within the triangle, then, there is space for maneuvering.

G   Bringing in Fiscal Policy

Central banks have a diverse array of tools to draw on in the conduct of monetary policy. Yet, these tools cannot be made to work toward achieving disparate goals. They can only be used in concert.

For example, suppose the domestic economy is underperforming for a negative output gap. This problem could be addressed by the central bank through any number of expansionary monetary policy actions: purchase government securities; purchase foreign reserve assets; lower the interest rate paid on excess reserves or the discount rate; or cut the reserve requirement ratio. Now suppose that externally the economy is facing upward pressure on the value of its currency. To stabilize the exchange rate, the actions called for are the opposite: sell government securities; sell foreign reserve assets; and so on. Thus, monetary policy alone cannot address both the internal and external imbalances. Indeed, contending with one problem will make the other problem worse.

For a situation like this, there is need of another policy arm. Fortunately, one exists in the form of fiscal policy. This is the subject of Chapter 12. Chapter 13 then looks at how monetary and fiscal policies can be combined to address internal and external imbalances jointly.

Data Note

Classification of monetary policy frameworks is from the International Monetary Fund *Annual Report on Exchange Arrangements and Exchange Restrictions*. This annual report reviews the policy frameworks, both de jure and de facto, of all IMF member economies. The de facto frameworks are reported in Table 11.1. An online database offers information by economy and year. For Taiwan, information on the monetary policy framework is drawn from the website of the Central Bank of the Republic of China (Taiwan).

For Charts 11.1 to 11.3, data on balance of payments reserve asset flows and foreign reserve stocks and on exchange rates are from the IMF International Financial Statistics database. Taiwan data are from the Central Bank of the Republic of China (Taiwan) Balance of Payments and International Investment Position database.

Data on Singapore exchange rates in Chart 11.4 are from the IMF International Financial Statistics database. Note that the Singapore monetary authority calculates its own NEER for policy purposes and hence its value will differ from the measure reported by the IMF, but not so much as to alter the general patterns discussed in this chapter. Singapore inflation and GDP growth measures are from the World Bank World Development Indicators database.

Bibliographic Note

A respected US textbook on monetary policy, in its 12th edition at this writing, is by Frederic Mishkin. Mishkin served on the US Federal Reserve Board of Governors during 2006–2008.

The case study on sterilization for Indonesia relies on Article IV Consultation reports of the IMF for 2010 and 2011. For the China case study, Article IV Consultation reports are not available because the Chinese government did not agree to the release of these reports in 2008 and 2009. A Bank for International Settlements working paper by Ma, Yan, and Liu offers an insightful analysis. Discussion of Hong Kong, Korea, and Vietnam in connection with Chart 11.2 also draws on IMF Article IV Consultation reports.

A post by Wiemer of May 5, 2021 on the *Asia Economics Blog* utilizes the framework developed in Chart 11.2 to illuminate the East Asian model for exchange rate–based stabilization policy. A post of July 16, 2021 assesses the exercise of expansionary monetary policy in response to the pandemic in light of the space for policy maneuver.

BIBLIOGRAPHIC CITATIONS

Central Bank of the Republic of China (Taiwan), 2020. Monetary Policy. www.cbc.gov.tw/en/np-443-2.html (accessed May 7, 2020).

Central Bank of the Republic of China (Taiwan), 2020. Balance of Payments & International Investment Position. https://cpx.cbc.gov.tw/Tree/TreeSelect?mp=2 (accessed May 7, 2020).

International Monetary Fund, 2009. Republic of Korea: 2009 Article IV Consultation. www.imf.org/external/pubs/ft/scr/2009/cr09262.pdf (accessed May 13, 2020).

International Monetary Fund, 2010. People's Republic of China – Hong Kong Special Administrative Region: 2010 Article IV Consultation. www.imf.org/external/pubs/ft/scr/2010/cr10345.pdf (accessed May 13, 2020).

International Monetary Fund, 2010. Indonesia: 2010 Article IV Consultation. www.imf.org/external/pubs/ft/scr/2010/cr10284.pdf (accessed May 13, 2020).

International Monetary Fund, 2011. Indonesia: 2011 Article IV Consultation. www.imf.org/external/pubs/ft/scr/2011/cr11309.pdf (accessed May 13, 2020).

International Monetary Fund, 2021. Annual Report on Exchange Arrangements and Exchange Restrictions 2020. www.imf.org/en/Publications/Annual-Report-on-Exchange-Arrangements-and-Exchange-Restrictions/Issues/2021/08/25/Annual-Report-on-Exchange-Arrangements-and-Exchange-Restrictions-2020-49738 (accessed October 9, 2021).

International Monetary Fund, 2020. AREAER Online. www.elibrary-areaer.imf.org/Pages/Reports.aspx (accessed May 7, 2020).

International Monetary Fund, 2018. International Financial Statistics. http://data.imf.org/?sk=4C514D48-B6BA-49ED-8AB9-52B0C1A0179B&sId=1390030341854 (accessed April 20, 2018).

Ma, Guonan, Xiandong Yan, and Xi Liu, 2011. "China's Evolving Reserve Requirements," BIS Working Papers No. 360. www.bis.org/publ/work360.pdf (accessed May 18, 2020).

Mishkin, Frederic S., 2019. *The Economics of Money, Banking and Financial Markets*, 12th edition (Pearson).

Wiemer, Calla, 2021. "The Exchange Rate in East Asia's Macro Stabilization Policy: It's Not Just China," *Asia Economics Blog*, May 5, 2021. http://acaes.us/blog/exchange-rate-in-stabilization (accessed December 28, 2021).

Wiemer, Calla, 2021. "Economics of the Pandemic, 2020 (Part III): Monetary Policy," Asia Economics Blog, July 16, 2021. http://acaes.us/blog/pandemic-2020-monetary-policy (accessed December 29, 2021).

12   Fiscal Policy

Fiscal policy involves managing government spending, taxation, and borrowing for purposes of macroeconomic stabilization. Fiscal policy works through both automatic stabilizers, based on countercyclical responses of spending and taxation to income fluctuations, and active management, particularly in response to severe negative shocks. Use of activist fiscal policy is limited by cumbersome decision-making processes, the countervailing effects of government borrowing on interest and exchange rates, and debt sustainability constraints.

Changes in government spending, taxation, and borrowing affect internal and external balance directly through aggregate demand and indirectly through the interest rate and the exchange rate. To a significant degree, fiscal policy works automatically as growth acceleration is tempered by rising taxes and declining transfer payments, and vice versa, growth slowdown is buffered by falling taxes and expanding transfer payments. A more activist approach is limited by difficulties of implementation, which nevertheless tend to be overcome in the face of severe negative shocks. In severe downturns, needed stimulus may be provided through government spending increases and tax reductions supported by borrowing, provided debt has been well contained during normal times. A moderate debt-to-GDP ratio affords the fiscal space for government to react when circumstances call for it.

We begin this chapter with a discussion of the fiscal policy transmission process and a comparison of the workings of fiscal policy and monetary policy. We then delve more deeply into the ramifications of the exchange rate regime and capital market openness for the transmission process. Fiscal policy, in principle, involves raising spending and lowering taxes when the output gap is negative and doing the opposite when the output gap is positive. This implies taking on debt when the economy slumps and paying it down when the economy booms. Human nature and the political process being what they are, however, debt buildup is in practice much easier than debt paydown. In light of these observations, we explore the nature of deficits, debt, and debt financing and then go on to consider guideposts for keeping debt financing in check to ensure fiscal sustainability. Vietnam provides the case study on fiscal sustainability. We further apply the concepts to examining the fiscal response of economies in Emerging East Asia to the trauma of the Great Financial Crisis. We end with thoughts on the coordination of monetary and fiscal policy in preparation for a rigorous examination of this topic in Chapter 13.

A   Fundamentals

Fiscal policy works through increases in government spending and cuts in taxes to boost an underperforming economy and conversely cuts in government spending and increases in taxes to rein in an overheating economy. Any shortfall between taxes and spending must be met through government borrowing which itself affects macroeconomic performance. Let us first look at the fiscal policy transmission mechanism, then draw back to consider broader issues of implementation and effectiveness by contrasting fiscal policy with monetary policy.

Fiscal Policy Transmission

Fiscal policy has its roots in the Keynesian notion that aggregate demand may fall short of the level needed to bring about full employment. Recall from Chapter 9, Equations (9.1) and (9.2), that in the Income–Expenditure Model, demand is given by type of expenditure as $C + I + G + X - M$ where consumption is a function of income after taxes stated as $C_0 + \beta(Y - T)$. Within this framework, aggregate demand can be boosted by raising government spending or by lowering taxes which has the effect of increasing after-tax income and thus consumption spending. Importantly, the stimulus does not stop with the initial spending increase or tax cut. There is a multiplier effect as an impetus to spending generates income that generates more spending and in turn more income, and so forth. Eventually, the effect dies out, though, as the increments to spending get smaller with each round due to some portion of income being saved.

In addition to government spending on goods and services, governments make transfer payments in support of social welfare programs. Insofar as the recipients of such transfers have lower incomes and spend a larger proportion of their incomes on consumption than those whose taxes fund the programs, overall consumption spending can be increased through tax and transfer schemes.

While the Keynesian focus is on stimulating an underperforming economy to achieve internal balance, the same principles apply under the opposing situation. For an economy that is overheating, the prescription is to cut government spending and increase taxes. Clearly this is more difficult politically. Yet there is a limit on the degree to which spending can be increased and taxes decreased as borrowing escalates. Even within that limit, government demand for loanable funds puts upward pressure on interest rates which crowds out private borrowing to the diminution of private consumption and investment spending.

Fiscal policy has a bearing on external balance as well as internal balance. A fiscal stimulus to aggregate demand causes imports to rise and exports to fall given a more vibrant home market. At the same time, government borrowing to support deficit spending puts upward pressure on interest rates inducing capital inflows to increase relative to outflows. The effects of trade flows and capital flows on the balance of payments are thus offsetting as a decrease in the current account balance is met by an increase in the financial account balance. A policy of fiscal restraint causes the reverse set of responses.

The effects of policy on internal and external balance are related through the equivalence that must hold between the domestic saving-investment gap $(S - I)$ and the export-import gap $(X - M)$. As the relationship was derived for Equation (4.8), investment and consumption were defined to absorb government spending. Let us now delineate the role of government in the economy. The GDP expenditure equation distinguishes government spending on consumption and investment, G, from private spending. And the equation for uses of income includes taxes, T, as an element. Setting the two expressions for GDP equal we have:

$$C + I + G + X - M = C + T + S. \tag{12.1}$$

Canceling the consumption terms and rearranging yields:

$$X - M = (S - I) + (T - G). \tag{12.2}$$

This equation holds that a surplus on the trade balance is matched by capital outflows deriving from some combination of an excess of saving over domestic private investment and a surplus of tax revenue over government spending. Conversely, a trade deficit would be matched by net capital inflows to fund some combination of domestic investment in excess of saving and government spending over and above tax revenue.

We could also think of this relationship as holding that a government deficit $(G - T)$ is met by a combination of saving in excess of domestic private investment $(S - I)$ and a trade deficit $(M - X)$ that mirrors a net capital inflow on the balance of payments:

$$G - T = (S - I) + (M - X). \tag{12.3}$$

More simply put, a government deficit is financed by a combination of domestic and foreign saving. How is this equivalency achieved in response to a fiscal stimulus? Higher domestic saving is induced by the increase in income deriving from the stimulus; private investment is crowded out as government borrowing pushes up interest rates; and further in response to higher interest rates, foreign capital is attracted and domestic capital is deterred from leaving. Conversely, a fiscal tightening is associated with the opposite set of outcomes: lower domestic saving; higher private investment; and reduced net capital inflows.

Monetary vs Fiscal Policy

The fiscal policy transmission mechanism has the advantage of working directly on the economy through government spending changes and at only a slight remove through tax changes that affect private income and in turn spending. By contrast, the workings of monetary policy are more indirect and less certain since a change in monetary base must be transmitted to an increase in bank lending to influence spending. During severe economic downturns, however, banks may have little desire to lend and businesses little motivation to borrow. Monetary policy under such circumstances has been likened to "pushing on a string." The central bank can push money into bank reserves, but if the reserves just sit on bank balance sheets, the stimulus dies.

In other respects though, monetary policy has advantages over fiscal policy. Most importantly, money supply management is wholly dedicated to the goal of macroeconomic stabilization. By contrast, government spending and taxation initiatives exist within an enormous and complex government budget aimed at achieving a vast multiplicity of goals that supercede macroeconomic stabilization in priority. Government undertakes spending in the service of many functions: It must provide a framework within which a market economy can operate; it must produce goods and services or regulate their production under circumstances where markets fail (e.g., public goods, natural monopoly, externalities, imperfect information); it must strive to achieve equity through social welfare programs. Increases and decreases in spending for the purpose of macroeconomic stabilization rest on top of all these more foundational goals. On the tax side, too, government has much else to consider: the need to fund its expenditures; effects on incentives; and consequences for equity. Macroeconomic stabilization is again an add-on. Finally, government must be attentive to the current and future impact of its borrowing on the tax-paying public and financial markets. This constrains the scope for fiscal policy action.

Relatedly, for monetary policy, decision-making is straightforward whereas for fiscal policy it is extremely cumbersome. Monetary policy is conducted by a handful of central bank authorities meeting periodically with little or no public accountability. Fiscal policy, by contrast, is conducted by large executive and legislative bodies embedded in a political process that is subject to public scrutiny. Quick reaction to ever changing circumstances is hardly the strong suit of such bodies.

Further, the political nature of government budgeting biases it toward expansionary policy and against contractionary resetting. Spending is easy to ramp up, but much harder to scale back. Similarly, taxes are easy to cut, much harder to raise. While monetary tightening, too, can inflict pain, such action is less transparent and therefore not so subject to politicization.

Of final note, both monetary and fiscal policy face limits to action on the stimulus side. For fiscal policy, the limit follows from the need to keep government debt in check. For monetary policy, the limit is the zero lower bound on interest rates, although the exercise of quantitative easing in response to the Great Financial Crisis showed this limit to be more flexible than previously thought.

B   Openness and Policy Effectiveness

Funding of government budget deficits must draw from a combination of domestic and foreign sources of capital. The degree of openness of capital markets thus matters in the process, as does the nature of the exchange rate regime. In this section we explore the implications for policy effectiveness considering in turn each of the four combinations of high vs low capital market openness and fixed vs floating exchange rates.

The analysis is supported with use of the IS–LM framework augmented by a balance of payments relationship (the Mundell–Fleming model) introduced in Chapter 9. For those not readily conversant in the model, the reasoning is manageable in verbal terms.

High Capital Mobility with Fixed Exchange Rate

We wish to consider the consequences of fiscal policy for national income taking first a situation where capital is highly mobile and the exchange rate is fixed. Figure 12.1, building on Figure 9.7, depicts a fiscal stimulus as a rightward shift in the IS curve. Recall that the IS curve captures equilibrium pairs of income and the interest rate as derived from the Keynesian expenditures equation. The downward slope of the IS curve indicates that as the interest rate falls, investment increases and hence so does income. An increase in government spending or a reduction in taxes is reflected in a rightward shift of the IS curve since higher income is associated with all levels of the interest rate.

The rightward shift of the IS curve results in a movement along the LM curve. The LM curve captures equilibrium pairs of the interest rate and national income based on money demand equaling exogenous money supply. An increase in the interest rate is associated with a higher level of income that induces the public to hold given money balances to meet liquidity needs as opposed to holding now higher yielding bonds. The movement along the LM curve that results from the fiscal stimulus brings about a higher interest rate and a higher level of income to maintain internal balance.

At the intersection of the IS′ and LM curves, the economy has moved off its BP curve implying an imbalance externally. The interest rate is too high relative to income to sustain

Figure 12.1 Fiscal stimulus with high capital mobility and fixed exchange rate

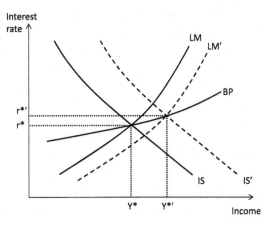

A fiscal stimulus shifts the IS curve to the right which results in a capital inflow to meet borrowing needs. This is met with foreign exchange purchases reflected in an LM curve shift to the right. A strong increase in income results.

external balance. As the interest rate overshoots, foreign capital flows in for an increase in the financial account balance that is not matched by a sufficiently large decrease in the current account balance. A bigger increase in income is needed to further decrease exports and raise imports to achieve external balance. Under a fixed exchange rate, the balance of payments surplus that results from the stimulus must be absorbed by the monetary authority purchasing foreign capital inflows. The resulting increase in the domestic money supply is represented by a rightward shift in the LM curve. The money supply increase lowers the interest rate, thus inhibiting net capital inflows, and raises income, thus decreasing the current account balance, to bring about external balance so that all three curves intersect at the same point, given by $Y^{*\prime}$ and $r^{*\prime}$.

The flat shape of the BP curve in Figure 12.1 implies that capital is highly mobile. The capital inflow generated by a small increase in the domestic interest rate requires a large increase in income to yield the necessary decrease in the trade account to preserve external balance. The combination of high capital mobility and a fixed exchange rate results in a big increase in income from the fiscal stimulus. This is because an expansionary monetary policy to preserve the exchange rate in the face of capital inflows amplifies the expansionary fiscal policy. Further, little domestic investment is crowded out from government borrowing because foreign capital responds so readily to a higher interest rate. Thus, fiscal policy is very effective in achieving economic growth under conditions of an open capital market and a fixed exchange rate.

High Capital Mobility with Floating Exchange Rate

Let us turn to the case of high capital mobility and a floating exchange rate represented in Figure 12.2. Again, a fiscal stimulus is represented by a shift in the IS curve to the right, and this puts upward pressure on the interest rate attracting a capital inflow such that at the intersection of IS' and LM, the economy is off its BP curve with a balance of payments surplus. Under a floating exchange rate, the value of the local currency rises in response to the capital inflow which induces a decrease in the trade balance to match the increase in the financial account balance. The increase in the value of the local currency is captured graphically as an upward shift in the BP curve to BP'.

This, however, is not the end of the story. Declining exports and competition from rising imports resulting from the higher domestic currency value feed back to reduce domestic demand, as represented by a leftward shift in the IS curve to IS''. The lower income then mitigates the increase in the exchange rate needed to resolve the external imbalance. The equilibrating process between income, the interest rate, and the exchange rate ultimately brings the economy to rest at $Y^{*\prime\prime}$.

In the extreme hypothetical case of perfect capital mobility, represented by a horizontal BP curve, the interest rate is determined entirely by global capital markets. In this situation, the rightward shift in the IS curve resulting from the fiscal stimulus generates a capital inflow that can only be offset in the trade account by a full reversion of income to its starting point, Y^*. The increase in income from the fiscal stimulus is thus entirely undone by a decrease in income due to lost exports and import competition hitting domestic production.

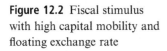 **Figure 12.2** Fiscal stimulus
with high capital mobility and
floating exchange rate

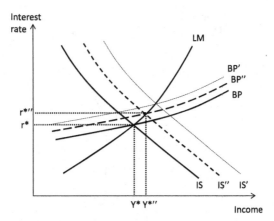

A fiscal stimulus shifts the IS curve to the right which
results in a capital inflow to meet borrowing needs. This
is met with an appreciation in the local currency reflected
in an upward shift in the BP curve. The currency
appreciation results in a decrease in the trade balance
that redounds back to the IS curve to moderate the
increases in income.

In general, then, in the case of high capital mobility and a floating exchange rate, the effect of a fiscal stimulus on income is undermined as capital inflows prompt currency appreciation that strikes at an economy's global competitiveness. As a result, the composition of aggregate demand shifts toward government spending and away from foreign and private domestic spending on tradable goods. Of final note, external financing of the fiscal deficit leaves a foreign currency debt burden that will require servicing into the future.

Under conditions of high capital mobility, the general conclusion is that a fiscal stimulus works much better if it is accompanied by a monetary stimulus. This occurs automatically under a fixed exchange rate. But even under a floating exchange rate, a complementary monetary stimulus can be instituted. The effect will be to moderate the interest rate increase and currency appreciation associated with a floating exchange rate. This will preserve more of the income gain from the stimulus and result in more of the financing of the fiscal deficit being provided domestically.

Low Capital Mobility with Fixed and Floating Exchange Rates

If barriers to capital mobility impede financing of the fiscal deficit from foreign funding sources, financing must be obtained from domestic sources. The situation of low capital mobility is depicted by a steep BP curve in Figure 12.3. The interpretation is that even a big increase in the interest rate draws little foreign capital and hence not much increase in income is needed to generate an offsetting reduction in the trade balance.

The rightward shift of the IS curve from the fiscal stimulus leads to an internal balance at the intersection of the IS′ and LM curves. To achieve external balance, however, would require a higher interest rate than the resulting $r^{*\prime}$. This is because at the higher income driven

Figure 12.3 Fiscal stimulus
with low capital mobility

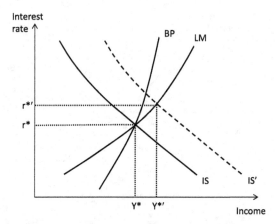

A fiscal stimulus shifts the IS curve to the right which
results in a steep rise in the interest rate with little
inflow of foreign capital. Government borrowing
crowds out private sector investment to limit the
increase in income. How the international payments
imbalance is resolved depends on the exchange
rate regime.

by the stimulus, the reduction in the trade balance is not met with a sufficiently large capital inflow. A balance of payments deficit results as exports decrease and imports increase.

Under a fixed exchange rate, the monetary authority must sell foreign currency and buy domestic currency to meet the balance of payments deficit. The resulting contraction of the money supply is captured by a leftward shift in the LM curve to a position intersecting with IS′ and BP. The ultimate result is a diminished increase in income from the stimulus. Foreign capital finances little of the fiscal deficit, and at a high interest cost. The upward pressure on the interest rate crowds out domestic borrowing to limit growth in income.

Under a floating exchange rate, the deficit in the balance of payments is resolved by a depreciation of the local currency that increases exports and decreases imports. With this, the BP curve shifts to the right and so, to a further degree, does the IS curve. Combined internal and external balance is ultimately achieved with an income somewhere above $Y^{*\prime}$ and an interest rate somewhere above $r^{*\prime}$. The initial fiscal stimulus is thus enhanced by currency depreciation that increases the trade balance controverting the effect of rising income to reduce it. In the final analysis, the fiscal stimulus, augmented by currency depreciation, achieves a strong gain in income, although this comes at a high interest cost for borrowing which must rely mainly on domestic funds diverted from the private sector.

Summary

To summarize, the effectiveness of fiscal policy depends on the openness of capital markets and the nature of the exchange rate regime. Table 12.1 outlines results under the various combinations.

Table 12.1 Effect of capital mobility and exchange rate regime on fiscal stimulus

Capital Mobility	Incipient External Imbalance	Exchange Rate Regime	Response to External Imbalance	Effect on Stimulus
high	net capital inflow > trade account decrease (BoP surplus)	fixed	monetary expansion	amplify
		floating	currency appreciation	diminish
low	net capital inflow < trade account decrease (BoP deficit)	fixed	monetary contraction	diminish
		floating	currency depreciation	amplify

A fiscal stimulus achieves its greatest effect on income under combinations of: (i) high capital mobility with a fixed exchange rate; and (ii) low capital mobility with a floating exchange rate. Under high capital mobility, a robust capital inflow to fund the fiscal deficit generates a balance of payments surplus that under a fixed exchange rate must be met with foreign exchange purchases by the monetary authority. This invokes a monetary stimulus that amplifies the fiscal stimulus. Under low capital mobility, the boost to income from the fiscal stimulus causes the trade balance to fall beyond the power of tepid capital inflows to match. Under a floating exchange rate, the balance of payments deficit is then resolved through currency depreciation that boosts exports and limits imports to provide further stimulus.

A fiscal stimulus is undermined under combinations of high capital mobility with a floating exchange rate and low capital mobility with a fixed exchange rate. Under high capital mobility, strong capital inflows in response to the fiscal stimulus cause a balance of payments surplus that under a floating exchange rate leads to currency appreciation and hence a mitigation of the income increase as exports fall and imports rise. Under low capital mobility the reduction in the trade balance that results from higher income causes a balance of payments deficit that with a fixed exchange rate prompts the monetary authority to buy local currency such that a monetary contraction undermines the fiscal stimulus.

C   Fiscal Balance and Debt

A deficit in the fiscal balance must be financed by the issuance of new government debt whereas a surplus in the fiscal balance affords the paying down of outstanding debt or the accumulation of reserve funds. Note that deficit and surplus are flow concepts whereas debt is a stock concept. We begin this section with definitions of fiscal notions and an analysis of how the fiscal balance responds to changes in national income to create automatic stabilizers. We then consider the various options available for debt financing and their consequences. Finally, we look at government debt levels for the economies of Emerging East Asia.

Fiscal Balance

The *overall fiscal balance* is the difference between total government revenue and total government expenditures including interest payments on debt and transfer payments made under social welfare programs. This is also known as the *net borrowing requirement*. The *primary fiscal balance* is total revenue minus expenditures excluding interest payments on debt. The primary balance is thus always larger than the overall balance, and may be positive even if the overall balance is negative.

Government revenue and transfer payments both vary as functions of national income. Revenue rises when income rises since economic activity is the basis for most taxation. Specifically, taxes defined on income, value added, profits, and sales all generate more government revenue as national income rises, and vice versa. Conversely, transfer payments are negatively related to national income. Transfer payments include outlays for poverty relief, unemployment compensation, and a variety of means tested social welfare programs. When economic performance is strong, transfer payments go down, and when it is weak, they go up. Formally, the relationship may be expressed as:

$$FB = R(Y) - G_F - Tr(Y) \tag{12.4}$$

where variable definitions are given in Figure 12.4.

As the figure shows, the fiscal balance is an increasing function of income since as income rises the positive contribution of revenue increases and the negative impact of transfer payments decreases. More government revenue and less spending as economic growth picks up imposes an automatic restraining effect on the economy. Conversely, as economic activity slows, government revenue falls and spending rises for a stimulatory effect. These built-in responses of taxation and spending to income changes kick in as

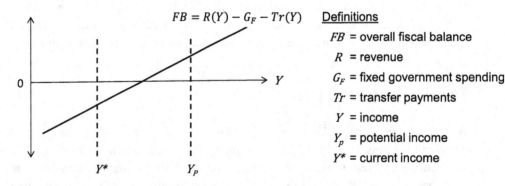

The fiscal balance is an increasing function of income, shown here in deficit at current income, Y^*, and in surplus at potential income, Y_P.

Figure 12.4 Fiscal balance response to income

automatic stabilizers to tamp down an overheating economy or boost up an underperforming economy.

Figure 12.4 identifies levels of income reflecting potential and actual performance. The economy depicted is underperforming at actual income Y^* relative to potential income Y_p. The current fiscal balance is negative, brought down by diminished tax receipts and inflated transfer payments relative to the reference point of potential output. If the economy were operating at its potential, the fiscal balance under the given tax and transfer regime would show a surplus. The fiscal balance at potential output is known as the *structural balance* or *cyclically adjusted balance*. Note that it is possible for an economy to have a structural deficit, which would be shown in the figure with a fiscal balance line that crosses the horizontal axis to the right of Y_p. The structural balance depends on how tax and transfer laws are specified with respect to income. The current balance, too, depends on tax and transfer laws, but is influenced in addition by the cyclical status of the economy relative to potential.

The *fiscal stance* of the government budget is defined with respect to the structural balance. A structural surplus is said to be contractionary, a structural deficit, expansionary. Note that in Figure 12.4, the fiscal stance is contractionary even though the government is running a current fiscal deficit.

Fiscal impulse refers to a change in the structural balance. A decrease in the structural balance brings about a positive fiscal impulse, or stimulus. Conversely, an increase in the structural balance brings about a negative fiscal impulse, or tightening. In the context of Figure 12.4, the economy could be pushed toward its potential with a spending increase or tax cut. Such a positive fiscal impulse would be represented by a downward shift in the FB function. Even at a cost of a larger current deficit, a positive structural balance (contractionary fiscal stance) could still be sustained.

Fiscal budget concepts
• overall balance = total revenue − total expenditures
• primary balance = overall balance + interest payments
• structural balance = overall balance at potential output
• automatic stabilizers: income-based taxes & transfers
• fiscal stance: based on sign of structural balance
• fiscal impulse: based on change in structural balance

Deficit Financing

Governments finance deficits by issuing debt securities. These securities may be sold to different types of buyers, each involving its own particular consequences for the economy depending on the impact on interest rates, the exchange rate, and the money supply. Specifically, government securities may be sold to: domestic non-bank entities; foreign entities; the central bank; or domestic commercial banks.

Domestic non-bank entities hold government securities as a low risk form of investment. Given limited domestic financial resources and imperfect capital mobility, sale of government securities to domestic private buyers crowds out financing for other purposes. Private sector demand for funds is more elastic with respect to interest rates than is government demand so private sector borrowers get squeezed out as interest rates rise. Crowding out is less severe the more open are capital markets to foreign sources of finance.

Under open capital markets the sale of government securities to foreign buyers, or the diversion of private entities to borrowing on the global market as they are crowded out of the domestic market, has its own drawbacks. Capital inflows push up the value of the domestic currency which discourages domestic production of tradable goods and services. Moreover, for government, as well as for some private borrowers, borrowing from abroad can result in a mismatch between debt service obligations in foreign currency and revenues generated in domestic currency. Should the domestic currency depreciate, debt servicing will become more difficult. Or, if the debt is short term with an expectation that it will be rolled over, the vagaries of global capital markets and international sentiment may impinge on access to funds. Many developing countries have ended up in crisis due to the "original sin" of relying on foreign borrowing. A final concern is that debt service on foreign borrowing involves payments between domestic residents and foreigners whereas for domestic borrowing the payments go from domestic residents as taxpayers to domestic residents as bond holders. In the latter case, the domestic recipients will be more inclined to spend their income in the home economy. The drawbacks of foreign borrowing do not obviate a role for it. Used judiciously, foreign funds can boost economic growth and generate returns sufficient to cover the costs.

A potential buyer of government securities is the central bank under an alluring process known as "money financing." The *seigniorage* of the central bank, or its power to create value out of thin air (provided overindulgence does not eat away at this power through inflation), allows it to buy government debt and, in effect, cancel the government liability since the central bank is itself an arm of government the net receipts of which revert to the fiscal budget. Under central bank financing, government debt is transformed into base money which supports broad money creation to add monetary stimulus to the initial fiscal stimulus. This relieves the upward pressure on interest rates from government borrowing and the resulting crowding out of private borrowing and/or drawing of foreign capital inflows. The extent to which government debt can be monetized is limited by the demand of the public to hold money balances in equilibrium with the money supply lest inflation be triggered. To ensure the central bank keeps a focus on this principle, its independence from government authorities with respect to money financing of government deficits is usually ordained. Otherwise, wiping away debt by printing money could prove all too tempting for incumbents pushing to get re-elected.

Finally, commercial banks may be buyers of government debt with implications that differ from purchase by non-bank domestic buyers. Commercial banks are motivated to hold government debt on their balance sheets due to its secure nature and potential use as collateral to support borrowing on financial markets. If purchase of government debt serves as an alternative to lending to private borrowers, the result is crowding out, the same as when non-bank lenders are involved. Alternatively, if commercial banks pledge their government debt to the central bank as collateral against borrowing, this increases bank reserves providing a basis for expanded bank lending to the private sector.

Governments must rely on a mix of sources for funding and look to market indicators to signal the relative costs. Too much reliance on central bank financing will result in inflation. Too much reliance on domestic finance will crowd out funding for private sector activities. And too much reliance on foreign sources will push up the value of the domestic currency to the detriment of traded goods production. Borrowing is constrained on all fronts. Markets signal the cost of trade-offs at the margin.

Government Debt in Emerging East Asia

There is no definitive threshold for how much government debt is too much. A variety of factors enter into the assessment. The trajectory of the debt-to-GDP ratio may be as important as its level. An economy with a moderate but rapidly rising debt ratio could be in more precarious straits than one with a higher but declining ratio. An economy with strong growth is better able to absorb debt servicing costs than one with slow growth. Poorer countries are at greater risk of running into debt servicing difficulties than richer ones. For developing countries, the focus should be on preserving sufficient fiscal space to ensure access to affordable credit in time of need should any shocks stress the government budget.

Debt-to-GDP ratios for the economies of Emerging East Asia are shown in Chart 12.1. Hong Kong and Singapore, despite their similarities in many respects, are outliers at opposite ends of the spectrum. At the low end, the Hong Kong government holds minuscule debt. By law, the territory is prohibited from running deficits, although the stricture may be open to interpretation as requiring fiscal balance over a period of time rather than strictly year by year. Nevertheless, the government budget was in surplus every year from 2004 to 2018, which resulted in a reserve accumulation of 40 percent of GDP. During a downturn, Hong Kong's economic interest would be well served by applying this reserve to fund a deficit, as indeed was done in 2019 and 2020.

Singapore's conduct of fiscal policy has been more responsive to economic circumstances with surpluses in some years and deficits in others. Its spending response to the pandemic was particularly aggressive as indicated by the debt-to-GDP ratio rising from 129 percent in 2019 to 155 percent in 2020. These high numbers are not worrisome because the Singapore government holds financial assets of roughly double its liabilities. Accumulation of government debt is thus not a sign of a history of chronic deficits. Rather, the government has issued debt even when running surpluses to provide safe assets for investors and to develop a market in these assets as a basis for pricing the risk of private sector borrowers. The savings captured in Singapore's Central Provident Fund are largely invested in government bonds.

The other economies included in Chart 12.1 show debt-to-GDP ratios in 2020 ranging from 33 percent for Taiwan to 68 percent for Laos. Much of Laos's public debt is owed to

Chart 12.1 Government debt, select economies, 2019–2020

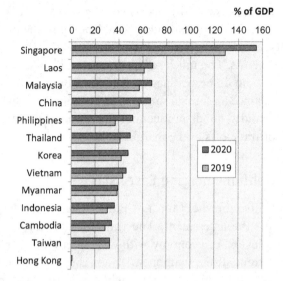

foreign lenders with China accounting for more than 40 percent of that. China has funded major energy and transportation projects in Laos under its Belt and Road Initiative. For these loans to be repaid, the projects will have to generate sufficient government revenue, either directly through user fees or indirectly through higher economic activity that expands the tax base. Recognizing that the limits of prudence have been reached, the Laotian government declared a moratorium on new investment projects in 2018. Still, at this debt ratio Laos has little capacity to absorb fiscal shocks and could be left at the mercy of its major creditors to renegotiate terms should its fiscal position come under duress.

Malaysia is next in line after Laos. With the Great Financial Crisis, the country's debt ratio rose sharply from 39 percent in 2008 to 50 percent in 2009, and continued to edge up over the next decade to hit 57 percent in 2019. With the pandemic, it leapt to 67 percent in 2020. Adding to the vulnerability, the government relies heavily on oil revenue which is subject to market fluctuations. A further concern is the accumulation of substantial off-budget liabilities. Recognizing the pressure on the country's fiscal space, authorities have articulated a strategy to expand revenue sources and improve tax administration.

China's debt ratio, showing at 57 percent in 2020, may not in fact be as sanguine as it seems. The IMF computed an "augmented debt ratio" for China of 73 percent in 2018 and projected this ratio to rise above 100 percent by 2024. This augmented ratio takes into account local government debt that is implicitly guaranteed by the center as well as other off-budget liabilities. Adding to future budgetary pressure is the rapid ageing of China's population. Countering these potential stress factors, however, the Chinese government is able to rely on ample domestic savings at low interest rates to fund its borrowing.

In the remaining cases, debt ratios were on the order of 30–40 percent in 2019 which left space for borrowing to ramp up in 2020 in response to the pandemic. Within this group,

Indonesia's position is more precarious than a debt-to-GDP ratio of 31 percent in 2019 would suggest. The country has relied heavily on foreign borrowing with non-residents holding about 60 percent of its government debt. Moreover, Indonesia's fiscal budget rests on irregular revenue sources such as oil exports and state-owned enterprise profits rather than on a broad and diversified tax base. Many such particulars enter into assessing a country's debt position and its space for fiscal maneuver.

D   Fiscal Sustainability

Government borrowing incurs interest and principal repayment obligations extending into the future. Meeting such obligations will require higher future taxes or lower spending than if the borrowing had not taken place. Debt service obligations can mount up ominously on the back of repeated borrowing to fund chronic oversized deficits. How much borrowing is, then, too much? A debt-to-GDP ratio that is on a continuously rising trajectory is clearly unsustainable. Thus, the formal notion of sustainability focuses on maintaining a stable ratio of debt to GDP at a medium-term time horizon on the order of two to ten years.

The orientation is toward the medium term to allow for flexibility in the short term. In the moment, the best laid plans must sometimes yield to unexpected developments. Larger-than-intended deficits in one year will require adjustment in the planned trajectory in future years to get back to a sustainable course. The medium-term sustainable target should allow sufficient fiscal space for unanticipated shocks to be absorbed with smooth reversion back to the sustainable path.

We begin this section by formally characterizing sustainability with reference to key macroeconomic factors. We then consider what happens if sustainability is breeched and unsustainability comes to a hard ending. Finally, we look at the Vietnam experience in which a sharply rising debt ratio appeared for a time to threaten sustainability and may yet prove challenging to contain.

Sustainability Condition

The formal notion of fiscal sustainability rests on the fiscal deficit following a path along which the debt-to-GDP ratio remains constant. Two factors are critical for their bearing on the size of the fiscal deficit that will meet this condition. Specifically, a faster rate of GDP growth will permit higher deficits to be absorbed. So, too, will a lower rate of interest.

The relationship is formalized in Box 12.1. The derivation involves finding the ratio of the deficit to GDP that will hold the ratio of debt to GDP, d_t, constant. The deficit is defined with respect to the primary balance relative to GDP, pb_t. A constant debt-to-GDP ratio is given by the condition $d_t - d_{t-1} = 0$. The strategy is to find an expression for pb_t in terms of d_{t-1} and parameters of the model that will yield this result.

Box 12.1 Fiscal sustainability formula

- Concept of sustainability:
  deficit/GDP is such that debt/GDP=constant

- Variables
  t = year index
  D_t = stock of debt $d_t = D_t/\text{GDP}_t$
  PB_t = primary fiscal balance* $pb_t = PB_t/\text{GDP}_t$
  g_t = real GDP growth rate
  π_t = inflation rate
  i_t = nominal interest rate
  r_t = real interest rate

- Sustainability requires: $d_t - d_{t-1} = 0$

*excludes interest payments

- Year on year debt increase:
$$D_t = (1 + i_t) \cdot D_{t-1} - PB_t$$

- Divide by GDP_t where:
$$\text{GDP}_t = (1 + g_t) \cdot (1 + \pi_t) \cdot \text{GDP}_{t-1}$$

$$\Rightarrow d_t = \frac{(1+i_t)}{(1+g_t)\cdot(1+\pi_t)} \cdot d_{t-1} - pb_t$$

- Note that: $\frac{1+i_t}{1+\pi_t} = 1 + r_t$

$$\Rightarrow d_t = \frac{1+r_t}{1+g_t} \cdot d_{t-1} - pb_t$$

- Subtract d_{t-1} from both sides:

$$\Rightarrow d_t - d_{t-1} = \frac{1+r_t-(1+g_t)}{1+g_t} \cdot d_{t-1} - pb_t$$

- Set equal to 0:
$$pb_t = \frac{r_t-g_t}{1+g_t} \cdot d_{t-1}$$

5

Start by defining debt in year t, D_t, as debt carried over from the previous year plus interest paid on that debt, $(1 + i_t) \cdot D_{t-1}$, minus the surplus in the current year, PB_t (where PB_t takes a negative value for a deficit). Then divide through by GDP in the current year and its equivalent given by GDP in the previous year times the nominal growth rate (the real growth rate plus the rate of inflation). This converts variables measured in levels into ratios to GDP. Simplifying and rearranging terms yields the desired condition for a constant debt-to-GDP ratio. Set that condition equal to zero and an expression may be derived for the primary balance relative to GDP in year t as a function of the debt-to-GDP ratio in the previous year, the real interest rate, and the real GDP growth rate. If the real interest rate exceeds the real GDP growth rate, sustainability requires that the primary fiscal balance be in surplus, while if the real interest rate is less than the real GDP growth rate, the primary fiscal balance can be in deficit without the debt-to-GDP ratio rising.

Note that under slow GDP growth when a fiscal stimulus is most needed, maintaining the same deficit deemed sustainable from a time of faster growth will cause the debt ratio to rise. If the slowdown in growth is temporary and the debt ratio of 50 percent affords a prudent fiscal space, the authorities may be able to preserve their fiscal stance through the slump and reassess the need for tightening in future years. If, on the other hand, slower growth has become the norm, the authorities will need to shift course to a smaller primary deficit over the medium term.

To convey a sense of the magnitudes involved, Table 12.2 presents examples. Suppose the target for a sustainable debt ratio is taken as 50 percent. As an optimistic scenario, suppose further that GDP growth is 7.0 percent a year and the real interest rate is 2.0 percent a year, as given by Case I. Under these conditions of high growth and a low interest rate, a primary deficit of 2.3 percent of GDP is allowable. Now consider the consequence of much lower growth at 1.0 percent a year under Case II. To maintain stability in the debt ratio at 50 percent, the primary balance must be in surplus in the amount of 0.5 percent of GDP. In Case III, let the growth rate return to 7.0 percent a year but raise the real interest rate to 5.0 percent. Under these conditions, a primary deficit of 0.9 percent of GDP can be accommodated. Finally, impose both the lower growth rate and the higher interest rate, and the debt ratio can be sustained only by running a primary surplus of 2.0 percent of GDP.

The overall deficit will necessarily be larger (or the surplus smaller) than the primary deficit. The overall balance is given as the primary balance minus the product of debt outstanding and the nominal interest rate. The values in Table 12.2 treat the nominal interest rate as equal to the real interest rate taking inflation as zero. But as long as inflation is low, the values will not differ much from those shown in the table. In Case I, a debt-to-GDP ratio of 50 percent and an interest rate of 2.0 percent imply an additional budgetary expense for interest of 1.1 percent of GDP for an overall deficit of 3.3 percent of GDP. With the higher interest rate of Case III, the interest expense reaches 2.6 percent of GDP. Thus, for a given growth rate, the primary balance must be higher to accommodate the larger interest payments and achieve a similar overall balance.

The derivation of Box 12.1 focuses on two key factors that bear on the relationship between a target debt ratio and the permissible deficit. In practice, complicating forces enter

Table 12.2 Effect of GDP growth and interest rate on sustainable primary balance

in percent

	Case I	Case II	Case III	Case IV
d_{t-1}	50.0	50.0	50.0	50.0
g	7.0	1.0	7.0	1.0
r	2.0	2.0	5.0	5.0
pb_t	−2.3	0.5	−0.9	2.0
overall balance (no inflation)	−3.3	−0.5	−3.5	−0.6

in. GDP growth will be even more favorable to achieving sustainability the more buoyant the tax system, where buoyancy refers to the potential for income growth to yield disproportionately higher tax revenue due to progressivity in the tax system. Further, the interest rate is not a given but will itself respond to changes in government borrowing with the degree of responsiveness depending on the economy's openness to capital inflows and the availability of domestic savings. Thus, the model must be taken as offering a rough rule of thumb with the actual budgeting process subject to ongoing observation and reassessment to keep debt at a prudent level.

Checks on Fiscal Unsustainability

If something is unsustainable, then it must end, one way or another. When a country's debt ratio is heading up and up on the back of excessive budget deficits as far as the eye can see, the preferable way to end it is with the authorities imposing discipline. This means embracing the pain of raising tax revenues and/or reducing expenditures to chart a new course.

Absent such deliberate action, an unpleasant ending will be forced. Government debt will become riskier causing interest rates on public sector borrowing to rise. Private sector borrowing will be crowded out, and GDP growth will slow. The central bank will come under pressure to monetize debt. This will cause inflation to rise, and debt will thereby be reduced in real terms. In the process, however, real incomes will fall, private investment will be discouraged, and capital will flee the country. If government is unable to rollover existing debt, it may go into default. This can lead to a full blown crisis. Creditors will need to work with authorities to negotiate a debt restructuring. With this, they will certainly impose conditions on further borrowing. The International Monetary Fund may need to step in with a rescue plan and impose conditions of its own.

The only way for the country to then climb back out of the hole it has dug itself into is to do what it should have done in the first place: establish a sustainable tax and spending regime. Clearly prevention is much the better strategy.

The Vietnam Case

Vietnam saw its ratio of public debt to GDP trend perilously upward from 24.8 percent in 2000 to 47.6 percent in 2016, as shown in the upper panel of Chart 12.2. From 2011 to 2016, the ascendance in the debt ratio was particularly sharp and unrelenting. The situation was more concerning than the narrowly defined measure of public debt suggests due to extra-budgetary guarantees of the debt of state-owned enterprises and government-backed financial institutions. The combined total of public and publicly guaranteed debt reached roughly 60 percent of GDP in 2016. This was in close striking distance of Vietnam's statutory debt limit of 65 percent.

Rising deficits from 2011 resulted from a combination of revenue decreases and spending increases relative to GDP, as shown in the lower panel of Chart 12.2. Budget deficits were in

Chart 12.2 Debt sustainability, Vietnam, 2000–2020

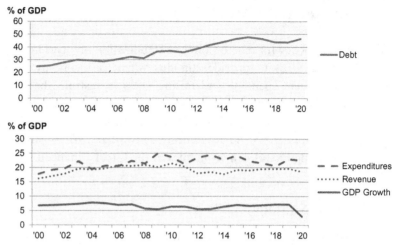

the 5–6 percent of GDP range from 2012 to 2015. Revenue weakened in part due to falling oil prices and reductions in import tariffs mandated by Vietnam's entry into various international trade agreements. Expenditure increases traced to a broad range of spending categories including wages and salaries of government employees, social security, capital investment, and national defense. Debt service costs also rose in conjunction with both the rising level of debt and a shift in the composition of debt from concessional to market-based.

From a peak in 2016, the debt ratio edged downward in 2017 and again in 2018. An important source of revenue growth during these years, however, was proceeds from the sale of shares in state-owned enterprises, which is inherently limited. More permanent revenue enhancement must come from broadening the tax base and improving tax administration. On the expenditures side, Vietnam has been burdened with an exceptionally high civil service wage bill that the government has sought to ease by downsizing the bureaucracy. It has also looked to achieve efficiency gains in public investment spending by reducing the number of projects and pushing for their more expeditious completion.

The downturn in the debt ratio was facilitated by strong GDP growth, in the neighborhood of 7 percent a year during 2015–2018. As elsewhere, the pandemic hit revenues in 2020 although the line was held against a rise in expenditures. Looking forward, a standard of 7 percent growth will be hard to maintain. Moreover, population ageing will increase the burden of social security spending, and climate change will also impose new spending demands. Upward pressure on expenditures and slower GDP growth suggest concerted efforts to raise tax revenue will be needed to keep the debt load in check.

Applying the formula of Box 12.1 with GDP growth taken at 5 percent and the interest rate at 3 percent, a debt-to-GDP ratio of 45 percent could be sustained with an overall fiscal deficit of 2.2 percent of GDP. The actual deficit was below that threshold in 2017–2018 at 2.0 percent, but exceeded it in 2019–2020. The situation is not dire, as it may have seemed a few years earlier, but bears watching.

E   Conduct of Fiscal Policy

Fiscal policy for macroeconomic stabilization involves increasing government spending and cutting taxes to provide stimulus when the economy slows and vice versa, reining in government spending and raising taxes to restrain the economy when it overheats. The scope for policy activism is circumscribed, and a general strategy must be framed in consideration of limitations, as we discuss in this section. Nevertheless, in time of crisis, an active approach can help to bring deliverance. We illustrate with a look at the response by Emerging East Asian economies to the Great Financial Crisis.

Policy Strategy

Many factors limit the potential for an activist fiscal policy. Decision-making processes with respect to fiscal budgeting are cumbersome and politically fraught. Because the politics of stimulus are so much easier to coalesce around than the politics of restraint, there is an inherent bias toward living beyond means and running up debt. Moreover, there are lags between assessing the state of the business cycle and taking action and further lags between taking action and getting an impact. By the time given policies kick in, they may no longer suit the circumstances. Nor are linkages between fiscal measures and economic activity clearly defined and readily exploited. Government can increase transfers or cut taxes, but if households and businesses do not spend their income gains, the multiplier effects will be muted and the policies will have little impact. All in all, fiscal policy does not lend itself to active fine–tuning year by year.

On the stimulus side in particular, policies are subject to economic limits. Governments pressing up against high debt-to-GDP ratios will lack space to increase deficit spending. Even governments that have maintained prudent fiscal space must be mindful of how public borrowing may crowd out private investment or draw inflows of foreign capital with consequences for the exchange rate and production of tradable goods.

In light of the limitations on fiscal policy, a reasonable strategy consists of three key pillars. First, allow scope for automatic stabilizers to work. Built into tax regimes and social welfare programs is an intrinsic mechanism by which revenues fall and expenditures rise during slowdowns, and vice versa during boom times. The fiscal impulse thus tends to move countercyclically over the course of the business cycle to push the economy back toward balance. The fiscal budget should therefore be managed with an eye to the structural balance as defined with respect to potential output. This means the actual budget balance should be afforded leeway to fluctuate from year to year with a medium-term perspective on the size of deficits.

Second, within the medium-term framework, fiscal management should be guided by the principle of sustainability. Sustainability is defined as a stable debt-to-GDP ratio at a level that allows adequate fiscal space to respond to crises. Setting a target level for the debt ratio involves judgment. Consideration must be given to economy specific characteristics that bear on growth potential, access to credit, and budgetary uncertainty. The critical impera-tive is that the debt ratio not be on a perpetually rising trajectory.

Third, in time of crisis, aggressive stimulus measures may be implemented conditional on previous adherence to the tenets of sustainability and fiscal space. Indeed, in extraordinary circumstance, aggressive stimulus measures may be resorted to even if fiscal foundations are less thanconducive. The most extraordinary of circumstances are upon us as of mid-2021 with a global pandemic. Governments worldwide have increased spending substantially even as they are beset with falling revenue, relying on borrowing and perhaps debt monetiza-tion as not previously imagined in view of the alternatives.

Policy Response to the Great Financial Crisis

The Great Financial Crisis offered a prime opportunity for the use of stimulatory fiscal policy in Emerging East Asia. The region was impacted through export losses and capital outflows even as domestic financial systems remained sound. Against this negative shock, fiscal stimu-lus found wide appeal to tide things over until trade recovered and global capital returned.

The fiscal response by economy is shown in Chart 12.3. The left panel gives the overall fiscal balance which captures both automatic stabilizers and policy action. A general pattern is visible of deficits spiking in 2009. The middle panel shows the structural balance to isolate the effect of policy changes. And the right panel shows the fiscal impulse which brings policy action into sharp relief.

Marked increases in the fiscal impulse in 2009 are broadly apparent indicating govern-ments acted boldly to increase spending and cut taxes. At the high end, the increases seen were 2.4 percent of GDP for Malaysia, 1.9 percent for Singapore, and 1.8 percent for Thailand. For most of the sample, the fiscal impulse quickly goes negative in 2010 and 2011 highlighting the temporary nature of the stimulus measures.

Hong Kong alone was out of sync with the rest of the region. This was due to the fiscal situation that transpired prior to the crisis. In 2007, Hong Kong ran an overall budget surplus of 7.3 percent of GDP. That the structural surplus was smaller than the actual surplus at 3.4 percent of potential GDP indicates the economy was functioning beyond a sustainable level. The stock and property markets were booming which generated fiscal revenue in excess of anticipated magnitudes. In response, the government acted in 2008 to return fiscal revenues to citizens and increase infrastructure spending. These measures show up as a strong positive fiscal impulse in 2008, and their partial lapse in 2009 as a negative fiscal impulse just as the rest of the region was moving to inject stimulus.

Over the period 2007–2011, Hong Kong and Singapore generally ran large fiscal surpluses, which is consistent with the positive net government asset positions of these economies discussed in connection with Chart 12.1. Against this backdrop, stimulus for Singapore during the Great Financial Crisis amounted to running a roughly balanced budget in 2009. By contrast, Malaysia was running substantial budget deficits prior to the crisis such that achieving a positive fiscal impulse meant deepening the deficit from 3.4 percent of GDP in 2008 to 5.9 percent in 2009. For China, Indonesia, the Philippines, and

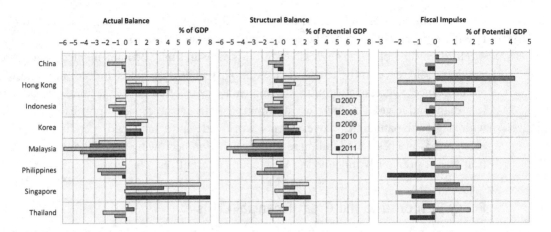

Chart 12.3 Fiscal policy response to the Great Financial Crisis, select economies, 2007–2011

Thailand, budgets had been in rough balance prior to the crisis, so implementing stimulus programs meant dipping into deficit to a not imprudent degree.

The East Asian response to the Great Financial Crisis epitomizes the exercise of fiscal policy to buffer the impact of a severe negative shock. In response to the shock, governments took active measures to increase spending and decrease taxes. On emerging from the crisis, these measures were then reversed. Prudent budgetary management during normal times can ensure availability of the fiscal space to act decisively in time of need.

F   Macro Policy Coordination

Fiscal policy and monetary policy have their respective strengths and weaknesses in the pursuit of macroeconomic stabilization. During the Great Financial Crisis, fiscal policy proved the go-to tool for warding off recession. In response to a negative shock, increased government spending can directly and immediately sustain employment and incomes, and well-targeted tax cuts can preserve standards of living and business viability. Monetary policy may not be as effective in such circumstances because reserves injected into the banking system will not necessarily be mobilized if, in the throes of a downturn, lenders and borrowers are reticent to take on risk. While fiscal policy tends not to be very nimble for use in fine-tuning over the normal course of the business cycle, a genuine crisis can spur governments to focus their energies and move swiftly in taking action.

For macroeconomic stabilization policy where only domestic balance matters (e.g., in the United States), monetary and fiscal policy serve essentially the same purpose of managing aggregate demand to keep an economy operating at its potential with low and stable inflation. For purposes of achieving domestic balance, either policy tool could be applied or both might be used in concert to achieve a given end – stimulus or restraint. For the economies of Emerging East Asia, however, macroeconomic balance must be viewed with respect to both internal and external dimensions. There are thus two objectives to be pursued simultaneously. For that, two policy tools must be implemented in complementarity. Policy coordination of this sort is the subject of Chapter 13.

Data Note

Data for Charts 12.1–12.3 are from the IMF World Economic Outlook database. A broader array of indicators is available in the IMF Fiscal Monitor database.

Bibliographic Note

John Maynard Keynes (1936) laid the foundation for understanding fiscal policy. Keynes framed the business cycle as being driven by aggregate demand such that when consumption and investment fall short of establishing full employment, government spending and taxation initiatives can provide the necessary boost.

The argument that with high capital mobility, fiscal policy is ineffective under a fixed exchange rate but effective under a floating exchange rate is due to Robert Mundell (1963). The argument is presented in standard graphical format in the textbook by Salvatore Dominick (2019).

The concept of "original sin" was put forward by Eichengreen and Hausman (1999) in reference to developing countries being compelled to borrow in foreign currencies exposing them to exchange rate risk and the potential for crisis. A series of related papers by the same authors and others followed this seminal work.

Discussion for particular economies of macroeconomic conditions and policy draws on IMF Article IV consultation reports.

A series of posts by Wiemer on the *Asia Economics Blog* tracks fiscal policy space and action with the unfolding pandemic. A post of August 14, 2020 contrasts the fiscal situation of Emerging East Asia going into the pandemic and the potential for response with the historic response to the trade shock that followed the Great Financial Crisis. A post of February 7, 2021 summarizes a webinar by Olivier Blanchard and Arvind Subramanian on the applicability to the developing world of the "New Fiscal Consensus," which promotes the use of fiscal stimulus, then applies the concepts to the economies of Southeast Asia to assess their potential to respond to the pandemic. And a post of July 16, 2021 examines fiscal space and its utilization one year into the ordeal.

BIBLIOGRAPHIC CITATIONS

Barry Eichengreen and Ricardo Hausmann, 1999. "Exchange Rates and Financial Fragility," NBER Working Papers 7418, National Bureau of Economic Research, Inc. www.nber.org/papers/w7418.

Blanchard, Olivier and Arvind Subramanian, 2021. "The New Fiscal Consensus," Ashoka Centre for Economic Policy. www.youtube.com/watch?v=RM_QXhBLwQ4 (accessed January 1, 2022).

International Monetary Fund, 2021. Fiscal Monitor, 2021. www.imf.org/external/datamapper/G_XWDG_G01_GDP_PT@FM/VNM?zoom=VNM&highlight=VNM (accessed August 5, 2020).

International Monetary Fund, 2021. World Economic Outlook database. www.imf.org/en/Publications/WEO/weo-database/2021/October (accessed December 22, 2021).

International Monetary Fund, various years. Article IV Staff Reports, various economies. www.imf.org/en/Publications/SPROLLs/Article-iv-staff-reports#sort=%40imfdate%20descending.

Keynes, John Maynard, 1964 [1936]. *The General Theory of Employment, Interest, and Money* (New York: Harcourt, Brace & World).

Mundell, Robert A., 1963. "Capital Mobility and Stabilization Policy under Fixed and Flexible Exchange Rates," *Canadian Journal of Economics and Political Science*, Vol. 29, No. 4 (Nov.), pp. 475–485.

Salvatore, Dominick, 2019. *International Economics*, 13th edition (Wiley).

Wiemer, Calla, 2020. "East Asia's Fiscal Response to Crisis, Then & Now," *Asia Economics Blog*, August 14, 2020. http://acaes.us/blog/east-asias-fiscal-response-to-crisis (accessed December 28, 2021).

Wiemer, Calla, 2021. "Economics of the Pandemic, 2020 (Part II): Fiscal Policy," Asia Economics Blog, July 16, 2021. http://acaes.us/blog/pandemic-2020-fiscal-policy (accessed December 28, 2021).

Wiemer, Calla, 2021. "The 'New Fiscal Consensus' As Per Blanchard & Subramanian Interpreted for Southeast Asia," *Asia Economics Blog*, February 7, 2021. http://acaes.us/blog/new-fiscal-consensus-interpreted-for-southeast-asia (accessed December 28, 2021).

13   Policy for Internal and External Balance

Macroeconomic balance is defined in two dimensions – internal and external. And two arms of policy are available to pursue balance – exchange rate policy, as a manifestation of monetary policy, and fiscal policy. In principle, with two tools and two objectives, a policy solution should be clear-cut, and sometimes it is. But sometimes matters are complicated by constraints on policy action and causes of imbalance that are structural rather than cyclical in nature.

Internal balance is achieved when GDP growth is at its potential and inflation is low and stable. External balance is achieved when the current account balance is, if not zero, then in some desired proximity of zero. Balance is a tenuous state of affairs against the constant buffeting of exogenous shocks and cyclical forces. When an economy veers off track, monetary and fiscal policies can be mobilized to steer it back. The two policy arms work at cross purposes meaning that for any particular combination of internal and external excess or shortfall, a specific combination of monetary and fiscal policy can be prescribed.

We begin this chapter by developing a graphical model that relates exchange rate policy, as a manifestation of monetary policy, and fiscal policy to internal and external imbalance. We then consider application of the model under various hypothetical scenarios. From there, we take up the case of Malaysia in the late 2010s to get a view into the complexities of implementing stabilization policy in the real world. The concluding section brings us to the culmination of a macroeconomics for Emerging East Asia.

A   Model of Internal and External Balance

The model of internal and external balance developed in this section is known as the Swan diagram for Trevor Swan who presented it in a 1963 paper. The graphical framework defines four zones of "economic discomfort" based on the four possible combinations of GDP growth underperforming versus overperforming relative to its potential and the current account overshooting versus undershooting relative to a target. Depending on where an economy finds itself within the Swan diagram, an appropriate mix of monetary and fiscal policies can be determined. The goal is to get to the sweet spot in the middle where internal and external balance exist in tandem.

Policy Objectives

The goal of internal balance involves GDP growth reaching its potential without tipping into inflationary overheating. Conceptually, potential is determined based on feasible contributions of labor, capital, and productivity growth. In practice, judgment is involved in envisioning what is achievable, with the limit becoming clear only when it is exceeded. At that point, bottlenecks develop and intensifying competition for resources causes prices to be bid up. The target range for inflation is typically viewed as being around 2–4 percent a year in the emerging economy setting.

Defining the goal of external balance involves some discretion. The preference in many countries is to aim for a degree of current account surplus. As shown in Box 5.1, East Asian economies on the whole, and China and Japan most notably, have run long-standing surpluses largely met by US deficits. One reason to sustain a surplus is that reliance on external demand can boost output and employment if domestic demand is insufficient to keep growth at potential. The drawback, however, is that a current account surplus implies a net capital outflow meaning that domestic saving is being used to fund investment abroad rather than at home. The associated capital outflow sometimes takes the form of reserve accumulation by the central bank, and since central banks do need to stockpile prudent levels of reserves, deliberate reserve building is a second possible reason to run a current account surplus. Alternatively, the outflow may reflect the decision of private agents to invest abroad on a net positive basis, in which case the domestic investment climate might bear improving. Finally, a third reason for targeting a current account surplus may be to preserve a buffer against tipping into deficit, implying net capital inflows with their attendant risk of reversal. In any case, a targeted current account surplus can be accommodated by the model as a standard of external balance, and so the choice of target may be regarded as flexible for purposes of the modeling exercise.

Policy Arms

Pursuit of internal and external balance rests on strategically combining fiscal policy and exchange rate policy within the Swan framework. A loosening of fiscal policy is achieved through an increase in government spending or a reduction in taxes. Such fiscal loosening stimulates GDP growth and at the same time reduces the current account balance as rising domestic demand means less is exported and more is imported. Conversely, a tightening of fiscal policy slows GDP growth and increases the current account balance.

On the exchange rate front, a depreciation in the domestic currency causes exports to rise and imports to decline so as to increase the current account balance. At the same time, GDP growth is stimulated by expenditure switching to domestic products as competition from imports is reduced and production for export expands. Conversely, an appreciation of the domestic currency reduces exports and raises imports to decrease the current account balance while expenditure switching to foreign products inhibits GDP growth.

The exchange rate serves in the Swan model as an instrument of monetary policy. The model is generalizable to a regime under which the monetary policy instrument is an interest rate, provided the exchange rate is flexible and capital markets are open. Targeting a higher interest rate is comparable to targeting a higher value for the domestic currency. The difference is that under the higher interest rate target, the central bank sells government securities rather than selling foreign exchange. Either way, monetary policy is contractionary. The higher interest rate motivates an increase in net capital inflows which indirectly pushes up the value of the domestic currency. A reduction in the current account balance follows, as desired. Targeting a lower interest rate is conversely equivalent to targeting a lower value of the domestic currency. With that, monetary policy is expansionary and hence GDP growth is stimulated and the current account balance increases.

Graphical Framework

The graphical framework for the Swan diagram is depicted in Figure 13.1. The policy space is defined by the fiscal stance on the horizontal axis and the real exchange rate on the vertical axis, taking the Malaysian ringgit for purposes of example.

An expansionary fiscal policy is reflected as a rightward movement within the graph. Fiscal loosening causes an increase in aggregate demand that moves the economy along a continuum from underperforming to overperforming relative to potential GDP growth. At the same time, it moves the current account balance from overshooting to undershooting relative to a target.

Figure 13.1 Graphical framework for balance

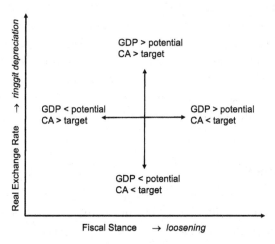

Fiscal loosening causes GDP growth to increase and the current account balance to decrease. Ringgit depreciation causes both GDP growth and the current account balance to increase.

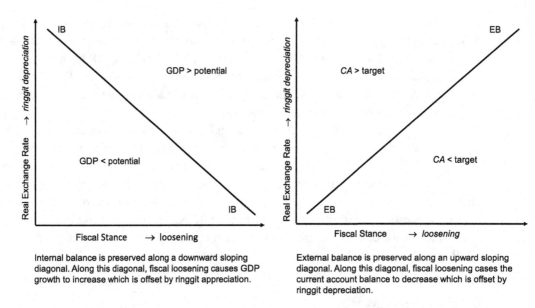

Internal balance is preserved along a downward sloping diagonal. Along this diagonal, fiscal loosening causes GDP growth to increase which is offset by ringgit appreciation.

External balance is preserved along an upward sloping diagonal. Along this diagonal, fiscal loosening cases the current account balance to decrease which is offset by ringgit depreciation.

Figure 13.2 Internal and external balance

Depreciation in the ringgit is reflected as an upward movement within the graph. Ringgit depreciation, commensurate with an expansionary monetary policy, moves the economy from underperforming to overperforming relative to growth potential and the current account balance from undershooting to overshooting of the target.

Within this framework, loci of internal and external balance are defined as in Figure 13.2. Internal balance is preserved along a downward-sloping diagonal that divides zones of GDP growth exceeding potential and falling short of potential. From a position on the diagonal, aggregate demand may be stimulated through loosening of the fiscal stance while ringgit appreciation has an offsetting contractionary effect to preserve balance.

External balance is preserved along an upward-sloping diagonal which divides zones of overshooting and undershooting of the current account target. From a point on the diagonal, fiscal stimulus causes the current account balance to decrease with this effect countered by ringgit depreciation to maintain balance.

The Swan Diagram

The diagonals for internal and external imbalance are overlaid to create the Swan diagram of Figure 13.3. The diagonals divide the graphical space into four "zones of economic discomfort," in Swan's parlance. It is possible to overshoot or undershoot with respect to both GDP growth and the current account balance simultaneously, or to overshoot on one and undershoot on the other. It is also possible to achieve balance in one dimension but be out of balance in the other dimension.

Figure 13.3 The Swan diagram

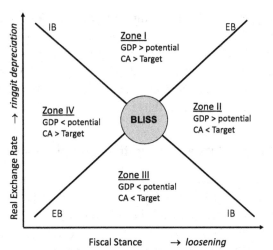

Overlaying the diagonals for internal and external balance
divides the graphical space into four zones characterized
by different combinations of internal and external
imbalance. The intersection of the two diagonals defines
the bliss point.

The policy objective is to move the economy to the state of "bliss" where the diagonals cross such that internal and external balance are achieved simultaneously. The Swan diagram offers clear policy prescriptions for doing so. Note, however, that any such outcome is always transitory. As an economy travels through time, it is constantly buffeted by shocks that disrupt any momentary state of bliss that might be attained. Management of macroeconomic stabilization policy must therefore be ongoing.

B   Model Application

Let us consider examples of macroeconomic imbalance of various sorts to see how the Swan diagram is applied.

Current Account Undershooting with Internal Balance

Suppose an economy is achieving growth at potential with inflation low and stable but the current account is hitting deficits of undesired level. Policymakers not schooled in the Swan diagram might look to resolve the external imbalance by relying on exchange rate policy in isolation. To increase exports and reduce imports in mitigation of the current account deficit calls for currency depreciation. This is achieved by the central bank selling domestic currency and purchasing foreign exchange.

The Swan diagram puts this policy action in broader context. A situation of internal balance combined with an excessive current account deficit is located on the IB diagonal in the lower right quadrant of the diagram. Depreciation of the domestic currency moves the economy in a vertical direction into Zone II which is characterized by GDP growth exceeding its potential. This results because the cheaper domestic currency promotes expanded production of exports and import substitutes. To avoid the consequent overheating, there is a need for fiscal tightening in conjunction with the currency depreciation to keep the economy on the IB diagonal, thus moving in a northwesterly direction.

Current Account Undershooting with Economic Overheating

Now consider the case where, again, the current account shows an excessive deficit but there is also an imbalance internally in the form of inflation picking up. This puts the economy in Zone II of the Swan diagram. A singular focus on the external imbalance would lead authorities to engineer a currency depreciation. The Swan diagram, however, points to a different strategy altogether. For an economy in Zone II, the goal is to move to the left, and that can be accomplished through fiscal tightening alone with no need for exchange rate adjustment. By reducing aggregate demand, the fiscal tightening restrains imports and encourages diversion of domestic production into exports. This narrows the current account deficit while at the same time reining in the overheating economy to reduce inflationary pressure.

Capital Inflow Shock from a Position of Overall Balance

As a third application of the Swan diagram, suppose an economy is in an initial state of balance both internally and externally. Then let it be hit with the shock of a large capital inflow. The capital inflow puts upward pressure on the value of the currency which ensures a rebalancing of international payments such that the increase in the financial account is offset by a decrease in the current account. At the same time, the loss of global competitiveness brought on by appreciation of the currency causes a slowdown in GDP growth. The effect of the capital inflow is thus to push the economy into Zone III.

Within the context of the Swan diagram, the prescribed policy response is clear: the authorities should push back on the currency appreciation to maintain the competitiveness of domestic products. This involves the central bank intervening in the foreign exchange market to absorb the money inflow. Balance in international payments is thereby sustained through central bank acquisition of foreign assets that matches the inflow of foreign capital aimed at acquiring domestic assets. The negative impact of the capital inflow on the current account balance and GDP growth is thus averted, and the economy remains at the bliss point.

C   The Malaysian Case

While the Swan diagram provides a useful analytical tool, reality tends to be more complex. We take as a case study the Malaysian situation of the late 2010s. First, we place the Malaysia of that period within the Swan diagram and draw the policy recommendations.

Then we consider the broader policy context and discuss the limitations on following through with these recommendations.

Application of the Swan Diagram

Malaysia achieved real GDP growth at a rate of 4.8 percent a year during 2015–2019. This was regarded by Malaysian authorities, with concurrence by the IMF, as being in line with potential. Inflation during the period averaged 1.9 percent a year. This record meets the standard for internal balance.

Externally, balance was more elusive, however, as shown in Chart 13.1. Malaysia's current account exhibited a consistent surplus position going back a decade. Relative to GDP, the surplus in 2019 at 3.4 percent was somewhat higher than in the preceding few years when it registered within a range of 2.2–3.0 percent. Reserve accumulation by the central bank played little to no role in balancing the surplus in recent years. Outflows on the financial account were the main balancing items in 2019 and 2020 whereas in the preceding few years the balancing element was lost to errors and omissions. The uptick in the current account balance in 2019 was due mainly to a decline in capital goods imports associated with weak domestic investment following a change in government in 2018 that brought project delays. The likely temporary nature of this disruption notwithstanding, underlying trend surpluses were assessed by the IMF as being excessive. In 2020, the pandemic shock compounded the current account surplus and financial account deficit but also swept Malaysia into the global recession from its previous position of internal balance.

Let us focus on the pre-pandemic years. The combination of internal balance and an excessive current account surplus places the Malaysia of this period on the IB diagonal in the upper left of the Swan diagram. This positioning implies a policy prescription of ringgit appreciation to narrow the external imbalance combined with fiscal loosening to compensate for the drag on the economy from diminished external demand. According to IMF modeling, undervaluation of the ringgit amounted to about 8 percent in 2019. Appreciation of the ringgit could be engineered by the central bank via intervention in the foreign

Chart 13.1 Balance of payments, Malaysia, 2010–2020

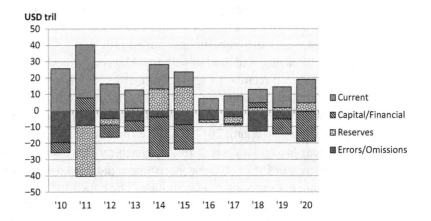

exchange market to purchase ringgit and sell foreign currency, and to a minor extent this did take place in 2018 and 2019. Alternatively, the central bank could sell government securities in association with a higher interest rate target which would indirectly raise the value of the ringgit. Under the former strategy, narrowing of the current account surplus would be offset by an increase in the official settlement balance; under the latter strategy, it would be offset by an increase in the financial account balance in response to the higher interest rate. Either way, getting to external balance while maintaining internal balance would call for Malaysia to tighten monetary policy and loosen fiscal policy.

Broader Policy Context

The policy recommendations offered up for Malaysia by the Swan diagram involve selling off central bank reserves and taking on additional government debt. Both recommendations presume the existence of a sufficient modicum of policy space. In selling reserves, the central bank must avoid compromising its capacity to respond to a negative balance of payments shock (e.g., a capital outflow or a drop in oil export prices). And in taking on more debt, the government must be mindful of sustainability concerns.

In the Malaysian case, central bank reserves in 2019 met basic standards of adequacy, although not with a large margin to spare. The public debt constraint, however, was already binding and indeed, to the point that the government had articulated a commitment to reducing its fiscal deficit to a target of 2.8 percent of GDP from 3.5 percent in 2019. The upshot is that a macroeconomic rebalancing strategy that involved fiscal loosening was not within the realm of consideration for Malaysia.

This does not mean all was lost. The imbalances the Swan model is designed to address are cyclical in nature. The premise is that an economy tends to fluctuate around norms of internal and external balance. When it deviates from these norms, monetary and fiscal policy can be implemented to deflect it back in a timely manner. In situations of sustained imbalance, by contrast, structural causes merit investigation. In the Malaysian case, overly large current account surpluses have a long history. In recent times anyway, such surpluses have not been motivated by a drive to accumulate foreign reserves on the part of the central bank. Rather, they reflect private domestic saving flowing out to support investment abroad. For structural solutions to the external imbalance, we must then look to lowering the saving rate or increasing the domestic investment rate.

Rates of saving and investment for Malaysia are shown in Chart 13.2. The current account balance relative to gross national income is equal to the difference between the saving rate and the investment rate. Over most of the 2010s decade, the current account surplus trended downward due to a declining saving rate against an investment rate that was fairly flat from 2012 until 2017. The investment rate then fell from 2018 as elections in May of that year brought an end to rule by the party that had held power since Malaysia gained independence in 1957. The new government put a hold on major infrastructure investment with the intent of rooting out corruption. The hoped-for return to trend was then subverted by the pandemic. Meanwhile, the saving rate continued trending downward which put it on

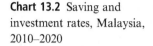

Chart 13.2 Saving and investment rates, Malaysia, 2010–2020

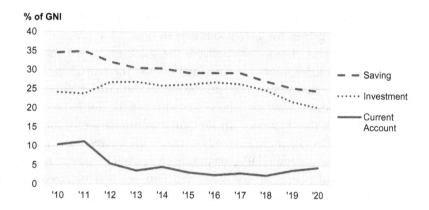

course to realign with a prospective recovery in the investment rate to historic norms. Such convergence would cause the current account surplus to disappear.

The decline in Malaysia's saving rate has been spurred by government policies that have encouraged consumption. Among these are policies aimed at raising the minimum wage and expanding social assistance programs to aid low income households. Still on the agenda is improvement in public support for health care which the pandemic has made more urgent. A stronger public health care system, and expansion in social insurance more generally, would reduce the need for precautionary saving and promote consumption as a driver of growth. Policies of this sort aimed at addressing structural factors underlying the saving-investment gap can work to resolve the external imbalance. This approach is better suited to the Malaysian case than one involving monetary and fiscal policy aimed at countering cyclical imbalances.

D   Conclusion

Both external and internal balance matter for stabilization policy in Emerging East Asia. The goal of internal balance is common to all economies. The goal of external balance takes on importance for those in which foreign trade and capital flows figure significantly and commitments must be made in foreign currency terms. Major shocks to any element of the balance of payments have ramifications for the exchange rate and hence for other elements of the balance of payments, with ultimate consequences for incomes and livelihoods. Foreign capital flows are particularly prone to volatility. Strong inflows carry the potential for disruptive flow reversals in the future. Sustained net outflows divert saving that could have been used to fund domestic investment instead. The external aspect of stabilization policy is motivated by these concerns.

Monetary and fiscal policy, as the two arms of stabilization policy, may be implemented to play distinctive expansionary and contractionary roles in pursuing balance in two dimensions. The role of monetary policy is most easily viewed through the instrument of the exchange rate. For example, on the external side an excessive current account deficit calls for the central bank to depress the value of the currency by buying foreign exchange so as to increase exports and decrease imports. On the internal side, the associated stimulus to production of tradable goods acts to raise GDP growth. The same reasoning applies if the instrument of monetary policy is the interest rate, provided the exchange rate is flexible and the capital account is open. Purchase by the central bank of government securities rather than foreign exchange lowers the interest rate which induces net capital outflows. The capital outflows then act to depress the value of the domestic currency, and the current account balance thus increases. In sum, an expansionary monetary policy, associated with a lower target for either the currency value or the interest rate, increases both the current account balance and the GDP growth rate. A contractionary monetary policy does the opposite.

Fiscal policy advances internal and external objectives in opposing combination. An expansionary fiscal policy involves an increase in government spending or a reduction in taxes. Internally, this increases aggregate demand to boost GDP growth. Externally, the current account balance is reduced as imports rise and exports decline in favor of satisfying domestic demand. In sum, an expansionary fiscal policy decreases the current account balance and increases GDP growth. A contractionary fiscal policy has the opposite effects.

Given the two arms of stabilization policy and the two dimensions in which balance is sought, clear-cut policy recommendations can be derived, at least in theory, for any combination of internal and external imbalance or balance. In practice, however, there are limits on the space for implementing countercyclical monetary and fiscal policies. Monetary policy of a contractionary nature requires the sale of foreign exchange when the exchange rate is taken as the policy instrument. For that, the central bank must have sufficient foreign reserves on hand not to compromise its capacity to respond to negative balance of payments shocks. Alternatively, the central bank could pursue a contractionary policy by selling government securities or even central bank bills. This approach requires that capital markets be open for an effect to feed through to the current account. On the other hand, fiscal policy of an expansionary nature requires the government to take on additional debt. For that, public debt outstanding must be managed within prudent bounds of sustainability.

A final qualification on the use of stabilization policy is that it is most usefully oriented toward nudging an economy back to balance when transitory shocks knock it off course. Deeper structural factors may be at stake for an economy that exhibits chronic external imbalances or growth underperformance. For external imbalance, structural causes must be sought in saving and investment behavior. Policies aimed at addressing such behavior will be more effective in resolving entrenched external imbalances than monetary and fiscal policies. Similarly for GDP growth that consistently falls short of expectations, policies aimed at underlying structural factors that bear on market functioning and productivity would better serve the need.

Data Note

Balance of payments data in Chart 13.1 are from the IMF International Financial Statistics database. Saving and investment data in Chart 13.2 are from the World Bank World Development Indicators database.

Bibliographic Note

The Swan diagram originated in a paper by Trevor Swan published in 1963. At that time, the international economic order rested on the Bretton Woods system of fixed exchange rates to the US dollar with the US dollar in turn tied to gold. Under this regime, manipulation of the nominal exchange rate was not a policy option, so the original diagram was framed with respect to the real cost of domestic relative to foreign goods rather than the exchange rate per se, and changes in relative cost were regarded as working through domestic money wage adjustments. The Swan model has since been adapted to incorporate the real exchange rate as the measure of relative cost between the home country and the rest of the world as, for example, in the textbook by Krugman and Obstfeld. These authors nevertheless continue to frame the discussion in terms of the historic Bretton Woods regime of fixed exchange rates without recognition of its applicability to the managed exchange rate regimes that prevail in Emerging East Asia in the present day.

Discussion of the Malaysian case draws from a Bank Negara Malaysia document and the Article IV Consultation report of the IMF.

BIBLIOGRAPHIC CITATIONS

Bank Negara Malaysia, 2020. Economic and Monetary Review 2019. www.bnm.gov.my/ar2019/emr-summary.php (accessed August 27, 2020).

International Monetary Fund, 2021. International Financial Statistics Database. https://data.imf.org/?sk=4c514d48-b6ba-49ed-8ab9–52b0c1a0179b&sId=1390030341854 (accessed December 22, 2021).

International Monetary Fund, 2020. Malaysia: 2020 Article IV Consultation Staff Report. www.imf.org/en/Publications/CR/Issues/2020/02/27/Malaysia-2020-Article-IV-Consultation-Press-Release-Staff-Report-and-Statement-by-the-49105 (accessed September 9, 2020).

Krugman, Paul and Maurice Obstfeld, 2006. *International Economics: Theory and Policy* (Boston: Pearson Education, Inc.).

Swan, T. W., 1963. "Longer-Run Problems of the Balance of Payments," in H. W. Arndt and W. M. Corden, eds., *The Australian Economy: A Volume of Readings* (Melbourne: Cheshire Press), pp. 384–395.

14 Macroprudential Policy

Macroprudential policy aims at safeguarding stability in the financial system. The system as a whole can become vulnerable to loss contagion even when institutions on an individual basis maintain strong balance sheets. Systemic risk tends to build and subside in cyclical fashion, with foreign capital flows contributing to the flux. Macroprudential policy pushes back against this ebb and flow through adjustment in financial regulation.

The Great Financial Crisis of 2008 hit the USA against a backdrop of output growth at potential with inflation low and stable. The macroeconomy appeared to be on a solid footing even as the financial system had become vulnerable to distress. Although the odd observer had warned of impending crisis, someone is always predicting crisis, generally wrongly. Most everyone was caught by surprise at the extent of the financial turmoil and the severity of the impact on the real economy. The lesson learned, or at least powerfully reinforced, was that preserving stability in the financial system requires careful attention to aggregate indicators and judicious regulatory intervention. Macroprudential policy serves this purpose.

Financial institutions have long been subject to regulation to contain risks to their own depositors and creditors. But even with institutions held to sound practices on an individual basis, the system as a whole may overshoot in creating credit and become fragile. Excesses may be concentrated in certain sectors, such as housing, or certain asset classes, such as foreign loans. Regulators have devised a variety of macroprudential policy instruments for use in guarding against such excesses. For example, loan-to-value caps on mortgages for home purchase restrict the loan amount to some portion of the home's value, with this portion lowered when the housing market is overheating or raised when the market is sluggish. For another example, limits on foreign borrowing by banks guard against the risk of straitened access to foreign exchange undermining capacity for debt service, with these limits adjusted based on the magnitude of foreign debt exposure in the aggregate.

A full rundown of the various instruments used to serve macroprudential purposes is reserved for the second section of this chapter. First, we elaborate on the function of macroprudential policy. Then once the policy instruments have then been laid out, we go on to discuss the institutional framework, both domestic and international, in which policy is conducted. That is followed by a survey of macroprudential policy use in Emerging East Asia with particular attention to the Korean case. Finally, we consider prospects for macroprudential policy to aid in averting and weathering crises.

A   Function

We begin this section by discussing the nature of systemic risk, why it tends to rise and fall in cyclical fashion, and how macroprudential policy functions to manage it. Global capital flows in and out of an economy can drive systemic risk, so we then take up the use of macroprudential policy to deal with this challenge. Finally, we consider how macroprudential policy overlaps with monetary policy and how the two policy arms may be coordinated.

Managing Systemic Risk

Financial risk takes on both micro and macro dimensions. At the micro level, risks of an idiosyncratic nature can threaten an individual institution without spilling over to other institutions. Regulatory policy curbs such idiosyncratic risk in a variety of ways to protect an institution's depositors and creditors. For example, capital adequacy standards ensure a sufficient equity position that an institution's owners will bear the brunt of any losses if loans go bad. Other examples include minimum requirements on the ratio of liquid assets to liabilities to ensure funds will be readily available to meet obligations and limits on foreign currency liabilities to guard against payment difficulties due to depreciation in the domestic currency. Many of these same types of regulations are incorporated into macroprudential policy to deal with risk on a systemic level, but with management oriented toward financial institutions in the aggregate.

At the macro level, risk extends to broad disruption in financial services due to asset markets freezing up or financial institutions failing in numbers. Once this process begins, contagion can break loose as loss of confidence breeds on itself. If holders of a particular asset type move to sell en masse and buyers are lacking, the price of the asset will collapse which can then trigger further pursuit of liquidity only to bring markets for other assets to the brink. Similarly, if a major financial institution becomes stressed, doubts can cascade to other institutions to set off waves of withdrawals and contraction of lending. Disruption can then spill over to the real economy as strained access to credit causes business activity to suffer with feedback in turn on the financial system as borrowers go into default.

Systemic risk rests on both structural relationships among institutions and cyclical processes involving feedback mechanisms over time. On the structural front, financial institutions rely on loans from one another. If one institution is unable to repay its creditors, those creditors in turn will have trouble repaying their creditors, and so on with broad ripple effects. Systemically important institutions that provide short-term wholesale funding to other institutions on a large scale can be particularly powerful drivers of broad shifts in credit conditions. With that, their failure can be catastrophic, and thus governments are loathe to allow it – "too big to fail," as it's known. Yet bailouts are very costly and send the wrong message on risk taking.

On the cyclical front, upswings and downturns tend to be self-reinforcing ... until, that is, they overshoot and the course reverses. In the upswing, credit expansion drives business growth which generates even more opportunities for credit and with that, even more business growth; in the downturn, credit tightening starves business activity which limits new opportunities for credit thus undermining activity even further. Feedback processes also come into play between credit and asset prices. An infusion of credit – to the economy broadly or in support of particular types of asset purchase – drives demand which pushes up asset prices. Higher asset prices in turn justify greater borrowing against the value of the assets. Feedback of this sort is commonly observed in housing markets where mortgage loans entitle the lender to take ownership of the property if the borrower defaults. Lenders and borrowers are reassured by rising property values, readily believing that prices can only go up. This belief itself can sustain momentum for quite some time. Eventually, however, property values diverge from rental returns to such a degree that the illusion is no longer viable and the bubble bursts. Once the tipping point is reached, the interaction runs in reverse: Property values begin to fall so lending tightens which undermines market demand causing prices to go into a downward spiral. Over the course of the cycle, risk builds as credit expands and prices boom, and then melts away during the bust that follows. This is true whether the boom and bust unfold in property markets or stock markets or foreign currencies or whatever.

Macroprudential policy aims to dampen the cyclical processes and impede the structural impulses among institutions that give rise to systemic risk. With respect to cyclical processes, the objective is to restrain booms and build resilience against busts. Under a home price boom, for example, authorities can lower the cap on the loan-to-value ratio for mortgages in order to tighten credit. They can also increase loan loss provisions that financial institutions are required to set aside so that if and when the bust comes and loans go into default, reserves are on hand to enable the institution to meet its obligations. With respect to structural linkages, the biggest source of risk derives from major institutions that supply funds broadly to other institutions. Policy action on this front involves identifying systemically important institutions and subjecting them to higher regulatory standards to strengthen their balance sheets against shock and forestall contagion.

Contending with Global Capital Flows

Systemic risk in emerging economies is aggravated by flows of global capital moving in and out, driven largely by external forces. Under pressure of inflows, domestic interest rates are depressed and asset prices are buoyed, and this encourages relaxation of lending standards. A mismatch results when borrowers incur obligations in foreign currencies against revenue streams in domestic currency. This mismatch carries risk associated with potential future depreciation in the local currency, a risk intrinsic to the dynamics of foreign capital pushing the value of the local currency up on its way in and down on its way back out. Should foreign loan inflows in particular come to a "sudden stop," continued debt service payment will require outflows that may be hard to keep up as the value of the domestic currency tumbles. This is especially so if borrowing was short term and must be paid back quickly rather than rolled over as may have been anticipated. Rising interest rates and falling asset prices will compound the economic hardship and financial stress.

Global capital flows to and from emerging economies are influenced by monetary policy in the major advanced economies and by the general vicissitudes of global risk appetite. When monetary authorities in the USA and the EU lower interest rates, investors go looking for higher returns worldwide; conversely, when those authorities raise interest rates, global capital retreats to safer ground. Other factors enter into the zeitgeist as well to influence mass psychology on risk taking. When risk sentiment is on, investors are eager to bet on emerging markets; when it shuts off, they seek safe harbor in the USA and Europe.

The volatility of global capital flows is captured in Chart 14.1 as measured by changes in foreign loan liabilities for Hong Kong, Korea, Singapore, and Taiwan (these being chosen for their longstanding openness to foreign capital and data availability). Inflows and outflows tend to move in sync across the four economies indicating the importance of outside factors in the direction and magnitude of flows. Two periods of sustained outflow stand out: 2008Q4 (fourth quarter) to 2009Q1; and 2015Q3 to 2016Q1. On the inflow side, movement was particularly strong in 2007 and was cumulatively substantial during the interim between the major outflow periods. Later years brought more quarterly volatility than seen previously. The outflow of 2008–2009 represented a flight from risk in the wake of the Great Financial Crisis. Similarly in 2015–2016, risk sentiment fell off, the provocation this time being a default on sovereign debt by Greece with ominous implications for the European Monetary Union. The prolonged inflows to emerging markets during the interim between these two risk-off events were motivated by low interest rates in the USA and Europe and the search by investors for higher yield.

Macroprudential policy can help to mitigate the impact of capital flow volatility on emerging market economies. The aim is to ensure that balance sheets of financial institutions

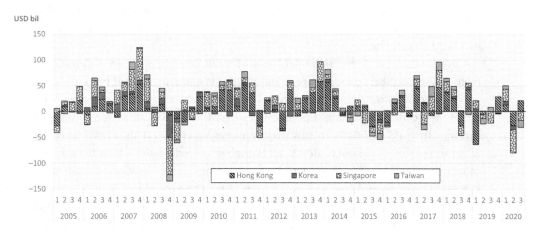

Chart 14.1 Change in foreign loan liabilities, select economies, 2005–2020

can withstand capital flow reversals and exchange rate fluctuations. Instruments for achieving this include limits on foreign borrowing and protections against currency mismatch. Standards can be tightened during periods of heavy capital inflow and loosened again when inflows subside or reverse direction. The key is to ensure capacity to maintain debt service payments under changing circumstances.

Coordinating with Monetary Policy

Macroprudential policy and monetary policy work with overlapping effect. Both bear on credit growth, asset prices, and risk taking. Monetary policy does so broadly through manipulation of the size of the central bank balance sheet with direct effect on interest rates and exchange rates and ultimate effect, with a lag, on output and inflation economy wide. Macroprudential policy takes a more targeted approach, pointing at particular types of assets and channels of credit with consequences mainly for financial stability and less feed through to output and inflation broadly.

If the financial cycle and the business cycle are hitting boom or bust in tandem, the two arms of policy can be used in a mutually reinforcing way to tighten or loosen as the case may be. But nuanced differences in how monetary and macroprudential policy play out also allow them to be used in complementary or offsetting fashion. For example, if the housing market is overheating with prices rising into bubble territory, macroprudential policy can be used to restrain home mortgage lending. The consequent cooling of home buying can, however, have knock on effects for construction, home furnishings, and appliances to impose a drag on the economy more broadly. To offset this, a more expansionary monetary policy can be implemented to sustain economic growth at potential.

For another example, if inflation is escalating, a tightening of monetary policy may be called for. In turn, however, rising interest rates may stress some borrowers with implications for the health of the financial sector. Macroprudential policy may then be taken up in counterpoint to ease regulatory costs on financial institutions. Conversely, a low interest rate policy implemented to stimulate a sluggish economy may encourage excessive risk taking in the financial sector. Under these circumstances, a judicious use of macroprudential policy can keep risk in check.

Coordinated use of macroprudential and monetary policies can also mitigate disruption from foreign capital flows. A capital inflow that is met with central bank purchase of foreign currency to stabilize the exchange rate has an expansionary effect on domestic money and credit. The central bank could potentially offset this with sterilization of the forex purchase through the sale of bonds to absorb the money increase. This would have the untoward effect, however, of keeping interest rates high and credit tight which would only encourage more capital inflows. On the other hand, foregoing the sterilization and allowing the money supply to increase and credit to expand could lead to excessive risk build up in the financial system. The stage is thus set for macroprudential policy tightening to tamp down financial excess in conjunction with monetary policy responding to absorb the capital inflow and stabilize the exchange rate.

Of final note, macroprudential policy shares with monetary policy a greater effectiveness in restraining booms than in stimulating recovery from busts. When the economy is slumping, monetary policy can bring down interest rates and give banks the capacity to lend, but capacity may not be enough to overcome widespread pessimism about the future. Similarly, macroprudential policy can ease regulatory standards and enhance incentives for lending, but financial institutions and their customers must wish to take advantage of these incentives. Fortunately, one more arm of macroeconomic policy stands ready to take up the mantle of stimulus in troubled times, and that is fiscal policy. The government can spend when no one else will, provided the it has maintained its creditworthiness and can borrow on manageable terms. Thus, the three arms of policy all have their places.

B   Policy Instruments

A great variety of macroprudential policy instruments has been utilized to varying degrees by the economies of Emerging East Asia. We begin this section by considering what qualifies as a macroprudential instrument. We then catalog the options and look at their implementation in the region.

Identification of Instruments

Classification schemes for macroprudential instruments can run to dozens of categories. In principle, inclusion should be based on applicability of an instrument to macroprudential purposes. The problem with this principle is that some prospective candidates can be applied to more than one end. For example, changes in reserve requirements are tallied in macroprudential data sources because they can conceivably be aimed at macroprudential goals even as their more standard purpose is to serve monetary policy.

Applying differentiated reserve ratios to foreign versus domestic currency deposits is more suggestive of a macroprudential than a monetary policy motive. For foreign currency deposits, the impact of changes in reserve requirements on domestic money supply is of little consequence such that the macroprudential motive of providing a buffer to meet potential capital outflows comes to the fore. Yet the case of differentiated reserve requirements on foreign currency deposits is not clear cut either. This instrument can be used as a capital control as well as a macroprudential instrument. Capital controls are discussed in Box 14.1.

Box 14.1 Capital controls

Capital controls are imposed by governments to limit the movement of funds across borders. As some macroprudential instruments can have this effect as well, the distinction comes down to intent. Conceptually, capital controls are motivated by a

Box 14.1 (cont.)

desire to preserve stability in the balance of payments and exchange rates; by contrast, macroprudential policies are meant to safeguard stability in the financial system. While the distinction is clear enough in principle, the outcomes with respect to external stability and domestic financial stability tend to comingle making intent difficult to discern merely from the fact of policy action.

China has made concerted use of capital controls in managing a gradual opening of its financial account on the balance of payments, pulling back or moving forward in response to exchange rate pressures. Foreign investment in China's stock market (renminbi denominated shares) was first permitted in 2002 under the Qualified Foreign Institutional Investment (QFII) program which set quotas on inflows and conditions on withdrawals. By 2012 the quota on QFII investment stood at just $30 billion. The years that followed saw aggressive increases until finally in 2020 the quota was lifted altogether, by which time QFII market capitalization surpassed $150 billion. On the outflow side, since 2010 individuals have faced a conversion limit on renminbi to US dollars of $50,000 a year. While this amount has been held fixed, the purposes for which conversion has been allowed and the strictness with which the rules have been enforced have varied in connection with the direction of pressure on the exchange rate. When the renminbi was depreciating in 2016, restrictions were tightened on the pooling of quotas among family and friends; conversely, in 2021 with the renminbi appreciating, consideration was given to allowing conversion for previously off-limits investment in foreign securities.

Identifying these Chinese measures as capital controls is straightforward enough since they pertain to the balance of payments and exchange rate stabilization; yet distinguishing capital controls from macroprudential policy is not always so easy. For example, limiting foreign borrowing by domestic banks serves both to inhibit capital inflows and to contain currency mismatches on bank balance sheets in mitigation of systemic risk. The same goes for requiring banks to hold higher reserves against foreign currency deposits than against domestic currency deposits. Such ambiguities are typically handled in data analysis by treating the measures as macroprudential policies when that is the subject of study and as capital controls when that is the subject of study, motivations being too difficult to discern and disentangle.

In identifying macroprudential policy instruments, the focus is on motive. In the policy formulation process, motive is explicit. The ambiguities arise only in the effort to analyze data absent recourse to the policymaking context. The ambiguities are, then, a caveat for data analysis rather than a problem for policy implementation, although when conducting policy there is a need to be aware of side effects implied.

Catalog of Options

A classification scheme for macroprudential policy instruments as they apply to financial institutions is presented in Table 14.1. We discuss elements of this scheme in turn.

Capital requirements have long been foundational to regulating individual financial institutions, and with the growing use of macroprudential policy have taken on a role at the aggregate level as well. The idea is to ensure owner equity is adequate to absorb prospective losses to a reasonable degree of likelihood. Capital requirements are specified as a ratio of capital to risk-weighted assets where heavier weights apply to riskier assets. Policy action involves adjusting the capital ratio or the risk weights in response to changing risk conditions in the financial system as a whole or in elements of the system. Additional capital buffers may also be applied, including

Table 14.1 Macroprudential policy instruments

Capital requirements & buffers	Capital requirement given as a ratio of equity to risk-weighted assets. Additional buffers may apply, including countercyclically such that the ratio rises as aggregate credit growth increases and is relaxed during an economic downturn. May vary by sector (e.g., household, corporate).
Limits on credit	Limits on credit growth or volume with penalties for exceeding. May vary by sector or be tailored by loan characteristics (e.g., maturity, size), institution characteristics, or other factors.
Liquidity requirements	Requirements on the ratio of liquid assets to liabilities.
Limits on leverage	Limits on leverage expressed as a ratio of some measure of debt to equity.
Loan loss provisions	Required allowance to be set aside against risk of loss on loan assets. May be dynamic such that reserves are built up faster during boom times. May vary by sector.
Borrower specific limits	Limits on loan-to-value ratios or ratios of debt service or loan size to borrower income. May vary by loan purpose (e.g., housing, motor vehicles, commercial real estate).
Tax measures	Taxes and levies on transactions, assets, or liabilities (e.g., stamp duties, capital gains taxes).
Foreign exchange regulations	Regulations on foreign exchange positions, exposures, funding, lending, or currency mismatch.
Restrictions on systemically important financial institutions	Measures applied to mitigate risk from systemically important financial institutions, both domestic and global (e.g., capital or liquidity surcharges).
Reserve requirements	Reserve requirements for macroprudential purposes, as distinct, in principle, from monetary policy purposes (although in practice, differentiation is difficult). May vary by currency.

countercyclical buffers that are increased during booms and decreased during busts. Capital requirements serve to create resilience in the financial system for weathering shock.

A number of instruments may be used to block the procyclical feedback between credit expansion and asset prices. A direct way of breaking this circuit is simply to impose limits on credit volume or credit growth, with possible specificity by loan purpose or borrower type. More indirect approaches work through lender incentives to both control credit growth and increase resilience against shock. For example, liquidity requirements mandate that institutions hold cash or other liquid but low-return assets against liabilities. This raises the cost of borrowing so as to mitigate the buildup of risk in connection with short-term wholesale funding through the financial market as opposed to more stable funding from deposits. Leverage ratios similarly discourage the reliance of financial institutions on borrowing and thus impede credit growth and the buildup of risk. Loan loss provisions involve the setting aside of funds against future losses, with these set-asides treated as a cost on an institution's income statement. Finally, taxes can be imposed on all manner of transactions or financial positions so as to discourage lending or particular sorts of risk taking.

Instruments based on features of the retail borrower can be put to targeted use in controlling credit growth. Restrictions are set with respect to borrower income or the value of the asset purchase the borrower is financing, commonly a home. These restrictions safeguard the solvency of both borrowers and lenders. Debt- (or debt-service-) to-income ratios and loan-to-value ratios can be lowered during periods of soaring asset prices to inhibit purchase and raised during periods of slumping asset prices to encourage purchase.

Instruments involving foreign currency are important in managing systemic risk deriving from foreign capital flows. These can take many forms, some already discussed but tailored by currency, including: limits on borrowing; limits on lending; loss provisions on loans; constraints on currency mismatch between assets and liabilities; taxes; or reserve requirements on deposits.

Systemically important financial institutions (SIFIs) are subjected to more stringent regulation. SIFIs are large institutions that play an oversized role in providing wholesale funding to other institutions. Their failure would reverberate throughout the financial system with serious consequences for the real economy as well. The "too big to fail" status of SIFIs implies the government would have to bail them out. To protect against any such eventuality, and the moral hazard a bailout would engender, special attention to standards must apply to SIFIs to ensure any excessive buildup of risk is quickly curtailed.

Finally, adjustment in reserve requirements can serve macroprudential purposes given that reserves act as security against deposits and thus help to contain systemic risk. Typically, however, the motivation is to manage growth of the money supply rather than to control systemic risk, and adjusting reserve requirements is thus generally intended to serve monetary policy rather than macroprudential policy.

In general, macroprudential policy instruments are designed to be adjusted over the course of the financial cycle or in response to the buildup of risk in particular realms. These instruments are readily tailored to meet specific risk threats: by sector; by activity; by locality; or by currency. This affords an abundance of options in policy implementation.

Circumstances may at times call for tightening on one front and loosening on another. Or, instruments may be used in complementary fashion, keeping adjustment incremental along each front to limit disruption.

Use in Emerging East Asia

Emerging East Asian economies have relied increasingly on macroprudential policy since the Great Financial Crisis, as have countries in the rest of the world. Use by instrument and by time period is shown in Chart 14.2, where use refers to discrete changes in the values of policy instruments and a distinction is made between tightening and loosening.

A number of observations are worth highlighting. First, tightening accounts for far more of the policy actions than loosening. One reason for this is that a newly established instrument can at its inception only be tightened, and not until it has been tightened to some degree can it be loosened with much relevance. Further, tightening and loosening are not symmetrical actions. Tightening serves to reduce risk and restrain credit growth whereas loosening does not simply do the opposite in the sense of increasing risk and stimulating credit growth; nor would increasing risk in the financial system ever be seen as a goal to be pursued. Rather, loosening comes most decisively into play when the financial system is under duress with loans going bad and credit drying up. Under such circumstances, relaxing constraints on financial institutions reduces their costs and gives them capacity to absorb losses. The reason for building buffers through macroprudential tightening is precisely to allow these buffers to be drawn on in times of stress so that collapse of financial institutions can be avoided. With the financial system in a downward spiral, risk does not increase upon the loosening of restrictions; rather, bad debts are unwound as the outcomes of risky undertakings are realized. By giving financial institutions space to absorb irretrievable losses, balance sheets can be restored to a sound footing on which credit growth can begin anew, and eventually macroprudential buffers can be rebuilt. Macroprudential policy has

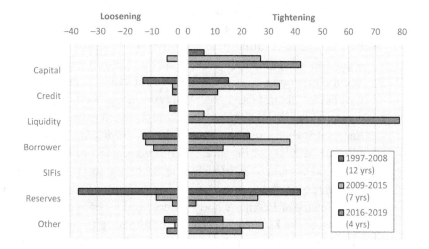

Chart 14.2 Macroprudential policy use by instrument, 1997–2019

taken off largely since the Great Financial Crisis. Within that time frame, compelling occasion for loosening of macroprudential regulations has, fortunately, not come to pass.

Second, changes in the reserve requirement ratio have seen heavy use going back decades, with loosening almost as common as tightening. This is predominantly a manifestation of monetary policy rather than macroprudential policy. That is, the motive was to influence growth in the money supply rather than to manage risk in the financial system. Remaining charts in this chapter thus exclude this instrument from the analysis.

Third, in the 2016–2019 period, use of capital requirements and liquidity regulations jumped sharply, and measures specific to systemically important financial institutions emerged on the scene. This represents new frontiers of policymaking opening up and being popularized. By contrast, credit controls and borrower-based restrictions have had a longer history, and with that loosening actions are more in evidence for these instruments. Indeed, in the recent 2016–2019 period, loosening was almost as common as tightening for borrower-based restrictions. These restrictions are commonly directed at the housing market where more balanced guidance can be exercised to good effect.

C   Policy Framework

The vast array of policy instruments available and the many related indicators to be monitored suggest that macroprudential policy is up against major bureaucratic challenges. Moreover, the ramifications of getting it wrong can spill over to other economies and even the world at large, as the Great Financial Crisis taught us. In this section, we consider the institutional framework, in both domestic and international aspects, that provides context for the conduct of macroprudential policy.

Domestic Institutions

No one model of governance predominates for managing macroprudential policy. All economies within our purview have established a macroprudential authority of some sort, but the specifics differ. The central bank generally plays a role, and so too do financial regulators with these regulators sometimes, but not always, housed inside the central bank. Within Emerging East Asia, the central bank is in charge of macroprudential policy in Cambodia, Indonesia, Laos, Malaysia, Singapore, Thailand, and Vietnam. In China, a commission directly under the State Council (China's cabinet) holds responsibility for financial stability with member units encompassing the central bank, the financial regulators, the Ministry of Finance, and other agencies. In Hong Kong, responsibility lies with the Financial Secretary assisted by the Secretary for Financial Services and the Treasury. In Korea, responsibility is shared among the central bank, the Financial Services Commission, the Ministry of Economy and Finance, and other agencies. In the Philippines, responsibility is vested in the Financial Stability Coordination Council which is chaired by the governor of the central bank and includes the heads of other agencies as members.

The central bank typically plays a key role in macroprudential policy due to the integral relationship between monetary policy and the financial system. Hong Kong is exceptional within Emerging East Asia in not having a discretionary monetary policy since money supply is dictated by the exchange rate peg. This undercuts the need for the monetary authority to play a role in macroprudential policy even as it elevates the importance of macroprudential instruments as tools of discretionary action. Adjustment of macroprudential regulatory parameters can affect the growth of credit where no scope exists in Hong Kong for manipulating the standard instruments of monetary policy – the interest rate and the exchange rate.

To inform policymaking, a large assortment of indicators must be monitored. Important among these are credit-to-GDP ratios, the rate of credit growth, asset prices, debt service costs relative to income, and foreign capital flows, all broken down along various lines into component parts. For none of these indicators do there exist clearcut thresholds that signify financial health or looming danger. Credit can increase for good reasons, for example: financial deepening as the financial system develops and becomes more sophisticated; broadening of financial inclusion as lower income households gain access to financial products; or rising standards of living generally. Beyond assessing magnitudes and trends then, analysts develop economic models and conduct stress tests. Stress tests are intended to reveal how the balance sheets of financial institutions would be impacted by shocks to such variables as interest rates, exchange rates, asset prices, foreign capital flows, or GDP growth. Macroprudential policy is aimed at ensuring resilience to these kinds of shocks to a reasonable degree of probability.

Armed with such data and analysis, decisions on how to adjust the instruments of macroprudential policy still come down to heavy reliance on judgment. Not a great deal is known about how adjustments in the instruments affect outcomes. The macroprudential policy toolbox has a relatively short history of use under fairly limited conditions. The empirical research done to date has focused mainly on dichotomous measures of policy action of the sort presented in the charts of this chapter; that is, an action is treated as a tightening or loosening of some instrument. Systematic data on the degree of tightening or loosening are scant.

In sum, the framework for conducting macroprudential policy involves diverse elements of government bureaucracy coming together to review data on a vast array of variables that are related to each other in complex ways and connected to policy instruments in poorly understood fashion.

International Institutions

Three international bodies provide guidance and support for the formulation of macroprudential policy. The Basel Committee on Banking Supervision focuses on banking. The Basel Committee was established in 1974 within the Bank for International Settlements, a "bank for central banks" headquartered in Basel, Switzerland. The Committee offers a forum for international cooperation and sets regulatory standards, articulated in a series of Basel Accords as detailed in Box 14.2.

Box 14.2 Basel Accords I, II, and III

The Basel Committee on Banking Supervision has promulgated three accords known as Basel I (1988), Basel II (2004), and Basel III (2009) aimed at providing guidance on bank regulatory standards.

Basel I was officially titled the Basel Capital Accord. Its focus was on establishing a capital adequacy standard that would ensure owner equity would bear the brunt of bank losses. The need for such a standard became apparent when the Latin American debt crises of the 1980s put the solvency of major international banks in jeopardy. Basel I set a minimum ratio for capital to risk-weighted assets at 8 percent. The challenge in crafting such regulation lies in assigning the risk weights to various asset classes, with this challenge compounded by ongoing innovation in financial products.

Basel II was designed to improve risk assessment in an evolving financial environment and to better ensure compliance with standards. Bank exposure to exchange rate fluctuations, commodity price movements, traded debt securities, and derivative products received needed attention in the risk calculus. In addition, review and disclosure protocols were strengthened.

Ultimately, however, these measures proved insufficient to prevent the Great Financial Crisis of 2008. In the aftermath, Basel III was formulated to go beyond the prior focus on capital adequacy and address leverage and liquidity risks. A bank can meet capital adequacy requirements under normal market conditions and still be unable to liquidate assets quickly enough to cover withdrawals or otherwise meet obligations when panic strikes and markets seize up. Basel III imposes limits on leverage, sets requirements for cash holdings, and places guardrails on maturity mismatches. Further, it provides for the identification of systemically important banks to be held to more rigorous standards.

The dynamism of the financial system is such that regulators are always struggling to keep up. Apart from the major overhauls of the three Basel Accords, the framework is subject to constant tweaking in view of new risk threats.

Membership in the Basel Committee encompasses 45 institutions from 28 jurisdictions. From Emerging East Asia, the following institutions are members: the People's Bank of China and the China Banking Regulatory Commission; the Hong Kong Monetary Authority; Bank Indonesia and the Indonesia Financial Services Authority; the Bank of Korea and the Korea Financial Supervisory Service; and the Monetary Authority of Singapore. Observer status is held by the Central Bank of Malaysia. Beyond its formal membership, the Committee networks with emerging economies to solicit input and seek consolidation of standards.

The imperative of creating an oversight body with a scope beyond banking became clear with the Great Financial Crisis. In 2009, formation of the Financial Stability Board (FSB) was endorsed by the G20 countries, and the organization was formally established in Basel, Switzerland in 2013. A precursor organization existed in the Financial Stability Forum, founded in 1999 by the G7 countries, but by 2009 the need for broader representation of emerging economies had become clear. The FSB has a broad mandate to promote international financial stability. It carries out this mandate by assessing vulnerabilities in the global financial system and advising on needed actions; promoting coordination and exchange among relevant authorities; and reviewing and coordinating the work of international standard-setting bodies.

Members of the FSB from Emerging East Asia include: from China, the Vice Minister of Finance, the Governor of the People's Bank, and the Chair of the China Banking and Insurance Regulatory Commission; from Hong Kong, the Chief Executive of the Monetary Authority; from Indonesia, the Assistant to the Minister of Finance and the Governor of Bank Indonesia; from Korea, the Governor of the Bank of Korea and the Chair of the Financial Services Commission; and from Singapore, the Managing Director of the Monetary Authority. In addition to national government officials, FSB membership extends to officials of multilateral organizations, among them the International Monetary Fund, the World Bank, the Bank for International Settlements, and the Basel Committee on Banking Supervision.

Finally, the International Monetary Fund contributes importantly to safeguarding global financial stability in a number of ways: monitoring financial policies, identifying risks, and advising the governments of its 190 member countries; assessing global financial developments and coordinating international responses; gathering systematic data on macroprudential policy and maintaining a public database; and conducting research for broad dissemination.

The Basel Committee, the FSB, and the IMF work closely with each other through integrated organizational structures. A strong institutional framework for overseeing the global financial system is vital given that systemic risk emanates not just nationally but internationally. Major financial institutions conduct business worldwide. Moreover, they conduct business with each other so the principle of systemic importance pertains internationally. For the health of the global financial system to be sustained, the same well-designed rules must apply to all internationally engaged institutions and confidence must prevail that all are abiding by these rules.

D   East Asian Experience

As noted in the discussion of Chart 14.2, Emerging East Asia has ramped up its use of macroprudential policy over time. In this section we break down the patterns by economy. We then focus on the case of Korea, an early adopter of macroprudential policy.

Cross-Country Comparison

Chart 14.3 shows use of macroprudential policy instruments by economy. As in Chart 14.2, a preponderance of tightening is evident, and this applies across all economies. Again too, an increasing use over time is apparent and applies to all economies. Note that each successive period pertains to a shorter span of years so on an annualized basis the increases from period to period are greater than the simple bar lengths reflect.

Hong Kong and China are revealed to be the heaviest users of macroprudential policy instruments. Hong Kong's recourse to these instruments was foreshadowed in the sub-section on domestic institutions where the lack of discretionary monetary policy was noted. Where the interest rate and exchange rate are not manipulable to influence the growth of credit, macroprudential instruments can serve this purpose. A monetary policy motive for active management of financial regulation thus looms large in Hong Kong.

China's use of the standard instruments of monetary policy is also constrained but for different reasons. The financial system in China is dominated by state-owned banks lending to state-owned enterprises such that the interest rate is not the foremost arbiter of credit decisions. Rather than targeting an interest rate then, the central bank steers policy with reference to monetary aggregates, as discussed in Chapter 11. Within this framework as well, macroprudential policy instruments become appealing tools of monetary policy.

The Hong Kong and China cases demonstrate the need for circumspection in interpreting the use of instruments identified with macroprudential policy. These instruments influence money supply growth even as they serve to manage risk in the financial system. In economies with flexible exchange rates and market-driven financial systems, the interest rate and/or exchange rate can take the lead in the conduct of monetary policy allowing for a more focused application of macroprudential policies on managing systemic financial risk.

Chart 14.3 Macroprudential policy use by economy, 1997–2019

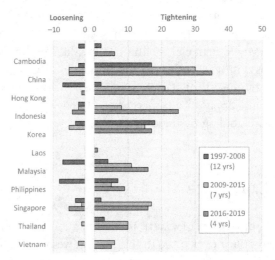

Note: Excludes reserve requirement adjustments.

The Korean Case

Korea was an early adopter of macroprudential policy, as Chart 14.3 illuminates. The country's long open financial account on the balance of payments and resulting reliance on foreign borrowing exposed it to crippling shocks with both the Asian Financial Crisis and the Great Financial Crisis. In the recovery from the Asian Financial Crisis, banks shifted their lending away from large corporations, which turned to the capital markets for financing, and toward households. Easy lending to support home purchases fueled a boom in housing prices that gained momentum with soaring prices justifying ever more lending. The authorities sought to break the cycle by imposing loan-to-value ratios in 2002. However, once lending solidified at a given loan-to-value ratio, the procyclical movement of credit and housing prices could re-ignite. In 2005 then, the authorities tried another tack by introducing debt-to-income ratios to rein in lending, income providing a more solid anchor than housing prices. These borrower-based instruments have been put to active use through the years, as Chart 14.4 shows. The authorities have leaned by turns to tightening or loosening as conditions warranted. Restrictions are manipulated specific to locality, lender type, and borrower characteristics.

The Great Financial Crisis called attention to the need for macroprudential instruments to manage foreign exchange risks. In the wake of the crisis, the flight of capital to safety left emerging market banks unable to rollover or repay short-term foreign currency loans as the value of local currencies fell. To limit the coupling of currency and maturity mismatches on bank balance sheets, Korea introduced a number of new safeguards. Specifically, a leverage cap was set on bank positions in forex derivatives (such as currency futures, forwards, and interest rate swaps), which create exposure to exchange rate risk. Further, a "macroprudential stability levy" was instituted to tax foreign currency debt at maturities of less than one year. Finally, a liquidity coverage ratio was imposed to require banks with foreign exchange liabilities above a certain threshold to hold liquid foreign currency assets against these liabilities. This package of forex instruments allows for exchange rate risk to be managed in different aspects.

By 2016, growing awareness of the risks associated with the interconnectedness of banks, and in particular the role of large institutions in providing wholesale funding, prompted measures directed at systemically important financial institutions. Korean authorities

Chart 14.4 Macroprudential policy use in Korea, 2002–2019

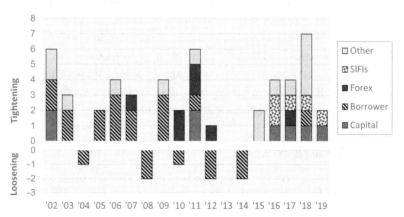

identified on bank and four bank holding companies as systemically important. These institutions are required to hold additional capital buffers.

Korea's macroprudential policies have succeeded in meeting key objectives: housing price increases have been contained; bank reliance on short-term foreign currency debt has been curtailed; and procyclicality between the financial cycle and the economic cycle has been weakened. The ultimate test of macroprudential management, however, lies in how well the financial system averts or weathers crises. On this, there is not yet a clear verdict.

E   Averting and Weathering Crises

As for crises that are successfully averted, we have no awareness; we are aware only of those that become manifest. Once a crisis erupts, the warning signs are always apparent in hindsight: a rapid buildup of credit relative to GDP; ballooning asset prices; widening mismatches by currency or maturity on balance sheets. Yet there are no hard and fast rules as to how much is too much for any of these indicators.

Macroprudential policy intervention involves a great deal of judgment. In monetary and fiscal policy as well, judgment is involved. But for these more established arms of policy, the objective is in the nature of fine tuning movement of the economy along a more or less identifiable path marked by economic growth at potential with inflation low and stable. Feedback on policy performance is ongoing; the policy toolkit is concise; and the mechanisms by which the tools work are fairly well understood. By contrast, for macroprudential policy the ultimate objective of building resilience is vaguely defined; timely feedback is absent; and the policy tools are multitudinous with their workings obscure.

As if these challenges to implementing macroprudential policy were not enough, the costs of restrictions are obvious, immediate, and borne by well-identified stakeholders while the benefits are nebulous, delayed, and felt by society at large. Macroprudential policies limit the current opportunities of businesses to make money. In exchange, the society of the future may possibly avoid the collapse of financial institutions and an economic recession. The titans of finance will tend to resist the impositions of macroprudential intervention. And given the rarity and unpredictability of financial distress, the political will to act against these vested interests will be difficult to marshall. Global standard-setting bodies have been helpful in elevating the decisions above the domestic political fray. The occasional financial crisis tends also to be a game changer in focusing consensus.

Crises when they do occur are damaging enough to leave deep and lasting impressions. The best that can be hoped is that we learn something from the experience. With that, we turn attention to the topic of crises in Chapter 15.

Data Note

The Bank for International Settlements is the source of data on changes in foreign loan liabilities in Chart 14.1

The International Monetary Fund maintains two overlapping databases on macroprudential policy that provide the source material for Charts 14.2–14.4. The Integrated Macroprudential Policy (iMaPP) Database is downloadable in a spreadsheet that contains monthly data from 1990 to an endpoint subject to updating (2016 for the analysis of this chapter). Policy actions are coded as +1 for tightening and –1 for loosening across 27 categories. The Data Query tool provides access to data from 2016 to the most recent year of compilation (2019 for the analysis of this chapter) in the form of detailed descriptions of policy actions that must be manually coded to conform with the iMaPP database, a process that involves judgment.

The IMF Data Query database also contains information on institutional frameworks for macroprudential policymaking that informed the discussion of domestic institutions.

Bibliographic Note

The multilateral organizations that oversee macroprudential policy are important sources of research and analysis. A 2013 International Monetary Fund paper provides an introduction. A 2017 Bank for International Settlements compendium of papers offers discussion of issues with contributions from Asian macroprudential authorities. A 2020 BIS paper considers macroprudential policy in emerging Asia in connection with foreign capital flows.

Insightful discussions of strategy for coordinating macroprudential, monetary, and exchange rate policies in the context of global financialization are to be found in Filardo et al. (2016), Obstfeld (2015), and Yellen (2014).

On the Korean case, the Bank of Korea website, an International Monetary Fund Technical Note (2020), and BIS (2017) are informative.

BIBLIOGRAPHIC CITATIONS

Bank for International Settlements, 2021. Basel Committee on Banking Supervision, www.bis.org/bcbs/index.htm (accessed February 2, 2021).

Bank for International Settlements, 2021. BIS Statistics Warehouse, Locational Banking Statistics Dataset. https://stats.bis.org/#df=BIS:WEBSTATS_LBS_D_PUB_DATAFLOW(1.0);dq=all%3FlastNObservations=6 (accessed February 18, 2021).

Bank for International Settlements, 2020. Capital Flows, Exchange Rates and Policy Frameworks in Emerging Asia, Asian Consultative Council, BIS. www.bis.org/publ/othp34.pdf (accessed March 17, 2021).

Bank for International Settlements, 2017. Macroprudential Frameworks, Implementation and Relationship with Other Policies, BIS Papers No. 94. www.bis.org/publ/bppdf/bispap94.pdf (accessed March 17, 2021).

Bank of Korea, 2021. Financial Stability. www.bok.or.kr/eng/main/contents.do?menuNo=400037 (accessed February 10, 2021).

Bloomberg News, 2021. China Mulls Easing Capital Controls on Offshore Investments, February 19, 2021. www.bloomberg.com/news/articles/2021-02-19/china-mulls-easing-capital-controls-on-offshore-investments (accessed February 25, 2021).

Filardo, Andrew, Hans Genberg, and Boris Hofmann, 2016. "Monetary Analysis and the Global Financial Cycle: An Asian Central Bank Perspective," *Journal of Asian Economics*, Vol. 46, pp. 1–16.

Financial Stability Board, 2021. www.fsb.org/ (accessed March 13, 2021).

Grigg, Angus and Lisa Murray, 2016. "China Tightens Controls on Moving Money Overseas," *Financial Review*, January 21, 2016. www.afr.com/world/asia/china-tightens-controls-on-moving-money-overseas-20160120-gma7g3 (accessed February 20, 2021).

International Monetary Fund, 2020. Integrated Macroprudential Policy (iMaPP) Database. www.elibrary-areaer.imf.org/Macroprudential/Pages/iMaPPDatabase.aspx (accessed November 29, 2020).

International Monetary Fund, 2020. Macroprudential Policy Survey Data Query. www.elibrary-areaer.imf.org/Macroprudential/Pages/ChapterQuery.aspx (accessed November 29, 2020).

International Monetary Fund, 2020. Republic of Korea, Financial Sector Assessment Program, Technical Note – Macroprudential Policy Framework and Tools. www.imf.org/en/Publications/CR/Issues/2020/09/18/Republic-of-Korea-Financial-Sector-Assessment-Program-Technical-Note-Macroprudential-Policy-49749 (accessed March 17, 2021).

International Monetary Fund, 2013. Key Aspects of Macroprudential Policy. www.imf.org/external/np/pp/eng/2013/061013b.pdf (accessed March 17, 2021).

Obstfeld, Maurice, 2015. "Trilemmas and Trade-Offs: Living with Financial Globalisation," BIS Working Papers No. 480. www.bis.org/publ/work480.pdf (accessed March 17, 2021).

Yellen, Janet, 2014. "Monetary Policy and Financial Stability," remarks at the 2014 Michel Camdessus Central Bank Lecture, International Monetary Fund. www.federalreserve.gov/newsevents/speech/files/yellen20140702a.pdf (accessed 17 March 2021).

Zhang, Longmei and Edda Zoli, 2016. "Leaning against the Wind: Macroprudential Policy in Asia," *Journal of Asian Economics*, Vol. 42, pp. 33–52.

15   Crises

The world is in crisis at this writing. A different sort of crisis it is, though, from the standard financial variety. Crises rooted in financial excess have played out recurringly for centuries. With experience, our understanding of their genesis and policies for addressing them have arrived at a certain orthodoxy. A pandemic is a much rarer event, rooted in non-economic causes and directly impacting the real economy. The policy response to the Covid pandemic remains an unfolding experiment.

Every now and then the normal ups and downs of the business cycle give way to a radical departure. An upswing in credit and asset valuation overshoots to such an extent that finally panic breaks out and the financial system collapses taking the real economy with it. Crises have played out along these lines for centuries without our figuring out how to prevent them despite the terrible losses they inflict.

Something has been learned, however, about the appropriate policy response to financial crises, with the essence of that knowledge dating back to the 1800s. The top priority must be to allay the panic. This is done by meeting the rush to sell troubled assets with adequate liquidity through generous monetary policy. Beyond that, effort must be made to tide over viable businesses and provide a social safety net for those falling into desperate straits. Fiscal policy is mobilized for these purposes.

We begin this chapter with a discussion of the nature of crises, first of the financial type, then of the real economy variety as embodied in the pandemic. We follow that with an overview of principles for policy response. Foundations thus laid, we examine the two crises that have rocked Asia broadly: the Asian Financial Crisis of 1997 and the Covid crisis, which of course is global in extent and ongoing as of this writing. We conclude with lessons, to the best of current understanding.

A   The Nature of Crises

The history of crises as written focuses on the financial type. In essence, an expansion of debt and a rise in asset prices interact with mounting frenzy to reach untenable levels. Finally, a realization dawns that the situation has gotten out of hand, and holders of overvalued assets move en masse to unload them causing prices to plummet. Panic ensues. Risk tolerance evaporates and investors rush to safe assets, especially cash. Banks shrink from lending; businesses fail; jobs are lost; spending dries up. The economy goes into a tailspin.

Variations on this theme are recognizable. Some crises are lodged in the domestic banking system or extend to domestic financial institutions more broadly. Some involve foreign borrowing and hit the balance of payments and exchange rate. Some pertain to sovereign debt. Often crises are multifaceted along these lines. Much of the analysis is generalizable, although at times distinctions need be drawn.

Crises arising from real shocks – pandemics, wars, natural disasters – possess origins beyond the economist's power to explain. The job then focuses on how to respond.

Financial Crises

In his classic work *Manias, Panics, and Crashes* first published in 1978, Charles Kindleberger sorted through the historical record going back nearly three centuries to discern patterns and formulate policy lessons. The earliest crisis in his compendium is the South Sea Bubble of 1720. The South Sea Company was granted a trading monopoly with Latin America by the British government in exchange for converting government debt securities to corporate stock, the idea being that the government would pay interest on the debt to the South Sea Company which would in turn pay dividends on the stock to shareholders. It was all a big swindle, according to Kindleberger (p. 84). Following past practice, the government quickly fell into arrears on its interest obligations, and the South Sea Company was in no position to make money on trade with Latin America since Spain and Portugal held the colonies and controlled the shipping. Yet the stock became a hot property with buy-in by everyone from the movers and shakers of society (Sir Isaac Newton among them) down to ordinary folk. Banks lent eagerly to support purchase on margin. New stock was issued to fund payment of dividends under a Ponzi scheme that could not long endure but worked splendidly in the moment. The stock price soared, rising from £128 in January of 1720 to over £1000 by August. And then the bubble burst. Within a month, the price dropped to £150 and by year end it leveled out at around £100. Great fortunes were made and lost. The case of the South Sea Bubble illustrates a fundamental principle of manias and panics: They materialize out of "general irrationality or mob psychology," people "gradually at first, then more quickly losing contact with reality" (p. 28). In the end, however, reality does prevail.

Kindleberger was an avowed fan of Hyman Minsky whose theory of the business cycle was expounded in Chapter 10. In Minsky's telling, a sound financial system tends to transform itself over time into one that is fragile. In good times, credit expands; asset prices rise; and maturity mismatches proliferate on balance sheets. This fuels an economic boom. Pursued to excess, however, the result can be disaster as ultimately the processes are obliged to reverse course. In the "revulsion" (Kindleberger's term), loans go into default; asset prices fall; and financial institutions fail. Painful as this is, the outcome will be a restoration of a sound financial footing from which to begin economic renewal.

With centuries of this pattern repeating itself, you would think the powers that be would have figured out how to stop it. And indeed, sometimes it appears as though they have. Chair of the US Federal Reserve Ben Bernanke gave a much ballyhooed speech in 2004 titled "The Great Moderation." The speech begins on this note: "One of the most striking features of the economic landscape over the past twenty years or so has been a substantial decline in macroeconomic volatility." Bernanke credited three factors for this moderation: structural change involving institutions, technology, and business practices; astute macroeconomic policy management; and good luck. In hindsight, we are all too aware that the greatest financial crisis to strike since 1929 lay just beyond the horizon.

It's not that there were no warning signs by way of the usual telltale indicators of debt levels and asset prices. The problem is that in the boom phase, success is all too easy to justify, per Bernanke, on grounds of institutional development, sound policies, and the like. In the approach to the Great Financial Crisis of 2008, the build up of sub-prime mortgage debt was ostensibly supported by the development of more sophisticated financial instruments to price and spread risk. Before that with the dot-com bubble of 2001, stratospheric price/earnings ratios on technology stocks were explained away as the information economy incorporating technological advances into expected future returns. Luckily, that bubble popped without inflicting broad damage to the real economy, losses being confined mainly to shareholders.

The title of a 2009 book on the history of crises captures well the human capacity to brush off the overreach of a boom: "This Time Is Different: Eight Centuries of Financial Folly." Authors Carmen Reinhart and Kenneth Rogoff present a comprehensive empirical analysis spanning 66 countries to ascertain the frequency, magnitude, and duration, as well as the causes and outcomes of crises. They distinguish among types of debtors and creditors to define three broad categories based on: domestic bank debt, extending to non-bank financial institutions in the modern context; domestic sovereign debt, including default via inflation that wipes away the real value of obligations; and debt held by foreign creditors bringing balance of payments and currency crises into the mix. These are not mutually exclusive, and indeed they commonly occur in combination. Emerging economies are especially prone to getting into trouble with foreign debt, as in the case of the Asian Financial Crisis. Latin American countries have been plagued by sovereign debt crises whereas Asian economies have done better in avoiding these in recent decades. That no country is too advanced to succumb to financial crisis was vividly demonstrated by the domestic banking (and shadow banking) crisis that erupted in the USA in 2008.

The Real Economy Shock of the Pandemic

The Covid-19 pandemic levied a direct hit on the real economy absent any prelude of financial excess. For most economies, the impact has derived more from measures to slow disease transmission than from the disease itself. Some East Asian economies, most notably Taiwan and Vietnam, showed quick success in identifying and quarantining infected individuals and then tracing their contacts to curtail spread, which allowed economic life to continue little abated. Others have imposed heavy lockdowns at great economic cost and with mixed results for disease transmission. The situation as of late 2021 remains fluid as new surges continue to erupt and clampdowns on activity are reinstated.

The pandemic and related public health interventions have hit both supply and demand sides of economies simultaneously. On the supply side, businesses have had to shut down or reduce operation, with travel and leisure sectors hit especially hard. Public transportation has been curtailed making it difficult for people to get to workplaces that do stay open. School closures have forced parents to preempt work with child care and home tutoring. On the demand side, consumers have avoided venturing out to patronize brick and mortar businesses, often under stay-at-home orders. Worries about the future have inhibited both household consumption and business investment.

While global pandemics are extremely rare – a century having passed since the last one – real economy shocks can derive from other sources. Natural disasters and wars are notable examples. Such shocks differ fundamentally from a pandemic in their devastating consequences for physical capital. A pandemic, by contrast, leaves the capital stock intact while inflicting a heavy human toll in death and morbidity. Implications for rebuilding and recovery are very different. Psychological trauma and trepidation about the future may factor in differently as well.

Importantly, even when a crisis emanates from a real economy shock, the financial sector can come under duress and contribute to its propagation. A financial crisis is caused by panic that debtors will not repay creditors. When businesses are being shut down or destroyed and workers are losing their jobs, the risk that loans will go bad escalates. Either borrowers must find sources of funds to meet their obligations, including taking on new debt; or creditors must absorb losses; or society as a whole, acting through government, must provide support. Approaching two years into the Covid pandemic, financial systems in Emerging East Asia have proven resilient. Some credit for this is due to prior improvement in prudential management that strengthened buffers to shock. Some credit is due also to government support policies during the course of the pandemic.

Recovery

A crisis causes businesses to fail, jobs to disappear, and with a financial crisis, lending to collapse. Recovery from the wreckage is a process, its speed depending on regeneration of confidence. Entrepreneurial risk taking, borrowing and lending, job creation – all depend on faith in the future. In the aftermath of a crisis, a sense of opportunity must take root, and once it does, markets will gear up to put resources back to work.

In a discrete sense, an economy may be regarded as having recovered once output reaches its pre-crisis level. More telling, however, is a comparison of the post-crisis and pre-crisis growth trajectories. A long-term drag on growth can result from "scarring," which may take a variety of forms. With respect to human resources, extended periods of unemployment can cause skill development to lag and attachment to work culture to deteriorate. Some workers may never regain their previous earnings potential. Under the Covid crisis, education losses due to school closures and uneven opportunities to learn from home will impact an entire generation of young people. But even under a crisis that does not shut down schools, the ability of families to invest in education suffers, diminishing prospects across generations.

With business failure as well, scarring can result, and may be especially pronounced under the Covid crisis where small businesses in the service sector have been hardest hit. Much of the productive value of such businesses resides in the operational knowledge and personal networks of proprietors, accumulated through years of experience. Such intangible assets may simply dissipate with the crisis even as physical assets are sold off and repurposed in the recovery. Put another way, the going-concern value of a business exceeds its liquidation value, with the difference irretrievably lost when the business goes under.

Finally, scarring may for a time leave a mark on entrepreneurial zeal and risk taking. Suffering serious, unanticipated loss tends to make people more cautious and less trusting going forward lest they become vulnerable again. In the pithy words of 19th-century intellect Walter Bagehot (recognized for his insight into business cycles in Chapter 10 and to be invoked again in the upcoming discussion of monetary policy): "Credit – the disposition of one man to trust another – is singularly varying. ... [A]fter a great calamity, everybody is suspicious of everybody; as soon as that calamity is forgotten, everybody again confides in everybody."

Some businesses may fall victim to a crisis despite having been healthy previously and holding promise of future viability post-recovery. Yet they are not able to sustain losses through the duration of the crisis and therefore default on debt, let go of workers, and sink into liquidation. With all the scarring such failure entails, investment in tiding over such businesses could be worthwhile. Yet a financial system under duress may not be equipped to provide the needed funds. That leaves government to take on the task. If appropriately timed and targeted, government support can prove a boon for post-crisis recovery.

Amid the dark clouds of a crisis, a silver lining can usually be found if one looks hard enough. The challenges and dislocations can help to catalyze innovation and hasten latent resource reallocation processes. Striking examples within emerging Asia under the Covid crisis include the rapid dispersion of electronic payment systems to all corners of society and the proliferation of efficient delivery services. Movement of government functions to electronic platforms is improving responsiveness and reducing opportunities for corruption. And (a favorite of the author) an explosion in bike riding in accordance with social distancing practices has been met in Metro Manila with extensive bike infrastructure development. The shift to a biking culture, if lasting, will bring real health and environmental benefits. Even a pandemic, then, presents opportunities for progress.

B   Policy Response

Once a situation reaches crisis proportions, policy must aim first and foremost at bringing about calm. In the recovery push beyond that, monetary and fiscal policy space will be constrained by the forces of external balance and the legacy of accumulated public debt.

Appeal may be made for outside assistance, but this will inevitably come with strings attached. Bailouts can help to turn the tide on the crisis, but risk sending a message that financial recklessness will be rewarded. We delve into these policy matters in this section.

Monetary Policy

In a financial crisis, the rush is on to unload troubled assets and seek the safe harbor of cash or the bonds of a trusted government, the US government largely playing this role in today's world. Even when crisis originated in the USA in 2008, US government bonds became the asset of choice. That meant the USA could respond to the crisis with heavy government borrowing and massive central bank purchase of government debt, with the dollar remaining strong all the while. Emerging economies do not have this luxury. There, authorities must be attentive to financial flows on the balance of payments in crafting a monetary policy response to crisis.

To get a sense of what is involved, consider first a crisis confined to the domestic financial system with no balance of payments consequences. To stem the panic, the monetary authority should step up as "lender of last resort," providing liquidity as needed to keep asset markets functioning and businesses operating. The original great thinker on crises, Walter Bagehot, put it this way in 1873: "The holders of the cash reserve must be ready not only to keep it for their own liabilities, but to advance it most freely for the liabilities of others. They must lend to merchants, to minor bankers, to 'this man and that man,' whenever the security is good" (p. 53). Easy access to funds will cure the panic and stabilize the economy.

A crisis involving foreign debt, however, calls for an altogether different monetary policy response. A sudden stop in foreign lending when creditors fear default will induce a net outflow of capital as payments on existing debt exceed new funding. The net outflows will cause the local currency to depreciate making repayment even harder. The process can quickly snowball as capital takes flight and the value of the currency plummets. To stem the panic of a balance of payments and exchange rate crisis, capital must be induced to stay through an attractive domestic interest rate. This means monetary policy should be tight, precluding "this man and that man" from getting loans.

Not uncommonly, crises encompass both domestic and foreign debt simultaneously, which creates a dilemma. The domestic crisis calls for monetary policy to be expansionary, the external crisis for it to be tight. Bagehot advised that in such situations priority be given to resolving the external crisis. The reasoning is that until the external panic is subdued, there is no hope of allaying the domestic panic. The interest rate must rise high enough to adequately compensate foreign capital such that the exchange rate is stabilized. Yet, at this elevated interest rate, domestic credit should be made readily available. In Bagehot's words: "What is wanted and what is necessary to stop a panic is to diffuse the impression that, though money may be dear, still money is to be had. If people could be really convinced that they could have money if they wait a day or two, and that utter ruin is not coming, most likely they would cease to run in such a mad way for money" (p. 66).

The key, then, is to re-establish confidence in the flow of credit. For foreign credit, this requires that the interest rate be sufficiently high to maintain risk-adjusted competitiveness internationally. Yet at the high rate of interest, the central bank as lender of last resort should ensure that loans are available for creditworthy borrowers who can pay the price. When the crisis does not hit the balance of payments, expansionary monetary policy and low interest rates will help to reassure domestic financial markets. Even then, however, balance of payments considerations will constrain the space for monetary policy. Interest rates in emerging economies must always be managed with an eye to foreign capital flows.

Fiscal Policy

As with monetary policy, the potential for fiscal policy to aid in recovery from crisis will be constrained by circumstances. If the source of the crisis traces to the private financial sector or a real economy shock with public finances remaining sound, there may be space for fiscal policy to provide stimulus. Just how much space will depend on past accumulation of debt, trend GDP growth, and the interest rate on government borrowing, as set forth in Chapter 11 and applied to the example of the pandemic crisis later in this chapter.

If, however, the source of the crisis is a sovereign default, then fiscal stimulus will not be an option. Further, for government finances to have reached such a state, space for monetary policy, too, may have been compromised. Long before government gets to a point of outright default, at least on domestic currency debt, it will almost certainly have resorted to the subtler tactic of relying on the central bank to monetize its debt. With that, inflation will rear up to eat away at the real value of the debt. This may work for a time to keep the tap flowing on government borrowing. Eventually though, accelerating inflation and rising interest rates will take a toll on the economy. When crisis hits against this backdrop, the central bank will have no leeway to expand the flow of credit to calm financial markets. With both monetary and fiscal easing foreclosed, the path to recovery will be difficult. To stabilize prices and re-establish government creditworthiness, the central bank will have to tighten and fiscal authorities will have to balance the budget. This will drive a painful recession. Disciplined follow-through, however, will be needed to pave the way to a sustainable recovery, supported by stable prices and a sound fiscal system.

If the sovereign debt troubles pertain to foreign rather than domestic currency debt, there is no inflating away the burden through monetization. More likely, a default will be accompanied by a balance of payments and exchange rate crisis as foreign capital inflows dry up. Re-establishing a sound footing under such conditions will likely involve negotiated commitments on fiscal policy in exchange for debt restructuring by foreign creditors.

Outside Assistance

The community of nations has developed institutions for handling balance of payments crises among its members. The International Monetary Fund plays the leading role. Beyond that, organizational structures have been evolving, and must continue to do so, to reckon with a changing international financial architecture.

The IMF was founded in the wake of the Great Depression and World War II in conjunction with the Bretton Woods system of fixed exchange rates. Under this system, a country's exchange rate peg could become misaligned with balance of payments fundamentals, and the IMF was tasked with then providing support to re-establish equilibrium. The Bretton Woods system dissolved in 1971 when the USA severed the dollar's link to gold which had served as the cornerstone of the framework. Under the more flexible exchange rate system that emerged, the IMF mandate is more broadly conceived as ensuring the stability of "the system of exchange rates and international payments that enables countries and their citizens to transact with each other." (from "The IMF at a Glance" on the IMF website) Under this mandate, the IMF monitors and advises on member country policies and provides assistance for resolving, or better yet pre-empting, crises.

For a country in or approaching crisis, an IMF rescue program involves new lending to the government tied to conditions on economic policies. The conditions are meant to restore macroeconomic stability and balance of payments viability, and with that to ensure a foundation for sustainable growth. IMF conditionality typically targets quantitative indicators that include: the primary fiscal balance; the level of government debt; the level of official reserves; and growth rates of monetary and credit aggregates. These targets are set within a program that prescribes policy reforms with respect to fiscal management and financial regulation and supervision. IMF oversight continues until the government has repaid its loans.

Once the IMF has quelled the emergency, a country's diverse creditors must negotiate feasible debt repayment terms, ideally in coordination with one another. Creditor countries have developed institutional structures for this purpose. The Paris Club was established in 1956, initially to renegotiate the troubled debt of Argentina. The organization has since evolved to include 22 mostly OECD member states. The focus is on debt extended by sovereign creditors to sovereign borrowers, including private borrowers with sovereign guarantees. Private creditors may sometimes be included in the negotiations as well. The principle of comparability governs Paris Club negotiations, meaning the same repayment terms must apply to all creditors.

The Paris Club construct has fallen increasingly behind the times as the diversity of creditors and instruments involved in lending to sovereign states has expanded. Notably, China's role as a creditor has grown rapidly with its lending tilted toward more at-risk borrowers, and China is not a Paris Club member. Further, loan agreements have become more complex, often containing provisions that privilege a given creditor over others or lay claim to specific assets or revenue streams as collateral. Most vexingly, confidentiality is sometimes imposed in the signing of agreements. These developments interfere with the Paris Club principle of comparability as a basis for debt renegotiation.

The Covid pandemic has focused attention on the need to redesign the framework for handling sovereign debt crises. Foreseeing that the stress of the pandemic could push some countries into default, the G20 on April 15, 2020 announced a "Debt Service Suspension

Initiative" (DSSI) identifying 73 low-income countries as eligible to seek relief (including Cambodia, Laos, and Myanmar). With a longer term view, on November 13, 2020 the G20 (of which China is a member) and the Paris Club jointly advanced a "Common Framework for Debt Treatments beyond the DSSI" committing member countries to adhere to the principle of comparability in debt renegotiation. Much remains to be worked out, however, within a context that has become more knotty than the Paris Club had to contend with historically.

The Moral Hazard Conundrum

If debtors – be they sovereign states or private financial institutions or non-financial corporations – expect to be bailed out should they run into trouble, their incentive to avoid running into trouble is considerably diminished. Debtors will take on more risk and be less concerned with managing risk knowing that on the upside they could win big and on the downside someone else will bear the cost. Undertakings may also be more prone to corruption and diversion of funds when a bailout provides a fallback. Yet a bailout is sometimes what it takes to clear the way for renewal when a situation becomes hopeless or to honor fairness when losses would spill over broadly onto innocent victims. This is the essence of the moral hazard conundrum.

What, then, is to be done by those charged with bringing a country back from crisis? The essential answer proposed by Kindleberger is to bailout when necessary but not to let borrowers know in advance that a bailout will be forthcoming. "The rule is that there is no rule" (p. 176). "The lender of last resort should exist, but his presence should be doubted" (p. 12).

C   Asian Financial Crisis

Much was learned from the Asian Financial Crisis about panics in emerging markets, and learned the hard way from mistakes made. Those mistakes involved both the initial creation of vulnerability and, once the crisis broke, the adoption of policies that aggravated rather than relieved it. In hindsight, it became clear things didn't have to get so bad.

Thailand and the Contagion

The charts in Chapter 1 that motivate this book vividly portray the breadth and depth of the trauma. In 1998, GDP contracted by 13.1 percent in Indonesia, 10.5 percent in Thailand, 7.4 percent in Malaysia, and 6.9 percent in Korea.

The crisis erupted on July 2, 1997 when Thailand broke with its peg to the US dollar after months of defending it against attack, and by the end of September the baht had lost 42 percent of its value. Thailand's depletion of foreign reserves and the incapacity of Thai borrowers to service their foreign debts set off a scare that reverberated across the region. Credit inflows froze, and other countries were caught up in the contagion.

Thailand had liberalized its financial markets in the 1990s and welcomed foreign capital. This helped to fuel spectacular growth averaging 9.5 percent a year over the decade leading up to the crisis. Foreign creditors were reassured by this record of success, as were domestic debtors who further took comfort in the exchange rate peg, confident they would be able to obtain the dollars they needed to meet foreign obligations at fixed cost in terms of baht. With the high-speed growth came booming property and stock markets, all driven by borrowed funds.

Foreign credit was being channeled through banks and less regulated non-bank financial intermediaries to support loans made in domestic currency. This created a mismatch on the balance sheet of the financial system between assets in domestic currency and liabilities in foreign currency. Moreover, the foreign borrowing was mostly short term while domestic lending was mostly long term creating a maturity mismatch as well. These mismatches made the financial system vulnerable to depreciation of the baht or sudden stops in foreign lending that would prevent rollover of short-term foreign debt.

By 1997, forces were conspiring against Thailand's development model. Export growth was slowing due to real exchange rate appreciation as rising inflation undermined the competitiveness of Thai products, especially against the Chinese juggernaut and Mexico's preferential access to the US market under the North American Free Trade Agreement. Government involvement in bank lending decisions was compromising returns, and perceived state guarantees of financial institutions were inducing excessive risk taking. Meanwhile, property and stock valuations were looking ever more dubious. Then, in late 1996 a major property developer defaulted on its loans and soon after so did a large corporation. Property and stock markets turned sharply downward on these triggers.

This marked a tipping point for foreign lenders who moved as a herd to get out of Thailand. As shown in the upper panel of Chart 15.1, the foreign borrowing item on the

Chart 15.1 Balance of payments flows, Thailand, 1990–2005

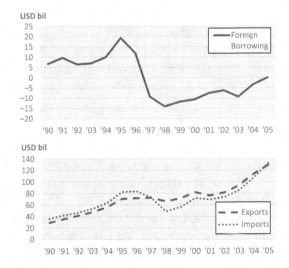

balance of payments, having peaked at \$19.3 billion in 1995 and holding strong at \$11.8 billion in 1996, dropped to \$-9.3 billion in 1997 as loan repayment exceeded new loan inflow. Indeed, the balance on foreign borrowing would remain negative until 2005. During the pre-crisis boom, strong foreign capital inflows funded large trade deficits, the gap widening notably in 1995–96, as shown in the lower panel of Chart 15.1. The post-crisis paydown of debt then required a sharp reduction in imports in 1998 followed by continued maintenance of a trade surplus until 2005.

As the crisis erupted, the net outward rush of funds put downward pressure on the Thai baht. Initially, the central bank stood by its peg, selling off foreign reserves to prop up the baht. Before long, however, the depletion of reserves reached a point where market players could foresee the futility of the effort and the scramble was on to unload the baht before its value crashed. This only compounded the pressure on the peg to accelerate the break.

Once the baht fell, contagion spread quickly across the region. While the worst hit countries – Indonesia, Korea, and Malaysia – showed similar excessive buildup of short-term foreign borrowing as Thailand, the herding behavior of panicked creditors blew the problem out of proportion with respect to underlying fundamentals. When everyone else is barreling for the exits, no one dares get left behind. The right policies might have mitigated the furor. Instead, the wrong policies inflamed it.

Policy Response

In a crisis driven by domestic debt, the central bank as lender of last resort can step in to calm a panic, exploiting its infinite capacity to print money. When the crisis involves foreign debt, however, the resources of the central bank are decidedly finite and, as in the case of Thailand, any appearance that foreign reserves are heading toward exhaustion only aggravates the situation. For recourse to deeper pockets, countries must turn to the IMF.

The IMF implemented its first program for Thailand in August 1997. The program involved a loan to support intervention in the foreign exchange market and repayment of foreign debt, conditioned on: balancing the fiscal budget; tightening monetary policy to raise interest rates; restructuring the financial sector; and instituting broad economic and governance reforms. Announcement of the package was meant to restore market confidence, most immediately by assuring a high rate of return on baht holdings so as to stabilize the exchange rate. But the program failed in this regard, and flight from the baht continued. In the face of ongoing crisis, the IMF ramped up its lending commitments and backpedaled on its conditions into the spring of 1998 when the situation finally normalized.

The initial requirement to balance the fiscal budget followed IMF practice arrived at through managing a series of crises in Latin America. But crises in that part of the world had derived from sovereign debt default on the heels of chronic oversized fiscal deficits. By contrast, before the crisis in Thailand, the government was running a surplus, its budget only dropping into deficit due to the economic downturn. The situation was as depicted in Figure 15.1 (adapted from Figure 12.4). With the economy at potential output (Y_p) pre-crisis, the Thai fiscal budget was in surplus, but went into deficit at crisis output (Y^*) as the

Figure 15.1 Fiscal balance under crisis with budget tightening

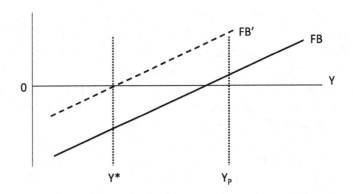

A crisis causes a movement along a given relationship between fiscal balance (FB) and income (Y) from a surplus at potential income (Yp) to a deficit at actual income (Y*). Budget tightening then causes a shift in FB to FB′ to restore budget balance at Y*.

economy moved along the initial fiscal budget (FB) line. Restoring balance would require raising taxes and cutting spending to shift the fiscal budget line upward (FB′). But these policies would be contractionary at a time when what was needed to restore confidence was stimulus. Unlike in Latin America, the pre-crisis tax and spending regime in Thailand was healthy and sustainable. Thus, an IMF mandate to change it was not reassuring.

Assessing the monetary policy mandate is more complicated. The reasoning behind the IMF's call for tightening was that higher interest rates would stem the money outflow and stabilize the baht. This follows Bagehot's prescription elaborated earlier in this chapter. The policy had its critics in the context of the Asian Financial Crisis, however. The concern was that restrictive domestic credit policies would cause failure of ultimately viable businesses and thus add to non-performing loans on bank balance sheets. Further, the drying up of trade credits would hit the imported inputs to production needed to sustain exports to yield the foreign exchange for debt repayment.

As for the IMF's broad mandates on economic reform, critics saw this as diverting administrative capacity to non-urgent tasks that while perhaps worthwhile in principle were better deferred. Bundling them into the IMF program arguably did more to unsettle markets than to calm them.

Policy Rethink

As the crisis failed to abate under the initial programs in Thailand and elsewhere, the IMF came around to relaxing its stance on fiscal policy. Not so on monetary policy, however. As for the economic reform policies, these were meant to be implemented over time rather than immediately anyway, so the IMF stood by them.

The IMF also came around to a more nuanced approach to opening the financial account on the balance of payments with an eye to preventing future crises. Countries hit hardest by the Asian Financial Crisis had all absorbed the economic orthodoxy of the day that foreign capital was to be welcomed. To be sure, foreign capital inflows bring many benefits: they support investment; they fund imports of production inputs, capital goods, and technology; and they promote competitiveness in the financial sector. On the downside, however, flows in and out can be volatile and can overwhelm the capacity of emerging economies to provide oversight.

The thinking on opening to foreign capital has evolved in recognition of these challenges. No question, inflows in the form of foreign direct investment are to be welcomed as they carry long-term commitments and bring with them technology and managerial talent. More ambiguously, for portfolio flows to be well handled, markets need to reach a certain maturity in depth and liquidity. But it was loan flows that caused the problem in Asia. In hindsight, regulation and supervision of the financial system were not up to managing foreign borrowing by financial institutions. With proper prudential oversight, the accumulation of currency and maturity mismatches on balance sheets would not have been allowed to happen. Developing the needed institutional capacity is a work-in-progress for many emerging economies, however.

Reaching an accommodative position on capital controls by the IMF has also been a process. Indeed, IMF chief economist from 2008 to 2015, Olivier Blanchard, in an interview with the *Washington Post*, described the scene within the organization as "trench warfare." What emerged under the gentler rubric of "capital flow management" was a recognition that a full opening of the financial account was not necessarily advisable at all times and in all places. The strategy, however, should be to move in the direction of liberalization against a backdrop of macroeconomic stability and sound prudential policy. Capital flow management measures should not be used as a substitute for getting these fundamentals right. To handle surges in capital flows, other instruments are to be preferred, specifically, the policy rate of interest, the exchange rate, and macroprudential measures. In a pinch, however, if a crisis situation seems to be gathering steam, capital controls may be invoked on an emergency basis.

In reality, many governments are more assertive in the use of capital controls than the IMF favors. China in particular exercises a heavy hand on capital flows, and arguably this has served well in the Chinese context.

D   Pandemic Crisis

The Covid pandemic has taken a heavy toll on some Asian economies while passing more lightly over others. The hit to real economic activity has been transmitted through multiple channels. Most fundamental, though not most decisive, is the channel of death and morbidity due to disease. More significant for economic outcomes is the channel involving mitigation measures against the spread of infection including business closures, stay-at-home orders, and public transportation shutdowns. Of mixed consequences is the foreign trade channel as exports of some manufactured goods have flourished while tourism and some other service exports have been decimated.

Fiscal and monetary policy responses have also factored into differing outcomes with policy space bearing significantly on the scope for action. In this section we apply concepts developed in Chapters 11 and 12 to analyzing macroeconomic policy initiatives in the Emerging East Asia region.

Fiscal Policy

The pandemic has cried out for increases in government spending to provide public health services, to support households that have lost their livelihoods, and to keep businesses afloat. Against these spending needs, revenues have been undercut by a shrinking tax base.

Changes in government revenue and expenditures in 2020 are shown in Chart 15.2. All 13 Emerging East Asian economies saw revenues decline, with the exception of Myanmar (if official statistics are to be believed). For Cambodia, Indonesia, the Philippines, and Vietnam, revenue drops exceeded 10 percent in 2020 relative to 2019.

The expenditure picture is more mixed. Singapore stands out for its extraordinary surge in spending. The government implemented five successive budgets in 2020 to raise spending by nearly 80 percent year on year, or about 20 percent of GDP. The Ministry of Finance credits this fiscal largesse with keeping a bad situation from becoming even worse, its estimates showing that a GDP contraction of 5.7 percent would have been larger by 5.5 percentage points without the fiscal intervention. The Singapore government had the luxury of being able to spend freely without regard for borrowing costs given substantial reserve funds accumulated through years of running budgetary surpluses. Moreover, the country possesses the administrative capacity to spend effectively at great speed and scale.

How much space a government has to spend in deficit depends on its fiscal sustainability position, as defined in Chapter 12. Recall that this is a function of three variables: the real

Chart 15.2 Change in public revenue and expenditures, select economies, 2020

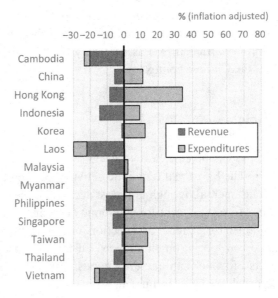

interest rate on borrowing (*r*); expected real GDP growth (*g*); and the debt-to-GDP ratio (*d*). These variables determine the primary balance (*pb*) that will hold the debt-to-GDP ratio constant (where the primary balance excludes interest payments on debt from the measure of expenditures). If the debt ratio is low initially, some space for it to rise may be incorporated into the reckoning of prudent borrowing.

As developed in Box 12.1, the fiscal sustainability condition is given as:

$$pb = \frac{r-g}{1+g} \cdot d. \tag{15.1}$$

A negative value for *r* – *g* implies a deficit on the primary balance is permissable under the sustainability condition. The lower the interest rate and the higher the GDP growth rate, the more space the government has for running a primary deficit while still preserving the debt ratio.

Values of the variables for Emerging East Asian economies are presented in Table 15.1. The real interest rate is taken as the nominal rate on 10-year government bonds minus the projected inflation rate for 2021–25 where all projections are from the IMF. The real cost of borrowing is negative for Hong Kong, Taiwan, and Vietnam. Indonesia faces the highest cost of borrowing at 6.3 percent in nominal terms and 3.4 percent in real terms, a key reason being its heavy reliance on foreign creditors. Promising growth projections give greatest advantage to Vietnam, China, and the Philippines.

Pre-pandemic, reported debt-to-GDP ratios across the region lay generally below a threshold that would cause concern (see Chart 12.1). A caveat, however, is that reported figures exclude off-budget spending (e.g., subsidies to money losing state enterprises) and contingent liabilities (e.g., pension obligations or prospective bailouts of failing financial

Table 15.1   Fiscal space determinants and utilization, 2020–25

in percent

	Interest Rate		GDP Growth	Debt/GDP	Primary Balance/GDP (*pb*)			
	Nominal 11/2021	Real (*r*) 2021–25	(*g*) 2021–24	(*d*) 2020	Sustainable d(r–g)/(1+g)	Actual 2020	2021	Projected 2022–25
China	2.9	0.9	5.9	66.3	–3.1	–11.2	–7.5	–5.9
Hong Kong	1.5	–0.9	3.7	1.0	0.0	–9.2	–3.7	–1.3
Indonesia	6.3	3.4	5.3	36.6	–0.6	–5.9	–6.1	–3.3
Korea	2.4	0.5	3.1	47.9	–1.2	–2.2	–2.9	–2.3
Malaysia	3.6	1.5	5.1	67.4	–2.3	–5.2	–5.9	–4.1
Philippines	5.1	2.1	5.9	51.7	–1.9	–5.7	–7.6	–4.5
Singapore	1.8	0.3	3.4	154.9	–4.7	–8.9	–0.2	2.0
Taiwan	0.6	–0.9	3.2	32.7	–1.3	–2.9	0.3	2.0
Thailand	1.9	0.6	3.3	49.6	–1.3	–4.7	–6.9	–3.4
Vietnam	1.9	–1.5	6.3	46.3	–3.4	–3.9	–4.7	–4.3

institutions). With an eye to these considerations, debt ratios in China and Malaysia become more worrisome going into the pandemic. All other economies showed existing space for their debt ratios to rise by standard benchmarks.

Despite its already stretched position, China responded aggressively to the pandemic running a primary deficit of 11.2 percent of GDP in 2020 and is projected to continue to run exceptionally large deficits in coming years. Next in line, Singapore and Hong Kong entered the pandemic essentially unconstrained in their spending given negligible prior debt in the case of Hong Kong and abundant government assets to offset high debt in the case of Singapore. Both took advantage of this latitude to ramp up their primary deficits to around 9 percent of GDP in 2020. At the opposite extreme, Taiwan and Korea kept their primary deficits below 3 percent of GDP which speaks to their successful containment of the disease as a basis for keeping their economies running. In all other cases, primary deficits reached a range of about 4–6 percent of GDP in 2020 with projections for even higher levels in 2021. These figures substantially exceed the sustainability threshold.

For the most part, the picture looking ahead through 2025, is for rising debt ratios given persistent gaps between projected primary deficits and the sustainability benchmark. Hong Kong, Singapore, and Taiwan are beyond concern with the latter two projected to revert to surplus budget positions soon. China and Malaysia were operating at the margin of prudence before the pandemic struck and have strained the bounds further with their pandemic responses. The Philippines entered the pandemic with a comfortable fiscal space but faced the deepest GDP contractions in the region and with that is incurring deficits at the upper reaches. Still, its growth projections are good and that is key to re-establishing a sustainable debt position.

A global emergency on a scale beyond living memory presents great pressure for governments to take on additional debt. Good fiscal management in normal times can ensure a comfortable space for this. The sudden decline in revenues caused by the pandemic is particularly difficult to weather without recourse to borrowing if performance of essential government functions is to continue. In addition, the pandemic necessitates increases in public health expenditures if the disease is to be subdued. Beyond these imperatives, public support for sustaining businesses and livelihoods through the upheaval of the crisis can mitigate scarring and smooth the way to recovery.

Monetary Policy

Emerging East Asia's response to the pandemic has rested largely on fiscal policy with monetary policy playing a facilitating role. In a financial crisis as opposed to a real economy crisis, central banks would play a vital role as lenders of last resort to maintain the smooth functioning of the financial system. Even under the real economy shock of the pandemic, central banks must be vigilant to ensure that balance sheets of financial institutions remain healthy with no serious build up of nonperforming loans.

In support of economic growth, central banks have eased by lowering policy interest rate targets and expanding asset purchases. This has helped to absorb the increased issuance of government securities. A broad uptick in growth rates in central bank assets in 2020 is visible

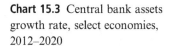

Chart 15.3 Central bank assets growth rate, select economies, 2012–2020

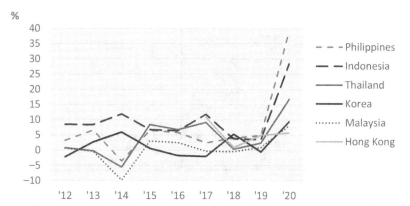

in Chart 15.3 Prior to the pandemic, asset growth rates typically ran at less than 10 percent a year. In 2020, this threshold was dramatically exceeded by the Philippines and Indonesia. In both countries, central banks took the extraordinary step of lending directly to the government thus relieving it of the need to sell securities on the open market with the central bank then making purchases from the public. This has ensured that greatly expanded government borrowing did not stress the absorptive capacity of securities markets.

Whether such large increases in central bank assets will be inflationary will depend on whether the impetus feeds into bank lending to then fuel increases in aggregate demand. Economic uncertainty surrounding the pandemic tends to crimp such feed through. Financial institutions prefer to build up safe holdings of reserves and government securities rather than lend in support of risky ventures, and businesses, too, are generally cautious about taking on capital projects.

Thus far, indications are that investors remain confident in Emerging East Asian currencies and satisfied with returns. Currency values have remained buoyant even as central banks have intervened to sell domestic currency and accumulate foreign reserves, as shown by the concentration of values for 2020 in the upper left quadrant of Chart 15.4. (Recall this analytical framework was developed in the chapter on monetary policy as Chart 11.2). Increases in reserve assets in 2020 were over 20 percent for Singapore and close to that for the Philippines. Only Indonesia experienced currency depreciation, and that was slight and with a push from the central bank buying foreign currency. The positive balance of payments positions with currencies generally stable or appreciating despite mostly weakening of exports suggest that global capital continues to be attracted to Emerging East Asia. That has given authorities space to keep interest rates low in pursuit of accommodative monetary policy.

Global liquidity was supported by expansionary monetary policy in the USA as the pandemic erupted. This allowed Asian central banks to follow suit in keeping interest rates low without concern for capital outflows. Should inflation pick up in the USA, however, the situation could change. If the Federal Reserve were to tighten monetary policy in response, rising interest rates in the USA would draw global capital away from emerging markets

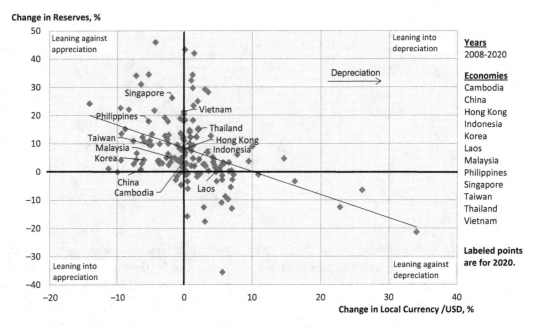

Chart 15.4 Reserves vs exchange rate, select economies, 2008–2020

putting pressure on central banks there to tighten as well. The race is on, then, to move forward jointly in vaccinating populations and pulling out of the crisis together with normalization of macroeconomic policies in sync.

E   Lessons

Past experience has imparted lessons about avoiding financial crisis and, too, about building capacity to respond when avoidance fails because one of the surest lessons about crises is that there will be a next time. We consider lessons with respect to three main policy areas: prudential policy; fiscal policy; and monetary policy.

Prudential policy. For avoiding financial crises, prudential policy is foundational, both at the micro level of individual financial institutions and at the macro level for the financial system as a whole. The foremost lesson from the Asian Financial Crisis is to guard against both currency and maturity mismatches on balance sheets. Short-term foreign borrowing channeled through the financial system concentrates exposure to risk on both fronts. Maturity transformation is an inherent function of financial institutions which is why prudential regulation imposes capital requirements and liquidity standards, as discussed in Chapter 14. Foreign currency exposure can similarly be managed with regulatory guardrails. Globally, financial flows to emerging markets tend to be procyclical, with inflows strengthening during the boom and outflows channeling money back to safe havens in the bust that follows. Macroprudential policy can help to moderate these ups and downs.

Fiscal policy. Keeping government debt within prudent bounds is key to both avoiding crisis and preserving space to respond when crisis hits. Foreign borrowing carries particular risk, although in recent times development of international bond markets in emerging economy currencies has helped reduce the risk. The sovereign debt crises of the 1980s and 1990s arose out of foreign currency loans going into default when the value of local currencies fell putting the cost of repayment beyond reach. The concept of "original sin" referenced in Chapter 12 refers to reliance on foreign currency borrowing to fund fiscal and current account deficits. Nowadays, emerging economy governments and businesses can readily borrow from foreign creditors in their own currencies, but even so, foreigners tend to be more fickle bondholders than locals making interest rates on foreign currency borrowing more volatile.

In advanced economies, the view has gained credence that with interest rates low and economies running slack amid the pandemic, authorities should dare to go big on fiscal policy. Whether this "new fiscal consensus" applies to emerging economies was the subject of a webinar discussion by Olivier Blanchard of France/USA and Arvind Subramanian of India, with the latter raising caveats. What is clear from Chart 15.2 is that under negligible burden of past debt, Singapore and Hong Kong have indeed gone big while most other economies in the region have been more mindful of the constraints imposed by their debt legacies. Just where limits of prudence have been exceeded will only become clear if and when inflation picks up and interest rates rise. Debt service will then take a greater claim on public resources. Yet being too conservative, either in responding to a crisis or in keeping debt low to preserve space for any future response, carries its own costs in terms of compromising economic growth relative to potential in the moment. Whatever lessons we have learned about fiscal policy, much guesswork remains as to how to find the right balance between excess and missed potential.

Monetary policy. The foremost lesson for monetary policy is that in a financial crisis the central bank must calm the panic above all else. Basic principles going back to Bagehot (1874) hold that in a crisis emanating from domestic debt, the central bank should step up generously as lender of last resort such that fundamentally viable financial institutions and other businesses do not fail. In a crisis involving foreign debt, however, the central bank must give priority to restoring confidence in the currency, and for this it must tighten credit, raising interest rates to stem capital flight and stabilize the exchange rate. Given the finite nature of central bank holdings of foreign reserves, achieving calm with respect to the currency may require outside help, notably from the IMF. Only when the panic surrounding currency valuation is subdued can creditors and debtors come together to negotiate feasible terms for loan repayment to lay a basis for economic renewal.

In fact, in the modern emerging market setting, the distinction between a crisis of domestic debt and a crisis of foreign debt is not likely to be clearcut. A crisis of domestic debt can easily spook foreign creditors to morph into a crisis of foreign debt. Thus, ensuring faith in the value of the currency must always command attention. Indeed, as a general rule in emerging economies, monetary policy space is constrained by global capital flows, except insofar as capital controls impede response to changes in market conditions or investor sentiment. Even in a crisis driven by a pandemic, then, the role of monetary policy is circumscribed.

Crises are rare enough that we tend to forget the lessons during long periods of calm. We are then blindsided when the moment comes. Thus has it been for centuries.

Data Note

Thai balance of payments data in Chart 15.1 are from the IMF Balance of Payments Statistics.

Government revenue and expenditure data in Chart 15.2 are from the IMF Fiscal Monitor database.

Central bank asset data in Chart 15.3 are from the IMF Monetary and Financial Statistics database.

Data on exchange rates and reserves for Chart 15.4 are from the IMF International Financial Statistics database except for Taiwan which are from the Republic of China (Taiwan) Central Bank.

Fiscal sustainability data in Table 15.1 are from the following sources: nominal interest rate on 10-year government bonds, the World Government Bonds database; Taiwan fiscal data, Republic of China Ministry of Finance; all else, IMF Fiscal Monitor database.

Figures on Singapore's response to the pandemic are from the Singapore Ministry of Finance.

Bibliographic Note

The landmark work on the history of financial crises is Charles Kindleberger's *Manias, Panics, and Crashes: A History of Financial Crises*. The first edition came out in 1978 with three further editions following by Kindleberger himself, and after his death three more by Robert Aliber as co-author. Introducing the fourth edition, Kindleberger acknowledged that "a fourth edition is perhaps not needed by readers but only as occupational therapy for the writer." Readers wishing to understand the essence of crises need look no further than Kindleberger's original book. This first edition lays out in fleet prose an analytical frame-work for understanding crises and fills it in with examples from history spanning the period 1719–1975. Alas, in subsequent editions, as every latest turn of events is injected, the narrative becomes fractured. Those wishing to learn about particular crises beyond 1975 would be better off consulting sources dedicated to those events.

The other epic work in the financial crisis canon is Reinhart and Rogoff's *This Time is Different: Eight Centuries of Financial Folly*, the title of which encapsulates the essential message. This book documents the history of crises in empirical terms to build on Kindleberger's narrative approach.

A recent retrospective on the Asian Financial Crisis and lessons learned is Takagi (2022). Standard sources from the time are Corsetti et al. (1998) and Radelet and Sachs (1998). The quote from Olivier Blanchard on trench warfare at the IMF is from Pearlstein (2015).

Discussion of institutions involved in foreign debt restructuring is to be found on websites of the G20 and the Group of 30.

Two posts by Wiemer on the *Asia Economics Blog* trace the economics of the pandemic, one dated July 16, 2020, the other December 2, 2021.

BIBLIOGRAPHIC CITATIONS

Bagehot, Walter, 1910[1874]. *Lombard Street: A Description of the Money Market* (New York: E.P. Dutton).

Blanchard, Olivier and Arvind Subramanian, 2021. "The New Fiscal Consensus." www.youtube.com/watch?v=RM_QXhBLwQ4 (accessed July 2, 2021).

Corsetti, Giancarlo, Paolo Pesenti, and Nouriel Roubini, 1998. "What Caused the Asian Currency and Financial Crisis? Part I: A Macroeconomic Overview; Part II: The Policy Debate," National Bureau of Economic Research, Working Papers 6833 and 6834.

G20, 2020. Communique. https://meetings.imf.org/~/media/AMSM/Files/SM2020/g20-communique.ashx (accessed June 16, 2021).

G20 and Paris Club, 2020. Common Framework for Debt Treatments beyond the DSSI. https://clubdeparis.org/sites/default/files/annex_common_framework_for_debt_treatments_beyond_the_dssi.pdf (accessed June 16, 2021).

Group of 30, 2021. Sovereign Debt and Financing for Recovery after the COVID-19 Shock: Next Steps to Build a Better Architecture. https://group30.org/publications/detail/4915 (accessed June 16, 2021).

International Monetary Fund, 2000. Recovery from the Asian Crisis and the Role of the IMF. www.imf.org/external/np/exr/ib/2000/062300.htm (accessed May 27, 2021).

International Monetary Fund, 2012. The Liberalization and Management of Capital Flows: An Institutional View. www.imf.org/external/np/pp/eng/2012/111412.pdf (accessed June 20, 2021).

International Monetary Fund, 2021. Balance of Payments and International Investment Position Statistics. https://data.imf.org/?sk=7A51304B-6426-40C0-83DD-CA473CA1FD52&sId=1390030341854 (accessed June 12, 2021).

International Monetary Fund, 2021. IMF Conditionality. www.imf.org/en/About/Factsheets/Sheets/2016/08/02/21/28/IMF-Conditionality (accessed June 15, 2021).

International Monetary Fund, 2021. International Financial Statistics. https://data.imf.org/?sk=4C514D48-B6BA-49ED-8AB9-52B0C1A0179B&sId=1390030341854 (accessed June 20, 2021).

International Monetary Fund, 2021. Monetary and Financial Statistics database. https://data.imf.org/?sk=B83F71E8-61E3-4CF1-8CF3-6D7FE04D0930&sId=1390030341854 (accessed May 20, 2021).

International Monetary Fund, 2021. The IMF at a Glance. www.imf.org/en/About/Factsheets/IMF-at-a-Glance (accessed July 10, 2021).

Kindleberger, Charles P., 1978. *Manias, Panics, and Crashes: A History of Financial Crises* (Basic Books).

Pearlstein, Steven, 2015. "The Smartest Economist You've Never Heard of", *Washington Post*, October 3, 2015. www.washingtonpost.com/business/the-smartest-economist-youve-never-heard-of/2015/10/02/8659bcf2-6786-11e5-8325-a42b5a459b1e_story.html (accessed June 18, 2021).

Radelet, Steven and Jeffrey Sachs, 1998. "The East Asian Financial Crisis: Diagnosis, Remedies, Prospects," *Brookings Papers on Economic Activity*, Vol. 1998, No. 1. https://doi.org/10.2307/2534670 (accessed June 19, 2021).

Reinhart, Carmen and Kenneth S. Rogoff, 2009. *This Time Is Different: Eight Centuries of Financial Folly* (Princeton University Press).

Republic of China Central Bank, 2021. Balance of Payments & International Investment Position. https://cpx.cbc.gov.tw/Tree/TreeSelect?mp=2 (accessed May 14, 2021).

Republic of China Ministry of Finance, 2021. Public Finance Statistics Database. https://web02.mof.gov.tw/njswww/webmain.aspx?sys=100&funid=edefjspf2 (accessed June 23, 2021).

Singapore Ministry of Finance, 2021. An Interim Assessment of the Impact of Key COVID-19 Budget Measures. www.mof.gov.sg/docs/default-source/default-document-library/news-and-publications/featured-reports/interim-assessment—covid-19-budget-measures-(19-feb-2021).pdf (accessed June 27, 2021).

Takagi, Shinji, 2022. "IMF Surveillance and Crisis Lending in Emerging Asia: A Crucible that Inspired an Intellectual Revolution, 1995–2010", in Hoe Ee Khor, Diwa C. Guinigundo, and Masahiro Kawai (eds.), *Trauma to Triumph: Rising from the Ashes of the Asian Financial Crisis* (Singapore: World Scientific).

Wiemer, Calla, 2021. "Economics of the Pandemic, 2020 (Part I): Covid Cases, Mobility Loss, and Exports," *Asia Economics Blog*, July 16, 2021. http://acaes.us/blog/pandemic-2020-cases-mobility-exports (accessed December 29, 2021).

Wiemer, Calla, 2021. "Economics of the Pandemic, 2021 Preliminary," *Asia Economics Blog*, December 2, 2021. http://acaes.us/blog/pandemic-2021-preliminary (accessed December 29, 2021).

World Government Bonds, 2021. www.worldgovernmentbonds.com/ (accessed June 25, 2021).

16 Epilogue

Macroeconomic stabilization in emerging economies calls for managing both internal and external balance within a policy space constrained by global capital flows and debt sustainability pressures. Emerging East Asia has crafted an approach to meeting this challenge that involves the exchange rate as policy instrument. But while the economics of the system have proven effective, the politics can run afoul of US strictures on currency manipulation. This is a source of ongoing tension.

Emerging East Asia has honed a well-functioning model for stabilization policy. Through a span of two decades between the Asian Financial Crisis and the Covid pandemic, the region sustained healthy growth with low inflation. External shocks from the bursting of the dot-com bubble in 2001 and the Great Financial Crisis in 2008 brought growth slowdowns, edging into modest contractions for a few, but recovery was quick (Chart 1.2). With the onset of the global pandemic in 2020, the region was, for the most part, well positioned to undertake supportive policies.

In this final chapter, we present a brief recap of the Emerging East Asia macro policy model. The model involves management of the exchange rate as a stabilization tool, which is fine as such. A problem arises, however, when the currency is "manipulated" to achieve advantage in trade. The USA has adopted a watchdog role on this front, putting threat of penalty tariffs at stake. A motivating factor in the writing of this book, as noted in the Preface, was the need for a textbook that would establish a basis for interpreting Asian exchange rate policy within a macro stabilization framework. With that framework in place, we take on the issue of currency manipulation.

And then we conclude.

A   Macro Policy in Emerging East Asia

The Emerging East Asia policy model is distinctive enough to warrant a textbook treatment of the subject. We recap the model in this section, then apply the framework to consider the region's positioning for responding to the macroeconomic shock of the pandemic.

Policy Model Recap

For the economies of Emerging East Asia, both external and internal balance demand attention in stabilization policy where external balance involves international payment flows on the current versus capital and financial accounts and internal balance pertains to growth versus inflation domestically. In US textbooks, external balance makes no appearance as a macro policy issue, nor does the exchange rate enter as a policy instrument. When a country prints the world's reserve currency and its payment obligations are denominated in that currency, external shocks are easily absorbed and the exchange rate can be left to go where it will. Emerging East Asian economies do not have that luxury. International payment obligations for the region are specified largely in foreign currency, and the exchange rate is pivotal for being able to meet those obligations. Maintaining confidence in the domestic currency is paramount in this setting.

To pursue balance in two dimensions, two arms of policy may be used in complementary fashion, as explained in Chapter 13. An expansionary monetary policy stimulates the economy and pushes the current account balance in a positive direction by lowering interest rates and the value of the currency whereas an expansionary fiscal policy also stimulates the economy but pushes the current account balance in a negative direction by raising interest rates and the value of the currency. The two arms of policy may thus be played off each other. For example, suppose an economy is operating with growth at potential and inflation low and stable, but the current account is in deficit to an undesired degree. The straightforward remedy for the current account deficit would be a central bank intervention to sell the domestic currency and buy foreign exchange. This has the undesired side effect, however, of inducing monetary expansion and thus stimulating the domestic economy which was initially in balance. To offset this unintended consequence, fiscal policy can be tightened, with the added benefit that this reinforces an increase in the current account balance.

Within this policy framework, the exchange rate acts in tandem with the interest rate. Either can be used as an instrument for targeting monetary policy; the two cannot, however, be made to work independently given an open capital account. Lowering a policy interest rate triggers a net capital outflow which depreciates the value of the local currency. On the other hand, intervening in the foreign exchange market to depreciate the currency causes an expansion in the monetary base which lowers the interest rate. The exchange rate can thus serve as a monetary policy instrument in the same way the interest rate does, the difference being the central bank intervenes in the foreign exchange market rather than in the domestic bond market. Empirical evidence presented in Chart 11.2 shows monetary authorities in Emerging East Asia have systematically intervened in the foreign exchange market to lean against shocks to external balance. Such action is integral to the conduct of monetary policy in the region.

The exercise of monetary and fiscal policy is subject to constraints in the Emerging East Asia context, with this topic, too, lying beyond the scope of US macro texts. Open capital markets limit the space available to manipulate interest rates in pursuit of internal balance without triggering cross-border capital flows that disrupt external balance. Indeed, Hong Kong and Singapore base their monetary policies entirely on exchange rate targeting given an inability to influence interest rates under their globally integrated financial systems. But the exchange rate, too, is of limited avail for stabilization purposes. Leaning against depreciation (or pushing for appreciation) requires the central bank to sell foreign currency against the hard limit of its reserve stock. On the other hand, leaning against appreciation (or pushing for depreciation) can be inflationary, or if the intervention is sterilized through bond purchases will impose interest costs on the central bank that may exceed the return on its holdings of safe foreign assets. As for fiscal policy, the big constraint is that creditors will become uneasy if public debt gets too high. Loss of confidence in the government's ability to meet its obligations can cause interest rates to rise and the value of the currency to fall with adverse repercussions for the economy.

Importantly, sound policy involves preserving latitude to respond to shocks. That means building a healthy trove of official reserves during good times and keeping government debt at a moderate level. This will ensure space for government to increase spending and maintain exchange rate stability should bad times hit.

Pandemic Response

Bad times did in fact hit with a vengeance in 2020. Lockdowns due to the pandemic undermined tax collection for most Emerging East Asian economies even as the need intensified for governments to spend on public health and social welfare programs. Externally, the impact of the pandemic on the region's exports was mixed as sales of some manufactures were strong while trade in services plummeted.

Fiscal space to respond to the crisis varied within the Emerging East Asia region (Table 15.1). Those well positioned (e.g., Hong Kong and Singapore) took advantage of it to ramp up government spending. Those with already high debt-to-GDP ratios either responded with more reserve (e.g., Malaysia) or tipped further toward imprudence (e.g., China). In between these poles, most of the region met the pandemic with budgets close to balance and sufficient fiscal space to raise deficits to around 4–6 percent of GDP without undue concern. Of course, as the pandemic stretches out, stress on government budgets will mount.

Space for monetary policy is influenced by global capital markets. Flows into Emerging East Asia remained buoyant in 2020 as evidenced by rising currency values coupled with increases in official reserves (Chart 15.4). An expansionary monetary policy in the USA kept interest rates low through the first year of the pandemic, which created space for Emerging East Asia to follow suit. However, should inflation threaten to take hold in the USA, a monetary tightening would not be far behind. That could prompt capital outflows from emerging economies and declining currency values with pressure to follow the USA in raising interest rates. Given uneven access to vaccines in the region, return to normal economic functioning will be staggered. Yet the USA will call the tune on monetary policy.

B   Woe to the "Currency Manipulator"

As the US trade deficit with China soared in the 2000-aughts, Americans became much exercised over China's exchange rate policy. Cries of "currency manipulation" resounded, the idea being that China was deliberately depressing the value of the renminbi for purposes of gaining an unfair advantage in exports. In this section, we consider the concept of currency manipulation and then examine the cases of China, Vietnam, and Taiwan.

Trouble with the Concept

Central bank intervention in foreign exchange markets does not in itself constitute "currency manipulation." As a technical matter, currency manipulation is all about intent, and intent is tough to prove. The IMF's Articles of Agreement stipulate that members shall "avoid manipulating exchange rates or the international monetary system in order to prevent effective balance of payments adjustment or to gain an unfair competitive advantage over other members" (p. 6). Under this rubric, the IMF has never designated any country a currency manipulator despite much pressure to do so. It is simply too difficult to distinguish *intervention* intended for macroeconomic stabilization from *manipulation* intended for gaining unfair advantage in trade.

This subtlety has not deterred the USA from applying the manipulator label. An investigation into currency manipulation by the US Treasury Department is triggered based on an economy meeting three criteria: net official purchases of foreign exchange exceeding 2 percent of GDP; a current account surplus exceeding 2 percent of GDP; and a bilateral trade surplus with the USA exceeding $20 billion. If the investigation finds in support of currency manipulation, the Treasury Department enters into bilateral engagement to seek remedies. The threat of penalty tariffs acts as leverage. The currency manipulator designation was officially applied to China in 2019 and 2020 and to Vietnam in 2020, and back in the 1980s and 1990s, to Korea, Taiwan, and China.

In its April 2021 report, the Treasury Department concluded that evidence was insufficient to designate any currency manipulators even though Vietnam and Taiwan had met all three criteria for investigation. Countries tagged for the watch list as meeting two of the three criteria included China, Korea, Malaysia, Singapore, and Thailand. The April 2021 report was the first of the administration of President Biden. There would seem to be plenty of room for different US administrations to interpret similar facts differently in reaching their conclusions given the ambiguity surrounding intentions. A role for politics cannot be denied.

The Macro Stabilization Argument

The US outcry over currency manipulation has been most vociferous with respect to China. The US Treasury Department designated the country a manipulator for three consecutive years from 1992 to 1994, then not again until 2019 and 2020. Incongruous as it may seem, between 1994 and 2018 the US trade deficit with China rose from $32 billion to $419 billion with no manipulator designations applied, then fell to $346 billion in 2019 and to $311 billion in 2020 with the designations reinstated.

Rather than trying to penetrate US motives and processes, let us consider the effectiveness of China's exchange rate policy from a macroeconomic standpoint for what that may suggest about intent. This subject was broached in Chapter 8, Section C, with a claim that China effectively steered its exchange rate toward a path of long-run stability. Against a surging current account surplus through the 2000-aughts and rising capital inflows following market liberalization toward the end of the decade, the Chinese central bank held the line against renminbi appreciation while building massive reserves (Chart 5.1). By 2015, however, the renminbi's tie to a rising US dollar brought a shift to perceived overvaluation relative to other currencies triggering fear of depreciation and inducing capital flight. Defending the renminbi against downward pressure cost the Chinese central bank nearly $800 billion of its $4 trillion in reserves within just two years. Since then, however, China's reserve trove has held steady against a stable renminbi and a current account surplus that in 2018–19 lay under one percent of GDP.

Did a low renminbi valuation during the 2000-aughts encourage exports and discourage imports to bring about large trade surpluses? No doubt. But was the trade imbalance a transitory aberration within the context of an exchange rate policy aimed at long-term stability? With the benefit of hindsight, a case for this can be made. China's trade surplus opened up in the 2000-aughts due to factors that raised the saving rate to drive a wedge between saving and investment, and strong net exports kept the economy going in the face of a shortfall in domestic demand. The major factors behind the rise in saving were transitory in nature, however, involving extraordinarily rapid growth in income and a demographic bulge that concentrated population in prime working and saving ages. As growth has slowed and the population has aged, the saving rate has come down, and with that the external imbalance has eased. Had the renminbi been allowed to appreciate under the pressure of the 2000-aughts, China's growth would have slowed and loss of confidence in an eventually overvalued renminbi could have resulted in even more precipitous capital outflows than those that actually materialized in 2015–16. China's exchange rate policy astutely avoided this fate and can therefore be justified on grounds other than "manipulation."

Vietnam was subjected to manipulator branding by the US Treasury under the Trump administration in 2020 but avoided this fate under the Biden administration on the strength of negotiations that had the country promising to refrain from engaging in "competitive devaluation." A latecomer to global trade, Vietnam has achieved quick success while yet remaining a small-time player in global capital markets. As a reforming command economy, its recourse to market forces for absorbing shocks is inhibited. Within this context, the country has kept a tight hold on its exchange rate relative to the US dollar even as this has led to changes in reserves that in percentage terms relative to a small base have run to extremes (Chart 11.1). By 2020, Vietnam had accumulated reserves of just 27.8 percent of

GDP, a modest stock by the standards of the region (Chart 11.3). Before it relaxes its exchange rate control, before it opens its capital markets, before it exposes its economy more fully to international engagement, Vietnam needs to build a reserve position that will allow it to defend its currency should the need arise.

Meanwhile, at the time of the manipulator charges, Vietnam was taking on supply chain relocations out of China in response to rising tensions between China and the USA. Such a positive shock to the balance of payments can be absorbed even under a stabilized exchange rate through increased imports or net capital outflows, but these responses take time. As with China then, within a longer-term context of adjustment to shock and the development of market mechanisms, Vietnam's exchange rate policy has been oriented toward macroeconomic stabilization. As such, the behavior does not qualify as "currency manipulation."

Taiwan was last designated a currency manipulator in 1992. Since then, its reserve accumulation has reached 83 percent of GDP putting it behind only Hong Kong, with its US dollar-backed monetary base, and Singapore (Chart 11.3). In 2021, Taiwan met all three conditions for an investigation by the US Treasury but escaped formal manipulator status. In taking a position of leniency, the Treasury noted in its report that the pandemic had "drastically affected global trade" (p. 1), favorably so for Taiwan's exports of semiconductors and high-tech equipment, and also highlighted Taiwan's success in controlling Covid transmission to keep its economy running relatively well. The Treasury went on to warn, however, that exchange market intervention has "resulted in a structurally undervalued exchange rate that has failed to adjust in the face of Taiwan's persistently large current account surpluses" (p. 4). Still, the Treasury recognized that Taiwan is a special case with respect to its need for buffers against risk pointing to its "geopolitical situation, its lack of IMF membership, and its dependence on imported energy and external demand" (p. 43). That brings us back to the point that building reserves as a buffer against risk is an essential aspect of macroeconomic stabilization policy in Emerging East Asia.

In sum, the economies of Emerging East Asia have managed their exchange rates consistent with the principles of macroeconomic stabilization laid out in this textbook. And that is okay.

C   Final Thoughts

The premise of this textbook is that as diverse as the economies of Emerging East Asia are in obvious ways, they can be subsumed within a common analytical framework for purposes of understanding macroeconomic phenomena – and a very different framework it is than the one presented in standard US texts. Key features of the framework are: attention to both internal and external balance; intertwining use of the exchange rate and the interest rate as monetary policy instruments; and management of policy under constraints imposed by international capital flows and government borrowing concerns. Implications of the framework are that the capacity to absorb shocks is strengthened by building a healthy stock of official reserves and by keeping public debt at a moderate level. Reserve accumulation depends largely on running current account surpluses. And that can provoke the ire of the USA. But a fair response is that US macro policy as expressed through the country's impact on interest rates and global capital flows is one of the most overbearing and uncertain elements of the global economic environment that emerging economies must contend with. Against the slings and arrows of US policy, then, reserves help provide resilience.

Finally, let us consider whether Emerging East Asia has honed an approach to macroeconomic policy that other emerging economies can learn from. A comparison with Latin America on the use of foreign exchange market intervention to lean against external shocks as viewed through the framework of Chart 11.2 would suggest so (see Wiemer and Meurer on the *Asia Economics Blog*, May 8, 2021). For Emerging East Asia, the data show a clear pattern of leaning against currency appreciation in the face of positive balance of payments shocks and against currency depreciation in the face of negatiave shocks. For Latin America, by contrast, the relationship between exchange rate movement and central bank intervention appears random. Relatedly, Latin American economies for the most part hold much lower reserves relative to GDP than Emerging East Asian economies making it harder for their central banks to intervene against currency depreciation. To develop the capacity that Emerging East Asia has for two-sided intervention, Latin American authorities would have to follow the East Asian model of running current account surpluses for an extended period to accumulate reserves. This may not be easy given the pushback East Asia has come up against.

Data Note

Figures on the US trade deficit with China are from the IMF Direction of Trade Statistics database.

Bibliographic Note

Bonham and Wiemer (2013) analyze the reasons for China's macroeconomic imbalances.

BIBLIOGRAPHIC CITATIONS

Bonham, Carl and Calla Wiemer, 2013. "Chinese Saving Dynamics: The Impact of GDP Growth and the Dependent Share," *Oxford Economic Papers*, Volume 65, Issue 1.

Congressional Research Service, 2020. Exchange Rates and Currency Manipulation. https://sgp.fas.org/crs/misc/IF10049.pdf (accessed October 20, 2021).

International Monetary Fund, 2020. Articles of Agreement. www.imf.org/external/pubs/ft/aa/index .htm (accessed October 21, 2021).

International Monetary Fund, 2021. Direction of Trade Statistics. https://data.imf.org/?sk=9d6028d4-f14a-464c-a2f2–59b2cd424b85&sId=1390030341854 (accessed October 22, 2021).

U.S. Department of the Treasury, 2021. Macroeconomic and Foreign Exchange Policies of Major Trading Partners of the United States. https://home.treasury.gov/policy-issues/international/ macroeconomic-and-foreign-exchange-policies-of-major-trading-partners-of-the-united-states (accessed October 21, 2021).

Wiemer, Calla and Roberto Meurer, 2021. "The Exchange Rate in East Asia's Macroeconomic Stabilization Policy: Contrast with Latin America," *Asia Economics Blog,* May 8, 2021. http://acaes .us/blog/exchange-rate-contrast-with-latin-america (accessed October 30, 2021).

Index

government debt, 248–249
  sterilization, 227–228
inflation
  and money. *See* money
  by economy, vs money growth, *101*
  expectations, 99, 189–190, 216
  pernicious effects, 103, 210
inflation targeting, 218
  and the Trilemma, 232
interest parity, 145–146
  covered, 146
  uncovered, 146
interest rate
  and asset prices, 128–129
  credit spread, 127
  determination, 126–127
  IS–LM model, 172
  real vs nominal, 126
  risk, 128
  term structure, 127
  yield curve, 127
internal balance, xxiii, 260–265
  fiscal policy effect on, 236–237
  monetary policy effect on, 211
international capital flows. *See* foreign
    capital flows
international investment. *See* foreign
    investment
international investment position
  by economy, *30*
International Monetary Fund. *See also*
    databases
  Article IV Consultation Staff Reports,
    233
  Asian Financial Crisis response,
    299–300
  crisis assistance, 296
  macroprudential role, 283
  on currency manipulation, 314
international trade. *See* foreign trade
inventories
  in GDP expenditures, 63
  planned vs unplanned accumulation,
    63, 164–165
investment
  in GDP expenditures, 62–63
investment banks, 113–114
IS–LM model, 171–175

Japan
  money-targeting monetary policy, 104

Juglar, Clement
  cause of depression, 182

Keynes, John Maynard
  aggregate demand, 99–100
  business cycle theory, 10
  Economic Consequences of the Peace,
    177
  euthanasia of the rentier, 178
  fiscal policy, 257
  General Theory of Employment,
    Interest, and Money,
    163, 179
  money and inflation, 100, 106
  on the long run, 98, 106
Keynesian Cross model, 164
Keynesianism, 161
  vs Austrian School, 187
  vs Monetarism, 103–104
Kindleberger, Charles, 290
  Manias, Panics, and Crashes:
    A History of Financial Crises,
    308
  on bailouts, 297
Korea
  bond market, 121
  foreign exchange market intervention,
    221
  macroprudential policy usage,
    285–286
    by instrument, *285*

labor market, 49–51
Laos
  bank finance dominance, 119
  government debt, 247–248
  inflation, 101
  monetary policy framework, 218
Latin America
  vs Emerging East Asia, 317
leaning against the wind, 158
liquidity preference. *See* money,
    demand, liquidity preference
loanable funds market, 126–127
Lucas, Robert
  rational expectations, 191

M0. *See* monetary base
M1–M3, 94
macroprudential policy
  and crises, 286

and the financial cycle, 279–280
challenges, 286
coordination with monetary policy,
  274–275
implementation, 281
institutions
  domestic, 280–281
  international, 281–283
instruments, 275–279
purpose, 272–274
usage, 279–280
  by economy, *284*
  by instrument, *279*
vs monetary and fiscal policy, 275,
  286
Malaysia
  balance of payments, *265*
  Bank Negara Malaysia as central
    bank, 91
  bank Z-score, 123
  government debt, 248
  Great Financial Crisis, fiscal response,
    255
  internal/external balance assessment,
    265
  monetary policy framework, 218
  policy space, 266
  saving and investment rates, *267*
  structural vs cyclical imbalances,
    266–267
Malthus, Thomas
  classical economics, 42
marginal efficiency of capital, 172
marginal propensity to consume (MPC),
  163
market
  equilibration, 38–39
  maker, 113
  power, 47–48
    efficiency effect, 49
Marshall, Alfred
  efficiency in markets, 40–41
  neoclassical economics, 42
  Principles of Economics, 54
microeconomics
  disconnect with macroeconomics, 4,
    53
Mill, John Stuart
  classical economics, 42
Mills, John
  business cycle theory, 11, 184–185

326   Index

Printed in the United States
by Baker & Taylor Publisher Services